The Crux of Refugee Resettlement

CROSSING BORDERS IN A GLOBAL WORLD: APPLYING ANTHROPOLOGY TO MIGRATION, DISPLACEMENT, AND SOCIAL CHANGE

Series Editors: Raúl Sánchez Molina and Nancy Anne Konvalinka

Mission Statement

By crossing political, social, cultural, and identity borders current migrants, refugees, and travelers meet challenges of globalization in their processes of displacement, incorporation, and adaptation to new settlements. These circumstances open up opportunities for anthropologists and members of related disciplines to work together with migrants, residents, and communities seeking to contribute to knowledge and action. This series seeks to address these challenges and their intersections with national, ethnic, gender, and generational identities by providing a range of interdisciplinary theoretical and methodological frameworks of how scholars and practitioners can approach not only knowledge, but also application. In addition, this series aims to show models of collaboration and interaction in economy, policy, social, and physical reproduction, health, labor market, education, and other social institutions.

Advisory Board

Books in Series

Identities on Trial in the United States: Asylum Seekers from Asia, by ChorSwang Ngin.
The Crux of Refugee Resettlement: Rebuilding Social Networks,
edited by Andrew Nelson, Alexander Rödlach, and Roos Willems

The Crux of Refugee Resettlement

Rebuilding Social Networks

Edited by
Andrew Nelson, Alexander Rödlach, and
Roos Willems

LEXINGTON BOOKS
Lanham • Boulder • New York • London

Published by Lexington Books
An imprint of The Rowman & Littlefield Publishing Group, Inc.
4501 Forbes Boulevard, Suite 200, Lanham, Maryland 20706
www.rowman.com

6 Tinworth Street, London SE11 5AL, United Kingdom

The cover photo was taken during an annual event, showcasing various refugee communities and connecting them with other groups, coordinated by the Midtown Utica Community Center (Utica, New York) at the Fort Stanwix National Monument (Rome, New York) in September 2016. The Center was founded to advocate for and support refugee and other low-income groups by providing educational and cultural programs and facilitating access to resources. This photo represents refugees' efforts to actively address challenges faced during the resettlement process through developing relationships with individuals from other communities (the "bridging" social capital discussed in this volume) while strengthening social networks within their own communities ("bonding" social capital).

British Library Cataloguing in Publication Information Available

Library of Congress Cataloging-in-Publication Data

Names: Nelson, Andrew (Lecturer of anthropology), editor. | Rodlach, Alexander, editor. | Willems, Roos, editor.
Title: The crux of refugee resettlement : rebuilding social networks / edited by Andrew Nelson, Alexander Rodlach, and Roos Willems.
Description: Lanham, Maryland : Lexington Books, 2019. | Series: Crossing borders in a global world | Includes bibliographical references and index.
Identifiers: LCCN 2018044213 (print) | LCCN 2018055119 (ebook) | ISBN 9781498588904 (Electronic) | ISBN 9781498588898 (cloth : alk. paper)
Subjects: LCSH: Refugees—Social networks—Case studies. | Refugees—Social conditions—Case studies. | Community organization—Case studies.
Classification: LCC HV640 (ebook) | LCC HV640 .C78 2019 (print) | DDC 305.9/06914—dc23
LC record available at https://lccn.loc.gov/2018044213

∞™ The paper used in this publication meets the minimum requirements of American National Standard for Information Sciences—Permanence of Paper for Printed Library Materials, ANSI/NISO Z39.48-1992.

Printed in the United States of America

We would like to dedicate this book to all resettled refugees worldwide for courageously entering unfamiliar territories and making them their own to the best of their abilities.

Contents

List of Figures and Table

FIGURES

TABLE

Introduction

Andrew Nelson, Alexander Rödlach, and Roos Willems

Amid the highest rise in the number of refugees ever recorded, the head of the United Nations High Commission for Refugees (UNHCR) called for "fundamental changes to allow for larger resettlement and humanitarian admission quotas" (UNHCR 2015b). The UNHCR defines *resettlement* as one of three durable solutions for refugees,[1] the other two being *voluntary repatriation* and *local integration* (in the country where the refugee applied for asylum status). *Resettlement* is considered the last option and refers to the selection and transfer of refugees from a country in which they have sought protection to a third country that has agreed to admit them as refugees with permanent residence status.[2] The status provided ensures protection against *refoulement* (i.e., the expulsion of persons who applied for refugee status) and entitle resettled refugees and their families or dependents access to rights similar to those enjoyed by citizens. Resettlement also carries with it the opportunity to eventually become a naturalized citizen of the resettlement country.

Under the best of conditions, resettlement is a difficult and life-changing experience for refugees that requires them adapting to a society, language, and culture significantly different from their own. Allowing for the fact that "home" is not just a geographic notion, but first and foremost a set of social relations, Marx defines a refugee as "a person whose social world has been disturbed" (1990, 190). Amid this disturbance, refugees rely on their pre-refugee understandings of individual, family, and social life that continue to influence their perceptions and behavior. Indeed, even as human beings will respond to crises or unfamiliar circumstances in innovative ways, their responses remain "set within the parameters specified by our perceptual frameworks [as human beings], and these are a function of our past" (Oliver-Smith 1986, 16). Refugees, resettled or not, will choose from those alternative behaviors that allow them to maintain their basic conceptions of what life is amid the turmoil and disruptions, a process that possibly (but not necessarily) leads to sociocultural change through innovative behaviors (Geiger 1993). Thus, within the process of resettling or reintegration in their new home countries, the reconstruction and reconfiguration of resettled refugees' social worlds and networks plays a pivotal role. Or, to refer to the title of this volume, the reconstruction of refugees' social networks is the crux of successful refugee resettlement.

ETHNOGRAPHIC PERSPECTIVE

We understand the resettlement experience in anthropological terms, and refugees as people who have undergone a forced *separation* and, unless or until they are *incorporated* as citizens into their host country (or have returned to their country of origin), find themselves in "transition," or in a state of "liminality" (Harrell-Bond and Voutira 1992). To use Turner's words, "[l]iminal entities are neither here nor there; they are betwixt and between the positions assigned and arrayed by law, custom, convention, and ceremonial" (1969, 95). Even upon acquiring citizenship and official incorporation in new countries, refugees often struggle to regain a sense of home and belonging. In other words, refugees have to deal with chaos; they have been forced to leave their established lives at home; often too, they have lost family members and are faced with the need to redefine their support systems. We maintain that the study of how refugees remake their support systems is not only central to understanding resettlement, but is also often achieved in spite of, rather than because of, policy. Hence, our goal is an applied one in that—as anthropologists—we focus on how refugees critique the bureaucratic conditions of their resettlement and generate their own community-centered solutions for remaking social networks and, thus, a sense of home. We consider the concept of *social capital* useful to identify and highlight core aspects of such remaking. Though there exists no commonly agreed definition of this concept, all definitions focus on norms and values as well as organizational and structural components of social networks.

The contributions in this volume follow recent calls in anthropology (Biehl and Petryna 2013) to apply the qualitative and ethnographic approach to draw attention to people's everyday struggles, which were largely absent in earlier studies of refugees. A large part of the body of refugee research is based on quantifiable data that fail to identify facets of refugees' lives crucial for program development, and ultimately result in short-lived approaches (Kopinak 1999; Whitmarsh 2013). Based on their findings and conclusions resulting from applying this approach, the authors of this volume problematize the legal definition of "refugee," further our applied understanding of the resettlement process, and make a strong case that this process can only be successful if the rebuilding of social networks and social capitals is recognized, prioritized, and actively supported by all stakeholders involved. The authors pay close attention to different forms of *bonding* and *bridging* social capitals and various types of social networks, arguing that their evolving and shifting relevance requires governmental and nongovernmental organizations to adopt a flexible approach originating from and responsive to refugee needs. In other words, it is necessary for resettlement organizations, policy makers, and funding agencies to focus on resettled refugees' *internal contexts*—their experiences and social and cultural backgrounds—as well as their *external contexts*—the places they live in and make sense of, their social networks and social capitals, enabling them to rebuild their lives, and the legal and socioeconomic realities they face.

Based on a participatory model to understanding resettlement, the authors argue that limitations of policies and institutional practices can be addressed by an anthropologically informed ethnographic engagement with refugee groups as they reconstruct their social networks in order to make sense of the new places they now inhabit. Policies should be based on the recognition that the refugees themselves are the experts of their own lives and needs for successful resettlement. Similarly, the practices of service providers working with refugees should account for the social and cultural complexities of the resettlement process instead of privileging technical and legal expertise over solidarity, cooperation, and a willingness to tackle challenges together. These highly personal and relational approaches would be not only more appropriate, but also more effective and integral to revitalizing resettlement programs in the twenty-first century.

In this volume, we use ethnographic approaches to understand the reconfiguration of social networks as a direct response to the structural limitations imposed by resettlement policies. Further, our focus on the dynamic relationship between "bridging" and "bonding" capital of networks (Putnam 2000) provides insights which not only critique current policy, but are also crucial to design effective interventions that aim to address social problems related to refugee resettlement. In our exploration of the resettlement of diverse refugee communities in various countries, we maintain that solutions to problems are most likely to be found in the strategies and adaptations of the communities facing these problems.

The geography of refugee populations and resettlement destinations emphasized in this volume reflects the flows of resettled refugees between 2007 and 2016, the decade in which its contributors conducted their research. The majority of the research comes from the United States, which accepted nearly 65 percent of all refugees resettled in third countries during a slightly longer (2004–2016) period (UNHCR 2017). Within the United States, a variety of resettlement contexts are discussed ranging from large metropolitan areas like Chicago and Dallas-Fort Worth, to midsize urban centers such as Omaha in Nebraska and Greensboro in North Carolina, to college towns like Columbus in Ohio and Burlington in Vermont, as well as to rust-belt cities of the upper Midwest, such as Utica in New York and Erie in Pennsylvania. Although the majority of cases come from US contexts, our goal is not to discuss US resettlement exclusively, but rather to critique and propose reforms on how third country resettlement is instituted more broadly. For comparative insight, we also included three case studies from large cities in the United Kingdom and Australia, as well as a smaller town in Canada.

The refugee groups studied in the volume reflect the general trends of refugee admissions to third countries for resettlement from 2004 to 2016 (UNCHR 2017). Of the twelve chapters, eight include reference to Nepali-Bhutanese refugees, a group that accounted for 11.3 percent of all resettled refugees worldwide.[3] Four chapters discuss Burmese refugees, who accounted for the highest number of resettled cases at 21.5 percent. Two chapters highlight Iraqi and Somali populations, who comprised 15.1 percent and 10 percent of all resettled, respectively. Beyond these four most represented groups, chapters also allude to refugees from Vietnam and Central Africa. Finally, one chapter adds to the discussion by questioning the politics of refugee designation with an ethnographic analysis of how involuntary migrants from Central America remake their lives in the United States in spite of not receiving refugee status.

Instead of attributing refugees only a passive voice, filtered and edited by the author, this volume includes the direct voices of refugees and service providers[4], commenting on conclusions drawn by the authors and their relevance and applicability to understanding and addressing issues faced by them. The fourteen authors of the chapter-ending commentaries reflect the variety of perspectives in refugee resettlement. Eight of the commentary authors are refugees, two of whom have also worked as service providers in resettlement. The other six have worked with refugees as case workers, administrators, and medical professionals in resettlement agencies, or as local politicians and educators. Although refugees and service providers occupy very different positions, we recognize both as integral to our call for a reformation of resettlement policy.

THE POLITICS OF RESETTLEMENT

The annual number of refugees submitted by the UNHCR for resettlement in third countries has increased considerably over the last twelve years, from 46,300 in 2005 to 145,500 in 2016 (UNHCR 2017). Since 2005, close to one million refugees have been resettled in twenty-eight countries. From this high number, the United States received about 50 percent, Canada and Australia each accepted approximately 10 percent, and European Union countries (mainly Sweden, Denmark, Finland, and Norway, who count for 75 percent of the EU's resettlement cases) granted entry to the bulk of the remainder (UNHCR 2015a). However, the UNHCR estimates that more than 1 million people are currently waiting to be resettled, a 50 percent increase since 2012. The ongoing problematic political crises surrounding many global conflicts strongly suggest that these numbers will continue escalating.

In spite of the increase, the current turn to the rightwing and anti-immigrant populism in many parts of Europe, Australia, the United States, and elsewhere suggests that resettlement policies will become ever more restrictive. Already in response to the backlash from her open-door policy for refugees in 2015, Germany's Chancellor Angela Merkel has greatly reduced the country's admissions of asylum seekers and refugees. Similarly, in his first week of Presidency, Donald Trump issued a 120-day suspension of the refugee admissions to the United States and reduced US admission totals by more than half the number reached in the last year of Obama's presidency. Even Scandinavian countries, often considered to be the most welcoming of refugees, have adopted more restrictive resettlement policies. Denmark, for instance, now encourages refugees to leave by paying them in exchange for returning to their countries of origin, or by seizing refugee assets to help pay for their resettlement. While such changes and new policies continue to have a dramatic effect on the acceptance of refugees for resettlement, in this volume we focus on the sociocultural context of resettlement policies for how they regulate and structure the everyday life of refugees. Namely, neoliberal policies of austerity have motivated cuts and reductions to resettlement programs, and effectively shifted the focus in resettlement from holistic notions of integration to increasingly narrow expectations of refugees as economic producers (Haines 2010; Ong 2003).

Nowhere is the austere support for refugee resettlement starker than in the United States. Since the country started its refugee program in 1970, it has gradually reduced funding for refugees from a maximum of three years of assistance to two years in 1987 and further to eight months by 1991 (Bruno 2011). While the United Kingdom offers an even shorter period of governmental support at six months, only the first three months are guaranteed in the United States. After three months, all funds are attached to job-seeking programs and behaviors. Refugees quickly learn that success is linked to finding employment and becoming self-sufficient. Keles (2008) refers to the US resettlement policy as "calculated kindness" in how it emphasizes immediate employment over the longer-term goals of language acquisition and social adaptation. This emphasis strips the resettlement process down to economic considerations, largely downplaying other factors, such as mental health, community cohesion, solidarity, safety, language acquisition, or educational attainment (Haines 2010). In the terms of Ong (2003, 9), refugees are quickly instructed that "[t]he most worthy citizen is a flexible *homo economicus,*" implying that citizenship is understood as economic production with the aim of reducing one's burden on society. This rush to economic independence produces what Besteman (2016, 104) calls an ironic contradiction of resettlement policy: "The very people who must present themselves as dependent recipients of charity in order to gain resettlement must, within the space of a few weeks, become economically independent and productive residents who make no demands on their American host communities."

In the United States, the objective of converting refugees from recipients into producers is assigned to the eleven Voluntary Agencies (Volags) who oversee the welcoming and settling of refugees in their first three months of arrival. Nawyn (2011) found that the goals of Volags and other nongovernmental organizations are constantly undermined by structural constraints placed upon them. In addition to finding employment during the first three months, refugees are expected during the same time period to also learn English and become comfortable using electronic devices, shopping at large grocery stores, navigating public transportation, paying bills and registering children for school. After three months, refugees become dependent on the limited support of the Office of Refugee Resettlement (ORR), which offers a few more months of assistance in the form of Temporary Assistance for Needy Families (TANF) and Refugee Cash Assistance programs. Participating in these programs requires one to find employment or attend job-training programs, and is only guaranteed until the eighth month after one's arrival.

While refugee assistance is the most limited in the United States versus the more generous packages of countries such as Canada or Australia (see, for example, Australia 2017), a harbinger of adjustments is imminent in various resettlement countries around the world. The cuts to resettlement programs are a product of the larger dismantling of the welfare state, an agenda to prioritize privatization, and promote the neoliberal ideologies of self-help, individual responsibility, autonomy and self-sufficiency. The individualizing agenda of neoliberalism is easily twisted to blame migrants, particularly poor ones, as the cause of their own poverty, as "unworthy citizens" (Negri and Hardt 2009, 45). Thus, federal mandates to accommodate diversity and welcome refugees are contradicted by cuts in economic assistance and a social climate of hostility toward refugees, not to mention racist xenophobia, culminating in what Besteman (2016, 137) calls a "bad faith effort of humanitarian rescue." Even after cuts, in this era of austerity and xenophobia refugees are often perceived as receiving a "free ride," being a drain on public services, and unwilling to work, learn English and adapt to American society.

The perceived fear of unproductive refugees is further manifested in the adoption of dispersal policies, in which governments purposefully scatter resettled refugee populations throughout the country as a way of promoting "assimilation." For instance, toward the goal of minimizing the possibility of enclaves, the United States government assigns resettlement locations with the objective of not overly "impacting" areas. Similarly, since 2004 in Australia, policies of "regional resettlement of refugees" or "dispersal of refugees" have led the Department of Immigration and Citizenship (DIAC) to resettle refugees without social or family ties to regional towns throughout the country (Johnston et al. 2009). More recently, Germany has started distributing refugee resettlement across the country based on a state quota system.

BRIDGING CAPITAL VERSUS BONDING CAPITAL IN RESETTLEMENT STUDIES

The pressure to achieve economic self-reliance and integration in a relatively short time forces refugee groups to rely on social networks internal to their community, or *bonding* social capital. Ironically, these outcomes run counter to the intentions of self-sufficiency and geographic dispersal policies, which are implicitly based on cultivating social networks with external groups, or *bridging* social capital. Indeed, many studies of refugee and migrant social networks have echoed Putnam's (1995) conclusion that bridging social capital is necessary for "getting ahead" while bonding social capital can only help communities "to get by." For instance, Morrice (2007, 166) asserts that "[e]thnic networks have the potential to be too insular with solidarity and so bounded that members can miss out on other resources and networks in the wider society. So while [bonding] social capital can be advantageous for communal survival, it can also, through network disadvantage, underpin disadvantage." Furthermore, other scholars have argued that bonding networks can promote the segregation and ultimate isolation of refugees (Finney and Simpson 2009), as well as confine them in low-paid employment (Jones et al. 2012). Motivated by this line of thinking, the United Kingdom's resettlement policy reversed course in 2005 from promoting the "bonding networks" of co-ethnic or co-national organizations to seeing such groups as problematic, even "separatist" (Cheung and Phillimore 2014). Following the United States and Australia, they then shifted to encourage "multi-ethnic services" to work against the seeming enclaving and separatist tendencies of new groups (Cheung and Phillimore 2013, 3).

Other scholars have, however, demonstrated that bonding social capital is not necessarily disadvantageous for successful resettlement (Cheung and Phillimore 2013; Bloch 2002; Bloch 2004). In particular, Cheung and Phillimore (2013) maintain that social capital of any kind, whether bonding or bridging, is always better than not having any. In their studies of refugee resettlement in the U.K., other factors such as language competency, pre-migration qualifications, and time in the country tend to be the most important indicators of future success. More directly, scholars have shown that bonding networks are central forms of support in the refugee experience. Lamba and Krahn (2003, 338) argue that "an objective network structure that links individuals in a social space must exist (e.g., a refugee's familial network structure)." For social capital to develop from network ties, the relationship must be positive and trusting, which can prove particularly difficult for refugees who have experienced trauma. Based on Giddens' (1990) distinction between "trust in specific individuals" versus "trust in abstract institutions or groups of people," Lamba and Krahn (2003, 338) draw attention to the importance of the former in the form of family support in refugee lives. Moreover, family ties serve as "structural links" to the host society, and can create "friendships, marriage prospects, employment opportunities, education information, access to accommodations, and financial aid." However, because refugee families do not always relocate as one unit, common household strategies may not be possible. Given the wide geographic spread of refugee families, social ties beyond the family-group are also necessary as solidarity with one's ethnic group is a *key factor* especially in economic adaption (Gold and Kibria 1993; Hung and Haines 1996; Light and Bonacich 1988; Portes and Bach 1985; Williams 2006). Lamba and Krahn (2003, 339) describe ethnic group networks as functioning in a similar manner to kin networks for how they provide access to employment, friendship, marital prospects, and accommodation. Gender differences in network characteristics also reveal important insights for understanding the importance of bonding social capital. Within certain refugee communities, women's networks tend to be more kin- and friend-centered, while men's ties develop in more formal settings, such as the workplace (Menjivar 1995).

FROM EITHER/OR TO BOTH/AND MODELS OF SOCIAL CAPITAL

The chapters in this volume engage in this debate to demonstrate how multiple forms of bridging and bonding social capital influence various social networks in response to refugee resettlement policies. Heinemann et al. demonstrate that policies should not focus on either bridging or bonding networks, but rather follow multifaceted approaches. Building on Bourgois' (2003) notion of the bicultural alternative, the authors show how refugees selectively choose between different forms of social capital depending on various circumstances and contexts. As Heinemann et al. state, the concept of the bicultural alternative "captures how individuals need to downplay or even deny membership in their primary sociocultural group in order to be accepted in another sociocultural group, but then must shift back to their primary cultural arena when they are with family and friends" (in this volume). Thus, contrary to Putnam (1995), successful resettlement does not follow a linear development from bonding to bridging social capital. Their research proposes that resettlement programs work to strengthen existing networks with kin and ethnic communities while also encouraging the establishment of networks within the wider social context. Rosales establishes that comparable patterns (referring to the experience of Maya migrants in the United States) can be identified in the settlement dynamics of involuntary migrants who are not officially recognized as refugees and consequently, do not qualify for formal resettlement. Thus, the theme of this volume is not only relevant to understanding resettlement patterns among recognized refugees, but also among other involuntary migrants. Corroborating Heinemann et al., Rosales argues that policymakers and organizations working with migrants need to focus on bonding as well as bridging social capital that tend to mutually reinforce or strengthen each other; because in the absence of one type of social capital, the development of other types of social capital is compromised. He further contends that effective social networks among migrant groups, who creatively highlight and strategically develop and use commonalities to nurture a shared identity and beneficial alliances, provide migrants and refugees with an additional type of social capital that is often overlooked and cannot easily be categorized as either bonding or bridging social capital. His chapter points at the limits of using categories such as bonding and bridging social capital, and refugees and involuntary migrants, reminding us that these are just "ideal types."[5]

Rosales and Heinemann et al. provide the larger context and background for the volume's critique for how resettlement is generally understood and specifically implemented through state and agency policy. They set the stage for the subsequent chapters that underscore the crucial importance of ethnography for understanding refugee resettlement dynamics and supporting appropriate programs that facilitate successful resettlement. These chapters focus more specifically on the policies of self-sufficiency, integration, and dispersal to demonstrate that although there is nothing inherently wrong with policies intending to facilitate bridging capital, in practice such policies often fail to account for cultural practices, suffer from insufficient funding, and result in many unintended consequences that are often contrary to their goals.

In Nelson's chapter on house-buying practices of Nepali-Bhutanese refugees in Fort Worth, Texas, refugees consider the resettlement agencies' lessons on self-sufficiency and economic independence to be alien to their cultural values and ultimately counter-productive to their goals of home ownership. In fact, house buyers reject the advice of agencies in order to cultivate cooperative "pooling" systems in which multiple sources contribute to each family's mortgage down payment. In a similar vein, Halsouet's chapter on young Nepali-Bhutanese women in Quebec secondary schools reveals how the Canadian educational system undermines its goals of integration by its lack of investment in immigration programs. As she shows, integration in and of itself is not the problem as the young refugee women are more than happy to enter classes with their Canadian peers. Rather, the problems stem from the lack of support for hired faculty to assist migrant children as well as a lack of training for teachers. Students, in turn, learn the "hidden curriculum" of self-help and self-discipline, which pushes them to rely more on their family and co-ethnic peers for scholastic support.

Similar to how the emphasis on economic independence and social integration is undermined by cultural miscommunication and insufficient funding, policies of dispersal fail to curtail social practices that favor the bonding networks of clustering. Despite being initially spread out by the resettlement process, refugees often relocate to create semi-enclaves of territorial solidarity, as scholars have found in both Canada (Simich 2003) and the United States (Besteman 2016). Moreover, within resettlement sites, agencies often contribute to the clustering of refugees by placing them repeatedly in the same neighborhoods. As the chapters by Lumley-Sapanski, Nelson, and Stadler each show, agencies have very little time and low budgets to find housing for refugees. Consequently, they often work with a small set of landlords and apartment complexes clustered in a few neighborhoods. Such neighborhoods tend to be poor, disconnected, and disproportionately consisting of non-white migrant populations. Besteman (2016: 108) refers to Haines' description of resettlement neighborhoods as part of some "other America," where struggles "to make ends meet means poor housing, dangerous neighborhoods, poor transport, and poor schools." Stadler identifies how Nepali-Bhutanese in Erie, Pennsylvania, are placed in predominantly African American neighborhoods, which are already imagined through racist ideologies as morally deficient and dangerous places. The structural neglect of inner-city poverty in Erie undermines the potential for bridging relations, pitting Bhutanese and their African American neighbors in a seemingly zero-sum game of competition rather than creating the conditions for solidarity to emerge. The socioeconomic disadvantages of dispersal policies are not just based on geography, but also relate to the access of information. In Stam's chapter on multiple refugee groups in Utica, New York, she demonstrates how dispersal leads not only to material poverty, but also to "informational" impoverishment. The refugees' informational deficit is rooted in their isolation from technology and access to necessary informal and formal information. As a result, the geographic and informational isolation of resettlement tends to disconnect refugees from opportunities for cultivating bridging capital. Ironically, the policy emphasis on dispersal and assimilation results less in the intended bridging networks, but instead reinforces bonding networks.

THE ROLE OF NON-STATE ACTORS

The research findings of this volume indicate that bridging capital is most effectively realized when not imposed through state-sponsored bureaucratic solutions, but more organically generated by non-state actors or developed in response to circumstances. One example is given by Sienkiewicz et al.'s description of the Settlement House model supported by the Center for New North Carolinians at the University of North Carolina at Greensboro. The researchers found that it was necessary to create physical spaces for inter-ethnic relations. If not made, refugees would be likely to migrate on to other cities where they had bonding capital of family or friends. Thus, rather than a result of state policy that facilitates assimilation and integration, the cultivation of bridging networks is often a consequence of the efforts of non-state agencies.

Relationships based on bridging capital can also develop in accidental and unintended ways as consequences of circumstances. For instance, Ramsay shows how the process of childbirth for central African refugees in Australia can reveal the "expansive potentialities of social networks." Giving birth reaffirms their identities as mothers rather than refugees and provides a connection with other women from both refugee and non-refugee backgrounds. In another case, Lumley-Sapanski found that among Iraqis in Chicago, bridging capital is established through necessity. As Iraqis in her study tended to be *free cases*—referring to individuals migrating individually without pre-existing family, kin or community ties at the location of resettlement as opposed to *anchor cases* arriving at a resettlement site that provides such ties—they are more likely to find housing and employment through networks based on bridging capital. However, for the far more common anchor case type of resettlement, like the Burmese in Chicago, the networks based on bonding capital informed housing choices.

Due to the lack of state support soon after their arrival, refugees become dependent on social networks. In fact, even before support ends, refugees often find more resources through the bonding social capital of personal networks and ethnic-based organizations than through the more formal Volags and NGOs (Gold 1992; Griffiths et al. 2005; Keel and Drew 2004). In particular, Community-Based Organizations (CBOs) adopt "quasi-formal"

(Nawyn 2011, 1521) roles, often based along ethnic or national lines that are concerned with the longer-term social and cultural adjustments of refugees. Support from co-ethnics or co-nationals is offered in culturally acceptable terms that challenge the individualist ideologies of formal resettlement policies. Besteman (2016, 212) notes that "[f]or people who prioritize community life and social networks over individualism, self-sufficiency means community independence rather than individual economic autonomy, and integration does not mean abandoning their values in a bid to become American." This observation tallies with the conclusion of a number of migration studies that find that the processes of integration and transnationalism are often mutually supportive (Carling and Pettersen 2014; Gropas et al. 2014).

Many of the chapters in our volume demonstrate that successful resettlement programs require engagement with and investment in CBOs. For instance, Yotebieng et al. have documented the efforts of a Volag in Columbus, Ohio, to leverage community participation and organizations in creating an effective mental health program. Other chapters look to how CBOs and other less formal networks develop programs on their own to not only provide necessary services, but to do so in a culturally specific fashion that is more likely to be trusted and utilized by refugees. Chase describes the benefit of CBOs structuring and facilitating programs that address community mental health and well-being in non-stigmatizing ways. Similarly, Stadler demonstrates how leaders of a Nepali-Bhutanese CBO in Erie, Pennsylvania, rework ideologies of neoliberal citizenship implemented through the self-sufficiency agenda of resettlement agencies to find "creative ways to labor" based on cooperative strategies for finding employment and transportation. In these cases, it is the bonding capital of networks that allows CBOs to more effectively translate or even transform the agencies' policies into strategies that work in everyday practices.

While networks based on bonding capital tend to be more likely to be trusted, they too can suffer from structural constraints. A central issue with bonding capital is exposed through its basis on the problematic category of community. As numerous scholars have argued (Amit and Rapport 2002; Chatterjee 1998; Chatty 2010; Massey 1994; Rapport and Overing 2000; Shaw 2008), there is no such thing as a discrete and homogenous community. Hoellerer's chapter demonstrates how the United Kingdom's policy to delegate resettlement support to nongovernmental bodies, such as the Refugee Community Organizations (RCOs), assumes that refugee communities would "naturally come together." She identifies a more Bourdieuian (Levien 2015, 80) model of social capital in which power is unequally distributed and contested. Cases of in-fighting, power struggles, and divisions resulted in many of the Nepali-Bhutanese RCOs splintering into multiple factions. Similarly, both Nelson and Stadler each demonstrate how differential status positions, often stemming back to pre-exile contexts, determine an unequal distribution of resources and knowledge of opportunities. Moreover, as Heinemann et al. found, early arrivals, known as "community anchors," can often become overburdened by expectations to help recent arrivals. They discovered that more recent arrivals were more likely to provide assistance rather than the more integrated first arrivals.

LAYOUT OF THE BOOK

Conceptual Frameworks

The first section of the volume discusses basic conceptual frameworks and provides some background on involuntary migration, such as the evolving and shifting nature of social networks and social capital and the problematic definition of a refugee versus a migrant. This section questions the differential valuation afforded to bonding and bridging forms of social capital in terms of the refugee resettlement process. Given the specific challenges of migrant integration in general and refugee integration in particular, coupled with the insecurity, isolation, and disorientation caused by experiences in their home countries, the reconstruction of bonding networks should be a first priority in the resettlement process (Smith 2013; Suter and Magnusson 2015). The two chapters in this section have corroborated this finding by illustrating how the relationship between the various types of networks is anything but stable, as refugees have to negotiate which type of social networks to create, nurture and engage with and from which form of social capital to draw. The authors formulate a number of recommendations for refugee agencies on how to support refugees and migrants while creatively supporting and cultivating different social capitals in specific situations.

In addition to establishing the foundational role of social capital and networks in the resettlement process, this section questions the category of refugee. Recently, it has been observed that internationally legally defined boundaries between the categories of refugees and migrants—which used to be considered clear-cut—have become blurred. This blurring is explained not only because "[s]tates have become increasingly concerned with the securitization of their borders against irregular migration" (Long 2009, 2), but also because individuals who qualify for refugee status, or for another form of international protection, may themselves have *mixed motivations* that cut across the conceptual dichotomy between a *forced flight* and *voluntary migration* (UNHCR 2007). Rosales' chapter on Mayan people fleeing Guatemala for the United States is an example of this blurring of legal categories. Despite escaping from the political atrocities in their home country, Mayan men and women are nevertheless considered and treated as migrants by the US immigration bureaucracy. By problematizing the dominant understanding and discussions about forced and voluntary migration, he provides a bottom-up contribution to the (usually top-down) refugee-migrant debate that reveals how supposedly voluntary migrants employ similar strategies of network reconstruction as do officially recognized refugees.

Mental Health and Wellbeing

The second section argues that issues related to mental health and well-being can best be recognized and addressed through a combination of community, neighborhood, and healthcare efforts. Traumatic events in refugees' countries of origin and during protracted stay in refugee camps generally result in loss of social and other capitals, exposing them to a wide range of physical, mental, and other health problems (Kim and Kim 2014). Stress experienced during resettlement takes further toll on their overall health and well-being, affecting adjustment to the host country (May et al. 2014). Social capital has been shown to significantly improve health and well-being of migrants in general and refugees in particular (Mahoney 2004; Olness 1998). The chapters in this section highlight exemplary cases of programs that increased refugees' social capital while also improving their health and well-being, arguing that service providers need to shift their conceptions of refugees from that of being vulnerable and passive to resilient and active.

The focus on refugees' mental health and well-being in these chapters is not new; a significant number of publications have explored a wide range of mental health issues among refugees (e.g., Harris and Zwar 2005). However, these chapters' ethnographic approach highlights how the creation, re-creation, and maintenance of social networks and (both bonding and bridging) social capital are crucial for resettled refugees' mental health and well-being. The participatory methods of anthropology readily connect to similar approaches in other academic and professional fields, such as the eco-systemic framework in the health professions, which makes the conclusions accessible to many involved with refugee health (Bronfenbrenner 1979; Guruge and Khanlou 2004).

Yotebieng et al. argue that programs that aim to increase a sense of well-being among resettled refugees, and particularly to support refugees with mental health needs, need to pay attention to the role of social networks and social capital in tapping into and enhancing refugees' resilience, as well as positively impacting their overall sense of well-being and mental health. These programs can be set up and run by refugees themselves (bonding), by governmental or nongovernmental organizations (bridging), or by all stakeholders together (bonding and bridging). Using participant-observation and interviews, Sienkiewiecz et al. explored a neighborhood-based program of "settlement houses" that facilitated three types of needs by nurturing the development of both bonding and bridging capital through addressing individual and household needs, communal needs within and among refugee communities, and the need to integrate into the local community. Receiving communities need to establish programs, such as resettlement houses, but are also encouraged to nurture the creation of programs by refugees themselves, tapping into refugees' agency and their knowledge and skills. Chase's ethnographic study of Bhutanese Nepali-speakers in refugee camps in Nepal and at a resettlement site in the United States examines community-based organizations run by refugees themselves and their impact on mental health and suicide rates. The organizations address distress through culturally salient patterns of belief and practices that alleviate stress and foster mental well-being.

Citizenship & Belonging

The third section explores the role of social networks in refugee belonging and identity vis-à-vis state and institutional factors. Refugees present a particular problem for a global social order organized by the nation-state, which presupposes rights and membership based on citizenship (Arendt 1994; Agamben 1998; Nyers 2006). Thus, refugees disrupt the "national order of things" (Malkki 1995) and, in turn, are seen by states as problems to be resolved through the process of repatriation back to home countries or resettlement in host countries. From the state's top-down perspective, resettlement creates questions about the allegiance of refugees to their new nation. They are imagined as either "Odyssean" outsiders, with continued ties to home country, or "Rubicon" insiders, who embrace their new identities (Joly 2002). Such either/or approaches reproduce the limitations of assimilation theories, which assume identity to be linear and singular (Rumbaut 1997), whereby one is considered either as incorporated insiders or excluded outsiders.

Anthropology's focus on bottom-up models has offered more flexible approaches to account for the multiplicity of identities emerging from the migrant's experience. For instance, anthropologists have applied the theory of hybridity (Bhabha 1994) to demonstrate how the liminal space of migrants in between home and host cultures allows for them to construct an alternative third identity (Yazdiha 2010). Similarly, the concept of transnationalism (Levitt 2001; Levitt and Glick Schiller 2004; Portes et al. 1999; Vertovec 1999; Ong 1999) recognizes the simultaneous links that migrant people maintain across borders and cultures. Missing from such concepts, however, is the processual and more personal nature of belonging that accounts for the intersection of multiple scales, places, and networks in the migrant ability (Malkki 1995; Shneiderman 2015) to become "at home in exile" (Graham and Khosravi 1997). For instance, a focus on belonging provides more attention to the possible internal divisions within groups, or networks of bonding capital, along class, gender, racial and religious lines, as well as the external, or bridging, links to other groups. Importantly, while refugee networks often conform to the logic and functioning of state-level immigration policy, they can also challenge it. Similarly, bonding and bridging networks can provide refugees with the material benefits of resources and social links of community, but they can also be exploitative and isolating.

The chapters by Hoellerer, Stam, Ramsay, and Halsouet speak to the limitations of state-level policy in creating a sense of belonging for resettled refugees. Hoellerer critiques how the United Kingdom's definition of "successful resettlement" reproduces a neoliberal model of outsourcing state programs to the bonding networks of community organizations in order to support refugees. As she shows, such models fail to account for the internal differences and conflicts of networks both within and between such organizations. The second chapter by Stam reminds us of the importance of recognizing the differences between refugee groups and argues for a contextual appreciation of each group. She documents the diversity of refugee strategies to gain information in a small town in upstate New York, and traces them back to each group's specific exile-generating conflict or event. Ramsay discusses how Central African women refugees in Australia conceive of giving birth as a step toward building future lives and connections in their new home in direct challenge to policies that fracture networks and families. Finally, Halsouet demonstrates how the Canadian educational policy of "socialization" is ill-equipped to meet the complex social needs of refugees in a small mono-ethnic town. Each chapter, in its way, highlights the importance of integrating both bonding and bridging social networks approaches for successful state policies.

Space & Place

The fourth section maintains that refugees are constantly in the process of emplacement, of actively making sense of one's place. Since the 1990s, anthropology and related fields have increasingly turned to questions of space and place to understand the refugee experience. Previously, ethnography often reproduced a sedentarist bias of assuming culture to be attached to territory (Gupta and Ferguson 1992), which had the effect of fixing "natives" in place (Appadurai 1988). As refugees are defined by their "homelessness" detached from territory and nation, sedentarist thinking has rendered them as abnormal, as people "out of place" (Malkki 1992). Such thinking has influenced the tendency of governments and resettlement agencies to imagine refugees as passive victims with little to no control over their lives in their new countries.

To correct for the limitations of sedentarist thinking, many scholars took a "spatial turn" to emphasize the increasing commonness of displacement and homelessness, and the general condition of mobility for much of humanity (Warf and Arias 2009; Gupta and Ferguson 1997; Clifford 1997). In a phrase, scholarship shifted from "roots to routes" (Friedman 2002). However, the turn toward mobility tended to dismiss the salience of attachments to territory and place. While paying greater attention to mobility offered a necessary step to attribute agency to refugees' movements (Malkki 1992), it rendered place to be the fixed, local and passive opposite of the more mobile, global, and active space (Lems 2014). However, as the geographer Doreen Massey (1994) has argued, place is much more than just local space, as it is entwined in global processes. Furthermore, Gielis (2009) understands place as the nexus of multiple translocal and transnational networks of social and economic importance. Thus, place carries significant meaning to people, even if they inhabit and interact in multiple social and physical spaces.

In this section, we maintain that refugees are constantly involved in the process of emplacement, or making of one's sense of place (Feld and Basso, 1996). Rather than a mutually exclusive binary, emplacement and displacement are linked processes occurring at the same time (Hammond 2004; Korac 2009; Lems 2014; Malkki 1992). Specifically, we show how both bonding and bridging social networks are central to the emplacement practices and strategies of refugees often in defiance of policies of dispersal that distribute refugees throughout a country with the goal of disrupting the possibility of enclaves forming. As such, home is much more than a physical place from which refugees are displaced; it is also a cultural process embedded in social networks and relations (Dudley 2011; Jansen and Löfving 2008; Pilkington and Flynn 1999). The anthropological methods of participant-observation and qualitative data are particularly insightful tools for identifying the agency of refugees in making places through networks.

The first three chapters of the volume demonstrate the spatial agency of refugees to move beyond the support of resettlement agencies in their strategies to remake their homes and reconnect their families and social networks in the new country. Nelson examines how, in contrast to the ideologies of economic independence instilled by resettlement agencies, Nepali-Bhutanese refugees employ social networks of dependence to purchase houses in the suburban outskirts of Fort Worth, Texas. Similarly, Lumley-Sapanski draws attention to how the circumstances of resettlement often determine which kind of social capital is drawn from in the secondary relocation decisions of Iraqi and Burmese refugees in Chicago. Stadler focuses on the strategies of Nepali-Bhutanese community organizations in Erie, Pennsylvania to uplift both their community and their marginalized neighborhood in spite of considerable structural restraints resulting from the post-industrial conditions of the rust-belt city.

Finally, in the volume-ending epilogue by Willems, she foreshadows the future of global refugee dynamics by pointing out that Europe is quickly becoming the center of third country resettlement. As such, she encourages European policy makers to learn from the lessons emphasized in this volume. In order to create conditions in which refugees can feel "at home" in resettlement, policies must listen to refugees to craft holistic programs that extend beyond economic production to prioritize the support and maintenance of social networks.

NOTES

1. The 1951 UN Refugee Convention defines a refugee as a person who is outside his or her country of nationality or habitual residence; has a well-founded fear of being persecuted because of his or her race, religion, nationality, membership of a particular social group or political opinion; and is unable or unwilling to avail himself or herself of the protection of that country, or to return there, for fear of persecution (UNHCR 2011: 3).
2. In some European countries, refugee status is increasingly given on a temporary basis, meaning that after an initial period of four or five years, the situation in the country of origin is re-evaluated and, when considered safe for return, refugee status can be withdrawn.
3. The name of this group is highly contested and debated. While some authors in this volume refer to this group simply as "Nepalese" or "Bhutanese" for the sake of demonstrating that both names refer to the same group of refugees, in the introduction we use the hyphenated term, "Nepali-Bhutanese."
4. The authors changed the names of interviewees and anonymized all identifying information.
5. The social theorist Max Weber argues that we need abstract concepts, which he calls ideal types, that help to create order in the seeming chaos of reality (Weber 1904). However, ideal types are not meant to refer to a specific reality in its totality, but rather to stress certain elements common to most cases of a given phenomenon. They are conceptual tools to be used to make sense of reality, while at the same time recognizing their inadequacy. In other words, categories and theoretical concepts understood as ideal types have a fictional reality and do not claim validity in terms of correspondence with each and every specific social reality.

REFERENCES CITED

Australian Government. 2017. "Department of Immigration and Border Protection." Retrieved from https://www.border.gov.au/Lega/Lega/Form/Immi-FAQs/is-there-any-support-to-help-me-settle-into-life-in-australia.

Agamben, Giorgio. 1998. *Homo Sacer: Sovereign Power and Bare Life*. Translation by Daniel Heller-Roazen. Stanford, CA: Stanford University Press.

Amit, Vered, Nigel Rapport, Thomas Eriksen, Katy Gardner, and Jon Mitchell. (2002). *The Trouble with Community: Anthropological Reflections on Movement, Identity and Collectivity*. London: Pluto Press.

Appadurai, Arjun. 1988. "Putting Hierarchy in its Place." *Cultural Anthropology* 3 (1): 36–49.

Arendt, Hannah. 1996. "We Refugees." In *Altogether Elsewhere: Writers on Exile*, edited by Mark Robinson, 110–119. Boston: Faber and Faber.

Besteman, Catherine. 2016. *Making Refuge: Somali Bantu Refugees and Lewiston, Maine*. Durham: Duke University Press.

Bhabha, Homi. 1994. *The Location of Culture*. London: Routledge.

Biehl, João and Adriana Petryna. 2013. "Critical Global Health." In *When People Come First: Critical Studies in Global Health*, edited by João Biehl and Adriana Petryna, 1–29. Princeton: Princeton University Press.

Bloch, Alice. 2002. *The Migration and Settlement of Refugees in Britain*. Basingstoke: Palgrave McMillan.

———. 2004. "Labour Market Participation and Conditions of Employment: A Comparison of Minority Ethnic Groups and Refugees in Britain." *Sociological Research Online* 9 (2): 1–19.

Bourgois, Philippe. 2003. *In Search of Respect: Selling Crack in El Barrio*. 2nd Edition. Cambridge: Cambridge University Press.

Bronfenbrenner, Urie. 1979. *The Ecology of Human Development: Experiments by Nature and Design*. Cambridge: Harvard University Press.

Bruno, Andorra. 2015. "Refugee Admissions and Resettlement Policy." *Current Politics and Economics of the United States, Canada and Mexico* 17 (3): 485–500.

Carling, Jørgen and Silje Vatne Pettersen. 2014. "Return Migration Intentions in the Integration-Transnationalism Matrix." *International Migration* 52 (6): 13–30.

Chatterjee, Partha. 1998. "Community in the East." *Economic and Political Weekly* 33 (6): 277–282.

Chatty, Dawn. 2010. *Dispossession and Forced Migration in the Middle East*. Cambridge: Cambridge University Press.

Cheung, Sin Yi and Jenny Phillimore. 2013. "Refugees, Social Capital, and Labour Market Integration in the UK." *Sociology* 48 (3): 518–536.

———. 2013. *Social Networks, Social Capital and Refugee Integration*. Research Report for Nuffield Foundation. Birmingham: University of Birmingham.

Clifford, James. 1997. *Routes: Travel and Translation in the Late Twentieth Century*. Cambridge: Harvard University Press.

Dudley, Sandra. 2011. "Feeling at Home; Producing and Consuming Things in Karenni Refugee Camps on the Thai-Burma Border." *Population, Space and Place* 17: 742–755.

Farmer, Paul. 2011. "Partners in Help." Retrieved from https://www.foreignaffairs.com/articles/haiti/2011-07-29/partners-help.

Feld, Steven and Keith Basso. 1996. *Senses of Place*. Santa Fe: School of American Research Press.

Finney, Nissa and Ludi Simpson. 2009. *Sleepwalking to Segregation? Challenging Myths about Race and Immigration.* Bristol: Policy Press at the University of Bristol.

Friedman, Jonathan, 2002. "From Roots to Routes: Tropes for Trippers." *Anthropological Theory* 2 (1): 21–36.

Geiger, Vance. 1993. *Refugee Cognitive Expectation and Sociocultural Change Theory.* Selected Papers on Refugee Issues: Volume 2. Arlington: American Anthropological Association.

Gielis, Ruben. 2009. "A Global Sense of Places: Towards a Place Perspective in the Study of Migrant Transnationalism." *Global Networks* 9 (2): 271–287.

Giddens, Anthony. 1990. *The Consequences of Modernity.* Palo Alto: Stanford University Press.

Gold, Steve. 1992. *Refugee Communities: A Comparative Field Study.* New York: Sage Publications.

Gold, Steve and Nazli Kibria. 1993. "Vietnamese Refugees and Blocked Mobility." *Asian and Pacific Migration Journal* 2 (1): 27–56.

Graham, Mark and Shahram Khosravi. 1997. "Home is Where You Make It: Repatriation and Diaspora Culture among Iranians in Sweden." *Journal of Refugee Studies* 10 (2): 115–133.

Griffiths, David, Nando Sigona, and Roger Zetter. 2005. *Refugee Community Organizations and Dispersal: Networks, Resources and Social Capital.* Chicago: University of Chicago Press.

Gropas, Ruby, Anns Tryandafyllidou, and Laura Bartolini. 2014. *Conceptualising the Integration-Transnationalism Nexus.* ITHACA Report. Florence: European University Institute.

Gupta, Akhil and James Ferguson. 1992. "Beyond 'Culture': Space, Identity, and the Politics of Difference." *Cultural Anthropology* 7 (1): 6–23.

———. 1997. "Beyond 'Culture': Space, Identity, and the Politics of Difference." In *Culture, Power, Place: Explorations in Critical Anthropology* edited by Akhil Gupta and James Ferguson, 33–51. Durham: Duke University Press.

Guruge, Sepali and Nazilla Khanlou. 2004. "Intersectionalities of Influence: Researching Health of Immigrant and Refugee Women." *Canadian Journal of Nursing Research* 36 (3): 32–47.

Hammond, Laura. 2004. *This Place Will Become Home: Refugee Repatriation to Ethiopia.* Ithaca: Cornell University Press.

Haines, David. 2010. *Safe Haven? A History of Refugees in America.* Kumarian Press.

Hannerz, Ulf. 1996. *Transnational Connections: Culture, People, Places.* London: Routledge.

Harrell-Bond, Barbara and Eftihia Voutira. 1992. "Anthropology and the Study of Refugees." *Anthropology Today* 8 (4): 6–10.

Harris, Mark and Nicholas Zwar. 2005. "Refugee Health." *Australian Family Physician* 34 (10): 825–829.

Hathaway, James. 1991. "Reconceiving Refugee Law as Human Rights Protection." *Journal of Refugee Studies* 4 (2): 113–131.

———. 1995. "New Directions to Avoid Hard Problems: The Distortion of the Palliative Role of Refugee Protection." *Journal of Refugee Studies* 8 (3): 288–304.

Hung, Nguyen Manh and David Haines. 1996. "Vietnamese." In *Refugees in America in the 1990s,* edited by David Haines, 305–329. Westport, CT: Greenwood Press.

Jansen, Stef and Staffan Löfving. 2008. *Struggles for Home: Violence, Hope and Movement of People*. New York: Berghahn Books.

Jones, Trevor, Monder Ram, Paul Edwards, Alexander Kiselinchev, and Lovemore Muchenje. 2012. "New Migrant Enterprise: Novelty or Historical Continuity?" *Urban Studies* 49 (14): 3159–3176.

Johnston, Vanessa, Katie Vasey, and Milica Markovic. 2009. "Social Policies and Refugee Resettlement: Iraqis in Australia." *Critical Social Policy* 29 (2): 191–215.

Joly, Danièle. 2002. "Odyssean and Rubicon Refugees: Toward a Typology of Refugees in the Land of Exile." *International Migration* 40 (6): 1–21.

Keel, Monique and Neil Drew. 2004. "The Settlement Experiences of Refugees from the Former Yugoslavia: Acculturation, Ethnic Identity, Ethnicity, Community and Social Network Development." *Community, Work & Family* 7 (1): 95–115.

Keles, Fethi. 2008. "The Structural Negligence of US Refugee Resettlement Policy." *Anthropology News* 49 (5): 6.

Kelly, James. 1987. "An Ecological Paradigm: Defining Mental Health Consultation as a Preventative Service." In *The Ecology of Prevention,* edited by James Kelly and Robert Hess, 1–36. New York: The Hawarth Press.

Kim, Isok and Wooksoo Kim. 2014. "Post-Resettlement Challenges and Mental Health of Southeast Asian Refugees in the United States." *Mental Health* 10 (2): 63–77.

Kopinak, Janice. 1999. "The Use of Triangulation in a Study of Refugee Well-Being." *Quality and Quantity* 33: 169–183.

Korac, Maja. 2009. *Remaking Home: Reconstructing Life, Place and Identity in Rome and Amsterdam.* New York and Oxford: Berghahn Books.

Lamba, Navjot and Harvey Krahn. 2003. "Social Capital and Refugee Settlement: The Social Networks of Refugees in Canada." *Journal of International Migration and Integration* 4 (3): 335–360.

Lems, Annika. 2014. "Placing Displacement: Place-making in a World of Movement." *Ethnos: Journal of Anthropology* 81 (2): 315–337.

Levien, Michael. 2015. "Social Capital as Obstacle to Development: Brokering Land, Norms, and Trust in Rural India." *World Development* 74: 77–92.

Levitt, Peggy. 2001. *The Transnational Villagers*. Los Angeles: University of California Press.

Levitt Peggy and Nina Glick Schiller. 2004. "Conceptualizing Simultaneity: a Transnational Social Field Perspective on Society." *International Migration Review* 38 (3): 1002–1039.

Light, Ivan and Edna Bonacich. 1988. *Immigrant Entrepreneurs: Koreans in Los Angeles, 1965-1982*. Berkeley: University of California Press.

Long, Katy. 2009. "Extending Protection? Labour Migration and Durable Solutions for Refugees." New Issues in Refugee Research: Research Paper No. 176. Retrieved from http://www.unhcr.org/4ad334a46.pdf.

Mahoney, Annette. 2004. "Introduction – The Health and Social Well-Being of Caribbean Immigrants in the United States." In *The Health and Well-Being of*

Caribbean Immigrants in the United States, edited by Annette Mahoney, 1–10. Binghamton: The Haworth Social Work Practice Press.

Malkki, Liisa. 1992. "National Geographic: The Rooting of Peoples and Territorialization of National Identity among Scholars and Refugees." *Cultural Anthropology* 7 (1): 24–44.

———. 1995. "Refugees and Exile: From 'Refugee Studies' to the National Order of Things." *Annual Review of Anthropology* 24: 495–523.

———. 1996 "Speechless Emissaries: Refugees, Humanitarianism, and Dehistoricization." *Cultural Anthropology* 11 (3): 377–404.

Massey, Doreen. 1994. *Space, Place and Gender.* Minneapolis: University of Minnesota Press.

Marx, Emanuel. 1990. "The Social World of Refugees: A Conceptual Framework." *Journal of Refugee Studies* 3 (3): 189–203.

May, Samantha, Ronald Rapee, Mariano Coello, Shakeh Momartin, and Jorge Arocho. 2014. "Mental Health Literacy among Refugee Communities: Differences between the Australian Lay Public and the Iraqi and Sudanese Refugee Communities." *Social Psychiatry and Psychiatric Epidemiology* 49: 757–769.

Menjivar, Cecilia. 1995. "Kinship Networks among Immigrants." *International Journal of Comparative Sociology* 36 (3–4): 219–232.

Merton, Robert. 1936. "The Unanticipated Consequences of Purposive Social Action." *American Sociological Review* 1 (6): 894–904.

Miller, Kenneth and Lisa Rasco. 2004. "An Ecological Framework for Addressing the Mental Health Needs of Refugee Communities." In *The Mental Health of Refugees: Ecological Approaches to Healing and Adaptation,* edited by Kenneth Miller and Lisa Rasco, 1–66. Mahwah: Lawrence Erlbaum Associates.

Morrice, Linda. 2007. "Lifelong Learning and the Social Integration of Refugees in the UK: The Significance of Social Capital." *International Journal of Lifelong Education* 20 (2): 155–172.

Nawyn, Stephanie. 2011. "'I Have so Many Successful Stories': Framing Social Citizenship for Refugees." *Citizenship Studies* 15 (6–7): 679–693.

Negri, Antonio and Michael Hardt. 2009. *Commonwealth.* Boston: Harvard University Press.

Nyers, Peter. 2006. *Rethinking Refugees: Beyond States of Emergency.* New York and London: Routledge.

Oliver-Smith, Anthony. 1986. *The Martyred City: Death and Rebirth in the Andes.* Albuquerque: University of New Mexico Press.

Olness, Karen. 1998. "Refugee Health." In *Handbook of Immigrant Health,* edited by Sana Loue, 227–242. New York: Plenum Press.

Ong, Aihwa. 1999. *Flexible Citizenship: The Cultural Logics of Transnationality.* Durham: Duke University Press.

———. 2003. *The Buddha is Hiding: Refugees, Citizenship and the New America.* Berkeley: University of California Press.

Pilkington, Hilary and Moya Flynn. 1999. "From 'Refugee' to 'Repatriate': Russian Repatriation Discourse in the Making." In *The End of the Refugee Cycle: Refugee Repatriation and Reconstruction,* edited by Richard Black and Khalid Khoser, 171–197. Oxford: Berghahn Books.

Portes, Alejandro. 1997. "Immigration Theory for a New Century: Some Problems and Opportunities." *International Migration Review* 31 (4): 799–825.

Portes, Alejandro and Robert Bach. 1985. *Latin Journey: Cuban and Mexican Immigrants in the United States*. Berkeley: University of California Press.

Portes, Alejandro, Luis Guarnizo, and Patricia Landolt. 1999. "The Study of Transnationalism: Pitfalls and Promise of an Emergent Research Field." *Ethnic and Racial Studies* 22 (2): 217–237.

Putnam, Robert. 1995. "Bowling Alone: America's Declining Social Capital." *Journal of Democracy* 6 (1): 65–78.

———. 2000. *Bowling Alone: The Collapse and Revival of American Community*. New York: Simon Schuster.

Rapport, Nigel and Joanna Overing. 2000. *Social and Cultural Anthropology: The Key Concepts*. London: Routledge.

Rumbaut, Ruben. 1997. "Assimilation and Its Discontents: Between Rhetoric and Reality." *The International Migration Review* 31 (4): 923–960.

Shaw, Mae. 2006. "Community Development and the Politics of Community." *Community Development Journal* 43 (1): 24–36.

Shneiderman, Sara. 2015. *Rituals of Ethnicity: Thangmi Identities between Nepal and India*. Philadelphia: University of Pennsylvania Press.

Simich, Laura. 2003. "Negotiating Boundaries of Refugee Resettlement: A Study of Settlement Patterns and Social Support." *Canadian Review of Sociology and Anthropology* 40 (5): 575–591.

Smith, Yda. 2013. "We All Bantu—We Have Each Other: Preservation of Social Capital Strengths During Forced Migration." *Journal of Occupational Science* 20 (2): 173–184.

Suter, Brigitte and Karin Magnusson. 2015. *Resettled and Reconnected: Social Networks in the Integration Process of Resettled Refugees*. Sweden: Malmö University, Malmö Institute for Studies of Migration, Diversity and Welfare.

Turner, Victor. 1969. *The Ritual Process: Structure and Anti-Structure*. Chicago, IL: Aldine Publishing Press.

United Nations High Commission for Refugees (UNHCR). 2007. "Refugee Protection and Mixed Migration: A 10-Point Plan of Action." Retrieved from www.unhcr.org/4742a30b4.

———. 2011. "The 1951 Convention Relating to the Status of Refugees and Its 1967 Protocol." Retrieved from http://www.unhcr.org/cgibin/texis/vtx/home/opendoc PDFViewer.html?docid=4ec262df9&query=1951unconvention.

———. 2015a. "UNHCR Global Trends 2014." Retrieved from http://www.unhcr.org/556725e69.html.

———. 2015b. "This is a Primarily Refugee Crisis, Not Only a Migration Phenomenon. Statement by UN High Commissioner for Refugees, Antonio Guterres, on the Refugee Crisis in Europe." Retrieved from http://data.unhcr.org/mediterranean/flash_read.php?ID=9.

———. 2017. 2016 Statistical Yearbook: Figures at a Glance. Retrieved from http://www.unhcr.org/en-us/figures-at-a-glance.html

United States Department of State (USDoS) (2016). *Fiscal Year 2015 Refugee Admissions*. Washington, DC: Bureau of Population, Refugees, and Migration.

Vertovec, Steven. 1999. "Conceiving and Researching Transnationalism." *Ethnic and Racial Studies* 22 (2): 447–462.

Warf, Barney and Santa Arias, eds. 2009. *The Spatial Turn: Interdisciplinary Perspectives*. London and New York: Routledge.

Weber, Max.1904. "Die Objektivität Socialwissenschaftlicher und Socialpolitischer Erkenntnis." *Archiv für Sozialwissenschaft und Sozialpolitik, Volume 19*. Tübingen: Verlag Von J.C.B. Mohr.

Whitmarsh, Ian. 2013. "The Ascetic Subject of Compliance: The Turn to Chronic Diseases in Global Health." In *When People Come First: Critical Studies in Global Health,* edited by João Biehl and Adriana Petryna, 302–324. Princeton: Princeton University Press.

Williams, Lucy. 2006. "Social Networks of Refugees in the United Kingdom: Tradition, Tactics and New Community Spaces." *Journal of Ethnic and Migration Studies* 32 (5): 865–879.

Yazdiha, Haj. 2010. "Conceptualizing Hybridity: Deconstructing Boundaries through the Hybrid." Retrieved from http://academicworks.cuny.edu/gc_pubs/314.

Part I

CONCEPTUAL FRAMEWORKS

Chapter 1

The Competing and Shifting Relevance of Social Capitals in Successful Refugee Resettlement

Laura Heinemann, Claire Herzog, Margo Minnich, Celeste Mitchell, Laeth Nasir, Alexander Rödlach, Chaitri Desai, and Melanie Kim, with commentaries by John Tluang and Govin Magar

The journey of a displaced person—a refugee—can be described as an ongoing process of losing, building, and maintaining social capital. The 1951 Refugee Convention defines a refugee as someone who, "owing to a well-founded fear of being persecuted for reasons of race, religion, nationality, membership of a particular social group or political opinion, is outside the country of his nationality, and is unable to, or owing to such fear, is unwilling to avail himself of the protection of that country" (UNHCR 1951). As refugees leave behind their homes, and with it their social networks and access to social capital, they often first migrate to a neighboring country where, by and large, they are expected to live in camps until being permanently resettled in a host country where they expect to start rebuilding their lives. Working together with countries willing to resettle refugees, the United Nations High Commission for Refugees coordinates the resettlement process. Because of limited quotas, scarce resources, complex bureaucracies, and international laws, relocation generally takes a long time and is riddled with complexities (UNHCR 2015).

According to representatives of resettlement agencies in Omaha, Nebraska, locally resettled refugees live on average for seventeen years in a refugee camp before being resettled in a host country, when returning home is not an option. Refugee camp conditions vary greatly, but can be characterized by a lack of resources, continued violence, and infectious diseases. At the same time, camps also facilitate some, if limited, access to social capital as children are born, friends are made, and networks are reestablished or created.

Nebraska is one of a number of states in the United States that has been chosen by the US government for the resettlement of refugees, owing to its low unemployment rate and relatively smaller communities. Highway signs with the slogan: "Nebraska . . . the good life" greet all who enter the state including newcomers, visitors, and residents alike. Omaha is the state's largest city. Located just west of the Missouri River, it enjoys a low cost of living and a successful, resilient economy with low unemployment rates that weathered even the most recent US financial crisis. It is, therefore, not surprising that the city attracts a significant number of new residents annually. In fact, Omaha saw a 4.2 percent increase in population between 2010 and 2013 (U.S. Census Bureau 2013). This population growth includes refugees, who are resettled by local nonprofit organizations referred to as *resettlement agencies*. Newly arrived refugees are assisted by their resettlement agency as well as governmental and nongovernmental organizations, such as Omaha Public Schools and local churches that motivate members to volunteer to assist the city's new residents. In addition to being a popular site for initial refugee resettlement, Omaha is also a *secondary migration* site. That is, refugees who were originally resettled in other cities often relocate to Omaha, encouraged by economic conditions and a desire to be close to kin and other members of their ethnic communities.

In 2012, former Omaha mayor Jim Suttle spoke at a public event referring to refugees as having access to "the Good Life" through initial or secondary resettlement in Omaha. He acknowledged that the resettlement process has not been easy and that "[a]s a city, we often struggle with language and cultural barriers, finding affordable and decent housing, and oftentimes employment for refugees" (Suttle 2012). Interconnections among refugees and to the larger community through social networks and social capitals are crucial to start a new life and to be part of "the good life." This is consistent with the findings of Cheung and Phillimore (2013) who note that the types of social connections developed and maintained by refugees can impact language acquisition, employment and even health status.

The process of leaving first one's home country and then refugee camps can fracture ties with friends, extended family members, and the larger community. Resettled refugees thus lose social capital in the form of supportive social networks and the associated dynamics of reciprocity and social trust, depleting both emotional social support and the instrumental support that would help them to navigate systems and solve problems (Keel and Drew 2004). Such loss can be traumatizing, and can further isolate individuals and communities already reeling from the conditions and experiences surrounding forced displacement. The maintenance and reconstruction of an extensive base of social capital, then, is essential for successful resettlement (Lamba and Krahn 2003). Although refugees are sometimes cast as perpetually dependent, they are in fact proactive in their own resettlement, drawing upon multiple forms of social capital throughout the process (William 2006). With often limited assistance from resettlement agencies and others, individuals and groups work to rebuild old and create new social networks and to regain social capital in their new home.

THE RESEARCH

Building from these perspectives, this chapter focuses on refugees' striving for and struggles with social capital. It draws from interactions with refugees and the resettlement agencies working with them in Omaha, Nebraska, in the context of two studies carried out by an interdisciplinary research team. The first study, spanning 2011 to 2013, was a health needs assessment of refugee communities, facilitated by a university-affiliated clinic.[1] The findings from this prompted a subsequent study in 2015[2] by the interdisciplinary team, to explore how social capital influences resettlement dynamics. Both studies utilized qualitative methods: observations, interviews, and focus group discussions. Study participants were selected through convenience and quota sampling to ensure that a wide range of groups and sub-groups were part of the studies. The audio-recorded conversations were transcribed verbatim and the resulting text analyzed, following the Grounded Theory approach (Corbin and Strauss 2008). The texts were coded using OpenCode 4.02 (Department of Public Health and Clinical Medicine 2013). The implementation of both studies as well as the interpretation of the resulting data was guided by faculty and staff at Creighton University, Lutheran Family Services—the primary resettlement agency in Omaha, and the YMCA, which provides programs tailored to refugee communities. The research group's community contacts were primarily resettled refugees from Bhutan and Myanmar (formerly Burma), particularly members of two major ethnic groups, the Karen and Karenni.[3]

REFUGEE RESETTLEMENT, SOCIAL NETWORKS, AND SOCIAL CAPITAL

The centrality of social capital for understanding resettlement dynamics calls for further exploration of this concept and its various dimensions. As an organizing framework, social capital theory affords important insights into the strengths of refugee communities as well as the barriers they can encounter when faced with a lack of social connections outside of the community (Smith 2013). But there also is some diversity among definitions of social capital (Keefer and Knack 2003). Woolcock (1998) for instance defines social capital in more general terms, as the norms and networks that enable collective action (also see Narayan 2005). This distinction between norms and networks corresponds in some respects with Uphoff's (1990) distinction between cognitive and structural components of social capital. Putnam (1993, 167), however, includes in his definition "features of social organization, such as trust, norms, and network that can improve the efficiency of society by facilitating coordinated action." Others, such as Coleman (1990), define social capital in terms of the quantity of obligations or informal "credit slips" between parties that are likely to be repaid, thus implicating both networks and norms. Suter and Magnussen (2015) remind us that social capital can be considered both a group and an individual resource. Bourdieu (1986) identifies economic, cultural, and social capital, each with its own relationship to social class, and emphasizes the dimensions of conflict and power. For Bourdieu, social capital is a resource in the social struggles that are carried out in different social arenas (Lawler 2011; Siisiäinen 2000). While the use of differing, vague, and inconsistent definitions, drawing sometimes on opposing social science and economic traditions (Siisiäinen 2000) has been criticized (e.g., Durlauf 2002), others argue that despite its vagueness, social capital motivates valuable research with significant policy implications (e.g., Sobel 2002).

Measuring social capital is complicated as the concept is related to networks and collective action but can exist outside of formal group membership (Rubenson 2011). In order to operationalize the concept, we refer to the World Bank's use of the concept of social capital, which includes five key dimensions as proxies for measuring social capital (Krishna and Shrader 1999). The first dimension is to assess groups and networks. Their effectiveness depends on aspects such as organizational elements, density and diversity of membership, and connections to other groups. The second is to systematically explore meanings and dynamics of trust and reciprocity, which greatly determine the efficiency of the groups and networks and how these relate to other groups and governmental and nongovernmental organizations (Fukuyama 1999, 16; Kreuter and Lezin 2002). The third dimension is collective action and its extent. The fourth dimension is social inclusion, an account of who in the community is included in collective action, decision-making, and access to services. The fifth dimension explores the ability of a community to communicate with its own membership, with other communities, and with members of their networks that live outside the community. Though these categories are not without their limitations, they consider and address major factors influencing the creation and maintenance of social capital. Our conversations with representatives of resettlement agencies and refugees focused on these dimensions.

Resettlement agencies can exert substantial control—both intentional and unintentional—over the social capital developed by refugees as they determine settlement (Simich 2003). When refugees arrive in their resettlement country, they need to quickly create both *bonding social capital* (i.e., social capital within a social network) and *bridging social capital* (social capital that *bridges* to other groups outside of the more immediate social network), as resettlement agencies taking cases from their national affiliates can provide support for only a limited time. According to case managers at an Omaha resettlement agency, refugees being resettled in the United States in 2017 received $1,125 per person and support services for the first ninety days, including rent and other needed resources. The support they receive in finding apartments, securing jobs, applying for federal aid, and some cultural competency instruction, amounts to formalized bridging social support. However, formal assistance ends by the end of the third month, after which resettled persons are expected to begin to pay their own rent and associated utilities, as well as repaying travel loans that enabled them to come to the United States. The assumption is that in this short time refugees will be able to acclimate to an entirely new cultural context and become self-sufficient. However, while government-sponsored official support is important, it rarely meets all of the needs of newly arriving refugees (Simich 2003).

ANCHOR CASES VERSUS FREE CASES

During the migration process from refugee camps to the United States, refugees have the opportunity to identify family or friends at potential resettlement sites as *anchor* relations. Those with such ties are then resettled at the location of the identified contact, and are referred to as "anchor" cases (Nawyn 2006). Refugees who do not have anchor relationships are identified as "free" cases (Nawyn 2006). The latter are often refugees that arrive in small numbers, such as the Kachin from Myanmar,[4] who comprise only a few families in Omaha, or refugees belonging to populations just beginning resettlement in the United States. Refugees arriving alone without existing relationships in the host community have limited access to bonding capital, which is social capital *within* their social network of kin, community, or both. These *free* cases can be relatively isolated and often struggle with creating social networks. Further, as a whole, people from smaller communities have smaller social networks which provide limited opportunity for the informal learning that can ease the transition to a new context (Morrice 2007). In contrast, *anchor* cases tend to have a high degree of bonding social capital, and can more easily re-establish larger social networks with extended family and their ethnic community. With greater bonding social capital and access to support from the community, one might infer that anchor case refugees enjoy a higher degree of bridging social capital and a smoother integration into the wider society. However, this hypothesis is complicated as tensions emerge between *bonding social capital* within refugees' in-group networks and *bridging social capital* with networks in the wider host community.

Such tensions have parallels in what Bourgois (2003, 170) calls the "bicultural alternative." This notion captures how individuals need to downplay or even deny membership in their primary sociocultural group in order to be accepted in another sociocultural group, but then must shift back to their primary cultural arena when they are with family and friends. Refugees navigate toward true bi-culturalism by carefully balancing a desire to be part of mainstream society, with maintaining identity and characteristics of their context of origin (Keel and Drew 2004). This marks a fine line that many in the community must walk. Movement too far into the mainstream culture of the new setting (i.e., through heavy use of bridging social capital) can make one vulnerable to accusations of betrayal of one's ethnic group, or outright rejection by one's home community, particularly if one is successful in mainstream society. Conversely, there is a risk of losing social capital in mainstream society if one emphasizes membership in the primary but more marginal social group (see Bourgois 2003).

While it is important to note that bridging and bonding capital are not mutually exclusive (Cheung and Phillimore 2013), we found evidence of the bicultural alternative at play in the communities we worked with. Within anchor case resettlement, this bicultural alternative manifests in negotiations of social capital within groups and outside the group, in the need to choose between bonding and bridging social capital—that is, between bonding within the indigenous culture brought over with the refugee group, and bridging to the host, or dominant culture. It comes to light in the everyday navigation of tensions surrounding finding and keeping work, making and keeping medical appointments, raising children and the myriad individual tasks required to assimilate into the new cultural context while maintaining relations within one's community of origin and across transnational migrant networks (see Williams 2006). Such tensions do not exist in the same way in free case resettlement, wherein refugees have arrived in the host community without already-existing ties, and therefore by necessity must build their bridging social capital in the absence of bonding social capital. This represents a different set of challenges that deserve greater attention but are beyond the scope of this chapter. Instead, we focus here on the shifting relevance of different social capitals in anchor case resettlement. Our relevant framing questions include: To what degree is bonding social capital readily available and accessible? How does one maintain and develop it? Can it erode over time? Does it ever become a drag on one's efforts to "bridge" out to other communities? Or is it more of a help?

THE LOCAL CONTEXT

Nebraska received 1,076 new refugee arrivals in the 2014 fiscal year according to the Office of Refugee Resettlement (ORR) (ORR 2015). The following graph illustrates the diversity of the 2014 cohort by country of origin. Although the data is for refugees resettled in the entire state of Nebraska, most of the individuals arrive and reside in Omaha, the primary resettlement location in the state. While the number of Iraqi, Congolese, and Syrian refugees is on the rise, by far the majority of refugees resettled in Omaha during the past ten years have been of Burmese and Bhutanese descent, with 4,560 and 1,308 arrivals, respectively (Refugee Processing Center, 2016).

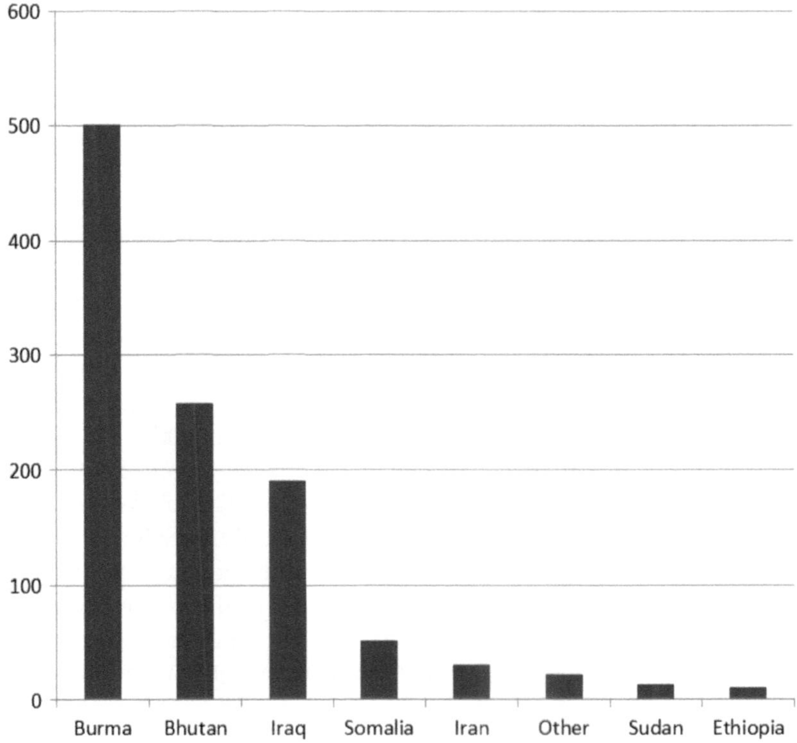

Figure 1.1 2014 Refugee Arrivals to Nebraska by Country of Origin. *Source*: Author-generated using data from Office of Refugee Resettlement 2015.

Among ethnic groups from Myanmar (Burma), the largest in Omaha is the Karen, followed by much smaller numbers of Karenni, Rohingya, Chin, Kachin, Burmese Muslim, and Burmese. Each group has its own language and cultural traditions. To communicate across ethnic groups, Burmese is the common language but many refugees have only a basic knowledge of Burmese or none at all. Most refugees from Myanmar spent an average of fifteen years living in refugee camps in Thailand after suffering extreme persecution and human rights abuses at the hands of the Burmese military. They began official resettlement to the United States in 2005. Access to the resettlement program overseas has now been closed and the arrival numbers for families from Myanmar are slowly decreasing. The majority of adults in this community have only a primary school education.

Bhutanese, who are ethnically Nepali, comprise the second largest group to arrive in the last ten years. Bhutan is a small Himalayan kingdom with a population of about 600,000. During the late 1980s, Bhutan's king instituted a "One Nation, One People" policy which essentially withdrew citizenship from all Bhutanese citizens who had migrated from Nepal generations before and maintained their Nepali language and customs in southern Bhutan. Within a very short period of time, 100,000 people were forcibly removed from the country and driven to form refugee camps in Nepal. The Bhutanese lived in the refugee camps for about eighteen years before resettlement began. While most Bhutanese adults over 40 or 50 years have little or no education, many of the younger Bhutanese were educated in the camps and learned English. A few were allowed to go to India to study. The majority of Bhutanese have now been resettled to third countries and arrival numbers are beginning to slow down.

Local resettlement agencies in Omaha are affiliates of larger, national voluntary agencies (VOLAGs) who contract with the US government to resettle refugees throughout the country at various resettlement sites and provide services facilitating the resettlement process. For example, Refugee Empowerment Center is an affiliate office of the Ethiopian Community Development Council (ECDC) in Arlington, Virginia, and Lutheran Family Services is an affiliate office of two national voluntary agencies: Church World Service (CWS) in New York and Lutheran Immigration and Refugee Services in Baltimore (LIRS). Local offices sign a cooperative agreement with these national agencies, and must fulfill a set of requirements outlined in the document. The agreement is very specific about the services the local office must provide to refugees and the timeline for fulfilling the requirements. All of the services are expected to be completed within ninety days, and failure to meet these requirements can lead to the cessation of refugee arrivals and/or revocation of the contract.

SOCIAL CAPITAL IN NINETY DAYS OR LESS

The services outlined in the cooperative agreement include preparing an apartment for newly arrived refugees or placing the refugees with relatives until securing an apartment. A culturally appropriate meal is to be served to the refugee upon arrival to the new US residence. Particular utensils and furniture must be made available, and there is a schedule of required visits and services that must be accomplished according to a specific timetable. All of these actions are documented and monitored closely in a national database accessible to the national office at any time.

One challenge facing the local agency is to search for a clean, safe apartment within the families' budget and appropriate to the size of the family. The process often involves cultivating relationships with reticent landlords who are leery of signing a lease with an unknown tenant from an unfamiliar country with no income, credit, or work history. In light of the constraints, refugees tend to be resettled in low-rent apartments, in low-income neighborhoods with access to public transportation. Refugees in Omaha often live in apartments clustered together, with approximately ten apartment complexes housing a sizable number of households of the same ethnic group. Our observations suggest that grouping according to ethnicity and language is more common than grouping according to other factors, such as nationality. For instance, both Burmese-speakers and Karenni-speakers come from Myanmar but, due to their experiences during the violent conflict in their home country they continue to mistrust each other.[5] Trust, as was mentioned earlier, is a key dimension for understanding social capital, and we return to this below.

Overall, agency case workers struggle to cover all the needs outlined in the cooperative agreement due to the extensive requirements and limited resources available to provide adequate and sufficient support. Certain services may be provided directly by the local agency, or may be referred out instead. These include referrals to English classes and employment services. Cultural orientation is provided to refugees at the refugee camp and again by the local agency within the first month of arrival to the United States, but the volume of information such orientation includes is so vast that it becomes unfeasible for refugees to retain it all. Interpretation is provided during orientation sessions and also throughout appointments with the local resettlement agency. The agency typically seeks to hire a community leader from the same ethnicity who can serve both as a case manager and as an interpreter for services. The agency also assists new arrivals with applying for a job, as well as accessing allotted cash, food, and medical benefits to which the individual and family may be entitled. Other forms of assistance such as helping children enroll in school are offered as well.

The specific requirements in the cooperative agreement to address refugee health care are comparatively limited. A health examination is required, but little else, and agencies often are left scrambling to help very ill individuals. Years of malnutrition and difficult conditions in the camps leave many new arrivals with serious medical and mental health needs within the first few months of resettlement, yet these necessities are not explicitly acknowledged in the cooperative agreement. Resettlement agencies often struggle to provide transportation to offices and clinics for the appointments and required health assessments and vaccinations within the first three months of arrival. After this initial time period the service is largely considered to be complete and refugees are then expected to meet their own needs in attending medical appointments.

The limits of this ninety-day window of time are consequential in daily life beyond health care as well. After ninety days, there is a policy-induced expectation that new arrivals can live in society without regular support from the agency. Recognizing that needs often persist beyond this time period, however, Lutheran Family Services in Omaha developed an extended program called "The International Center of the Heartland," which provides limited assistance with specific needs for refugee families beyond the initial ninety-day resettlement phase. The staff at the International Center also help secondary migrants to Omaha with applying for government benefits, accessing medical care in some cases, and with referrals to onsite legal services.

When relatives are nearby, such as in anchor cases, they likewise are expected to serve as an ongoing resource for newly arrived individuals. This, coupled with the spatial concentration of refugees in apartment complexes and neighborhoods, facilitates the creation of bonding capital, but not necessarily of bridging capital. Physical closeness reduces isolation at the same time that it reduces the need to ask for support from others. For example, one community leader said during an interview, echoing what we heard elsewhere: "If you live close to your relatives, you get out of your isolation easily as you just walk to them. Otherwise you need to ask for transport." This is particularly true for the early months after arriving at the resettlement site, but is also true for later. Thus, refugees generally try to get an apartment or house near their relatives or in-laws. However, this is not always easy as one refugee mentioned to us: "Some do not move. If they move they have to go to the office and sign a contract with the other landlord. That's too complicated and they say, 'Okay! We'll stay.'" Such evidence suggests that programs raising awareness among refugees about their legal rights and providing assistance when they want to move or when they face other problems with their landlords can have a positive ripple effect regarding their access to social capital. One refugee told us the following: "One of my friends, he has been there almost three years. The stove was broken and he called the landlord and the landlord said ‘okay, tomorrow I will come and fix it,’ but he never came. So, some people, they do not understand that oh, it’s very hard for them to go and ask someone who can read and write, everyone has jobs, has their own time.”

Indeed, the importance of finding and maintaining paid employment is a factor that intersects several dimensions of resettlement. As Torezani, Colic-Peisker, and Fozdar (2008) found, refugees view job training as an opportunity to build their networks, and employment can facilitate the development of bridging social capital. However, pressures to obtain a job as soon as possible can also leave refugees prone to sacrificing English-as-a-Second-Language classes and attending cultural orientation and professional training in favor of work hours. Koyama (2013) found that English competency is a significant factor facilitating entry in the workforce and integration into American society. But Cheung and Phillimore (2014) found that multiple factors play a role in both employment and integration.[6] For many individuals with overseas work experience, their training may not translate into similar work in the United States, whether or not their English language skills are adequate. For professionals, the situation is frustrating as doctors, dentists, engineers, and teachers must requalify in the United States, an arduous process many cannot complete. These individuals may find work in their field as assistants or they may work in retail, warehousing, or manufacturing to meet the immediate demands of supporting their family.

Among the states with the lowest unemployment rates, Nebraska is home to many large meat processing facilities for nationally recognized brands such as Tyson, Cargill, ConAgra, and Hormel as well as numerous other production manufacturing plants. Like generations of immigrants before them, many refugees strive to support their families through work in these factories. Though the work is hard manual labor, individuals with limited English proficiency are able to learn the skills required to maintain employment in this occupation. Since so many refugees work at the same factories, they use social capital networks to conserve resources by carpooling, for example. Further, since many of the refugees work together in the same place, they have the same time off on weekends to spend time with family and social networks.

Despite the provision of specific and intensive services by the agencies, the refugee resettlement model also depends on assistance from the host community. The local agency is expected to recruit and train volunteers to support the newly arrived individuals and families. Volunteers are often individuals and families from religious institutions and civic organizations. The volunteers can serve as a source of bridging capital to the refugees by helping them navigate the culture and systems of their new home, but these programs are not consistently coordinated and are prone to gaps in services. Though the goal is for every refugee arrival to be supported through volunteers, refugees who are identified as lacking social capital, such as those who arrive as free cases, are often prioritized by the agency to be assigned a volunteer. In spite of this effort by the resettlement agency to prioritize assigning volunteers to these individuals, however, a common perception was voiced by a leader from the Karen (Myanmar) community referring to the free cases: "they get nothing."

The enlistment of volunteers to bridge the social capital divide could be more effective if this process was both more coordinated and more attuned to refugees' strengths and capacities. Resettlement agencies have a mediating role in shaping social supports (Simich 2003), but as Lamba and Krahn (2003) note, most refugees themselves also actively participate in building and maintaining social networks. To insure that free cases, and indeed all refugees, receive the support needed to successfully integrate into the community, refugee and humanitarian agencies must develop standardized volunteer responsibilities, training curricula and agreements to be used by local resettlement agencies to facilitate a more sustainable and consistent volunteer support network. A more formalized process would also have volunteers better prepared not only to recognize and respond to needs, but also to support and augment the existing capacities of refugees who can be proactive participants in their successful resettlement (Williams 2006).

SHIFTING RELEVANCE OF SOCIAL CAPITAL NETWORKS

Notably, new Karen and Bhutanese arriving today face a different reality than those who arrived a few years ago, who were regularly offered an enthusiastic and individualized welcome. Representatives of the resettlement agency, together with volunteers from the wider community, and members of the ethnic group, once received new arrivals at the airport, wearing traditional ethnic dress and waving national and regional flags. After several years of weekly arrivals and increasingly busy community members, however, this rarely happens now as of writing in 2018. Current arrivals now join much larger networks with varying degrees of social integration and no longer arrive to the same special attention. And although volunteers from churches are continually recruited to provide support to newly arrived refugees and tend to be very passionate about providing this support, their commitment varies widely and often wanes over time.

The various sources of social capital themselves can shift rather rapidly over the course of resettlement. As agencies provide support required through the cooperative agreement for just ninety days, and only a minor ongoing supportive role afterwards, they work primarily to facilitate the (re)building of social capital during the initial stage of resettlement. In addition to the agencies, resettled refugees mainly draw upon four types of social support networks: relatives and in-laws (kin), members of their ethnic groups, neighbors, and religious organizations. The relevance of these likewise ebbs and flows, both for individuals and for communities.

Networks of neighbors, ethnic communities, and religious groups tend to be reinforced by other factors, such as relationships that were developed in refugee camps. These networks' characteristics were influenced by cultural patterns, beliefs, and practices, sharing a common language, as well as experiences since leaving the homeland. Kin provide significant support during the initial months but might assume a lesser role afterwards. In contrast, networks of neighbors are increasingly approached by refugees over time to provide support, facilitated by geographical proximity. Similarly, ethnic networks that often overlap with religious networks tend over time to increasingly provide social support for their members, such as transport and interpretation services. With increased social distance, the dynamics of providing social support are altered. While these dynamics among closely related kin and in-laws are influenced by a generalized form of reciprocity, a higher degree of social distance among neighbors and members of ethnic and religious organizations results in a different type of reciprocity that is more akin to market-based principles.

Increasing numbers of members in an ethnic association can nudge clearer delineations of access to organized forms of support. For example, in its early days, the community-based organization, Karen Society of Nebraska, was effectively, if unofficially, comprised of all Karen in Omaha. As the community has grown, the Karen Society has now formalized its membership, implemented a more formal dues structure, and requires membership in order to receive assistance, for example, with funeral costs (which has been an important benefit provided by the society). Observing such changes and their relevance for refugees encouraged us to further explore them as well as their implication for programs and policies, as we discuss here.

ANCHORING AND UNMOORING SOCIAL CAPITAL

Even though most refugees arriving in Omaha have an anchor, the need to acquire the language of the host country, to access transportation, and soon to pay rent and other expenses cannot be met by anchors alone. While those who arrived a few years ago may wish to provide support to other community members, they have meanwhile other responsibilities. They might have children in school and take part in school events; they often must work long hours; and they may have moved some distance from the areas of the city where new refugees commonly are resettled.

Such dynamics are not always recognized and responded to by resettlement agencies, which operate on the notion that available anchors and existing networks will provide new arrivals with the necessary bonding social capital. Ideally, this bonding capital in turn would assist new arrivals to adapt to and integrate more easily into the wider society. At the time of a refugee's arrival, resettlement agencies try to ascertain the level of assistance an anchor indicates he or she can provide by interviewing those individuals indicated by the new arrival as potential sources of support. Case workers follow this necessary protocol but are also aware that an anchor might not be able or willing to provide the necessary level of support. They frequently hear what members of refugee communities also mentioned to us during conversations and interviews. For example, one refugee noted that "the agency thinks it is okay, they have relatives; so, whatever they need, relatives will help them." Anchors are aware of their importance for new arrivals. One interviewee noted that: "people who have come later are lucky because we are already here. If they need help, we can help them so they don't have the same problem we had when we first came." However, there is evidence of misunderstandings between the agency and anchors about the exact responsibilities involved in the relationship.

Anchors may not want to appear uncooperative for fear that it would trigger a delay or denial of their friend or relative's resettlement, and thus they might agree to provide assistance beyond their capability. The agency might have the understanding that the anchor is providing assistance, but circumstances can prevent the anchor from providing the services they initially agreed to provide, such as transport to medical appointments scheduled by the agency which may be at a time when a member of the family is using the car to go to work.[7] There is evidence that some anchors feel overwhelmed, particularly those with good English and professional skills and a relatively high degree of integration into society who are more often than others asked to provide support. They become worn out and can encounter the dilemma of not being able to sufficiently provide for their own family because of providing social support to other refugees. In a context of scarce resources to meet the needs of a growing community, already-established individuals and networks struggle to balance their responsibility for newer arrivals, with other realities and demands of daily life. While free case refugees undoubtedly face tremendous challenges re-building social capital upon resettlement, anchor case refugees are not in all cases coddled by anchoring networks.

A more nuanced understanding of anchor cases, recognizing that anchors' ability and willingness to provide assistance to other refugees changes over time, is therefore necessary to determine what programs and services an agency needs to provide to new arrivals. Our research strongly suggests that anchors who are themselves fairly new arrivals and not yet fully integrated in the wider society tend to be sources of strong support, while their ability and willingness to provide support wanes over time as they integrate more fully into mainstream society. We repeatedly heard statements such as the following: "Who is more likely to help the newly arrived refugees? It is the people who have been here for a shorter time, let's say six months."

A prominent theme emerging from our informal conversations and more formal interviews and focus groups is that refugee families who have lived in the United States for several years can be *less* likely to provide assistance to newly arrived refugees. Our interlocutors generally reasoned that an increased level of integration in society as well as adaptation to the day-to-day demands of work, school, and so on, tended to pose a barrier to providing such assistance. In short, they have become busy and involved in the expectations of daily American life and, subsequently, do not have the time to provide adequate support and assistance to new arrivals, including to anchor cases. In a sense, then, acculturating to a dominant mainstream way of life in the United States constrains and unmoors access to bonding social capital for successfully resettled refugees, who have moved out of apartments where clusters of their relatives, in-laws, and other members of their ethnic and religious groups live. It also compromises access to bonding social capital for new arrivals. And moreover, working and living in a more middle-class milieu does not easily and automatically facilitate the building of bridging social capital with neighbors and coworkers outside of one's own ethnic community.

It is widely considered a sign of success when people are able to rent or buy a house instead of living in an apartment, and indeed, some resettled refugees are purchasing single-family homes. Resettlement agencies and Omaha public officials generally regard refugees' purchasing and moving into homes as very positive and an indicator of the success of the resettlement process.[8] However, such mobility can also have a downside, particularly vis-à-vis the rest of the community. When resettled refugees living in an apartment complex "lose" individuals who speak English well, are able to understand bills and other correspondence sent by mail, to drive a car, or just to babysit their children, they lose social capital.

Further, community members may experience isolation after moving when their new home is far away from where other refugees live. One family living in a suburban area of Omaha said they had no neighbors who were refugees and saw their refugee friends much less than they used to. Even though this family was able to drive to visit kin and friends from their ethnic community and attend the religious services of their church, they experienced some degree of social isolation. This left them with decreased access to bonding social capital without necessarily having increased access to bridging social capital. Successfully resettled refugees thus might struggle to maintain a balance between being a member of the wider society and providing support to members of their ethnic and kinship networks.

More established members of the community might even apply pressure on new arrivals such as relatives in need of support, and others, to become independent. One community leader identified a common sentiment: "Okay, when I first came I had to do like that, so when you come you have to do like that, too." In other words, those who arrived earlier and could not rely on anchors to provide them with social support and bonding social capital, feel that new arrivals should not rely overly on their support. There is some degree of resentment among earlier arrivals that new arrivals may have it easier than they did. Another community leader explained that: "most of the relatives just say 'oh you have to work, you have to find work quickly, because you have to pay for your apartment, you have to pay for everything, you have to pay for yourself.' This causes a lot of stress, particularly if they cannot find a job or lose a job. They worry, 'okay, if we lost our job, how can I now pay for rent?'"

As anchor cases, particularly those who are close kin and in-laws, tend to reduce their social support, other networks become important sources for social capital for newly arrived refugees. However, these are guided by different dynamics of trust and reciprocity. While a more generalized form of social capital is common among closely related individuals, market-based principles tend to be more common among those other networks that are characterized by increased social distance. Our observational and interview data indicate an emergent informal local economy beginning to take shape along the contours of social capital. Social networks can be potential sources of short-term financial help, but established community members—even relatives—can be reluctant to lend money, and might charge substantial interest, as one interviewee explained: "if you give me $500, I will give you next month $550." Another participant adds: "And sometimes even the neighbors, we have to pay them for transportation," with payment made in the form of cash, but also by trading food, transportation, and babysitting responsibilities. Further, given the stakes involved in securing employment within ninety days of arrival in the United States, experienced community members have carved out a niche offering their services to find a job, to facilitate the paperwork for receiving job benefits and so on, in exchange for cash. New arrivals might in fact pay large sums; as one interviewee described, "Some people pay them a few hundred dollars to help find a job."

For both anchor and free cases, programs offered and services provided by agencies are of particular importance during the first months, but the awareness that some of these programs are only available for a particular period of time causes a significant amount of stress to new arrivals, their anchors, and case workers in agencies, who are aware that this one-size-fits-all approach to programs is not adequate for all refugees. For example, the policy-driven expectation that refugees should be employed and financially self-supported within three months after arrival is problematic. This major source of stress and anxiety is compounded by language barriers, lack of transportation (which can become a major dilemma in a car-dependent city like Omaha), and other obstacles. Fearing the significant consequences of missing an appointment or a job interview, when faced with an obstacle, refugees must determine who to ask for help, as one interview relayed: "do you call your relatives, contact your neighbors, or the agencies?"

During our conversations, it became apparent that when several sources of support are available, including access to various forms of social capital, new arrivals are better able to fulfill this expectation within the timeframe provided. The availability of multiple sources of support also tends to reduce stress among all involved. One leader of a refugee Community-Based Organization (CBO) explained that "the ninety-day deadline to find a job and start paying bills is a big stressor, [but] the more connections new arrivals have, the more likely it is that they meet this deadline." In other words, resettlement policies need to work in unison with other sources of social support providing both bonding and bridging social capital. Among the most important sources for social capital are community leaders who are in demand for their access to bridging social capital, often because of their English language ability and their ties outside of the community. One leader said: "I don't mind to help people who come to me. They call me because I got a contact from Health and Human Services whom I can call or email directly and then they can get benefits right away, even though you know agency cannot get it on time, I can do it earlier than [the] agency."

But there are other complex stakes involved in accessing social capital. For example, religious organizations often provide support to those who join the church or the temple. Overall, all Christian communities have had much more access to bridging social capital through American-born Christians, many of whom are very interested in helping people who have been persecuted because of their religious convictions. As one participant noted: "they don't help people who don't go to their church. They will not help others if they don't join. Christians won't help a Buddhist or different ethnicities." Our observational data suggests that the promise of greater access to resources and social capital indeed results in both Buddhist-to-Christian and Hindu-to-Christian conversions among Nepali-Bhutanese with some regularity. In a context of scarce resources, the differential support among religious faith groups is also at least partly a function of the growing size of the Christian refugee communities, which are now numerous enough to be able to divide into more specific denominations and churches that focus on their own members.

In sum, while refugees who arrive with ties to an anchor in the resettlement site can benefit from access to an already-established community, their efforts to join networks and rebuild social capital are complicated by changing dynamics related to their anchors' successful resettlement, resettlement policies and programs, and the social networks they are part of. The scarcity of resources available to agencies, anchors, and social networks is a major challenge for all parties aiming to establish adequate access to both bonding and bridging social capital. In light of this, for policies to be most successful, they must engage with and foster multiple sources of social support and social capital, and the specifics and duration of programs must also respond to the dynamic and shifting relevance of social capital within communities.

WORKING ACROSS (AND AMONG) GROUPS

Refugees are not a single, homogeneous group, but belong to very diverse ethnic, linguistic, religious, and social groups coming from unique situations and having different experiences during their journey as refugees from their homeland, via a refugee camp, to the host country. Successful resettlement hinges on careful attention to the particular cultural, linguistic, and historical dimensions of a community, and to the contours within and between communities. Refugees' efforts to re-create social capital at resettlement sites can be informed by the circumstances, relationships, and networks developed in refugee camps. For example, the Karen in particular have re-worked some of the organizational patterns they established in the refugee camps, as well as the sociopolitical skills gained in Myanmar during conflict with the main government, to develop an effective zoning system in the neighborhoods where they now reside. Similar to the system used in refugee camps, each zone has a community leader who serves as a contact person for members residing in the zone, and also serves as a link to the larger ethnic community. However, groups vary in how they are able to establish such organizational webs.

While the Karen in Omaha have created an effective system of zones in this manner, the Karenni community was unable to create such an effective type of organizational structure. Our research data indicate that this can be at least partially explained through circumstances prior to their arrival: The Karenni originate from a very rural part of Myanmar and arrive in camps with lower levels of education as well as fewer individuals with highly developed leadership skills. Of the ten refugee camps in Thailand, the Karenni lived in camps farthest north, in areas that were difficult to reach, especially during the rainy season. They, therefore, had less contact with nongovernmental organizations (NGO), and less access to education and other services compared to the Karen, who were in more central camps that were more easily accessible. Arriving in Omaha, the Karenni were often confused with the Karen and lumped together with them, though they are culturally and linguistically a distinct ethnic group.[9] Thus, the Karenni have had less access to bridging social capital and have experienced relative disadvantage since 2008, when the first Karenni arrived in Omaha. This only recently is beginning to change with the arrival of stronger community leaders and the development of leadership in the Omaha community over time as resettled Karenni have gained confidence as well as English language skills.

Some refugee leaders who have access to bridging social capital will avail this capital only to those who share the same religious beliefs or belong to the same social group (or caste)—that is, with whom they share bonding capital. But we also observed creative bridging between ethnic groups. For example, the leader quoted above, regarding his contact at Health and Human Services, does not expect to be paid and will offer his assistance to members of other social groups and religions. He explained this through his education: "I went to school where they taught us equality, but some people, they didn't, so they are thinking the old way" (with "the old way" referring to discrimination based upon inclusion in a social or ethnic group). Offering another example, Burmese-speaking and Karenni-speaking refugees experienced considerable tension and even violence between their ethnicities in their countries of origin, which might influence their relationship and how they mutually provide support for each other at resettlement sites. However, simplistic understandings of these specifics can misrepresent realities. The complex relationship between these two groups—both in their homeland and at the resettlement site—is influenced by other factors too, such as religion. Most of the Karenni in Omaha belong to the Roman Catholic Church. They do not have a priest speaking their language and, therefore, sometimes rely on a Burmese-speaking priest from a neighboring city to lead religious services for them. And in other instances, we likewise see bridging across ethnic groups on the common ground of religion. While most Karen in Omaha are Baptist, those Karen who are Catholic do celebrate some religious services together with Karenni Catholics, despite differences in language and culture. In other words, we need to carefully attend to the multiple factors that determine relationships among groups and the resulting provision of social capital.

DISCUSSION AND CONCLUSION

One of the major themes emerging from our research is the complex interconnections between bonding and bridging social capital. Putnam's (2000) distinction between "bonding social capital" and "bridging social capital" seems to have particular resonance with our data. As the two concepts imply different resources, forms of support, and obligations, drawing on both of them requires access to different types of networks, familiarity with them, and ease in being part of them (Ferlander 2007). Further, it has been observed that moving from *bonding* to *bridging* social capital can be problematic as the development of bridging social capital often compromises and limits bonding social capital (Leonard 2004).

This resonates with Bourgois' concept of the "bicultural alternative" (Bourgois 2003). We observed these dynamics with refugee communities, who generally enter the United States with a lower socioeconomic status, and whose upward mobility is often tied to moving away from their cultural group, both figuratively and in some cases, literally. At the same time, this deprives them of access to bonding social capital, and subsequently, compromises their ability to develop supportive relationships outside their ethnic group in order to have access to bridging social capital. While generally, bonding social capital might eventually facilitate access to bridging social capital, refugees need to carefully negotiate the two forms of social capital. An unbalanced emphasis on bonding social capital may compromise the ability to access bridging social capital. The same is true when too much emphasis is given to bridging social capital, which leads to reduced access to bonding social capital, which in turn may then negatively influence bridging social capital.

We also must recognize that refugees' attempts to access various forms of social capital do not occur in a social vacuum. They are influenced by societal realities. Refugees deal with existing divisions among social groups in the low-income residential areas where they often live, particularly during their first years after arrival. Benson (1990, 383) argues that "cultural and linguistic differences and class antagonisms raise the greatest barriers to interaction." This phenomenon may be occurring between other minority and refugee populations in Omaha, making attempts by refugees to join social networks outside their kin, ethnic, and religious group difficult, and accessing bridging social capital problematic. Pickett and Wilkinson (2009) find that if social capital is only shared among members of a circumscribed network but not with other groups in society—in other words, substantial bonding capital but little bridging capital—it can undermine social cohesion, leading to poor social outcomes. Similarly, Szreter and Woolcok (2004) argue that a healthy society has a balanced distribution of different forms of social capital, including high levels of support, information exchange, tolerance, accessibility and empowerment both within and among groups and networks.

In addition, funding constraints make it difficult to ensure adequate support by agencies as well as other governmental and nongovernmental organizations. Under current government policies and funding regulations, new arrivals are expected to work and become self-sufficient within three months; afterward, resettlement agencies might continue limited support if needed, but only if resources are available; other new arrivals have priority. Similarly, anchors are expected to help but often themselves struggle and are limited by time and finances. Neighbors and ethnic networks are available to provide assistance but might also expect some form of compensation. Religious networks try to assist their members first but may be unable to assist others. In short, resource constraints among those who might be able to assist refugees results in inadequate provision of both bonding and bridging social capital, and meanwhile fall short of augmenting refugees in their own efforts. This can set up new arrivals for difficulties or even outright failure regarding adaptation and integration.

In light of these findings, our research underscores the importance of programs that simultaneously (1) minimize the effects of major stressors on refugees being resettled, (2) strengthen existing networks with kin and ethnic communities, and (3) encourage the creation of stable networks with the wider society. We suggest that successful resettlement will become a solid outgrowth of programs that combine these three dimensions, by supporting refugees to creatively negotiate different social capitals in specific but ever-changing situations.

COMMENTARY

John Tluang

When we first came to the United States, I and the other members of the Chin community lost all of our social capital and experienced a sense of loss of control. We did not know how to do anything by ourselves. We did not know anything about American culture. But, little by little we learned how to adapt to the culture and Western dress. The pressure to find a job is great for new refugee arrivals, but once employed, refugees can purchase a car after six months on the job. Having a car alleviates much of the stress faced by families, such as relying on others for transportation for daily needs, medical appointments, and emergencies. You write about developing bridging social capital with the new community. We developed bridging social capital with our neighbors and American community members by integrating into the US workforce. Since we have been in the United States, our culture has changed including an improvement in our living standard. Our children growing up in the United States are different and, in fact, more polite in their interactions with the family.

COMMENTARY

Govin Magar

You write about the loss of social capital when refugees settle into their new country. We experienced this when we came to the United States from Bhutan. Similar to many of the first arrivals, we lost our social capital and were waiting for the rest of our family members to arrive to the United States. During this time, we had nothing to do and felt lost. There was definitely confusion surrounding the responsibility of the person or persons introducing us to the United States. We experienced many of the things you write about. This individual was not always related to the new arrival, such as the true “anchors,” and was not always willing to cover expenses that were incurred before the individual or family began receiving food and cash assistance benefits. For example, food stamps did not typically arrive until one month after arrival, and families are only provided with one week of groceries. The agreement between this individual and the resettlement agency does not accurately describe the responsibility of this individual. In a car-dependent city like Omaha, we really struggled with transportation. We were unable to buy groceries and found it difficult to navigate the local bus system. Our social structure, the bonding and bridging social capital that you write about, is still constantly changing. For example, the same individuals who acted as leaders overseas did not assume leadership roles when we came to the United States. Individuals who were not leaders overseas became leaders in the United States. This may have had a destabilizing effect on our group, limiting our bonding capital, as the highly educated people who were held in esteem as leaders overseas kept to themselves in the face of the uncertainty surrounding the new, unknown culture. Another factor that may have held the expected leaders back was not being able to fully communicate in English to help the Bhutanese community build bridging social capital. However, things changed when we started school to learn English. At school, we met new Bhutanese friends and together planned social gatherings around our shared cultural practices. These gatherings fostered the building of bonding social capital for everyone. And, in learning English, we were able to build bridging capital with our American neighbors. It is true that we encourage the newer cohort to learn how to use the buses and do other things for themselves so they will learn about the culture and not lack the knowledge needed to become self-sufficient while building bridging capital with our new community.

NOTES

1. IRB#: 11-16249.
2. IRB# 695028-2.
3. Among members of these groups, ethnic identity takes precedence over national identity.
4. The Kachin live in Northern Burma, close to the Chinese and Indian borders. They are a much smaller population than the Karen and Karenni. For the last

seventeen years, until March 2016, their leadership had a truce with the Burmese authorities, and so little displacement was experienced by this population. In addition, those who were displaced tended to cross the border to China, where they were not officially welcomed, but were largely tolerated. Those that did travel had to go through China to Thailand to come to the camps.

5. Similar observations were made for Somali Bantus and mainstream Somali groups.

6. Also, see Beaman's (2012) analysis of social network dynamics and labor market outcomes among resettled refugees in the United States.

7. Based on such observations, it would be important to develop innovative ways to assess more accurately how much social support anchor cases can provide and how the level of social support changes over time.

8. A few refugees from Myanmar and Bhutan in Omaha have passed the real estate exam and now help community members purchase their own homes.

9. This echoes other missteps made in the past. For example, when Somali Bantu refugees came to Omaha in 2004, they were assigned a Somali-speaking caseworker who did not speak the same primary language as the Somali-Bantu (Mai Mai and Mizgua languages are spoken by the Somali-Bantu) and on top of the language and cultural differences, this caseworker was ethnic Somali and there can be tension between the groups due to the history of Bantu enslavement by the Somalis. This led to enormous misunderstandings which still affect the level of trust between the refugees and the larger community.

REFERENCES CITED

Abdi, Cawo Mohamed. 2014. "Threatened Identities and Gendered Opportunities: Somali Migration to America." *Signs* 39 (2): 459–83.

Beaman, Lori. 2012. "Social Networks and the Dynamics of Labour Market Outcomes: Evidence from Refugees Resettled in the U.S." *Review of Economic Studies* 79: 128–61.

Benson, Janet. 1990. "Good Neighbors: Ethnic Relations in Garden City Trailer Courts." *Urban Anthropology and Studies of Cultural Systems and World Economic Development* 19 (4): 361–86.

Bourdieu, Pierre. 1986. "The Forms of Social Capital." In *Handbook of Theory and Research for the Sociology of Education,* edited by John Richardson, 241–58. New York: Greenwood Press.

Bourgois, Philippe. 2003. *In Search of Respect: Selling Crack in El Barrio.* New York, NY: Cambridge University Press. Print.

Cheung, Sin Yi and Jenny Phillimore. 2013. "Social Networks, Social Capital and Refugee Integration." Research Report for Nuffield Foundation.

———. 2014. "Refugees, Social Capital, and Labour Market Integration in the UK." *Sociology* 48 (3): 518–36.

Coleman, James. 1990. *Foundations of Social Theory.* Cambridge: Harvard University Press.

Corbin, Juliet and Anselm Strauss. 2008. *Basics of Qualitative Research: Grounded Theory Procedures and Techniques*. 3rd Ed. London: Sage.
Department of Public Health and Clinical Medicine. 2013. *OpenCode 4.02*. Software Program. Umeå: University of Umeå, Sweden.
Durlauf, Steven. 2002. "Bowling Alone: A Review Essay." *Journal of Economic Behavior and Organization* 47: 259–73.
Ferlander, Sara. 2007. "The Importance of Different Forms of Social Capital for Health." *Acta Sociologica* 50 (2): 115–28.
Fukuyama, Francis. 1999. *The Great Disruption—Human Nature and the Reconstitution of Social Order*. New York: The Free Press.
Jindra, Michael. 2014. "The Dilemma of Equality and Diversity." *Current Anthropology* 55 (3): 316–34.
Keefer, Philip and Stephen Knack. 2003. *Social Capital, Social Norms, and the New Institutional Economics*. MPRA Paper 25025. Retrieved from http://mpra.ub.uni-muenchen.de/25025/1/MPRA_paper_25025.pdf.
Keel, Monique and Neil Drew. 2004. "The Settlement Experiences of Refugees from the Former Yugoslavia: Acculturation, Ethnic Identity, Ethnicity, Community and Social Network Development." *Community, Work & Family* 7 (1): 95–115.
Koyama, Jill. 2013. "Resettling Notions of Social Mobility: Locating Refugees as 'Educable' and 'Employable.'" *British Journal of Sociology of Education* 34 (5–6): 947–65.
Kreuter, Marshall and Nicole Lezin. 2002. "Social Capital Theory: Implications for Community-Based Health Promotion." In *Emerging Theories in Health Promotion Practice and Research: Strategies for Improving Public Health,* edited by Ralph DiClemente, Richard Crosby, and Michelle Kegler, 228–54. San Francisco: Jossey-Bass.
Krishna, Anirudh and Elizabeth Shrader. 1999. *Social Capital Assessment Tool*. Washington, DC: The World Bank.
Lamba, Navjot and Harvey Krahn. 2003. "Social Capital and Refugee Resettlement: The Social Networks of Refugees in Canada." *HIMI/RIMI* 4 (3): 335–60.
Lawler, Steph. 2011. "Symbolic Capital." In *Encyclopedia of Consumer Culture,* edited by Dale Southerton, 1418–21. London: Sage.
Leonard, Madeleine. 2004. "Bonding and Bridging Social Capital: Reflections from Belfast." *Sociology* 38 (5): 927–44.
Morrice, Linda. 2007. "Lifelong Learning and the Social Integration of Refugees in the UK: The Significance of Social Capital." *International Journal of Lifelong Education* 26 (2): 155–72.
Narayan, Deepa. 2005. *Measuring Empowerment: Cross-Disciplinary Perspectives*. Washington, DC: The World Bank.
Nawyn, Stephanie. 2006. *Making a Place to Call Home: Refugee Resettlement Organizations, Religion, and the State*. Dissertation, Department of Sociology, University of Southern California.
Nohr, Emily. 2012. "How Many Refugees Are There In Nebraska?" *Mosaic: News and Information for Nebraska's New Americans*. Retrieved from http://cojmc.unl.edu/mosaic/2012/05/04/refugees-nebraska.

Office of Refugee Resettlement. 2015. *Fiscal Year 2014 Refugee Arrivals*. Geneva: UNHCR. Retrieved from https://www.acf.hhs.gov/orr/resource/fiscal-year-2014-refugee-arrivals.

Putnam, Robert. 1993. *Making Democracy Work: Civic Traditions in Modern Italy*. Princeton: Princeton University Press.

———. 2000. *Bowling Alone: Collapse and Revival of American Community*. New York: Simon & Schuster.

Refugee Processing Center. 2016. "Admissions and Arrivals." Retrieved from wrapsnet.org.

Rubenson, Daniel. 2011. "Social Capital." In *Encyclopedia of Power*, edited by Keith Dowding, 612–13. London: Sage Publications.

Siisiäinen, Martti. 2000. *Two Concepts of Social Capital: Bourdieu versus Putnam*. Paper presented at the ISTR Fourth International Conference, Trinity College, Dublin, Ireland.

Simich, Laura. 2003. "Negotiating Boundaries of Refugee Resettlement: A Study of Settlement Patterns and Social Support." *CRSA/RCSA* 40 (5): 575–91.

Smith, Yda. J. 2013. "We Are All Bantu—We Have Each Other: Preservation of Social Capital Strengths during Forced Migration." *Journal of Occupational Science* 20 (2): 173–84.

Sobel, Joel. 2002. "Can We Trust Social Capital?" *Journal of Economic Literature* 55: 139–54.

Steed, Camille and Alexandra Moscu. 1994. *A Street of Dreams*. DVD. Lincoln: Nebraska ETV Network.

Suter, Brigitte and Karin Magnusson. 2015. "Before and After: New Perspectives on Resettled Refugees' Integration Process." In *Resettled and Connected? Social Networks in the Integration Process of Resettled Refugees*, edited by Brigitte Suter and Karin Magnusson, 55–144. Malmö: Malmö University.

Suttle, Jim. 2012. *Nebraska: "Welcome to the Good Life."* Audio Speech. Retrieved from http://www.acf.hhs.gov/programs/orr/the-mayors-corner-mayor-jim-suttle-omaha-ne.

Szreter, Simon and Michael Woolcock. 2004. "Health by Association? Social Capital, Social Theory, and the Political Economy of Public Health." *International Journal of Epidemiology* 33 (4): 650–67.

Torezani, Silvia, Val Colic-Peisker, and Farida Fozdar. 2008. "Looking for a "Missing Link": Formal Employment Services and Social Networks in Refugees' Job Search." *Journal of Intercultural Studies* 29 (2): 135–52.

UNHCR. 1951. *Convention Relating to the Status of Refugees*. New York: United Nations.

Uphoff, Norman. 1990. "Understanding Social Capital: Learning from the Analysis and Experience of Participation." In *Social Capital: A Multifaceted Perspective*, edited by Partha Dasgupta and Ismail Serageldin, 215–49. Washington, DC: The World Bank.

U.S. Census Bureau. 2013. *ACS Demographic and Housing Estimates*. 2009-2013 5-Year American Community Survey. Washington, DC: United States Government. Retrieved from http://factfinder2.census.gov.

Wilkinson, Richard and Kate Pickett. 2009. *The Spirit Level: Why Greater Equality Makes Societies Stronger*. New York: Bloomsbury Press.

Williams, Lucy. 2006. "Social Networks of Refugees in the United Kingdom: Tradition, Tactics and New Community Spaces." *Journal of Ethnic and Migration Studies* 32 (5): 865–79.

Wolf, Eric. 2010. *Europe and the People Without History*. Berkeley: University of California Press.

Woolcock, Michael. 1998. "Social Capital and Economic Development: Toward a Theoretical Synthesis and Policy Framework." *Theory and Society* 27: 151–208.

Chapter 2

Guatemalan Mayas in the American Midwest

Creative Intercultural Networking

Martin Renzo Rosales and Juana Domingo Andrés, with commentary by Claire Herzog

Juana Domingo Andrés, a Q'anjob'al[1] woman born in the town of Santa Eulalia,[2] in the Department of Huehuetenango, Guatemala, arrived in Omaha, Nebraska, in 1995. With the support of one of her brothers, she moved to this city after several months in Los Angeles, where she arrived from Guatemala in 1994. In Omaha, Domingo Andrés started working as a regular employee at a meat processing plant, a far cry from her days in Guatemala where she founded and was the director of a Catholic school. She said that, by the time of her arrival in Omaha, she met other immigrants who, like her brother, had arrived in the city during the mid-1980s. These people had fled the military regime that was violently ruling their country through the repression of individuals and communities, to the extent being accused of committing acts of genocide[3] (Falla 1992; Amnesty International 2014; Spanish Federal Court 2008). Domingo Andrés also noticed that, after the end of the civil war in Guatemala in 1996, immigrants from that country kept coming to Omaha looking for better economic conditions.

Since the moment she settled in Omaha, Domingo Andrés started a new life with opportunities and challenges that were simultaneously old and new for almost any immigrant (learning the law of the land, adjusting to the cultural idiosyncrasies of the US Midwest, looking for a job, and dealing with her status as resident). By 2007, after observing the diverse problems and needs of their fellow migrants, Domingo Andrés, her husband Luis, and others pondered what could be done to help other Q'anjob'al to navigate their new place of residence and, as a result, founded the community organization Pixan Ixim (Spirit of Corn). Since then, this organization has been engaged in a series of networking initiatives of active collaboration with diverse individuals and organizations that support fellow Q'anjob'al immigrants in their process of understanding and assuming the implications of living in Omaha,[4] regardless of their status as refugee seekers or economic migrants.

With the slogan *Reinforcing Our Roots, Living Our Maya Heritage*, Pixan Ixim has been facilitating the connection not only among the Q'anjob'al residing in Omaha, but also between them and other organizations and institutions in the United States, and between the Q'anjob'al in Omaha and those remaining in their original town of Santa Eulalia in Guatemala. Furthermore, Pixan Ixim has fostered relationships with other indigenous groups in the United States, more specifically the Omaha Nation. By analyzing the actions of immigrants like Domingo Andrés and organizations like Pixan Ixim, this chapter will present a case in which we will revisit some conceptual categories, such as migrant, refugee, and asylum seeker/asylee,[5] and appreciate the practical dynamics of networking that a group of Q'anjob'al have developed to build, restore, sustain, and increase their social capital.

The Q'anjob'als' experience in Omaha, represented by Pixan Ixim, shows several commonalities with the experiences of refugees, as well as other documented and undocumented immigrants. It also exposes the politicization in the United States of the blurred boundaries between the categories of refugees and immigrants when applied to people coming specifically from certain conflict Latin American countries. In addition, this case reveals a singular insight for the discussion of distinctive migration rights for Native Americans that goes beyond the contemporary legal framework of modern states. Considering all these aspects, the Mayas in Omaha have been developing creative strategies of social adaptation in the United States by simultaneously bonding, bridging, and linking social capital through networking within and outside their ethnic or sociocultural context (Morrice 2007).

CONTEXT: IMMIGRANTS AND REFUGEES FROM LATIN AMERICA IN THE UNITED STATES

The growing presence of Latin American immigrants in the United States has been serving as an opportunity to reshape the misleading and simplistic perception held by the common population and popularized by the media, of who these immigrants are beyond the image of the stereotypical Spanish-speaking mestizo almost exclusively identified as Mexican. This presence is also helping to spread awareness of the demographic and cultural diversity within each country of that region and the different backgrounds and dynamics of the migration experience of many of the people coming from there (Sanabria 2007; Portes 2011; Rumbart 2011; Le Baron 2012).

Latin America is a demographically diverse region: by 2012, it was estimated that 126.21 million of people of African descent lived in Latin America and the Caribbean, versus 39.16 million in North America (World Bank 2012). It is also home to more than 45 million of Native Americans (United Nations 2010) who possess cultures, traditions, and languages totally different from that of the dominant Spanish- or Portuguese-speaking societies of Central and South America (Winn 2006, 3). The Economic Comission for Latin America (CEPAL) has recognized 826 indigenous groups in this region, and has estimated that more than 200 groups are living in voluntary isolation (United Nations 2010). The percentages of indigenous people listed by CEPAL in countries like Bolivia (62.2 percent), Guatemala (41 percent), Peru (24 percent), Mexico (15.1 percent), and Panama (12.3 percent) are indicators of the demographic relevance of these groups. In Guatemala alone, twenty-two different Maya groups add up to a population of more than four million people of Native American origin (Brown and Odem 2011).

It is important to remember that the political violence that has affected Guatemala since 1960 has been a crucial catalyst in the increase of forced migration from there to the United States. Other migratory waves have been triggered by critical economic conditions, natural disasters, or widespread post-civil war criminality (Tienda and Sanchez 2013; Jonas 2013; Ribaldo 2016; Hiskey, et al. 2016). Among those who have emigrated from Guatemala, the Maya population deserves special attention. It has been estimated that about 500,000 Maya have migrated to the United States (Brown and Odem 2011). To give perspective to the magnitude of this migration of Native Americans from Guatemala, Alan Le Baron noticed that, according to the US 2010 census, the Native American population was estimated at 5.2 million, but, when compared with other Native American groups, if considered as a single group, "Maya in the U.S. could possibly be larger than the combined two largest groups of currently recognized Native Americans, the Navajo and the Cherokee" (2015).[6]

MAYAS AND THEIR CULTURE OF MIGRATION

Research about a "culture of migration," in which migration is considered a part of a series of embedded values of a community and among several socially accepted and encouraged behaviors, has been referred to in several sources (Timmerman, Hemmerechts, and De Clerck 2014; Brettell 2015, 155). Lutz and Lovell (2000) have pointed out that, throughout the centuries, migration has been and still is part of the historical life experience of the Maya people, who have been moving across the borders of many contemporary national political units. More explicitly, they said that "migration is a crucial element in the story of Maya survival . . . a rational, multidimentional reaction to the daily challenge of survival, whether the challenge arose last year, a decade ago, or in the wake of the Spanish conquest almost five hundred years ago" (Lutz and Lovell 2000, 11–12). This aspect of the perception of migration as embedded in the culture of the Maya people has been presented by Luis Marcos, one of the leaders of Pixan Ixim. He argues that this practice should be considered an ancestral characteristic of the Maya groups that sets them apart from other types of immigrants coming to the United States (Marcos and Domingo Andrés 2015).

MAYA MIGRATION TO OMAHA SINCE THE 1960s

Several sources have documented different aspects of the migration of people from Maya communities from Mexico and Guatemala to locations in North America as diverse and widespread as Los Angeles, Florida, Houston, Georgia, and Vancouver (Falla 1992; Burns 1993; Foxen 2007; Goldin 2011, Loucky and Moors 2000; Nolin 2002). All of these references relate the Guatemalan migrations to the political, social, and economic factors which, since the 1960s have forced many of the migrants to move out of their homeland looking for a safer home, better socioeconomic conditions, and additional supporting resources for their fellows back home. The zenith of this migration was reached between the mid-1970s and 1980s during the military governments of Generals Romeo Lucas García (1978–1982) and Efraín Rios Montt (1982–1983) (Falla 2000; Burns 1993; Loucky and Moors 2000). By that time, inspired by the challenges of a devastating earthquake that affected Guatemala in 1976, Maya communities had developed self-help networks[7] and a stronger sense of identity that in different ways contested the military repression.

It is argued that this network of solidarity was interpreted by the Guatemalan army as a sign of the subversive nature of the Maya population, which led the military to suspect them of supporting the leftist guerrilla groups that were operating in the mountainous Maya regions (Jonas 2013). To intensify its fight against the guerrillas, the Guatemalan government implemented a policy of scorched earth (*tierra arrazada*) (Amnesty International 2014). Between 1960 and 1996, over 200,000 people were killed in the country's internal armed conflict, including an estimated 40,000 who were subjected to forced disappearance. Countless others suffered torture including sexual violence. The UN-sponsored Commission for Historical Clarification concluded in its 1999 final report that State forces, and groups allied to the state, were responsible for 93 percent of documented human rights violations and an estimated 83 percent of victims of the internal armed conflict were Indigenous Mayan people. The 1999 report also stated that a culture of racism had led to Indigenous peoples being viewed as "the enemy within." As a result of this military action, it was estimated that, during the 1980s alone, about half a million Guatemalan people were internally or externally displaced (Fabri 2000). Some 150,000 fled to Mexico, but, according to the United Nations High Commissioner for Refugees, only a third of them settled in refugee camps and were identified there as refugees (UNHCR 2011).

In 1996, a peace agreement was signed between the Guatemalan government and the Marxist rebel army, the Guatemalan National Revolutionary Unit. This peace agreement put an official end to the armed conflict in that country, but led to a set of contradictory consequences that pushed another wave of Maya migrants to the United States. On the one hand, the agreement signified positive achievements in terms of demilitarization, the creation of a civilian police force, the establishment of a human rights commission, and the discussion of the rights of indigenous people (Brown and Odem 2011). On the other hand, the postwar governments failed to address properly the issue of land distribution, and they were negligent in the implementation of effective policies that would relieve the lives of exclusion and poverty lived by the majority of the Maya population. The Free Trade Agreements between Guatemala, other Central American countries, and the United States, and the implementation of neoliberal policies, created additional vulnerabilities for small rural producers and workers in cities. In addition, the presence of mining and hydroelectric projects in traditional Maya territories produced collateral tensions.

In fact, since the year 2000, Mayas have been forced to migrate because of the expansion of mines and hydroelectric projects that are expelling the population from their ancestral lands (Amnesty International 2014). There is a persistent dynamic of governmental repression against people protesting not only because of the pollution, exploitation, and deprivation of their lands and rivers, but also against the increasing poverty and illness among the population. The Guatemalan legal system seems to be ineffective in protecting the lives and rights of Mayas and in prosecuting the perpetrators of acts of violence against Maya environmental activists. This has forced more Mayas to look for other spaces of social and economic freedom where they could thrive without being repressed (Ibid.). When people are forced from their homeland not because of the pressure of a blatant and violent political persecution, but because of economic policies that exclude them from the basic elements of a life lived with dignity, the formal concepts of either "refugee" or "migrant" are insufficient to capture the need to flee from the conditions that undermine their rights.

MIGRANT, ECONOMIC MIGRANT, REFUGEE, OR ASYLEE?

Considering this panorama, what is the best term to describe the status of the Maya diaspora in the United States? At first, their status should be determined according to the conditions that motivated their migration, either forced or voluntary; however, not all the known terms seem to be appropriate to describe the complexity of their condition. Terms widely used, like migrants, economic migrants, refugee, asylum seeker, and asylee, have different connotations depending on the historical and sociopolitical contexts in which they have been defined or their association with different juridical areas: immigration law, refugee law, and citizenship. In addition, there are differences between how the US government and international organizations define these basic terms.

In its Glossary on Migration, the International Organization for Migration (IOM 2004),[8] argues that some definitions in the field of migration are frequently vague, controversial, or even contradictory. According to this document, as migration is a phenomenon that traditionally has been addressed nationally, the usage of certain terms tends to vary from country to country or even among the officers of sending and receiving countries, border authorities, and governmental and nongovernmental organizations, and even migrants themselves (IOM 2004, 3). Despite this observation, they see a common element present in the definitions of the term *migrant* used by different organizations, which is the freedom that the person has when deciding to migrate (IOM 2004, 40; UNHCR 2011).

In addition, the United Nations High Commissioner for Refugees defines a *migrant* and *economic migrant* as: "a person who . . . voluntarily leaves his country in order to take up residence elsewhere. . . . If he is moved exclusively by economic considerations, he is an economic migrant and not a refugee" (UNHCR 2011). However, the IOM goes beyond the UNHCR definition of economic migrant, and uses the following:

> A person leaving his/her habitual place of residence to settle outside his/her country of origin in order to improve his/her quality of life. This term may be used to distinguish from refugees fleeing persecution, and is also used to refer to persons attempting to enter a country without legal permission and/or by using asylum procedures without bona fide cause. It also applies to persons settling outside their country of origin for the duration of an agricultural season, appropriately called seasonal workers. (IOM 2004, 21)

A *refugee*, according to the 1951 Refugee Convention, is a person who, "owing to a well-founded fear of being persecuted for reasons of race, religion, nationality, membership of a particular social group or political opinion, is outside the country of his nationality, and is unable to, or owing to such fear, is unwilling to avail himself of the protection of that country" (UNHCR 2016). In Latin America, this definition has been extended to include "persons who have fled their country because their lives, safety or freedom have been threatened by generalized violence, foreign aggression, internal conflicts, massive violations of human rights or other circumstances which have seriously disturbed public order" (Cartagena Declaration 1984).

The US Citizen and Immigration Services (USCIS) of the Department of Homeland Security summarizes as follows the criteria that, according to US law, describe a *refugee*:

- Is located outside of the United States.
- Is of special humanitarian concern to the United States.
- Demonstrates that they were persecuted or fear persecution due to race, religion, nationality, political opinion, or membership in a particular social group.
- Is not firmly resettled in another country.
- Is admissible to the United States. (USCIS 2016)

The difference between the two definitions is obvious: while the UN Convention of 1951 focuses on the situation of a person fleeing from persecution in their home country, regardless of where the person is settled, US law emphasizes that the physical location of the person should be outside the United States. In addition, US law stipulates that the situation of the person looking for refuge should be of *special humanitarian concern* to the United States. This concept is of course subject to different interpretations given that the humanitarian criteria agreed upon internationally are not always shared by US authorities, or may be overruled by certain national political interests.

When addressing the different legal frames of reference regarding the concepts associated with migration in general and refugees in particular, Julian Lim (2013) distinguishes between historically contested areas: immigration law, refugee law, and citizenship. According to Lim, "in the last century, exclusion has been a defining criteria in the development of U.S. immigration law, while refugee law has effectively become an alternative pathway to admission for certain immigrants who would otherwise be excluded" (Lim 2013, 1014). Lim argues for a complementarity of these different legal areas in ways that could cover certain legal vacuums.

The process of covering legal voids has not been exempt from conceptual or practical tensions. While US refugee law has adopted the 1951 Convention's definition of *refugee* and the related concept of *non-refoulement*, which protects individuals from being sent back to their place of persecution, US immigration law on the other hand is based on "the right of a sovereign state and its political community to make decisions about inclusions" which "are often advanced through self-interested claims of ethnic, cultural, political and economic preferences" (Lim 2013, 1040). This could partially explain why, even though the majority of immigrants who left Guatemala between the mid-1970s and 1990s were fleeing political violence or ethnic persecution, they were not granted political asylum by the US government who categorized them as economic migrants (Brown and Odem 2011).

According to the American Migration Council, an *asylum seeker* is the person who is requesting asylum, while an *asylee* is the person granted asylum (American Migration Council 2016). The USCIS on the other hand, uses the terms *asylee* and *asylum seeker* interchangeably to describe:

> an alien in the United States or at a port of entry who is found to be unable or unwilling to return to his or her country of nationality, or to seek the protection of that country because of persecution or a well-founded fear of persecution. Persecution or the fear thereof must be based on the alien's race, religion, nationality, membership in a particular social group, or political opinion. (U.S. Citizenship and Immigration Services 2018)

While we acknowledge the semantic distinction between the terms *asylum seeker* and *asylee* stated by the American Migration Council, for the analysis of the case presented in this chapter, we will use the definition officially applied by the USCIS, considering its official authoritative role in granting legal status to the different categories of immigrants in the United States.

The USCIS defines *asylum status* as "a form of protection available to people who: a) meet the definition of refugee, b) are already in the United States, and c) are seeking admission at a port of entry" (USCIS 2015). In other words, in the United States, the location of the individual is what determines the distinction between refugees and asylum seekers. So, refugees are outside the United States at the moment of their assessment for relocation, and asylum seekers or asylees are already in US territory or at a port of entry when they raise their request for that special status. Having a legal migration status is not a requirement for asylum seekers to apply for protection. Another difference in the United States between those people who have been granted the status of refugee and asylum seekers/asylees is that refugees *must* apply for a permanent resident status (green card) after one year in the United States, while asylees/asylum seekers have the option to do so.

Starting in 1965, US immigration policy toward Latin America has been inconsistent in terms of either limiting or supporting immigration from certain countries. During the 1980s, the ideological affinities between the right-wing military regimes in Guatemala and El Salvador and the Reagan administration that supported them influenced US policy toward refugees moving from these countries. This affinity became even more controversial because, during this period, the Reagan administration denied 98 and 97 percent of asylum petitions from Guatemalans and Salvadorans, respectively (Hipsman and Meissner 2013; Jonas 2013). In contrast, people who fled countries like Nicaragua or Cuba, whose governments were opposed by the US administration, were granted asylum status easily.[9]

Despite the setbacks in the process of being accepted by US government officials as refugees or asylum seekers/asylees, some Mayas and other Central Americans fleeing from persecution did receive the support of different agencies, organizations, and institutions that challenged attempts to undermine the accounts of those fleeing violence and oppression in their countries of origin. Religious activists for instance had an important role by declaring their communities, or congregations, sanctuaries for refugees coming from Guatemala and El Salvador and forcing the invocation and reinterpretation of laws in meaningful ways. Their actions in favor of those migrants fulfilled US and international regulations that were, in fact violated by the US government itself (Bibler Coutin 2011, 577). Most of the Mayas in Omaha as well have never been granted the official status of refugees or asylum seekers despite escaping from political, economic, or ecological violence, and they also did not receive the special types of government assistance for relocation that other refugees in Omaha did receive (as reported by Laura Heinemann et al. in this volume). Hence, the Mayas in Omaha necessarily have had to rely more heavily on the use and building of social capital needed to fill that gap by developing solidarity networks very similar to those they had in Guatemala.

TRANSNATIONAL MAYA IMMIGRANTS IN OMAHA, NEBRASKA: RUPTURES, SUTURES, AND THE BUILDING OF SOCIAL CAPITAL

In spite of the challenges encountered in their process of relocation, Mayas in Omaha developed a set of strategies that are helping them to adapt, negotiate with, and survive in the US sociocultural context, while at the same time preserving their connections with Guatemala, as such complementing the existing research in the field of transnational migration. In her study about Guatemalan refugees and immigrants in Ontario, Canada, Catherine Nolin (2002) commented on the dynamics of what she calls "refugee transnationalism," which is defined as "the process by which immigrants and refugees forge or maintain multi-stranded social relations that link together their places of origin and places of settlement" (Nolin 2002: 61). According to Nolin, this transnationalism implies also a shift from an exclusive focus on "connections" to the study of "ruptures and sutures" of identity and sense of belonging. This approach is useful because it captures the realities of migrant lives not as static events frozen in time, but as dynamic and evolving processes. Nolin relates *rupture* to the "discourses of exile, migration, place-making, and identity." By contrast, *sutures* in immigrant lives are created in the processes of identity renegotiation that are established through "points of attachment, temporary identification, and place-making strategies" in the new context (Nolin 2002, 62).

As Nolin rightly says, "the ruptures of refugee lives, emerged as the spaces of loss through death, disappearance, and departure of leaders, teachers, and activists." As such, a rupture could mean the end of relations, interactions, shared experiences, or memories built with others in the homeland (Nolin 2002, 60). The rupture also implies the geographical distancing from the familiar, the homeland, and starting anew in a different context. Among the members of the community, rupture also triggers initiatives of ensuring their adaptation to the social, cultural, legal, and economic context of the host place. One clear rupture experienced by the Mayas who left their homes was triggered by the extensive repression they suffered in Guatemala (Falla 1992; Burns 1993; Goldin 2011; Lutz and Lowell 2000).[10] In many cases, the trauma associated with that experience became difficult to communicate verbally, even years after the events had occurred. The political violence or the memories of direct repression affected people's reluctance to return to their homeland or speak about the brutal events that led to their departure.

Nolin points out that after a time of settling in their new homeland, these refugees proceed to *suture*, which is the process of growing new affective and effective roots and forging new alliances and connections in the new setting. These connections and alliances, which will be explored later when analyzing the topic of social capital, foster the refugees' sociocultural adjustment and integration into the new context, while at the same time providing ways to preserve their connections with symbolic or real spaces for cultural identity (Nolin H. and Lovell 2000). Although several voids created during the episode of rupture could not be recovered, new points of connection between the new and old homeland and the past and present were created instead. In the case of the Maya immigrants in the United States, these points of suture have taken the forms of practical and connective symbolic actions. Practical skills, such as learning English, strategies for finding a job, getting a house, becoming familiar with the US legal system and sociocultural norms, and becoming engaged in local community and religious organizations, coexist with symbolic actions of identity affirmation, such as the use of traditional Maya costumes in special occasions, communication in the native language, and the ritual expression of their ancestral spirituality.[11] The learning of new practical skills also has been useful for the preservation and communication of the symbols of their ancestral identity, as it can be seen in the use by the

Q'anjob'als in Omaha of electronic communication and social media to keep in touch with fellows in Santa Eulalia or in other parts of Guatemala either in Spanish or in the Q'anjob'al language. In fact, Pixan Ixim has its own web page and a Facebook account where information and updates about its activities are posted and where people can contact its leadership.

The process of what Nolin calls suture also leads to a flexible identity that moves across a spectrum of multiple sociocultural definitions, independent of the simple identification with the homeland or a specific ethnic group. We find, for instance, many of these individuals who, when living within the borders of Guatemala, were self-identified as member of a specific Maya group like Mam, Q'anjob'al, Kekchi, Chuj, Quiché, and so on. However, when in the United States, as they share with others several forms of discrimination as well as the need for affirmation or recognition of specific common rights, they become Maya, or Guatemalan, or even Hispanic. As Domingo Andrés and Marcos stated: "if the condition of speaking Spanish is seen as a convenient tool to prevent discrimination, many fellows could assume in many instances, sometimes reluctantly but other times without internal conflict, the Mexican, Hispanic or Latino identity" (2015). However, there are instances in which the sense of indigenous identity supersedes any other ethnic identity not directly associated with their cultural heritage, and the individuals "actively resist a public miscategorization of being part of the Hispanic community" and position themselves mainly as indigenous people seeking refuge in the United Sates (Hiller, Linstroth and Ayala Vela 2009). From the process of suture described by Nolin, we can observe some outlines of what we call the building of social capital.

RESETTLEMENT AND AGENCY: BONDING, BRIDGING, AND LINKING SOCIAL CAPITAL IN OMAHA

According to Robert Putnam, the definition of social capital is as follows: "features of social organization, such as networks, norms, and trust, which facilitate coordination and cooperation for mutual benefits" (1995, 67). The concept has been adopted for analytical purposes by a wide array of disciplines, including sociology, economics, psychology, public health, and disaster studies (Hawkins and Maurer 2010). In the field of migration studies, social capital has been understood as an encompassing concept that describes the endowment of personal and sociocultural resources that immigrants have and put into action in diverse ways and circumstances in order to be effectively engaged into to the sociocultural context of their new place of residence (Palloni, Massey, and Ceballos 2001; Erel 2001; Lamba and Krahm 2003;

Morrice 2007). Cheung and Phillmore (2013) describe the concept of social capital simply as "the concrete help and resources garnered from networks."

Social capital has been considered as a theory useful to explain the factors affecting the decision to migrate (Portes 1997; Palloni, Massey, and Ceballos 2001). An understanding of social capital also elucidates interpersonal networks developed in the course of the movement of people across national borders; such movement generates a "self-perpetuating dynamic that progressively reduces the costs and risks of future migration" (Massey and Riosmena 2010, 298). More specifically, social capital theory would say that, despite the usual high cost and risk associated with migration for the first member of the community that successfully migrates abroad, a social connection with him or her becomes an important source of social capital (i.e., access to information, assistance, and material support) that other members of the community take advantage of for future migrations at reduced costs and risks (Lamba and Krahm 2003). In another chapter of this book, Heinemann et al. address in more detail the discussion about social capital, and like them, we have assumed the use of the term as a conventional, but somewhat limited, way to address a complex set of resources related to the network of relationships that refugees build when circumstances force them to relocate.

The "push/pull" factors that influenced the migration to Omaha expose the relevance of social capital as a factor that simultaneously promotes migration and gathers the members of a diasporic community who have been threatened or discriminated against elsewhere. Linda Morrice (2007) has addressed the distinction between *bonding*, *bridging*, and *linking* forms of social capital. She refers to *bonding capital* as the ties that connect individuals with those of similar demographic characteristics or affective closeness (friends, close relatives, neighbors, and work colleagues). *Bridging capital* refers to the ties that connect them with other groups more distant in terms of sociocultural or economic background. *Linking* social capital refers to the individuals' connections with "contacts outside of their own social milieu, who have relative power over them and from whom they draw upon resources, ideas, and information" (Morrice 2007, 162; Hawkins and Maurer 2010, 1780). In the study that is the focus of this chapter, bonding, bridging, and linking are categories that represent, sometimes partially, different types of connections within and between groups that either could be mutually excluding or overlapping.

According to Domingo Andrés, many of her fellow Q'anjob'als, on the one hand, felt pushed from locations in the United States where they experienced unemployment and racial discrimination from US citizens and other immigrants from Latin America. On the other hand, they felt pulled to Omaha because of their contacts with relatives or compatriots from Santa Eulalia who had arrived previously to this city and who were able to endure the demanding conditions of working in meat-packing companies. After having adapted to a type of job quite different from what they were used to in Guatemala and other parts of the United States, those who first arrived in Omaha encouraged other relatives and friends to move to this city by ensuring them mentorship and connections to be inserted in the job market. After, and even while, finding job stability, many of the newcomers start to participate in social groups and religious and other community organizations in which they become connected with other fellow immigrants with whom they engage in the process of building more social capital.

BONDING CAPITAL AMONG THE Q'ANJOB'ALS

The majority of the Q'anjob'al Mayas in Omaha are people who already have an original sociocultural and geographical base for bonding capital: Santa Eulalia, the community from which where they come. They also share a common ethnic identity that becomes apparent through symbolic expressions and active actions of solidarity. Some symbolic expressions are shown in community events and celebrations by, for example, the use of traditional dresses in public places and the common practice of Maya spirituality, even with some blending with colonial Catholicism. In this regard, one example that unifies several symbolic elements of the Q'anjob'al identity is the celebration of the feast of Santa Eulalia[12], the Catholic patron saint of the namesake town from where almost all the Q'anjob'als in Omaha came. In fact, the feast of Santa Eulalia is the main social event of the Q'anjob'al community in Omaha. It is prepared and organized with anticipation and pride and requires extensive coordination and collaboration among many members of the community.

This celebration is where the dynamics associated with bonding, bridging, and linking capital are on full display and the sense of belonging to a unique community takes front seat. This celebration also shows how a Catholic devotion introduced by Spanish missionaries in the highlands of Guatemala some centuries ago has been appropriated by many of the Q'anjob'als to such a level that it has become a symbol of their ethnic identity. Celebrated every year in the second week of February, this is the event at which many Q'anjob'als coming from different parts of Omaha and other surrounding towns gather and socialize by performing several activities: common prayer, meal sharing, and listening and dancing to traditional music played with the marimba. Coordination of the actions of different people is crucial for the success of the celebration: fundraising; finding and reserving the location of the celebration; advertising the event; preparing the food; organizing the program of activities during the event; assigning of the different performing roles; rehearsing and performing the traditional dances; contacting, rehearsing, and performing of the marimba players; or, even transportation of the marimba from Guatemala. These are some of the apparently simple actions that require an important investment of time and coordination of people, not to mention financial resources.

Language is a symbolic aspect of the event and serves as a metaphor of the simultaneous experience of bonding and bridging capital. As other non-Q'anjob'al guests[13] are invited, the organizers of the event are careful to guarantee that the non-Q'anjob'al speakers can understand prayers and other statements that are expressed in that language; therefore, those parts of the activities that require it are interpreted or spoken in English or Spanish. Even though language is an important element of ethnic identity, it yields precedence to the sense of connection with the ancestral place of origin or with other traditional symbols. These other symbols are used to create a trans-generational bonding between first and second generations of Q'anjob'als. I was able to witness an example of this during a Santa Eulalia celebration held in 2013, when noticing the behavior of young Q'anjob'al girls born in the United States. Like any second-generation kid, they tended to speak English instead of Q'anjob'al to communicate with peers and even with their parents. However, I noticed that they felt equally comfortable wearing the *corte*, the traditional skirt worn by Maya women. They also joined other young Q'anjob'al boys, now native English speakers, when dancing with the rest of the community to the rhythm of the marimba, a traditional instrument played by Maya musicians. Later in life, these second-generation Q'anjob'als probably will be more assimilated to the mainstream Anglo culture, and even the current appreciation and acceptance of these ancestral symbolic elements will be diminished; however, at the moment, part of that sense of a distinctive identity has been passed down to them thanks to this collective effort to reproduce a celebration associated with the traditions and values forged in a remote homeland.

The bonding capital of the Q'anjob'als also could be seen from a transnational perspective in the two-way exchange and transfer of resources and expertise between Mayas in Omaha and those in Guatemala. The easy communication between these communities by air transportation, telephone, and social media has facilitated these connections. Here are some recent examples: in 2013, Alvaro Ramazzini Imeri, bishop of Huehutenango, came to Omaha to participate in the second conference of the International Day of the Indigenous People and celebrated a mass for the Q'anjob'al community. Since 2014 until the time of writing, Fr. Mat Xun, a Catholic Q'anjob'al priest, has been coming to Omaha to preside over the mass for the feast of Santa Eulalia in Q'anjob'al with the community. During their visits, both religious leaders not only preside over liturgical activities for the community, they also hold conversations with families and individuals, participate in community gatherings, and share first-hand information about the situation in

Santa Eulalia. In response, the Q'anjob'al community in Omaha has been able to organize fundraising activities to provide substantial financial support for the construction of a new Catholic church in Santa Eulalia and other projects.

The bonding capital built in Pixan Ixim has been crucial to providing moral support to the members of the community who face health issues or problems with the US legal system. For instance, home or hospital visits to other Q'anjob'als who are sick is a common practice. This practice of moral solidarity also is evident when members of the community who are able to visit Santa Eulalia pay a visit to the relatives of other Q'anjob'als living in Omaha. The same could be said about visits to those members of the community who are in prison or facing legal issues in Guatemala. In 2014, in reaction to a judicial case in Santa Eulalia against a group of Q'anjob'al leaders, the leadership of Pixan Ixim was able to serve as liaison between Q'anjob'al lawyers and the office of the Inter-American Commission for Human Rights in Washington, D.C., to coordinate advisory and advocacy support.

The solidarity of the immigrants in the United States is also coming from Guatemala. In December 2016, a Maya scholar residing in Guatemala, who had a PhD in social psychology, was invited to collaborate on research about health assessments in the Maya community in Omaha. She interviewed more than fifty members of the community and was able to provide some counseling to women in need. During the month she stayed in Omaha, her room and board were covered by Pixan Ixim in exchange for her expertise in interviewing, transcription, data coding and analysis.

WORKING ON BONDING AND LINKING CAPITAL FOR MIGRATION PURPOSES: THE CASE OF ROLANDO LORENZO-NICOLAS

In addition to the collaboration deployed for the successful organization of a community celebration, the concrete impact of bonding capital has also been seen through long-lasting actions of solidarity in which the dynamics of bonding and linking social capital seemed to converge. In 2015, Lorenzo-Nicolas, a Q'anjob'al activist who was part of the leadership of Pixan Ixim in Omaha was informed that he was going to be deported to Guatemala for the second time.[14] However, this process was halted thanks to the active support of Pixan Ixim and the use of the legal resources available in the US court system. Lorenzo-Nicolas arrived in Omaha as an undocumented immigrant in 1998 and was initially deported to Guatemala near the end of 2005. In April 2006, Lorenzo-Nicolas came back to the United States, again without documents, after spending about five months in his native Santa Eulalia, where he observed the repression suffered by his fellows. In 2007, he became involved with Pixan Ixim and joined its leadership team. By that time, Pixan Ixim was opposing a mining project that was affecting Santa Eulalia and surrounding communities. Operating in Guatemala as part of the Gobierno Ancestral Plurinacional (Ancestral Plurinational Government) or GAP, Pixan Ixim unsuccessfully demanded that the Guatemalan government stop the mining project. The refusal of the government to proceed accordingly triggered a series of demonstrations by the locals in Santa Eulalia, which were violently repressed by military and police personnel. Detentions, harassment, and threatening of other Maya leaders, and even the kidnapping and then killing in April 2013 of activist Daniel Pedro, a local leader of Pixan Ixim in Santa Eulalia, were the evidence of an escalating conflict in which the indigenous leaders were bearing the brunt of the repressive tactics.

On January 6, 2015, Lorenzo-Nicolas received a removal order, an official notice informing him of his imminent deportation, from the US Department of Homeland Security (DHS). Fearing for his security because his public activism with Pixan Ixim in Omaha was well known in Guatemala; Lorenzo-Nicolas filed an application for withholding of removal[15] and protection under the Convention against Torture. After providing arguments supporting his claim, and with the support of the leadership of Pixan Ixim, the Migration Court blocked his removal from the United States.

This case is considered by the leadership of Pixan Ixim a huge step in the direction of US recognition of the persistent danger that members of the Maya community could experience in Guatemala even after the civil war. The bonding capital accumulated through the relationship between Lorenzo-Nicolas and other members of Pixan Ixim provided him the law services and community support he needed to successfully complete a migration procedure; he would have not been able to afford it individually. The linking capital accumulated by Pixan Ixim through the understanding of and access to the US legal system, and the bridging capital resulting from their connection with legal advisers, provided the institutional support that reversed Rolando's vulnerable position and has set a legal precedent for other possible claims against the deportation of other Maya activists. In addition, it helped give some visibility to the struggles of the people of Santa Eulalia in order to defend their rights in Guatemala.

BRIDGING CAPITAL: Q'ANJOB'AL NETWORKS IN THE MIDWEST

In the United States, the bridging capital that connects the members of the Maya community with other groups, agencies, and institutions is a resource that has facilitated access to services provided by extra-ethnic networks with which Pixan Ixim has established relationships at different levels. As of 2015, Pixan Ixim has built a growing network of evolving alliances with diverse organizations and institutions in the United States, Omaha, and Guatemala (Marcos and Marcos 2015), including:

a. The Catholic Church: At the national level, Pixan Ixim was originally associated with the National Office of Pastoral Maya, which was under the umbrella of the Office of Migration and Refugee Services of the United States Conference of Catholic Bishops (USCCB). After lobbying to acquire a status that was more in line with their allegiances with other Native American communities, the role of this office was assumed by the office of Native American Affairs. At the city level, the connection has been with the archdiocese of Omaha, the Ixim Group (Spirit of Solidarity),[16] and the Jesuit Community of Creighton University. The parish of Saint Francis of Assisi has become the main center of activities for the Maya community. Its facilities have served as space for organizing meetings, training sessions, and prayer services. It also offered provisionally a space for housing Q'anjob'al youth.
b. Universities: Through diverse partnerships, Pixan Ixim has been able to coordinate recurring training programs (e.g., English as a second language, migration issues), youth mentoring, and health issues (e.g., formation of health promoters and courses on mental health and first aid). The main partners are The Center for Reduction of Health Disparities of the University of Nebraska Medical Center (UNMC) and the Center for Promoting Health and Health Equity and the Department of Cultural and Social Studies at Creighton University.
c. Other Local Organizations: Pixan Ixim was able to get the assistance of Justice for Our Neighbors, which provided advice for migration issues, the Seventh-Generation Fund and the Omaha Community Foundation, which provided financial support.
d. The Omaha Nation: This group provided support and affinity for the reaffirmation of the Maya identity as a Native American group by promoting sociocultural exchanges.
e. The Plurinational Ancestral Government of the Akateko, Chuj, Popti', and Q'anjob'al Maya Nation: Composed of different Maya groups that historically have been autonomous, this is a movement of political affirmation within Guatemala formed to gain a public voice and demonstrate unity in a country where, despite being a majority, Mayas are treated as second-class citizens and perceived as fragmented ethnic units.

Even after acknowledging some difficulties,[17] these different alliances have been instrumental in providing the Q'anjob'als in Omaha with diverse spaces for bonding and bridging social capital, which have helped them to adapt and thrive in this city with different levels of success.

BEYOND SOCIAL CAPITAL CATEGORIES AND CONTEMPORARY MIGRATION STATUS OF NATIVE PEOPLE IN THE AMERICAS

Ongoing interactions between Q'anjob'als, other Maya groups from Guatemala, and Native Americans in the United States have created supporting networks that combine elements of bonding and bridging social capital. These spaces of social capital have also provided the leadership of Pixan Ixim with new insights about the migration rights of Native people from different parts of the Americas.

Pointing out, correctly, some particularities of the cultural and ethnic backgrounds that distinguish Mayas from US Native Americans could be an appropriate argument to consider the result of their interactions as another example of bridging capital, exemplified by the appointment of formal ambassadors between the Omaha Nation and the Maya Ancestral Government.[18] However, there are some overarching characteristics that could place these groups, at least theoretically, within a common category: the shared ancestral identity of being the direct descendants of the original inhabitants of the continent, with religious and cultural expressions, and links of communication that predate those introduced by the Europeans. These native groups also share a common history of dispossession, oppression, and marginalization by the European colonizers and their descendants. More recently, all over the continent, these native groups are in danger of losing their ancestral identity due to the overwhelming influence of the non-indigenous majority. These common experiences have set into motion between the Mayas and members of the Omaha Nation dynamics of interactions akin to bonding social capital.

One result of this interaction in the United States is the elaboration of the argument defending the migration rights of native peoples coming from other parts of the Americas. In this regard, the claim made by the Pixan Ixim leadership in Omaha is that Mayas, and therefore Q'anjob'als, should be recognized by the US legal system as members of a Native American nation has become part of the Maya arguments in favor of their right to migrate to the United States. The argument says that this right is a prerogative granted by their status as indigenous people, as established by their traditions and the history of interethnic interactions that predate the existence of the modern states in the Americas. Taking advantage of the linking capital built with international organizations that have framed the legal criteria for indigenous rights, Luis Marcos emphasizes in his argument in favor of migration regulations that consider the special conditions of indigenous people and the relevance of the United Nation Declaration on the Rights of Indigenous people (UNDRIPS). Article 36 of this declaration states:

1. Indigenous peoples, in particular those divided by international borders, have the right to maintain and develop contacts, relations and cooperation, including activities for spiritual, cultural, political, economic and social purposes, with their own members as well as other peoples across borders.
2. States, in consultation and cooperation with indigenous peoples, shall take effective measures to facilitate the exercise and ensure the implementation of this right. (The United Nations General Assembly 2007)

These two parts of this article are references for the new input that the leadership of Pixan Ixim is giving to the discussion about the migratory status of Mayas in the United States. Luis Marcos argues that the US government should acknowledge in its national legislation these rights that have been acknowledged internationally. This is a position supported by Alan Le Baron, who asserted:

> for all people in the United States, considering the Maya as Native Americans gives opportunities to re-imagine the debate over immigration and the immigration conflict between Anglos and Hispanics (Latinos) in the United States by remembering that all the Americas have experienced the "original sin" of the conquest and the subsequent oppression of the Amerindians, which continues unresolved in most all areas of the Americas. (LeBaron 2015)

Article 36 is the basis of the dialogue and cooperation between the Maya leadership and the Omaha Nation. However, the expectation of the leverage that could be built with the combination of bonding and bridging capital coming from this relationship could face some hurdles from the long history of the groups' rights being ignored or dismissed. Despite some advances in the acknowledgment of indigenous rights, the evidence promotes skepticism. For example, by 1995, Robert Fairbanks wondered how realistic it was to expect a respectful recognition by the state of Native American sovereignty (Fairbanks 1995/1996). Twenty years later, the question about how modern states effectively address the issue of sovereignty or autonomy of indigenous groups is still a work in progress, and the political context in the United States at the beginning of 2018 could make this endeavor more challenging.

The installation in February 2017 of a new US government that has promised a more restrictive migration policy increases the sense of uncertainty about the effectiveness of the alliances between indigenous groups for the purpose of migration rights. In this context, the Maya strategy of bridging social capital with different agents could provide alternative spaces for agency and maneuvering in a potentially more hostile context. However, there is no room for naiveties. Pixan Ixim also would face the natural challenges of the dynamics that are common in many organizations: internal divisions, changes in the intensity and relevance of the relationship with other stakeholders, and the changes in vision and mission associated with the aging and replacement of the leadership of the organization and the first generation of Maya immigrants.

In general terms, and in addition to the challenges mentioned above, the Mayas' experience and arguments have introduced another element to the discourse about migration: how to catalog the migration rights of a group whose heritage, despite having as a traditional place of geographic location a Latin American country, is not mainly Hispanic and whose existence predates the colonial settlements, but, as has happened with the Native Americans in the United States, has been victim of the abuse and oppression of European colonizers. Alan Le Baron (2015) has summarized the challenges of this particular area of inquiry in the following terms:

> Inside the United States, the Maya become part of the larger questions concerning immigration policy and immigration justice. As a new ethnic group in the United States, questions emerge on how they affect previous social and race relations. For the children of the Maya, it becomes a question of education and how to overcome the limitations of the home life and successfully compete with children of non-immigrant and non-indigenous parents. In addition, indigenous immigration from Latin America should inspire questions about who belongs to the Latino family in the United States; while reminding us about Latino and Hispanic inter-ethnic and class divisions.

The complexity of this case ultimately encompasses something that is, on the one hand, common among migrants and refugees, such as the emotional and practical spaces of ruptures and sutures triggered by migration and the different ways to exercise their agency in the new setting. On the other hand, in the case of the Q'anjob'als in Omaha, their concerns about and struggles for justice and prosperity in their ancestral homeland (Santa Eulalia, Huehuetenango) are as appreciated and passionately pursued as their claims and actions to protect their rights to migrate and live with dignity, freedom, and preservation of their ethnic identity either in Omaha, Nebraska, or elsewhere in the United States.

COMMENTARY

Claire Herzog

Rosales and Domingo Andrés examine in their chapter the complexities surrounding the migration of Mayas to the United States, specifically the Q'anjob'al community in Omaha, Nebraska. As they point out, whether migrants are deemed immigrants, refugees, asylees/asylum seekers, or economic migrants is highly influenced by politics and ideological affinities toward particular governments. Regardless of terminology, many of the observations about networking, social capital, ruptures and sutures, and a community's efforts to retain their culture in a new country are applicable to other immigrant and refugee groups.

The situation faced by the Maya in Guatemala parallels that of some refugees in Omaha, especially those from Burma (Myanmar) who also resided in rural areas in the homeland and were considered inferior, experienced internal and external displacement, and were subjected to development projects such as dams that damage their ability to sustain themselves. These minority ethnic groups, which in Omaha primarily include the Karen, Karenni, Chin, and Kachin, have also heavily relied on creative networking and social capital to make the transition to the United States.

Each of the aforementioned ethnic groups has formed its own community organization to support activities similar to that of Pixan Ixim. As the authors also mentioned, those formally resettled as refugees have a distinct advantage of being connected with a resettlement agency for a short time upon arrival and often continue to rely on that agency for occasional needs for years to come. However, the language barrier is also significant, as many refugees speak uncommon ethnic languages and may be forced to communicate in a second language in which they are not completely fluent, which puts them in a similar situation as Q'anjob'al who may need to use Spanish to access interpreters. This can make it difficult to create bridging or linking social capital and forces families to rely more heavily on bonding with their own communities, although those community members trying to assist newcomers often have many gaps in the knowledge needed to navigate various situations in a new country.

Another interesting similarity can be found in the relationship between the Catholic Church and the Karenni community. As the authors mention, they found the Q'anjob'al follow the "common practice of Maya spirituality even with some blending with colonial Catholicism." The same can be said for the Karenni who encountered Catholic missionaries in the refugee camp and have formed a connection with a Catholic church in their neighborhood, though they can also be found practicing animist beliefs.

The authors equally point out the push/pull factors influencing migration of Q'anjob'al to Omaha. The pull factors are very similar to those that have led to Omaha being home to the largest Sudanese community in the United States, as well as one of the largest populations of ethnic minorities from Burma. Both of these refugee groups experienced high "secondary migration," in which they were initially resettled in another city, then migrated to Omaha to join family and friends from the same refugee camp, and pursued the job opportunities in meatpacking that were not as readily available in the first city of placement.

The account of the experiences of the Q'anjob'al in Omaha is an important contribution to the understanding of migrant acculturation. The section about their rights as indigenous people provides a unique addition to the discussion. It is important to understand the various factors that impact a community's ability to thrive to support and strengthen that effort.

NOTES

1. The Q'anjob'al is one of the thirty distinctive groups that belong to the Maya family who populate most of Guatemala and part of the south of Mexico, Belize, and part of Honduras. Just in Guatemala, there are twenty-two Maya groups.

2. Santa Eulalia is the name used by the colonizers for the Maya town of Jolom Konob' (Head of the People), a center where the Maya leaders and elders used to meet to discuss community and administrative affairs.

3. According to Amnesty International, between 1960 and 1996, more than 200,000 people were killed in the country's internal armed conflict, including an estimated 40,000 who were subjected to forced disappearance. Countless others suffered torture, including sexual violence. The UN-sponsored Commission for Historical Clarification concluded in its 1999 final report that state forces, and groups allied to the state, were responsible for 93 percent of documented human rights violations, and that an estimated 83 percent of victims of the internal armed conflict were Indigenous Mayan people. The 1999 report also stated that a culture of racism had led to Indigenous peoples being viewed as "the enemy within."

4. In 2013, Pixan Ixim was granted tax-exempt status as a nonprofit organization.

5. Definitions of each of these terms will be provided later on in the text.

6. According to the US 2010 Census, the populations of Navajo and Cherokee people reported were 286,731 and 284,247, respectively. See: https://www.census.gov/history/pdf/c2010br-10.pdf.

7. This practice of communal solidarity in Guatemala was the base of the building of social capital among Mayas when they migrated to the United States.

8. By June 2017, this publication was under revision and being updated.

9. Susan Bibler Coutin witnessed cases whose development supports her argument on the political influence in the interpretation of refugees' experiences. She comments how on asylum hearings, "US government representatives depicted Central Americans' accounts of persecution as something other than the threat of violence, or as a type of violence that could not be linked to race, religion, nationality, social group membership, or political opinion" (Bibler Coutin 2011, 576–577).

10. As mentioned previously, by the early 1980s alone, about 150,000 individuals—mostly Mayas from the highlands—were killed or disappeared during the civil war, and the Guatemalan army has reported the destruction of 440 villages from the highlands at that time (Jonas 2013).

11. In several homes where their ancestral spirituality is still appreciated, the elders are used to praying using candles, burning resin, copal resin, and incense.

12. This is the name of a Catalonian Catholic saint whose devotion was introduced in Guatemala by the Spaniards colonizers in the seventeenth century.

13. These guests are Hispanic and Anglo members of the Omaha community, organizations, or representatives of agencies that have been supporting Pixan Ixim and with which this organization has been building bridging capital.

14. This is a summary collected from file # A078-357-132 on the case of the withholding of removal of Rolando Lorezo-Nicolas, raised to the Immigration Court of the Executive Office for Immigration Review, US Department of Justice. October 1, 2015.

15. A *withholding of removal* is a legal procedure that a person requests for the prohibition of his removal to the country where he "would feel that his life or freedom would be threatened on account of race, religion, nationality, membership in a particular social group, or political opinion" (Assylum and Withholding of Removal Relief Convention Against Torture Protections 2009).

16. Not to be confused with Pixan Ixim, the Ixim: Spirit of Solidarity is a local group of American missionaries who organize mission trips to rural parishes in Guatemala and coordinate the connections between the diocese of Huehuetenango and the archdiocese of Omaha.

17. Not all the alliances have been able to stand the test of time and, in certain cases, the connections have been based on circumstantial needs and have been short-lived or reassumed according to specific situations.

18. Since 2017, the Mayan embassy to the Omaha Nation has been located in the building that Pixan Ixim has been renting in Omaha.

REFERENCES CITED

American Migration Council. 2016. "Asylum in the United States." Retrieved from https://www.americanimmigrationcouncil.org/research/asylum-united-states.

Amnesty International. 2014. *Mining in Guatemala: Rights at Risk*. National Report. London: Amnesty International.

Bibler Coutin, Susan. 2011. "Falling Outside: Excavating the History of Central American Asylum Seekers." *Law and Social Inquiry* 36 (3): 569–596.

Brettell, Caroline. 2015. "Theorizing Migration in Anthropology: The Cultural, Social, and Phenomenological Dimensions of Movement." In *Migration Theory: Talking Across Disciplines*, by Caroline Brettell and James Hollifield, 148–174. New York: Routledge.

Brettell, Caroline and James Hollifield. 2015. "Introduction. Migration Theory: Talking across Disciplines." In *Migration Theory: Talking across Disciplines*, edited by Caroline Brettell and James Hollifield, 1–35. New York: Routledge.

Brown, William and Mary Odem. 2011. "Living Across Borders: Guatemala Maya Immigrants in the US South." *Southern Spaces: A Journal about Real and Imagined Spaces and Places of the US South and their Global Connections*. Retrieved from https://southernspaces.org/2011/living-across-borders-guatemala-maya-immigrants-us-south.

Burns, Alan. 1993. *Maya in Exile: Guatemalans in Florida*. Philadelphia: Temple University Press.

Cartagena Declaration. 1984. "Cartagena Declaration on Refugees," Colloquium on the International Protection of Refugees in Central America, Mexico, and Panama

in Cartagena de Indias, UNHCR, 44. Retrieved from http://www.unhcr.org/en-us/about-us/background/45dc19084/cartagena-declaration-refugees-adopted-colloquium-international-protection.html.
Cheung, Sin Yi and Jenny Phillimore. 2013. *Social Networks, Social Capital and Refugee Integration*. Research report for Nuffield Foundation. Birmingham: University of Birmingham.
Erel, Umut. 2010. "Migrating Cultural Capital: Bourdieu in Migration Studies." *Sociology* 44 (4): 642–660.
Fabri, Antonella. 2000. "Space and Identity in Testimonies of Displacement: Maya Migration to Guatemala City in the 1980s." In *The Maya Diaspora: Guatemalan Roots, New American Lives*, edited by James Loucky and Marilyn Moors, 56–72. Philadephia: Temple University Press.
Fairbanks, Robert. 1995/1996. "Native American Sovereignty and Treaty Rights: Are They Historical Illusions?" *American Indian Law Review* 20 (1): 141–149.
Falla, Ricardo. 1992. *Masacres de la Selva*. Guatemala: Editorial Universitaria.
———. 2000. *Quiché Rebelde*. Austin: University of Texas Press.
Foxen, Patricia. 2007. *In Search of Providence: Transnational Mayan Identities*. Nashville: Vanderbilt University Press.
Frank, Andre Gunder. 1966. "The Development of Underdevelopment." *Monthly Review* 18 (4): 17–31.
Goldin, Liliana. 2011. *Global Maya:Work and Ideology in Rural Guatemala*. Tucson: The University of Arizona Press.
Hawkins, Robert and Katherine Maurer. 2010. "Bonding, Bridging and Linking: How Social Capital Operated in New Orleans following Hurricane Katrina." *British Journal of Social Work* 40 (6): 1177–1193.
Haynes, Paul. 2009. "Before Going Any Further with Social Capital: Eight Key Criticisms to Address." Ingenio: Instituto de Gestión de la Innovación y del Conocimiento. Retrieved from http://www.ingenio.upv.es/sites/default/files/working-paper/before_going_any_further_with_social_capital__eight_key_criticisms_to_address.pdf.
Hernandez, Ester. 2006. "Relief Dollars: US Policies toward Central Americans, 1980s to Present." Edited by Immigration and Ethnic History Society. *Journal of American Ethnic History* 25 (2/3): 225–242.
Hickey, Maureen. 2015. "Modernization, Migration, and Mobilization: Relinking Internal and International Migrations in the 'Migration and Development Nexus.'" *Population, Space and Place* 22 (7): 681–692.
Hiller, Patrick, J. P. Linstroth, and Paloma Vela. 2009. "'I am Maya, not Guatemalan, nor Hispanic' – The Belongingness of Mayas in Southern Florida." *Forum: Qualitative Social Research* 10 (3): 1–23.
Hipsman, Faye and Doris Meissner. 2013. "Immigration in the United States: New Economic, Social, Political Landscapes with Legislative Reform on the Horizon." Migration Policy Institute. Retrieved from http://www.migrationpolicy.org/article/immigration-united-states-new-economic-social-political-landscapes-legislative-reform.
Hiskey, Jonathan Abby Córdoba, Diana Orcés, and Mary Malone. 2016. *Understanding the Central American Refugee Crisis: Why They Are Fleeing and How U.S.*

Policies are Failinng to Deter Them. Migration Report. Washington D.C.: American Immigration Council.

Horevitz, Elizabeth. 2009. "Understanding the Anthropology of Immigration and Migration." *Journal of Human Behavior in the Social Environment* 19 (6): 745–758.

International Minority Rights Group. 2008. "World Directory of Minorities and Indigenous Peoples-Guatemala: Maya." Retrieved from http://www.refworld.org/docid/49749d163c.html.

IOM, International Organization for Migration. 2004. *International Migration Law – Glossary on Migration 1*. Geneva: International Organization for Migration. Retrieved from http://publications.iom.int/books/international-migration-law-nde g1-glossary-migration.

Jonas, Susanne. 2013. "Guatemalan Migration in Times of Civil War and Post-War Challenges," Migration Policy Institute, March 27. Retrieved from http://www.migrationpolicy.org/article/guatemalan-migration-times-civil-war-and-post-war-challenges.

Kearney, Michael. 1994. "From the Invisible Hand to the Invisible Feet: Anthropological Studies of Migration and Development." *Annual Review of Anthropology* 15: 547–565.

Lamba, Navjot and Harvey Krahm. 2003. "Social Capital and Refugee Settlement: The Social Networks of Refugees in Canada." *Journal of International Migration and Integration* 4 (3): 335–360.

Le Baron, Alan. 2012. "When Latinos are not Latinos: The Case of Guatemalan Maya in the United States, the Southeast and Georgia." *Latino Studies* 10: 179–195.

———. 2015. "Maya in the US." Latino Connection Georgia. May 25. Retrieved from https://lcfgeorgia.org/maya-in-the-us-by-alan-lebaron-phd-the-maya-heritage-community-project.

Lim, Julian. 2013. "Immigration, Asylum, and Citizenship: A More Holistic Approach." *California Law Review* 101 (4): 1013–1077.

Loucky, James and Marilyn Moors. 2000. "The Maya Diaspora: Introduction." In *Guatemalan Roots: New American Lives*, edited by James Loucky and Marilyn Moors, 1–10. Philadelphia: Temple University Press.

Lutz, Christopher and George Lovell. 2000. "Survivors on the Move: Maya Migration in Time and Space." In *The Maya Diaspora: Guatemalan Roots*, New American Lives, edited by James Loucky and Marilyn Moors, 11–34. Philadelphia: Temple University Press.

Marcos, Luis and Juana Marcos. (2015). Communidad Maya Pixan Ixim and Its Presence in Omaha, Nebraska (March 18). Interview by M. Renzo Rosales.

Massey, Douglas and Fernando Riosmena. 2010. "Undocumented Migration from Latin America in an Era of Rising U.S. Enforcement." *The Annals of the American Academy of Political and Social Science* 630: 294–321.

Morrice, Linda. 2007. "Lifelong Learning and the Social Integration of Refugees in the UK: the Significance of Social Capital." *International Journal of Lifelong Education* 26 (2): 155–172.

Nolin-Hanlon, Catherine and George Lovell. 2000. "Flight, Exile, Repatriation, and Return: Guatemalan Refugees Scenarios, 1981-1998." In *The Maya Diaspora:*

Guatemalan Roots New American Lives, edited by James Loucky and Marilyn Moors, 35–55. Philadelphia: Temple University Press.

Nolin, Catherine. 2002. "Transnational Ruptures and Sutures: Questions of Identity and Social Relations among Guatemalans in Canada." *Geography and Refugees* 56 (1): 59–67.

OSEA. 2004-2016. "Maya or Mayan? Comment on Correct Terminology and Spelling," The Open School of Ethnography and Anthropology. Retrieved from http://www.osea-cite.org/program/maya_or_mayans.php.

Palloni, Alberto, Douglas Massey, and Miguel Ceballos. 2001. "Social Capital and International Migration: A Test Using Information on Family Networks." *American Journal of Sociology* 106 (5): 1262–1298.

Papademetriou, Demetrios. 2004. "The Shifting Expectations of Free Trade and Migration." In *NAFTA's Promise and Reality: Lessons from Mexico for the Hemisphere*, edited by John Audley, Demetrios Papadimitriou, Sandra Palaski, and Scott Vaughan, 39–60. Washington, D.C.: Carnegie Endowment for International Peace.

Passel, Jeffrey and D'Vera Cohn. 2016. *Overall Number of U.S. Unauthorized Immigrants Holds Steady Since 2009*. Washington DC: Pew Research Center.

Portes, Alejandro. 2011. "America and Its Immigrants: A Game of Mirrors." *Proceedings of the American Philosophical Society* 155 (4): 418–432.

———. (1997). "Immigration Theory for a New Century: Some Problems and Opportunities." *The International Migration Review* 31 (4): 799–825.

———. (2012). "Tensions that Make a Difference: Institutions, Interests, and the Immigrant Drive." *Sociological Forum* 27 (3): 563–578.

Putnam, Robert. 1995. "Bowling Alone: America's Declining Social Capital." *Journal of Democracy* 6 (1): 65–78.

Ribaldo, Clare. 2016. *Gangs in Central America*, CRS Report Prepared for Members and Committees of Congress. Washington DC: Congressional Research Service.

Rostow, Walt. (1960). *The Stages of Economic Growth: A Non-Economic Manifesto*. Cambridge: Cambridege University Press.

Rumbart, Rubèn. 2011. "Pigments of Our Imagination: The Racialization of the Hispanic-Latino Category." Migration Information Source, April 27. Retrieved from http://www.migrationpolicy.org/article/pigments-our-imagination-racialization-hispanic-latino-category.

Sanabria, Harry. 2007. "Anthropology of Latin America and the Caribbean." In *Anthropology of Latin America and the Caribbean*, edited by Harry Sanabria. New York: Routledge.

Spanish Federal Court. 2008. "Summary of Genocide Proceedings before the Spanish Federal Court Round One February 4-8, 2008." Retrieved from https://nsarchive2.gwu.edu/guatemala/genocide/round1/summary1.pdf.

The United Nations General Assembly. 2007. *Declaration on the Rights of Indigenous People*.

Tienda, Marta and Susana Sanchez. 2013. "Latin American Immigration to the United States." *Daedalus* 142 (3): 48–64.

Timmerman, Christiane, Kenneth Hemmerechts, and Helene Marie-Lou De Clerck. 2014. "The Relevance of a 'Culture of Migration' in Understanding Migration Aspirations in Contemporary Turkey." *Turkish Studies* 15 (3): 496–518.

U.S. Citizenship and Immigration Services. 2018. "Asylee." Retrieved from https://www.uscis.gov/tools/glossary/asylee.

U.S. Department of Justice, Executive Office for Immigration Review. 2009. "Asylum and Withholding of Removal Relief Convention Against Torture Protections." Fact Sheet, January 15. Retrieved from https://www.uscis.gov/ilink/docView/SLB/HTML/SLB/0-0-0-1/0-0-0-11261/0-0-0-14927/0-0-0-15242.html.

UNHCR, UN High Commissioner for Refugees. 2011. "Handbook and Guidelines on Procedures and Criteria for Determining Refugee Status under the 1951 Convention and the 1967 Protocol Relating to the Status of Refugees." Retrieved from http://www.refworld.org/docid/4f33c8d92.html.

United Nations, Comisión Económica para América Latine y el Caribe (CEPAL). 2010. Los pueblos indígenas en América Latina. Retrieved from Https://www.cepal.org/infografias/los-peublos-indigenas-en-america-latina.

———. (2016). "UNHCR Viewpoint: 'Refugee" or 'Migrant"-Which is Right?," July 11. Retrieved from http://www.unhcr.org/en-us/news/latest/2016/7/55df0e556/unhcr-viewpoint-refugee-migrant-right.html.

USCIS, US Citizenship and Immigration Services. 2015. "Refugee & Asylum." Retrieved from https://www.uscis.gov/humanitarian/refugees-asylum.

———. (2016). "Refugees." Retrieved from https://www.uscis.gov/humanitarian/refugees-asylum/refugees.

———. n.d. "Service Law Books Menu/Immigration and Nationality Act." Retrieved from https://www.uscis.gov/ilink/docView/SLB/HTML/SLB/0-0-0-1/0-0-0-29/0-0-0-101/0-0-0-195.html.

Velasco, Andres. 2002. "Dependency Theory." *Foreign Policy* (133): 44-45.

Winn, Peter. 2006. *Americas: The Changing Face of Latin America and the Caribbean*. Los Angeles: University of California Press.

World Bank. 2012. African Diaspora. Retrieved from https://siteresources.worldbank.org/INTDIASPORA/Resources/AFR_Diaspora_FAQ.pdf.

Zong, Jie and Jeanne Batalova. 2016. Migration Policy Institute. April 14. Retrieved from http://www.migrationpolicy.org/article/frequently-requested-statistics-immigrants-and-immigration-united-states.

Part II

MENTAL HEALTH AND WELL-BEING

Chapter 3

Re-Imagining Home

Resilience and Social Networks among Resettled Refugees in Columbus, Ohio, United States

Kelly Yotebieng, Surendra Bir Adhikari, Jaclyn Kirsch, and Jennifer Kue, with commentaries by Angela Plummer and Jhuma Acharya

> I just came back from a meeting with the Somali community, and something stood out to me. After explaining that Columbus, Ohio hosted the third largest Somali population in the world outside of Somalia, rivaled [in the United States] only by Minneapolis, she went on to note, "That is why you never see a Somali waiting for the bus." This seems important; something about the length of time and the size of the community is creating connections for newly arriving Somali refugees that allows them to find their way in this new country. Need to think about how this experience can be built on for the new, but large and growing, Bhutanese-Nepali refugee population among others . . .
>
> Yotebieng's Fieldnotes (2013)

FIGURING IT OUT: PROJECT DESIGN IN AN UNFAMILIAR COMMUNITY

Bringing aboard decades of combined experience in humanitarian and international development work with refugee populations worldwide, the authors of this chapter were all left with more questions than when they started. A wealth of literature seeks to address the humanitarian context of refugee populations in the developing world, the source of most displacement as a result of civil strife, ethnic cleansing, and wars (see Fiddian-Qasmiyeh et al. 2014; Turner 2016; Agier 2011; Colson 2003; Malkki 1995). However, despite our background in the literature, and our practical experience, we felt that the focus on vulnerability was only one side of the story. We wondered, what of their resilience?

Curiosity to know more gives rise to a myriad of research questions, such as: *to what extent do the policies and programs of service providers best leverage the enormous strengths that lie within social networks?* Or to explore, *to what extent does existing social support infrastructure, such as finding an established community in a refugee's place of resettlement, account for disparities seen in mental health and social adjustment among resettled refugee populations?*

We decided to explore these issues further when Yotebieng, a medical anthropologist, was hired by a refugee resettlement agency in Columbus, Ohio, to oversee the design and implementation of a mental health screening and referral program. She was new to Columbus, new to the field of refugee resettlement, and freshly coming from over a decade working in Central Africa. Understanding her disadvantage in lacking contextual knowledge, Yotebieng initiated a series of activities including participant observation and reviews of attendance at stakeholder meetings. Her engagements included the implementation of unstructured interviews with refugee resettlement case workers, refugee community members, and service provider agencies.

During this process our team came together. Yotebieng connected with Kue, a public health researcher trained in mixed methods and previously a refugee from Laos. She then met Adhikari, a Nepali medical sociologist and mental health administrator from the Ohio Department of Mental Health and Addiction Services. And finally, she engaged Kirsch, at the time as a program intern who was pursuing her dual Master's degree in social work and public health. Our combined interdisciplinary experience and common research interest in resilience building led us to embark on building this program together. Over the course of trying to figure it out, we arrived at several exploratory findings. We believe these key findings, the focus of this chapter, will serve as advocacy for increased collaboration between refugee community groups, resettlement agencies, social scientists, and policy and decision makers. It will also help to promote an active resettlement model built on previous research which address adjustment and health issues in the context of refugee resettlement (Peisker et al. 2003; Lamba and Krahn 2003; Heinemann et al., this volume).

RESILIENCE THEORY AND OPPORTUNITIES FOR ANTHROPOLOGISTS

Resilience theory is a promising research framework that examines the protective or enabling factors that allow individuals and communities to actively mitigate and cope with challenging situations (Obrist et al. 2010; Panter-Brick 2014; Ungar 2013; Garmezy 1991; Kimhi 2014; Berkes and Ross 2013; Ungar 2015, 2013). Adger (2000) goes further to distinguish resilience related to the ability of groups or communities to cope with external stressors resulting from social, political, and environmental change as social resilience. The bourgeoning framework of resilience is a tool for social scientists to examine the strengths and practices of social networks and their potential to improve individual and community-level well-being. Yet, resilience theory often tends to focus on individual attributes, attempting to link them with biology, or external attributes. We were unable to find much research focusing on how resilience is built, the role that individual agency and social networks play in determining one's own destiny. Below we discuss how research on refugee social networks contributes to the continuing development of social resilience theory.

Resilience is an increasingly pervasive buzz word in the humanitarian world. However, less has been done to understand its meanings and manifestations in different contexts, ways in which factors that lead to resilience as a protective factor can be identified and measured, and how it may be fostered or hampered by social networks (Panter-Brick 2010; 2014; Marchezini 2015; Ungar 2013; Heinemann et al., this volume). These are questions for which ethnographic methods are well poised to explore.

We posit that in the framework of resilience theory, we have much to learn from refugees in terms of their abilities to continue their lives, and even thrive after being exposed to enormous, often prolonged, adversity. We believe there is empowering potential in this framework. It allows us to shift our research focus and position refugees and their social networks as active agents in building their new lives, rather than simply as passive recipients of services (Lamba and Krahn 2003; Willems 2005). Aggregate research suggests resilience be examined at and between individual, community and national levels, including the interactions between these levels (Kimhi 2014; Noltemeyer and Bush 2013; Ungar 2013). While all three levels can be examined individually, this chapter is specially focused on the interaction between individual and community levels, and specifically, the importance of tapping into social networks to build individual resilience among refugees.

Applying Resilience to Social Networks and Mental Health and Wellness Programs

There is select research (Waterworth et al. 2014; Simich et al. 2003; Arévalo et al. 2015; Heinemann, et al., this volume; Kue et al. 2016) that highlights positive health benefits related to social support and the existence of social structures at both the individual and community levels. This includes literature which posits links between social networks and mental health as a powerful tool to mitigate stress (Kawachi and Berkman 2001; Turner et al. 1983; Greenblatt et al. 1982; Kuo and Tsai 1986; Fiori et al. 2006; Seeman 1996). Other research demonstrates (a) that social support facilitates employment and ability to meet basic needs, reduces stress, and improves physical and mental health; (b) that support from others reduces loneliness and despair; and (c) that immigrants perceive adequate support as exerting a positive influence on their health (Stewart et al. 2010; Heinemann et al., this volume). Furthermore, Albert et al. (1998) posit links in health-seeking behavior and access to mental health care services in individuals who are members of established and large social networks.

Often closely related to mental health and wellness, there also appear to be economic benefits for refugee communities when social networks exist. This is especially the case when there are *tenured* members or individuals in higher-level positions within a variety of industries (Beaman 2012; Lamba et al. 2003; Cheung and Phillimore 2014; Torezani et al. 2008; Smith 2013). Takeda et al. (1996) conducted research among Iraqi refugees to examine *internal* (from within existing community social networks) and *external* support in terms of their roles in supporting psychological and economic adaptation during resettlement; and found that internal social support was the better predictor of psychological adaptation. These findings are also echoed in Heinemann et al.'s (this volume) notions of bonding within and between groups.

The case of Somali refugees in Columbus, Ohio, exemplifies the relatively rapid integration of resettled individuals as a result of a preexisting large and established refugee community. This stood out in stark contrast to refugees resettled from other nations,[1] who either found no community to integrate into, or are exposed to newer and yet-to-be established communities, as demonstrated in the following excerpts from Yotebieng's fieldnotes:

> Just came back from a volunteer English lesson for a group of women from the Democratic Republic of Congo. Most are relatively new arrivals, and their community seems to still be small, and struggling to meet their basic needs, let alone provide substantial support to new arrivals. One individual was looking for help to purchase school materials for her children and seemed anxious as she wasn't sure who to ask to borrow money. (Yotebieng's Fieldnotes, 2013)

EMPOWERMENT OF AND LEARNING FROM SOCIAL NETWORKS: TOWARD REAL PARTNERSHIP

There are potentially enormous impacts of handing responsibility back to refugee individuals or community instead of perpetuating the status quo of treating these individuals as passive recipients of services (Patel 2000). After all, the communities know best what their needs are and what barriers they are vulnerable to in addressing these needs. Better partnerships, beyond simply a relationship of service provision, are needed between refugee resettlement agencies and service providers with refugee individuals, families, and communities. Our case study explores how social scientists can be more involved in developing and supporting these partnerships.

Building an Ethnographically Informed Refugee Health and Wellness Program

In 2013, a refugee resettlement agency in Columbus, Ohio spearheaded the Refugee Health and Wellness Program to implement a mental health screening and referral program for newly arriving refugees who either were coming directly from war-torn countries like Iraq or had spent most of their lives in camps, like the Bhutanese-Nepali and Somali. This stemmed from numerous conversations between resettlement agency staff and community leaders that mental health was an issue they wanted to better address in their communities.

This wellness program was patterned after the Pathways to Wellness Program, which used the Refugee Health Screener 15 (RHS-15), a predictive screening tool for anxiety, depression, post-traumatic stress disorder (PTSD) and adjustment-related disorders in refugees (Hollifield et al. 2013). Individuals whose scores exceeded 12 (or a positive score) in the RHS-15 were referred to counseling services which worked closely with the resettlement agency to build their capacity in working with the different refugee populations they were serving. The rest of the program design was flexible, offering an opportunity for our ethnographic research. The World Health Organization's 2013–2020 Mental Health Action Plan urges service providers to critically examine barriers in the context of mental health or other basic services and to devise culturally appropriate strategies to address these barriers. The incorporation of ethnographic methods in the formative stage of this project allowed us to fully understand the context, stakeholders, and service gaps from both the refugees and social service providers' perspectives. As we discovered several social networks among the refugee communities over the course of our initial participant observation, we recognized that working with social networks would allow us to understand and address social determinants of health as well as help to decrease stigma and ensure acceptability and effectiveness of subsequent interventions.

Ohio hosts a large and diverse network of refugee communities including one of the largest Bhutanese-Nepali refugee communities in the United States due to both primary and secondary migration.[2] Refugee resettlement agencies for the most part are called to provide assistance for the first three months of a refugee's arrival in the United States, with some limited assistance afterward as other grant funding permits. This understandably is a very expeditious timeline to expect self-sufficiency from newly arrived refugees. Beiser et al. (2010) rightfully acknowledge that resettlement is actually an extremely long and ongoing process. This challenges agencies to identify sustainable supportive services in the community, and provide needed connections between individuals and these services, so that the refugees have access to support as needed beyond the initial three-month period that falls within the refugee resettlement agency's mandate. It is precisely within this framework, as a sub-recipient to one of the national VOLAGs (Voluntary Agencies), we applied for an Office of Refugee Resettlement–funded mental health screening and referral program for refugees that were within their first five years in the United States.

The program employed a mixed method participatory action research methodology in the development of its activities. We identified and worked with refugee-led, community-based organizations to identify their primary concerns and perceived gaps related to mental health in their community. At the beginning, we conducted exploratory ethnographic methods including participant observation and unstructured interviews and revisited these approaches as part of a mid-term evaluation. The qualitative research was complemented by a longer quantitative survey on mental health and health seeking behavior specific to the Bhutanese-Nepali clients, the largest refugee group being resettled by the agency.[3] All authors participated and took notes of their observations in different community-sponsored events (e.g., religious celebrations, marriages, and cultural festivals, including New Year) as well as cultural awareness activities organized by the City Health Department. Engagements also included exploring existing social networks and meetings with organizations of the Iraqi, Bhutanese-Nepali, and Somali communities in particular, the three largest communities that the agency was serving and resettling. We used a resilience framework and analyzed our data in the broader social structures that influence refugee's mental health and wellness. We developed an open coding scheme based on emergent themes in the data. The first author coded all field notes using MaxQDA and wrote memos to draw attention to remarkable events and to identify relationships emerging between codes.

The Somali community, the largest refugee community in Ohio, had multiple community groups, religious centers, and social networks that were well organized. The Iraqi community, relatively new, had one central community group with an impressive number of ongoing activities. This community had already built relationships with existing social service agencies and schools, provided afterschool care among other services, and had several social media sites where they provided information to and about their community. The Bhutanese-Nepali community association was recently established and was brimming with new ideas to assist the community, but lacked the resources and fully dedicated personnel to implement many of them.

After getting to know the community, all authors began to probe and ask more questions about mental health to better understand the specific problems that had led to so many community members requesting support from the refugee resettlement agency. Though the investigation led to the finding of a pervasive theme of loneliness as a result of the communities being disconnected from their social networks, there also was happy comingling among community members when they were able to come together during different community events. Simultaneously, the RHS-15 screenings revealed that many individuals had high scores, indicating elevated levels of anxiety and depressive symptoms. However, many did not accept referral to mental health services. In our dialogue with the bilingual and bicultural caseworkers from the communities themselves as well other community members, it became apparent that the lack of interest in referrals was primarily attributed to enormous stress, pressure, and a long list of barriers and challenges common to newly resettling refugees. The referrals for counseling and medical appointments were perceived as an added, and unnecessary, stress.

Many refugees also noted that they often were either unfamiliar or felt uncomfortable with the concept and experience of counseling or therapy. One 35-year-old woman from Iraq noted: "I am strong, look what I have been through already, I am not crazy and am not sure what talking to someone will do to help me." As we continued to participate in community events and got to know some of the refugee-led community-based organizations, they began to suggest alternative programs to support mental health in their communities. These activities focused on solidifying social networks by bringing together community members that may be experiencing similar stressors, and allowing them to comingle. Suggested programs included parenting groups, yoga sessions, community adjustment support groups, music sessions, and exercise classes.

Across diverse nationalities served by the agency, women more often reported "feeling isolated and lonely." Men are normally the household members who are able to attend English classes through the resettlement process. Additionally, men are typically the ones to initially secure employment, which often leaves the women at home to take care of the children and with little ability to socialize and connect with others. An Iraqi female participant in her early thirties reported: "I rarely if ever leave my home" and "I am most hours of the day alone in my apartment for fear of getting lost." She stated: "My only reason for coming as a refugee was to give my children a better life but I would like to return back to where I came from once they have grown up." Another Bhutanese-Nepali woman, thirty-two, who had had recently given birth reported feeling like: "I have no one to talk to and no one to lean on to help me with my child."

Both of these testimonies emphasize the importance of social networks. They also highlight an opportunity: the potentially critical role resettlement agencies and service providers can play in assisting newcomers, especially women, who may be coming from places where they had more social support and interaction. No participants interviewed had undergone formal counseling, but several reported participating and being interested in more alternative wellness programs like yoga, music, and support groups in order to meet with other people and get out of their homes.

After twelve months of implementing the RHS-15 screening, referrals, and alternative wellness activities aimed at bringing individuals together, we conducted a mid-term evaluation consisting of interviews with eighteen individuals who initially had high scores on the RHS-15. Our continued participant observation with the communities highlighted that the Iraqi and Somali communities had built strong community associations where individuals could be referred for different needs. However, the Bhutanese-Nepali community organization expressed some distress related to substance use, drinking and driving, mental health issues including attempted suicides, and highlighted the need for additional attention to be paid to their community. At the beginning of the project, the scores from the RHS-15 alone would not have led us to pay focused attention to this community, as they did not differ dramatically from other communities. However, our ethnographic methods allowed us to uncover their unmet needs, which were essentially boiling under the surface. A few weeks after this discussion, we were alerted of an attempted suicide in the community. We needed to better understand how to build resilience in this particular community whose social networks were eager for the support, but all of us were unsure of where to start.

We conducted two separate focus group discussions with the Bhutanese-Nepali community where we asked the community about what they considered to be their biggest health issues, their experiences with local health services, if they have ever experienced discrimination, and importantly, what needs they defined as most critical including ideas on how they could be best addressed. One major finding that emerged from this exercise included the appreciation of the activities that brought community members together while helping to create bridges with resources and other individuals from outside of their communities. This finding echoes the strengths of bonding and bridging activities revealed by the other contributions in this volume. This included the music and yoga classes, parenting groups, and community outings to gardens and temples, which had been piloted at the community's suggestion during early phases of our ethnographic research. A reoccurring theme hinged on the need to continue supporting the community to build its own infrastructure with the suggestion of a community center evoked on several occasions.

Recognizing that numbers talk, we recognized that we needed to complement our ethnographic findings with quantitative data that would allow for the community and refugee resettlement agencies to leverage toward policy change and funding decisions to fill some of the emerging needs among Bhutanese-Nepali refugees in the area. The Ohio Department of Mental Health and Addiction Services (OhioMHAS) suggested conducting a comprehensive mental health and well-being survey. Consequently, a survey was implemented in the summer of 2014 with OhioMHAS' financial and technical support to the refugee service provider agency. This was a timely move especially given that the Bhutanese-Nepali refugee population was growing rapidly.

The instrument was patterned after a US Centers for Disease Control and Prevention (CDC) survey was used in 2012 (Ao et al. 2012) to study resettled Bhutanese-Nepali refugees in six states. It was comprised of 181 questions including 7 new questions on income, general health, and tobacco use (Adhikari et al. 2015). The survey was conducted with 200 individuals from the Bhutanese-Nepali refugee community who were recruited from the two principal neighborhoods where the majority of the population resided using convenience and snowball sampling methodologies. While we recognize the limitations of the convenience and snowball sampling, given the resources available and the fact that there has been no accurate census of the Bhutanese-Nepali refugee community, we believe that the chosen neighborhoods would be fairly representative of it. Any respondent who did not consent to be interviewed or who was not able to respond due to physical or mental impairment was excluded. Surveys had side-by-side translation in Nepali language and were conducted in the participant's home with no family members present. They were implemented by twenty Nepali-speaking interviewers, whom each received three hours of intense survey administration training in Nepali from the refugee resettlement agency and OhioMHAS.

ADDITIONAL INSIGHT INTO SOCIAL NETWORKS

The ethnographic methods were the foundation for the referral mechanism, activity design, and continued program evaluation of the Refugee Health and Wellness Program. They also helped us to identify specific needs that could be addressed by the aforementioned quantitative instrument. A look at responses to some of the measures on social networks based on the quantitative survey with the Bhutanese-Nepali refugee community provides an interesting perspective (table 3.1). What is important from a policy standpoint and an area to build upon is that an overwhelming majority (90.9 percent; n=181) of 199 respondents agreed or strongly agreed that there are people they can depend on to help them if they really needed help (Adhikari et al. 2015).

Importantly, in its implications for the potential role of social networks in supporting mental health, among 164 responses to the question: "if you were

Table 3.1 Selected Social Support Measures (Adhikari et al. 2015)

Statements (n)	*% Agreed/Strongly Agreed*
Lack emotional closeness with another person (N = 196)	20%
Have no one to turn to for guidance in times of stress (N = 200)	13%
Not respected for their skills and abilities (N = 200)	14%
There are people they can depend on to help them if they really needed help (N = 181)	91%

feeling like life was not worth living which would you be most likely to do," 67 percent said they would seek out a friend or relative, followed by merely 19 percent who would go to a mental health professional. Only 9 percent mentioned they would seek help from a physician or medical practitioner and about 5 percent said they would seek help from other resources such as: clergy, crisis hotline, self-help group, self-coping or try to ignore their thoughts of not wanting to live anymore. It became apparent that resources typically provided during crisis were not those which would be sought out by this community or perceived as useful in a time of need. Corroborating the Bhutanese-Nepali refugee community's call for a community center to provide continued support to their community, this presents a great opportunity to leverage these community strengths.

THE RESETTLEMENT AGENCY'S RESPONSE: APPLYING ANTHROPOLOGY TO BETTER SUPPORT SOCIAL NETWORKS

In addition to implementing activities suggested and requested by the community as noted above, during the formative phase of our ethnographic research, we began to meet with the Iraqi, Somali, and Bhutanese-Nepali community associations to identify ways to build on and continue to support existing social networks. The Somali case demonstrates the success that refugees can achieve in resettlement when a strong community infrastructure is waiting for them upon arrival. Because of their long standing in the community and their resilience, the Somali community has demonstrated success in opening businesses, contributing to the local economy, and integrating into every facet of social life, including political and decision-making levels of Columbus. In general, the Somali community has more supportive resources available, including multiple community associations, and social support programs geared toward their needs.

However, when individuals arrive to Columbus, they may not know about these resources immediately and they might struggle to get connected to their communities. We observed that once individuals became integrated, they tended to seek out the resettlement agency's Wellness Program less and less, and preferred to access support from within their own communities. This led the refugee resettlement agency to make a change in the way cultural orientation and outreach was conducted. During cultural orientation, representatives from community groups, were invited to come and introduce themselves, talk about what they do, and exchange contact information so that individuals would begin to form a reliable, community-based network.

DISCUSSION

Analysis of the specific issue of mental health in the framework of social networks using a resilience lens leads us to some important insights. A resilience framework allows us to explore different coping strategies employed by individuals and communities, and how they enable well-being in these communities. It allows us to explore how we can better understand not only what social suffering does to people, but what people do when their world is dramatically altered (Das 2007) and how in the face of trauma or adversity do some "stay strong while others crumble" (Kleinman 2006, 73). The agency of individuals and social networks became front and center in resilience theory. More than something inherent or biological, it focused on a community member's ability to overcome stressors and effectively lead what s/he feels to be meaningful and productive lives in her/his new home. We observed that resilience was something that could be actively built, bolstered, and supported. Individuals within social networks were brimming with their ideas of the root causes of the mental health issues they were seeing, and also sharing ideas on how to address them. By supporting them in implementing these ideas, be it a community center, or activities such as yoga, music, and other activities, we had shifted the focus of our program from one focused on needs (i.e., finding mental health support) to one focused on building upon community strengths. We feel that if we had approached this program development with a different lens, focusing only on a quantitative needs assessment, we would have missed these important opportunities and perhaps implemented a simple screening and referral program focused only on clinical services. This approach would have mistakenly imposed a biomedical model on a problem that the community had their own distinct ways to address.

Panter-Brick (2014) advances that understanding resilience within a society includes the specific, creative mechanisms that make a society successful. Ethnographic methods allow us to explore the patterns and mutual influences of factors within and between the individual, community, and national levels (Panter-Brick 2014). Weisner et al. (1997) further suggest that it is especially important for social scientists to explore the productive ways in which households and social networks are adapting to social change if we truly want to understand how to both theorize and build resilience. Further ethnographic research into the intersections between social networks and resilience can allow for resilience scales to be built and integrated into future studies.

Our research with the Somali, Bhutanese-Nepali, and Iraqi refugee communities in Columbus, Ohio, especially the ethnographically informed focus and mixed method approach with the Bhutanese-Nepali community, provides clarity to the statement that community and social relationships are central to their perceived mental health. This research underscored that service providers and refugee resettlement agencies can be more effective in promoting resilience and positive coping models related to mental health for individuals within communities by building on community strengths.

The strategic approach that the Wellness Program took as a result of this research was to foster or enhance collaboration within networks and families. While perhaps not pure community-based participatory action research, the study participants were involved in formative research conducted during program development and evaluations. This allowed them to identify tangible needs and stressors and leverage available community resources. Ethnographic methods allowed us to identify sources of stress that needed to be addressed to build resilience, including challenges related to welfare benefits that an individual is eligible for, access to language classes, and childcare and employment. The program's social worker proceeded with individualized case management services, where an individual's needs were noted during intake and effectively combined with observations from the formative research, and an action plan was developed to address these stressors.

At the culmination of the research noted above, and after observing the ability of the Somali refugee community in Ohio to integrate more effectively to the post-migration environment, we challenged ourselves to explore answers to questions such as: (a) how to support other refugee communities to experience similar relative success; and (b) how to help provide more long-term and sustainable social adjustment support to other refugee communities in Ohio.

CONCLUSION AND POLICY IMPLICATIONS

This case study provides important insight and suggestions for mental health program development, using a resilience framework, in other communities. Taking the example of refugees resettled in Columbus, Ohio, we have demonstrated the value in employing an ethnographic approach to understand how social networks are organized within the different refugee communities, these networks' perceived needs and gaps for their communities, their strengths, and how to effectively connect these social networks with the resources that will allow them to meet their needs. This allowed us to identify simple, but important, actions that we could take early on, including inviting community organizations to take part in the federally mandated Cultural Orientations for refugees implemented by refugee resettlement agencies as an opportunity for new arrivals to make connections with existing social networks, and hear from them directly "keys to success" and other tips as they begin their new lives.

This could not have been achieved by an anthropologist, or by ethnography alone, but both played a role in identifying the additional information needed (including quantitative data), and identifying resources from within other professional social networks, including local universities, social support, state, and federal agencies. We argue that this model can prove effective within other resettled refugee or immigrant populations, and the results, as they center on supporting existing social networks rather than creating new ones, have the potential to continue after the funding is completed.

Anthropologists, social scientists, and community social networks are valuable stakeholders in effective and successful integration of resettling communities (Pham 2013) and, in this case, allowed for the construction of an integrated approach, combining both clinical screening and referrals with community-defined activities (e.g., support for childcare, yoga, exercise, supplementary English classes, etc.) that leveraged and brought together strength and resilience from within social networks, to address mental health well-being of refugee communities.

The role anthropologists and ethnographic approaches can play in engaging community social networks is an important one. They not only bring in diverse perspectives for a more holistic approach, but they can also help to identify, and devise ways to address cultural and linguistic barriers between refugee communities and mainstream service providers (Kue et al. 2016). This can have a tremendous impact on leveraging refugees' resilience at every step of the refugee resettlement process. Community members' engagement in research and the design of programs geared toward them leads to a more robust evaluation of their impact, enabling policy and decision makers to gauge programmatic effects and evaluate the financial sustainability of self-sufficient communities.[4]

COMMENTARY

Angela Plummer and Jhuma Acharya

The project examined within the context of this chapter is housed within Community Refugee and Immigration Services' (CRIS) refugee resettlement program. It spurred out of an earlier need, which we identified in working with our clients. While we observed that there were issues that merited attention, we were unsure exactly how to proceed, and decided to take action by seeking resources for this program, which in its first years included this research that allows us to better understand the strengths and resilience of our communities, and more specifically, the specific determinants that we could draw upon in the implementation of our own mental health and wellness activities.

For refugees to become self-sufficient and fully integrated into the community it is critical that impediments to health and well-being are reduced or eliminated. We noticed anecdotally for many years that a large minority of refugees experience multiple, distressing somatic and psychological symptoms, and poor mental health, and it is with this concern in mind, that we began our program. Yet, we were unsure of what activities would be most appropriate to address these needs, and this is where the important ethnographic research and exploration of social networks came in handy.

The CRIS Refugee Wellness Program sought to transform central Ohio into a community where the mental health needs of refugees are fully met. In our project's efforts to transform central Ohio into a community where refugees may become self-sufficient more quickly and more fully integrated into the community, the process and recommendations of this research were critical in allowing us to demonstrate the need to support the refugee-led community organizations and other grassroots initiatives to re-establish, strengthen, and support social networks as an appropriate way to in turn support the resilience and coping strategies of the individuals being resettled into those communities. In fact, it was in part when working with this chapter's researchers that we began inviting those communities to cultural orientations for new arrivals to establish connections early, as well as inviting them to project stakeholder meetings so that their voices could be heard as we analyzed our progress to date and tried to identify solutions to improve. As noted earlier, at the time we implemented the program no mental health screening was being done in Ohio, but our efforts helped bring attention to the need and now the screening is being done as a component of the overall health screening at the State level.

Lastly, it was in large part because of the efforts undertaken in this research that the Bhutanese-Nepali Community Association of Columbus was able to raise its visibility and secure several grants to implement a community center, a place where we are building on the strengths of our social network to implement programs that support the mental health, wellness, and overall integration and well-being of our community.

We are grateful for the opportunity to work with the dedicated anthropologists, social workers, public health professionals, and sociologists who made this research possible, and we look forward to continuing our collaboration in our efforts to better understand and therefore best adapt our services to our ever-changing, diverse community of new Americans.

NOTES

1. While not part of this study, given the relatively small size of their population as compared to the Somali, Bhutanese-Nepali, Iraqi populations, and other smaller groups are still struggling to organize themselves as communities, including groups from the Democratic Republic of the Congo, Rwanda, Burundi, and the Central African Republic.

2. Ohio is also host to refugees from other countries experiencing violent conflict including Iraq, the Democratic Republic of Congo, Central African Republic, Afghanistan, and Syria (Ohio Refugee Services 2016: http://jfs.ohio.gov/refugee/index.stm#pop).

3. For the quantitative portion of the investigation, Institutional Review Board (IRB) was approved by the Ohio Department of Mental Health and Addiction Services (#2014–7, April 4, 2014).

4. We would like to thank Community Refugee & Immigration Services, especially Angela Plummer, Executive Director, and Sarah Miller, former Refugee Health and Wellness Program Manager for their support of this research and commitment to ensuring the utmost quality of their programs. We also would like to thank the Office of Refugee Resettlement, Administration for Children and Families, US DHHS via our partner Church World Services for providing the funding that allowed the Refugee Wellness Program to take shape and be a learning opportunity for resettlement agencies and other organizations providing support to resettled refugees. I would also like to thank Dr. Jennifer Syvertsen and Ashley Bersani for their critical feedback and analyses of the different iterations of this research.

REFERENCES CITED

Adger, William Neil. 2000. "Social and Ecological Resilience: Are They Related?" *Progress in Human Geography* 24 (3): 347–364.

Adhikari, Surendra Bir, Kelly Yotebieng, Jhuma Acharya, and Jaclyn Kirsch. 2015. *Epidemiology of Mental Health, Suicide and Posttraumatic Stress Disorder among Bhutanese Refugees in Ohio, 2014*. Ohio Department of Mental Health & Addiction Services, Community Refugee and Immigration Services. Columbus, OH. Retrieved from http://mha.ohio.gov/Portals/0/assets/Research/Reports/Bhutanese-Refugee_MH_Suicide_PTSD_Report_April%202015.pdf.

Agier, Michel. 2011. *Managing the Undesirables*. Cambridge: Polity.

Albert, Maya, Thomas Becker, Paul Mccrone, and Graham Thornicroft. 1998. "Social Networks and Mental Health Service Utilisation-A Literature Review." *International Journal of Social Psychiatry* 44 (4): 248–266.

Ao, Trong, Eboni Taylor, Emily Lankau, Teresa I. Sivilli, Curtis Blanton, Sharmila Shetty, Barbara Lopes-Cardozo, Jennifer Cochran, Heidi Ellis, and Paul Geltman. 2012. *An Investigation into Suicides among Bhutanese Refugees in the US 2009-2012: Stakeholders Report*. Atlanta: Centers for Disease Control and Prevention.

Aréval, Sandra, Katherine. Tucker, and Luis Falcón. 2015. "Beyond Cultural Factors to Understand Immigrant Mental Health: Neighborhood Ethnic Density and the Moderating Role of Pre-migration and Post-migration Factors." *Social Science & Medicine* 138: 91–100.

Beaman, Lori. 2012. "Social Networks and the Dynamics of Labour Market Outcomes: Evidence from Refugees Resettled." *The U.S. Review of Economic Studies* 79 (1): 128–161.

Beiser, Morton. 2010. "Compassionate Admission and Self-defeating Neglect: The Mental Health of Refugees in Canada." *Canadian Issues / Thèmes Canadiens*. Summer: 39–44. Retrieved from http://canada.metropolis.net/pdfs/immi_health/Immigrant%20Mental%20Health%20-%20pgs39-44.pdf.

Berkes, Fikert and Helen Ross. 2013. "Community Resilience: Toward an Integrated Approach." *Society & Natural Resources* 26 (1): 5–20.

Cheung, Sin Yi and Jenny Phillimore. 2014. "Refugees, Social Capital, and Labour Market Integration in the UK." *Sociology* 48 (3): 518–536.

Colson, Elizabeth. 2003. "Forced Migration and the Anthropological Response." *Journal of Refugee Studies* 16 (1): 1–18.

Das, Veena. 2007. *Life and Words: Violence and the Decent into the Ordinary*. Berkeley and Los Angeles: University of California Press.

Fiddian-Qasmiyeh, Elena, Gil Loescher, Katy Long, and Nando Signoa. 2014. *The Oxford Handbook of Refugee & Forced Migration Studies*. Oxford: Oxford University Press.

Fiori, Katherine, Toni Antonucci, and Kai Cortina. 2006. "Social Network Typologies and Mental Health Among Older Adults." *The Journals of Gerontology Series B: Psychological Sciences and Social Sciences* 61 (1): P25–P32.

Garmezy, Norman. 1991. "Resiliency and Vulnerability to Adverse Developmental Outcomes Associated with Poverty." *The American Behavioral Scientist* 34 (4): 416–430.

Greenblatt, Milton, Rosina M. Becerra, and E. A. Serafetinides. 1982. "Social Networks and Mental Health: An Overview." *The American Journal of Psychiatry* 139 (8): 977–984.

Hollifield, Michael, Sasha Verbillis-Kolp, Beth Farmer, Eric C. Toolson, Tsegaba Woldehaimanot, Junko Yamazaki, Annette Holland, Janet St Clair, and Janet SooHoo. 2013. "The Refugee Health Screener-15 (RHS-15): Development and Validation of an Instrument for Anxiety, Depression, and PTSD in Refugees." *General Hospital Psychiatry* 35 (2): 202–209.

Kawachi, Ichiro and Lisa F. Berkman. 2001. "Social Ties and Mental Health." *Journal of Urban Health,* 78 (3): 458–467.

Kimhi, Shaul. 2014. "Levels of Resilience: Associations among Individual, Community and National Resilience. *Journal of Health Psychology* 21 (2): 164–170.

Kleinman, Arthur. 2006. *What Really Matters: Living a Moral Life Amidst Uncertainty and Danger.* New York: Oxford University Press.

Kue, Jennifer, Sudarshan Pyakurel, and Kelly Yotebieng. 2016. "Building Community-Engaged Research Partnerships with Bhutanese-Nepali Refugees: Lessons Learned from a Community Health Needs Assessment Project." *Practicing Anthropology* 38 (4): 37–40.

Kuo, Wen and Yung-Mai Tsai. 1986. "Social Networking, Hardiness and Immigrant's Mental Health. *Journal of Health and Social Behavior* 27 (2): 133–149.

Lamba, Navjot and Harvey Krahn. 2003. "Social Capital and Refugee Resettlement: The Social Networks of Refugees in Canada." *Journal of International Migration and Integration / Revue de l'intégration et de la migration international* 4 (3): 335–360.

Malkki, Liisa. 1995. *Purity and Exile: Violence, Memory, and National Cosmology among Hutu Refugees in Tanzania.* Chicago and London: The University of Chicago Press.

Marchezini, Victor. 2015. "The Biopolitics of Disaster: Power, Discourses, and Practices." *Human Organization* 74 (4): 362–371.

Noltemeyer, Amity and Kevin Bush. 2013. "Adversity and Resilience: A Synthesis of International Research." *School Psychology International* 34 (5): 474–487.

Obrist, Brigit, Constanze Pfeiffer, and Robert Henley. 2010. "Multi-layered Social Resilience: A New Approach in Mitigation Research." *Progress in Development Studies* 10 (4): 283–293.

Panter-Brick, Catherine. 2010. "Conflict, Violence, and Health: Setting a New Interdisciplinary Agenda." *Social Science & Medicine* 70 (1): 1–6.

———. 2014. "Health, Risk, and Resilience: Interdisciplinary Concepts and Applications." *Annual Review of Anthropology* 43 (1): 431–448.

Patel, Vikram. 2002. *Where There is No Psychiatrist.* Cambridge: The Royal College of Psychiatrists.

Pathways to Wellness. 2013. *Refugee Mental Health Bibliography: The National Partnership for Community Training.* SeaTac: Pathways to Wellness.

Peisker, Val Colic and Farida Tilbury. 2003. "'Active' and 'Passive' Resettlement: The Influence of Support Services and Refugees' own Resources on Resettlement Style." *International Migration* 41 (5): 61–91.

Pham, Thao. 2013. "Anthropology and Social Work: Moroccan Immigrant Women in Spain." *Practicing Anthropology* 35 (4): 22–25.

Seeman, Teresa. 1996. "Social Ties and Health: The Benefits of Social Integration." *Annals of Epidemiology* 6 (5): 442–451.

Simich, Laura, Morton Beiser, and Farah Mawani. 2003. "Social Support and the Significance of Shared Experience in Refugee Migration and Resettlement." *Western Journal of Nursing Research* 25 (7): 872–891.

Smith, Yda. 2013 "We All Bantu – We Have Each Other: Preservation of Social Capital Strengths during Forced Migration." *Journal of Occupational Science* 20 (2): 173–184.

Stewart, Miriam, Edward Makwarimba, Morton Beiser, Anne Neufeld, Laura Simich, and Denise Spitzer. 2010. "Social Support and Health: Immigrants' and Refugees' Perspectives." *Diversity in Health & Care* 7 (2): 91–103.

Takeda, Joe. 1996. "The Effect of Internal and External Social Support on Refugee Adaptation: Psychological and Economic Adaptation of Iraqi Refugees." Dissertation. University of Tennessee, Knoxville.

Torezani, Silvia, Val Colic-Peisker, and Farida Fozdar. 2008. "Looking for a 'Missing Link': Formal Employment Services and Social Networks in Refugees' Job Search." *Journal of Intercultural Studies* 29 (2): 135–152.

Turner, Jay, Gail Frankel, and Deborah Levin. 1983. "Social Support: Conceptualization, Measurement, and Implications for Mental Health." *Research in Community & Mental Health* 3: 67–111.

Turner, Simon. 2016. "What is a Refugee Camp? Explorations of the Limits and Effects of the Camp." *Journal of Refugee Studies* 29 (2): 139–148.

Ungar, Michael. 2013. "Resilience, Trauma, Context and Culture." *Trauma, Violence & Abuse* 14 (3): 255–266.

———. 2015. "Resilience Research Center:" Retrieved from http://www.resilienceresearch.org/about-the-rrc/resilience/14-what-is-resilience.

Weisner, Thomas, Candice Bradley, and Philip Leroy Kilbride. 1997. *African Families and the Crisis of Social Change*. Westport: Bergin & Garvey.

Willems, Roos. 2005. "Coping with displacement: Social Networking among Refugees." In *Displacement risks in Africa: Refugees, Resettlers and Their Host Populations*, edited by Gebre Ohta, 53–77. Balwyn, Australia: Trans Pacific Press.

Chapter 4

Reconstructing Social Ties

The Multiethnic Engagement Patterns of Refugees Residing within a North Carolina Settlement House

Holly Sienkiewicz, Tracy Nichols, Sharon Morrison, and Maura Nsonwu, with commentary by Margaret Evans and Natacha Nikokeza

Increased cognizance of global refugee crises and subsequent resettlement to Europe, Canada, and the United States has intensified interest in integration policies and local community cohesion. While integration remains a much-contested term, the U.K. Home Office defined it as a "dynamic, multifaceted two-way process which requires adaptation on the part of the newcomers, but also the society of destination" (2003, 113). Existing migration theories often emphasize the multifaceted components of integration including economic, social, and cultural aspects (Zetter et al. 2002; Ager and Strang 2008). Though in practice, economic integration remains the focal point of many resettlement programs—especially those in the United States. The overarching goal of North Carolina's Refugee Assistance Program cites the attainment of "early economic self-sufficiency" as a primary goal (NCDSS 2013); however, early economic self-sufficiency may hinder the social and cultural components of integration. While globally refugee resettlement programs have always encouraged economic integration (Korac 2003), the benefits of social integration in the resettlement process have garnered recent attention (Goodson and Phillimore 2008).

Since Putnam's seminal work on social capital, the concepts of social bonding and social bridging have become common discourse in refugee resettlement practice (Putnam 2000; Simich et al. 2005; Yan and Lauer 2008). There is renewed emphasis on both bridging and bonding with Morrice stating that successful bridging and bonding are "key to both the definition and achievement of integration" (2007, 167).

Beyond integration, Szreter and Woolcock (2004) argue that social bridging and bonding are vital to the health and well-being of resettled refugees. It is often presumed that refugees are at an increased risk for mental health conditions, an assumption attributed to tumultuous pre-migration experiences associated with refugee status (Schweitzer et al. 2006). Risk factors such as war, torture, genocide, terrorism, natural disasters, and famine contribute to a higher incidence of mental health issues such as post-traumatic stress disorder (PTSD), anxiety, depression, and somatization than witnessed in the general population (Schweitzer et al. 2006; Lindencrona, Ekblad, and Hauff 2008; Gerritsen et al. 2006).

Distressing events occurring in premigration settings subsequently contribute to one's mental health status; however, postmigration challenges account for much of resettled refugees' present-day stress (Miller 1999). Postmigration stressors include issues such as financial concerns, acculturation, loss of traditional ways of life, and forced modernization (Miller 1999; Miller and Rasco 2004). In Schweitzer et al.'s (2006) assessment of Sudanese refugees resettled in Australia, they note that the most commonly reported post-migration stressors pertain to worry regarding family back home, employment status, and acculturation challenges. Additional postmigration stressors include experiences of prejudice and discrimination and dismal housing conditions (Pumariega, Rothe, and Pumariega 2005). The combination of such stressors has the potential to negatively impact one's mental and physical health, and refugees lacking support of their own ethnic community were significantly more likely to experience depression than refugees with ties to ethnic communities (Beiser 1993). Increased social engagement and social support have the potential to alleviate and possibly negate symptoms associated with mental and physical health ailments (Uchino 2009; Rook 1984).

THE SETTLEMENT HOUSE MODEL AS A SOCIAL SUPPORT INTERVENTION

Refugee integration with wider society is unlikely to occur without intentional initiatives specifically designed to promote inter-connectivity. Targeted community interventions are necessary to foster between group inter-ethnic cohesion (Daley 2007). Implementation of the settlement house model as a community-based intervention is one way of promoting social bridging and bonding among resettled refugee populations. The settlement house model hails from the social work field and was established with the intention of connecting historically marginalized groups with social services within the parameters of their own neighborhoods. Four primary tenets comprise a functioning settlement house including: 1) programming is offered within walking distance of residents targeted for service delivery; 2) programming is implemented for family members of all generations; 3) programming is flexible and based on community needs; and 4) programming promotes and celebrates cultural diversity (Fisher 2005). English language courses, child care, employment assistance, information and referral services, and health education programs are commonly offered through settlement houses (Yan 2004).

Responses to address integration concerns include the development of broad policies and conceptual frameworks. While these tools are useful, they do not address community cohesion and integration at the local level, nor do they focus on specific interactions of diverse ethnic groups (Daley 2007). Few studies have examined the social engagement patterns of resettled refugees and local communities (Castles et al. 2002) and those that have often limited reporting to one or two ethnic groups (Yu et al. 2007). Furthermore, integration occurring within the settlement house model has not been adequately explored. While settlement houses have a long history of connecting immigrant communities with host societies (Addams 1999), little is known about intra- and inter-ethnic interactions and the degree in which they occur within this model (Yan and Lauer 2008).

By examining interactions occurring within a settlement house model, practitioners will have a better understanding of aspects likely to increase social bridging and bonding. This knowledge can advise refugee resettlement practice at state and local levels, and researchers can advocate for integration strategies likely to increase engagement contributing to enhanced mental and physical health outcomes for resettled refugees.

ETHNOGRAPHIC APPROACH

The reconstruction of refugees' social networks post-resettlement remains a relatively unexplored area of research. We conducted a focused ethnography to better understand the social engagement patterns of multiethnic resettled refugees residing within a settlement house. Data collection within a focused ethnography occurs over a shorter period of time and examines a specific angle of a social problem or social processes within a community (LeCompte and Schensul 1999; Boyle 1994); thus, we did not examine every aspect of refugees' lives post-resettlement but narrowed the scope to explore social network construction.

Historically Guilford County has been the largest refugee receiving county in the state of North Carolina resettling over 800 refugees each year (UNCG CNNC 2014). The Magnolia Manor[1] Community Center operated under an adapted version of the settlement house model. Housed in three consecutive units within an apartment complex, the Magnolia Manor Community Center functioned under the auspices of a local nonprofit agency providing support services to resettled refugees. The apartment complex consists of 178 individual units and housed approximately 250 refugees or 80 percent of the total population. Apartment management donated the units to the nonprofit agency with the understanding that two area resettlement agencies would place refugees within the complex, thus, raising occupancy rates. Due to unforeseen circumstances, the Community Center permanently closed ten weeks after the study began.

Data were collected over eight months. Nearly one hundred hours of observation were conducted in locations including English language classes, community gardens, parking lots and outdoor space. In addition to participant observation, formal interviews were conducted with thirty-six individuals including residents from Burma (10), various African countries (9),[2] and Vietnam (9), past refugee residents (2), Center staff (2), Center volunteers (2), and apartment managers (2). Informal conversations took place with no less than 115 Community Center staff and volunteers, apartment staff, and refugee, immigrant, and non-immigrant residents.

Refugees living at Magnolia Manor were grouped into three primary categories based on group similarities while simultaneously taking their differences into consideration. Nine refugees from six different African countries were interviewed. The authors acknowledge the hundreds of ethnicities and languages comprising the African continent; however, African refugees at this site bonded over shared language and similar cultural identities. The main groups from Burma consisted of the Chin and Karen. While the ethnic groups speak different languages and practice different cultures, they were grouped together because of shared resources available for refugees specifically from Burma regardless of ethnicity. All participants from Vietnam identified as ethnically Vietnamese. Comparison groups were formed based on observed social networks. Results represent a co-construction of events informed by both emic (insider) and etic (outsider) perspectives.

Due to the nature of this ethnography, refugees from a range of different backgrounds and cultures participated in this study. Fortunately, two of the three interpreters used were native to the ethnic communities being interviewed. Therefore, they served a dual role as cultural brokers and interpreters for the study. If misunderstandings became apparent during interviews, the interpreters interjected to help clarify any confusion.

Recruitment was affected by my past experience at the site. I taught cultural orientation classes at the Magnolia Manor Community Center the year it opened—three years prior to the beginning of this study. A prolonged absence from direct service involvement with the Center allowed me to re-enter the scene with a relatively fresh outlook, while pre-established connections facilitated access to the setting. While teaching, I met and maintained relationships with several refugee families. Families still residing at the complex introduced me to newer residents. Prior trust established with the refugee community helped me to build rapport with newer arrivals throughout this study.

POST-RESETTLEMENT INTEGRATIVE MODEL OF SOCIAL ENGAGEMENT

By examining observed and reported patterns of intra- and inter-ethnic interactions within the boundaries of the settlement house, various types of social networks emerged through three forms of social engagement: functional, communal, and exploratory. Figure 4.1 illustrates the Post-Resettlement Integrative Model of Social Engagement (PRIMSE). The model portrays each engagement type with its corresponding interactions. Several interaction types reside in more than one type of engagement. This is represented by their placement within the overlapping circles. For example, Lessening Hardship and Assisting Others are represented in both Functional and Communal Engagement, while Testing the Waters overlaps with Exploratory and Communal Engagement. In addition, several interaction types may start in Functional or Exploratory Engagement but may lead to Communal Engagement. These relationships are depicted by dotted arrows. Figure 4.1 highlights how the results are interconnected and often mutually dependent on one another.

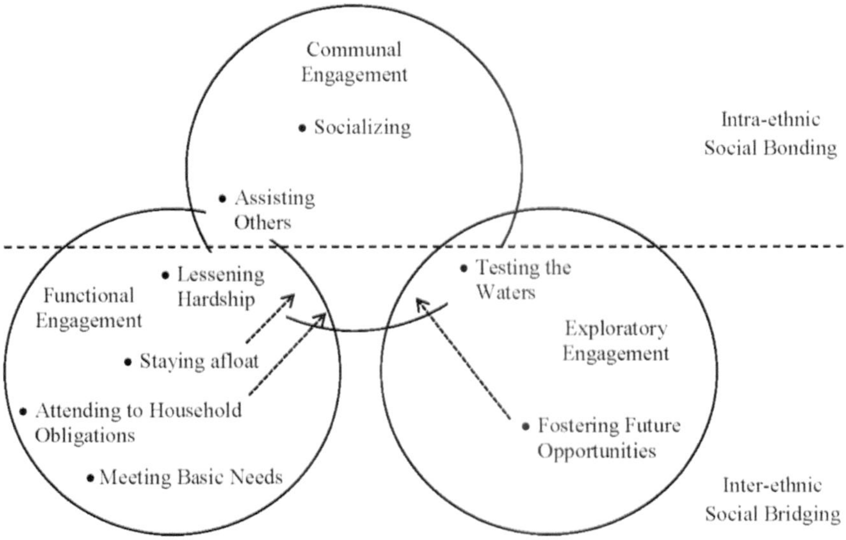

Figure 4.1 Post-Resettlement Integrative Model of Social Engagement. *Source*: Author-generated.

Functional Engagement

Functional Engagement is a pragmatic approach to engagement. Refugees that partook in this type of engagement carried out activities essential to their individual well-being or the well-being of their immediate family. Functional Engagement is comprised of interactions necessary to subsist in the United States. Interactions are demarcated into the following categories: Meeting Basic Needs, Attending to Household Obligations, and Staying Afloat.

Meeting Basic Needs

Bernadette, a refugee resettled from the Democratic Republic of Congo, experienced several maintenance concerns in the two-bedroom apartment she rented. Our field notes depict a common scenario for refugees living in low-income housing:

> Water from the neighbor's apartment was leaking into Bernadette's living room. Meseret (a refugee from Ethiopia) seemed appalled by this. She asked if the apartment had any other problems. Bernadette mentioned cockroaches and said that the apartment management never seems to finish this job. They start to spray and then they stop. The cockroaches are always there. Meseret was encouraging Bernadette to complain about this to the management. Bernadette shrugged her shoulders and changed the subject.

This scenario illustrates Bernadette's hesitancy to contact apartment management to report maintenance issues—even those not caused by her or her family. She is reluctant to engage with apartment staff and bring up questions and concerns that she may have.

Meeting Basic Needs occurred when refugee residents did not want to initiate contact with other parties, but felt compelled to do so. If not for the situation in need of resolution, the groups would not interact with one another. Interactions pertaining to Meeting Basic Needs tended to be sporadic. They occurred intra- and inter-ethnically, but were more common between inter-ethnic populations. All three major refugee groups at Magnolia Manor took part in interactions Meeting Basic Needs; these interactions occurred most frequently with apartment management. Examples of this type of interaction included communicating maintenance concerns and explaining late rent payments.

Attending to Household Obligations

Interactions stemming from Attending to Household Obligations were the by-product of a primary action. If not for the chore or obligation, interactions would not have occurred. Interactions were not forced like they were with Meeting Basic Needs, but they consisted of surface-level gestures and greetings.

> Honorine, a 40-year-old mother physically separated from her husband during an attack on their village in the Central African Republic, stood immediately outside her apartment unit taking out her daughter's braids. Lahn, a 71-year-old man from Vietnam, walked by with a bag of trash. He placed it in the dumpster and then walked back. Honorine waved and said, "Hi. How are you?" The man smiled, waved, and walked back into his apartment.

Interactions of this type required minimal effort. They tended to occur sporadically, but routines could develop from interactions of this type. Interactions while Attending to Household Obligations occurred both intra- and inter-ethnically and at times evolved into prolonged social encounters that lead to Communal Engagement. African, Burmese, and Vietnamese refugees all experienced this type of interaction. Examples within this category included greeting or receiving greetings from other residents while disposing of trash, preparing food, working on a vehicle, or waiting for the bus.

Staying Afloat

Many refugee women of differing ethnicities met weekly to make crafts to be sold at local fairs. The volunteer coordinating this group observed changing behavior over time.

> The women would sit in groups based on their countries of origin—the Vietnamese with the Vietnamese, the Burmese with the Burmese, and the Africans all together . . . the groups were very exclusive and talked amongst themselves in the beginning but . . . this gradually began to change—especially if one woman was viewed as the expert in a particular craft or trade. The other women would begin asking "experts" various questions about that craft.

Interactions pertaining to Staying Afloat were a by-product of another action or behavior that contributed to a family's economic well-being. Interactions required minimal effort and were often superficial; at times, they could potentially transpire into genuine relationships. Staying Afloat interactions occurred repeatedly over an extended period of time with the same individuals. They occurred both intra- and inter-ethnically and were primarily observed among Burmese and Vietnamese women. Examples of this type of interaction included conversing with others while knitting, sharing gardening tips, or explaining craft techniques.

Communal Engagement

Communal Engagement consists of interactions that helped refugees prosper individually and collectively. The emphases of interactions were no longer solely related to individual or family needs. While some Communal

Engagement interactions described below also constitute Functional Engagement, the foci of the interactions have shifted from individual necessities to the assistance and support of other refugees. Refugees that took part in Communal Engagement advanced beyond basic survival mode and began to settle into their new life in the United States.

Communal Engagement consists of the following interactions: Lessening Hardship, Assisting Others, and Socializing.

Lessening Hardship

A group of elderly Vietnamese women regularly completed routine tasks together such as grocery shopping. Field notes captured the following regularly-occurring scene: "Ngon, Long, and Phuong are out walking. They must be going to Food Lion. The three women consistently go grocery shopping together." While grocery shopping together could be done for social purposes, none of these women were comfortable speaking English; therefore, going to the store together was easier than going alone. Together they were able to help one another navigate the shopping trip.

Interactions to Lessen Hardship occurred simply to make life easier for oneself, while simultaneously advancing the positions of others. At times refugee residents pooled their collective knowledge to accomplish certain tasks or figure out a problem. These interactions were a byproduct of the primary action and their focus pragmatic. Interactions to Lessen Hardship consisted of individuals joining with others to improve their own well-being; interests of the individual remained primarily self-serving. Resultantly, Lessening Hardship could be categorized as both Functional Engagement and Communal Engagement. Lessening Hardship interactions were likely to be surface level, but evolved into deeper interactions at times. They were also usually sporadic, but could progress into regular occurrences. Interactions of this type occurred intra-ethnically. African and Vietnamese women in particular were observed participating in this type of interaction. Examples of interactions to Lessen Hardship included sharing apartments and women grocery shopping and figuring out how to make social service appointments together.

Assisting Others

Several single mothers from various countries in central Africa residing within the apartment complex routinely helped each other out. The following observation, captured by our field notes, was a regular occurrence with refugees within the apartment complex: "On my way out I ran into Sylviane. She was with Honorine right outside of Honorine's apartment. Both stopped and waved. Sylviane was driving Honorine to work." Assisting Others consisted of sharing both tangible and intangible resources with others—typically one's neighbors. This type of interactions entailed refugee residents appropriating resources amongst the larger group. Assisting Others is the first interaction described that was not the byproduct of a different action; the primary action included aiding others in need. When Assisting Others, the focus shifted from interactions that benefitted oneself and one's immediate family to interactions benefitting others. Interactions that Assist Others could be viewed as a form of collective survival. This category is distinct from Lessening Hardship, because refugee residents Assisting Others did not tangibly gain from the interaction; motivations appeared altruistic and genuine. Assisting Others tended to occur continuously over time. Interactions under this category were more common amongst one's own ethnic group but could be displayed inter-ethnically as well. African and Burmese refugees at Magnolia Manor were more likely to engage in interactions of this type. Examples of interactions to Assist Others included offering a ride to those lacking transportation, sharing tools and gardening supplies, babysitting one another's children, and communicating information about crime.

Socializing

Within the complex there was a group of elderly Vietnamese men who routinely socialized together. Field notes capture the following scene: "Three Vietnamese men are now sitting outside of Phuong's apartment facing the garden. All three lawn chairs are aligned in a row so that none of the men are facing each other and all share the same view. They are laughing and their voices are echoing throughout the apartment complex." The men depicted in the scene above enjoyed spending time together. They tended to socialize at the end of the day when all other chores and obligations had been completed.

Socializing interactions occurred when residents recruited others or were physically recruited to participate in some sort of group activity. Socialization with others was one of the main reasons for partaking in the activity. This interaction is different from Assisting Others, because power differentials between those Socializing were more balanced than those Assisting Others. Refugees Assisting Others had something that other refugees did not; whereas, both parties contributed equally when Socializing. Interactions of this kind tended to be genuine and occurred continuously. Socializing was more likely to take place onsite within refugees own ethnic communities. At times, former residents of Magnolia Manor came back to partake in these interactions. Refugees residing in the U.S. for longer durations were more likely to display this type of interaction and often solicited new arrivals to participate in social activities. Refugees from all three groups Socialized. Examples of Socializing interactions included participating in walking groups, sharing tea outside, welcoming new arrivals, and participating in soccer games or other sports activities.

Exploratory Engagement

Exploratory Engagement helps refugees prosper at the individual level, but surpasses traditional survival mentalities by emphasizing integration into the U.S. While Communal Engagement fostered prosperity in the sense that refugees were participating in activities that benefitted more than the individual, the focus of Exploratory Engagement is on individual integration and inclusion in one's new society. Refugees that partook in Exploratory Engagement participated in cultural activities, customs, and norms different from their own. Exploratory Engagement consisted of the following interactions: Testing the Waters and Fostering Future Opportunities.

Testing the Waters

Testing the Waters consisted of attending events outside of one's cultural norms. Interactions under this category at Magnolia Manor were solely initiated by American staff or volunteers at the Community Center. Refugee residents, intrigued by these events, often attended out of curiosity. Fatima, a refugee resident of the complex resettled from Sudan described the following scenario: "Yeah, [Jehovah's Witnesses] used to come to me for Bible study. I meet them in Magnolia Manor Center and they ask me if I believe in God . . . and then I called them, please . . . I want to know better, and they used to come to my home and teach me Bible study. I'm not a Jehovah's Witness . . . but there's something I want to know from them."

Testing the waters overlaps slightly with Communal Engagement; Exploratory Engagement is emphasized, however, as residents were actively going outside of their norms to try something new. Communal Engagement during these events was minimal. Interactions tended to be surface-level and activities under this category occurred only sporadically. Events were exclusively inter-ethnic, although degree of participation varied by ethnicity (e.g. attendance of multiple refugee groups, attendance by native-born Americans and Vietnamese refugees only). Testing the Waters typically took place onsite at Magnolia Manor before the Community Center closed or transportation was provided by those initiating the event. All three major refugee groups partook in these types of interactions. Attending baby showers and dinner parties were examples of Testing the Waters.

Fostering Future Opportunities

This category pertained to interactions designed to Foster Future Opportunities for integration. While the Community Center was open, these interactions consisted of onsite English for Speakers of Other Languages (ESOL) classes and cultural orientation sessions. After the Community Center closed interactions that Fostered Future Opportunities occurred almost exclusively offsite in the form of ESOL and citizenship classes. From field notes: "I drive up and see a congregation of Vietnamese residents. There is a large white van coming the other way. . . . The van is from the Senior Resource Center. It stops to pick up the residents. Seven Vietnamese men and one woman get in the van. They smile and wave to me as they climb in."

Fostering Future Opportunities could lead to Communal Engagement. In their true form interactions of this type tended to be surface-level but occurred regularly. Interactions that Fostered Future Opportunities occurred most commonly in structured settings, but could occur in non-structured settings as well. Refugees from all groups took part in these types of interactions. Examples of these types of interactions included attending ESOL and citizenship classes, seeking assistance with ESOL homework, and learning how to use public transportation from inter-ethnic others.

Contextual Variances to Functional, Communal, and Exploratory Engagement

Across the board refugees from parts of Africa, Burma, and Vietnam tended to take part equally in different types of engagement and interactions. There were, however, interactions where participation based on ethnic group and gender differed. This occurred with Staying Afloat, Lessening Hardship, and Assisting Others.

Staying Afloat

At Magnolia Manor, interactions classified as Staying Afloat were typically displayed by women. Women were more likely than their male counterparts to stay at home; therefore, it was easier to witness interactions of this type amongst female residents. Men might partake in this type of interaction while at work, however, it was beyond the scope of the study to explore this.

Staying Afloat interactions were not observed amongst African refugee residents either. Many African families at Magnolia Manor were headed by single mothers employed offsite. Thus, they were less likely to be observed partaking in this type of interaction onsite. They also had less time available for gardening and supplemental income activities (e.g. making crafts to sell). The few African women that gardened typically tended to their plots alone.

The Burmese were more likely to engage in Staying Afloat interactions, although not all occurred onsite. A local church supported the Burmese population at Magnolia Manor. Once a week, the church hosted activities for Burmese women and children; the women attended a sewing group, while the children received homework help. The women in the sewing group learned to use sewing machines and collectively produced items to sell at local craft fairs.

Lessening Hardship

The bridging Communal and Functional Engagement interaction of Lessening Hardship occurred most frequently among women. Women at Magnolia Manor were more inclined to work through problems together, whereas men often resorted to solving problems on their own. Lessening Hardship was not observed amongst Burmese refugees. The Burmese had been resettled at Magnolia Manor for several years, resulting in a large presence of families with significant time spent in the U.S. Multiple families were well versed in U.S. systems and were likely to assist others if needed. Therefore, newly arriving refugees were less likely to have to solve problems from scratch. Ms. Biak expressed: "I like this place because [there are] a lot of Burmese people . . . so [if] I need help, they come and help me." Because of the large presence, there was higher probability that a Burmese resident in the complex knew the solution to a particular problem, that resident just had to be located and asked for assistance.

Assisting Others

The Vietnamese were regularly observed working through problems together but were never seen Assisting Others. The Vietnamese at Magnolia Manor were much older than other refugee residents. Only one out of nine Vietnamese refugees interviewed was employed; most lived solely on social security income and the supplemental income earned making crafts. After the Community Center closed, two Vietnamese couples each received a donated washing machine and dryer from members of their church. Due to water and electric costs, however, these couples did not share their machines. Other Vietnamese residents were observed washing clothes by hand. The Vietnamese may not have Assisted Others, because as a group they had fewer tangible assets to physically Assist Others with. They worked to solve problems together, but had few resources to share with one another.

Implications of the Community Center's Closing

Refugee residents of all ethnicities expressed confusion when the Community Center closed. Many assumed that all apartment complexes in the U.S. had Community Centers like the one at Magnolia Manor and never realized the possibility of the Center closing. All refugees residing at Magnolia Manor were affected by the closure; however, residents were affected differently based on certain group characteristics.[3]

Refugees of African Origin

The loss of functional and exploratory opportunities was apparent amongst African families—especially those headed by single mothers. African families relied on case management and tutoring services offered through the Community Center more than other refugee groups; parents expressed concern about their children's education in the absence of afterschool tutoring. The Community Center had filled a void for many of the fragmented African families residing at Magnolia Manor.

Refugees from Burma

Refugees from Burma were the least affected by the Community Center's closing, in part, because they received supplemental services through a local church. Burmese families practicing Islam, however, were disproportionately affected by the closing. Muslim youth were less likely to attend offsite tutoring services provided by the church, opting for assistance from Community Center staff and volunteers instead. Regardless of religion, many Burmese parents were illiterate. Because of this, the Center played a crucial role assisting youth with homework, when their parents could not.

Vietnamese Refugees

The Vietnamese were significantly affected by the Center's closing as well mostly due to their age. Because the Vietnamese were older and less likely to be employed, they were home during the day and more likely than other groups to use the Community Center. Vietnamese were the primary attendees of the onsite ESOL classes. They were acutely aware of their need to achieve basic English proficiency within seven years in order to take the naturalization test and retain current benefits.

Vietnamese women were affected by the closing more so than men. All but one woman interviewed reported experiencing motion sickness while using public transportation. Because of this, women were less likely to leave the apartment complex than men. Men attended several offsite activities hosted by a local senior center, but women typically did not participate in these events. Vietnamese women, thus, were the hardest hit by the loss of the Community Center in terms of Exploratory Engagement.

The closing of the Community Center mid-study affected engagement patterns of refugees at Magnolia Manor. The loss of cultural interactions associated with Exploratory Engagement was most apparent. Refugee residents at Magnolia Manor were not likely to engage with non-refugee neighbors due to minimal English language proficiency and fear. Participants frequently expressed that their language skills were not yet at a point where they felt comfortable engaging with native English speakers. Others were fearful to interact with native speakers because they could not easily determine of their neighbors "to whom was good or to whom was no good." Before closing, the Community Center provided residents with opportunities to ask cultural questions and practice their English skills with native speakers in a nonthreatening environment.

Social Networks within the Settlement House Model

Findings indicate that resettled refugees engaged in both intra-ethnic social bonding and inter-ethnic social bridging when residing within a settlement house. While instances of both social bonding and bridging occurred, engagement types differed depending on the ethnic composition of those involved in the interaction. The settlement house model promoted three types of social engagement: Functional, Communal, and Exploratory Engagement. This model encouraged social bonding through Communal Engagement facilitated by geographic proximity. It advanced steps at social bridging and Exploratory Engagement through culturally-oriented service provision and Functional Engagement through income-generating activities. A combination of all three types of social engagement is critical for the successful integration of resettled refugees.

Although desired, many resettled refugees had few, if any, opportunities for social engagement with wider society. Of the refugees that actually connected with members of the local community, the majority of interactions resulted in Functional Engagement only (Goodson and Phillimore 2008) and did not transcend Exploratory Engagement. Daley found similar results in her 2007 study of community cohesion and refugee integration at the local level. Inter-ethnic interactions remained superficial failing to promote meaningful relationships or influence change in attitude (Daley 2007). Exploratory Engagement emphasizes the importance of establishing "weak ties" through social bridging and the influence that they can have on sharing knowledge and establishing new identities (Williams 2006).

The void occurring from foregone opportunities for Exploratory Engagement was most apparent when the Community Center closed. The Vietnamese were disproportionately affected by the loss of access to onsite ESOL classes and face time with native English speakers. Because many African and Burmese refugees were employed, they were more likely to receive small doses of exploratory interactions while at work when employed with others from different backgrounds.

Prior to its closing, Community Center activities falling under the exploratory domain served as primary mechanisms for connecting refugee residents at Magnolia Manor. Resettlement agencies assisted refugees to become

Functionally Engaged in their new society, and Communal Engagement often occurred naturally over time, since refugees were typically resettled within just a handful of apartment complexes throughout the city. While opportunities for Exploratory Engagement existed outside the settlement house, the ways in which this type of engagement was offered did not meet the needs of all residents—particularly the aging Vietnamese community. Successful integration cannot be completed without Exploratory Engagement.

Social Networks and Health

Social relationships influence individuals in many ways and contribute to one's sense of identity, confidence levels, and overall health and well-being (Dupuis-Blanchard et al. 2009). The benefits associated with social engagement and social support are not exclusive to a particular population or specific disease. Social engagement via social support benefits refugee populations in a number of ways such as increasing feelings of empowerment, easing social integration, building networks, sharing problems and experiences with others, and decreasing stress (Simich et al. 2005). While the establishment of supportive relationships is a component of successful relocations (Sugihara and Evans 2000), resettled refugees experience many barriers to social engagement in their new setting. At a time when social support is needed most, few refugees have the social networks intact to help mitigate stress associated with a transnational migration.

Health is a general indicator of successful integration (Ager and Strang 2008). The engagement types discovered in this study align closely with health promotion tenets. From a health promotion perspective, the combination of economic (i.e. functional), social (i.e. communal), and cultural (i.e. exploratory) capital are essential to one's health and well-being (Abel 2007); the unequal distribution of any of these types of capital can affect health opportunities at both individual and collective levels further exacerbating health inequities. Thus, the settlement house model through its promotion of functional, communal, and exploratory engagement can be viewed as a health promotion intervention in addition to its longstanding history as a social work intervention.

Policy Implications

Findings emphasize the importance of having easily accessible community space that allows resettled refugees the opportunity to engage in social bridging and bonding activities. Community space such as this brings refugees and the wider community together and may help promote the "process of reconstituting family and social support networks [that] assures emotional and material stability throughout many months and years of resettlement" (Simich 2003, 581–2).

Refugee admission and family reunification policies also have to be re-examined by governments sponsoring refugee resettlement. While governments may try to resettle extended families in locations near to one another, this is not executed in practice. If opportunities to re-establish social networks are inadequate upon resettlement, many refugees may elect to migrate to a secondary location in effort to find additional support networks; this involves further disruption to refugees being resettled and the local communities hosting them. This underscores the need for governments to modify their admission and family reunification policies placing a greater emphasis on resettling extended family members in the same geographic locations (Lamba and Krahn 2003).

Establishing various types of social support and experiencing different types of engagement early in resettlement is imperative for newly arrived refugees. Successful integration is bound by time. There is a finite window of one to two generations for immigrant families to attain middle class status; typically, if it does not occur within this timeframe, it is unlikely to occur at all (Portes and Rumbaut 2001). The establishment and implementation of community centers in areas with high concentrations of refugees may facilitate the reconstruction of social networks with multiethnic refugees and the wider society post-resettlement.

CONCLUSION

The Post-Resettlement Integrative Model of Social Engagement may serve as a useful guide when examining social networks of resettled refugees. Its parameters go beyond the traditional economic benchmarks of integration heavily relied on by many communities receiving refugees. Distinguishing three main categories of social engagement that can be further deconstructed into eight different forms of interactions allows for a deeper understanding of the nuances associated with re-establishing social networks post-resettlement. The model provides resettlement staff and volunteers working with refugees a framework to guide integration strategies and policies, promote public health practices, and provide them with potential social engagement goals to strive for.

Successful integration requires that refugee populations interact with a variety of people of different backgrounds in order to experience the multiple forms of engagement presented. Each form of engagement contributes to the multi-faceted process that constitutes integration. Social bonding with intra-ethnic communities helps to retain a sense of identity at a time when refugees are likely to feel lost and overwhelmed, while social bridging presents opportunities to promote new knowledge and foster confidence. The settlement house at Magnolia Manor fostered cultural diversity and inter-ethnic social bridging. However, when the Community Center closed, residents lost opportunity for all onsite exploratory engagement. While the apartment complex remains diverse, it is experienced in the form of small ethnic enclaves dispersed throughout the complex as opposed to inter-ethnic mingling.

Individuals experiencing forced displacement are at an all-time high; given current trends, refugees will continue to resettle in the United States, Canada, and throughout Europe. Refugees have a history of disrupted social networks and often arrive to their new country with physical and mental health ailments. While increased social network size and enhanced social support have the potential to alleviate negative physical and mental health outcomes, resettled refugees often lack such networks and support arriving with little, if any, of their social network intact. A more comprehensive understanding of the social engagement of refugees within a settlement house will assist local communities and resettlement agencies make informed decisions about future integration strategies. Furthermore, a better understanding of refugee social engagement patterns may inform new programs or influence the ways in which existing programs are executed. As a public health intervention, the settlement house has the potential to enhance the depleted social networks of refugee residents.

COMMENTARY

Margaret Evans and Natacha Nikokeza

The backgrounds and personal histories of resettling refugees may vary greatly, but one thing is common to all new arrivals: they leave behind family, friends, and belongings when starting a new life. Upon arrival they must find a job, familiarize themselves with a society and culture that are different from their own background, create a new network of friends and acquaintances, and learn a new language. During the adjustment process, they experience successes, but they are also likely to experience alienation, loneliness, frustration, and racism.

As early as 1952, the United Nations Economic and Social Council defined integration as a gradual process by which new residents become active participants in the economic, social, civic, cultural, and spiritual affairs of a new homeland. It is a dynamic process in which values are enriched through mutual acquaintance, accommodation, and understanding. It is a process in which both the migrants and their compatriots find an opportunity to make their own distinctive contributions (Kage 1962). It is very much this definition to which settlement housing subscribes.

Existing as a *safe haven* for individuals who have resettled in a new community and culture, the settlement house model provides support for Maslow's foundational need for security and freedom from fear for individuals fleeing persecution (Maslow 1943). For women, children, and the elderly in particular, the close proximity of community centers and programs provided for those who need support, assists in alleviating the economic, social, political, and cultural barriers that prevent individuals from achieving holistic self-sufficiency.

Community centers operate as an entity which increases social capital and fosters empowerment for individuals on both individual and collective levels. For individuals originally from developing communities with limited access to resources and decision-making opportunity, community centers exist as a place to recognize strengths through skill development, thus fostering the ability to provide for *self and others* through an enhanced network of resources and increased social and economic well-being.

Taking into consideration the emphasis on economic self-sufficiency, community centers exist as an extended platform that aid in building social, cultural, and economic resources by and with immigrant and refugee communities. It is through the emergence of community centers that immigrants and refugees realize their full potential in a new society, and that society realizes the benefits that immigrants and refugees bring.

NOTES

1. The site and interview participants are all referred to by pseudonyms.
2. Henceforth referred to as "African" refugees; while this group was comprised of refugees from 6 different countries, many bonded over shared languages. The authors acknowledge the thousands of languages and ethnicities that comprise the African continent; however, African refugee participants in this study bonded over shared identities. This is what was used as the basis for group comparisons.
3. Again, these classifications are not to trivialize the differences of refugees from different parts of Africa, but to focus on similarities and along the lines of how social networks naturally formed at the research site.

REFERENCES CITED

Abel, Thomas. 2007. "Cultural Capital in Health Promotion." In *Health & Modernity: The Role of Theory in Health Promotion*, edited by David McQueen, Ilona

Kickbusch, Louise Potvin, Jurgen Pelikan, Laura Balbo, and Thomas Abel, 43–73. New York: Springer Science & Business.

Addams, Jane. 1999. *Twenty Years at Hull House.* Boston: Bedford/St. Martin's.

Ager, Alastair and Alison Strang. 2008. "Understanding Integration: A Conceptual Framework." *Journal of Refugee Studies* 21 (2): 166–191.

Beiser, Morton. 1993. "After the Door has been Opened: The Mental Health of Immigrants and Refugees in Canada." In *The International Refugee Crisis*, edited by Vaughan Robinson, 213–227. Basingstoke: Palgrave Macmillian.

Boyle, Joyceen. 1994. "Styles of Ethnography." In *Critical Issues in Qualitative Research Methods*, edited by Janice Morse, 159–185. Thousand Oaks: Sage Publications.

Castles, Stephen, Maja Korac, Ellie Vasta, and Steven Ventorec, 2002. *Integration: Mapping the Field.* London: United Kingdom Home Office.

Daley, Clare. 2009. "Exploring Community Connections: Community Cohesion and Refugee Integration at the Local Level." *Community Development Journal* 44 (2): 158–171.

Dupuis-Blanchard, Suzanne, Anne Neufield, and Vicki Strang. 2009. "The Significance of Social Engagement in Relocated Older Adults." *Qualitative Health Research* 19 (9): 1186–1195.

Fisher, Robert. 2005. "History, Context, and Emerging Issues for Community Practice." In *The Handbook of Community Practice,* edited by Marie Weil, 34–58. Thousand Oaks: Sage.

Gerritsen, Annette, Inge Bramsen, Walter Deville, Loes van Willigen, Johannes Hovens, and Henk van der Ploeg. 2006. "Physical and Mental Health of Afghan, Iranian and Somali Asylum Seekers and Refugees Living in the Netherlands." *Social Psychiatry and Psychiatric Epidemiology* 41 (1): 18–26.

Goodson, Lisa Jane and Jenny Phillimore. 2008. "Social Capital and Integration: The Importance of Social Relationships and Social Space to Refugee Women." *The International Journal of Diversity in Organizations, Communities, and Nations* 7 (6): 181–193.

Kage, Joseph. 1962. *With Faith and Thanksgiving: The Story of Two Hundred Years of Jewish Immigration and Immigration Aid Effort in Canada, 1760–1960.* Montreal: Eagle.

Korac, Maja. 2003. "Integration and How We Facilitate It: A Comparative Study of the Settlement Experiences of Refugees in Italy and the Netherlands." *Sociology* 37 (1): 51–68.

Lamba, Navjot and Harvey Krahn. 2003. "Social Capital and Refugee Resettlement: The Social Networks of Refugees in Canada." *Journal of International Migration and Integration* 4 (4): 335–360.

LeCompte, Margaret D. and Jean J. Schensul. 1999. *Designing and Conducting Ethnographic Research.* Volume 1. Walnut Creek: Altamira.

Lindencrona, Fredrik, Solvid Ekblad, and Edvard Hauff. 2008. "Mental Health of Recently Resettled Refugees from the Middle East in Sweden: The Impact of Pre-Settlement Trauma, Resettlement Stress and Capacity to Handle Stress." *Social Psychiatry and Psychiatric Epidemiology* 43 (2): 121–131.

Maslow, Abraham. 1943. "A Theory of Human Motivation." *Psychological Review* 50 (4): 370–396.

Miller, Kenneth. 1999. "Rethinking a Familiar Model: Psychotherapy and the Mental Health of Refugees." *Journal of Contemporary Psychotherapy* 29 (4): 283–306.

Miller, Kenneth and Lisa Rasco. 2004. *The Mental Health of Refugees: Ecological Approaches to Healing and Adaptation.* Mahwah: Lawrence Erlbaum Publishers.

Morrice, Linda. 2007. "Lifelong Learning and the Social Integration of Refugees in the UK: The Significance of Social Capital." *International Journal of Lifelong Education* 26: 155–172.

North Carolina Division of Social Services. N.d. "The North Carolina Refugee Assistance Program." Retrieved from http://www.ncdhhs.gov/dss/refugee.

Portes, Alejandro and Ruben Rumbaut. 2001. *Legacies: The Story of the Immigrant Second Generation.* Berkeley: University of California Press.

Pumariega, Andres, Eugenio Rothe, and JoAnne Pumariega. 2005. "Mental Health of Immigrants and Refugees." *Community Mental Health Journal* 41 (5): 581–597.

Putnam, Robert. 2000. *Bowling Alone: The Collapse and Revival of American Community.* New York: Simon & Schuster.

Rook, Karen. 1984. "Promoting Social Bonding: Strategies for Helping the Lonely and Socially Isolated." *American Psychologist* 39 (12): 1389–1407.

Schweitzer, Robert, Fritha Melville, Zachary Steel, and Philippe Lacherez. 2006. "Trauma, Post-Migration Living Difficulties, and Social Support as Predictors of Psychological Adjustment in Resettled Sudanese Refugees." *Australian and New Zealand Journal of Psychiatry* 40 (2): 179–187.

Simich, Laura. 2003. "Negotiating Boundaries of Refugee Resettlement: A Study of Settlement Patterns and Social Support." *Canadian Review of Sociology* 40 (5): 575–591.

Simich, Laura, Morton Beiser, Miriam Stewart, and Edward Mwakarimba. 2005. "Providing Social Support for Immigrants and Refugees in Canada: Challenges and Directions." *Journal of Immigrant Health* 7 (4): 259–268.

Sugihara, Shiho and Gary W. Evans. 2000. "Place Attachment and Social Support at Continuing Care Retirement Communities." *Environment and Behavior* 32 (3): 400–409.

Szreter, Simon and Michael Woolcock. 2004. "Health by Association? Social Capital, Social Theory and the Political Economy of Public Health." *International Journal of Epidemiology* 33 (4): 650–667.

Uchino, Bert. 2009. "Understanding the Links between Social Support and Physical Health: A Life-Span Perspective with Emphasis on the Separability of Perceived and Received Support." *Perspectives on Psychological Science* 4 (3): 236–255.

UNCG Center for New North Carolinians. 2014. "Guilford County Refugee Arrivals by Country of Origin." Retrieved from https://cnnc.uncg.edu/wp-content/uploads/2015/01/Refugee-Arrival-Numbers-FY-2014.pdf.

Williams, Lucy. 2006. "Social Networks of Refugees in the United Kingdom: Tradition, Tactics and New Community Spaces." *Journal of Ethnic and Migration Studies* 32 (5): 865–879.

Yan, Miu Chung. 2004. "Bridging the Fragmented Community: Revitalizing Settlement Houses in the Global Era." *Journal of Community Practice* 12 (1–2): 51–69.
Yan, Miu Chung and Sean Lauer. 2008. "Social Capital and Ethno-cultural Diverse Immigrants: A Canadian Study on Settlement House and Social Integration." *Journal of Ethnic & Cultural Diversity in Social Work* 17 (3): 229–250.
Yu, Soojin, Estelle Ouellet, and Angelyn Warmington. 2007. "Refugee Integration to Canada: A Survey of Empirical Evidence and Existing Services." *Refuge* 24 (2): 17–34.
Zetter, Roger, David Griffiths, Nando Sigona, and Margaret Hauser. 2002. *Survey on Policy and Practice Related to Refugee Integration.* Oxford, European Refugee Fund Community Actions.

Chapter 5

Community-Based Organizations and Psychosocial Care in the Bhutanese Refugee Diaspora

Liana E. Chase, with commentary
by Madhu Neupane

SHIFTING PARADIGMS IN REFUGEE MENTAL HEALTH

The past few decades have seen a major shift in how we think about the mental health of refugees, and in particular the relevance of formal mental health interventions developed in Western contexts (Watters 2001). A wealth of literature now suggests that the experience and classification of mental or emotional suffering, as well as the methods of care most effective in treating it, vary significantly from one sociocultural context to another (Kirmayer 1989; Kleinman 1981). As a result, therapeutic approaches developed and tested within Western host societies may be less effective or appropriate for refugee populations of non-Western backgrounds (Tribe 2005). There is also evidence that these approaches may fail to meet the needs that refugees themselves identify as most important, such as in the domains of housing, employment, and basic safety (Summerfield 1999). Stigma and a range of financial and logistical barriers may furthermore prevent refugees from accessing available mental health services (Miller 1999).

Alongside this growing cognizance of the limitations of formal mental health services, scholars have called for further recognition of the strengths and resilience of refugees. Pathologizing models that locate disorder in the individual—thereby framing refugees as inherently vulnerable—have given way to frameworks that emphasize the social and environmental determinants of mental health problems and conceptualize refugees as active agents in the pursuit of mental health and well-being (Lewis 2011; Bonanno 2004;

Rousseau et al. 1998). In line with this thinking, mental health researchers have begun to develop and evaluate intervention models that build upon and develop existing resources within refugee communities (Ryan, Dooley, and Benson 2008; Miller and Rasco 2004).

Social networks comprise one such community resource that has been extensively linked with mental health outcomes in recent years. Best practice guidelines on the treatment of populations affected by "complex emergencies" such as forced displacement now call for the strengthening of social networks as a first tier of mental health intervention, prior to offering focused or specialized mental health support (Inter-Agency Standing Committee 2007; Psychosocial Working Group 2003; Rousseau et al. 2011). Initiatives that strengthen social networks may be particularly pertinent in the context of refugee resettlement. As detailed in the Heinemann et al. chapter in this volume, recently resettled refugees often experience a significant loss of "social capital," defined as the social networks and norms that enable collective action (Woolcock 1998). By definition, resettled refugees have been forcibly extricated from social networks in their countries of origin, and many experience a second loss of the social networks developed while living in refugee camps when they resettle. As such, strengthening existing social ties and fostering the generation of new ones may represent a crucial element of mental health promotion efforts in resettled refugee communities.

As formal networks of refugee individuals, refugee community-based organizations (CBOs) offer one promising avenue to strengthening social networks and attendant mental health benefits (Mitchell and Correa-Velez 2009; Espinoza and Ferguson 2006). However, in the mental health literature to date, refugee CBOs have mainly been investigated as potential partners to be engaged within more formalized, professionalized mental health interventions, rather than primary sites of mental health and psychosocial care in and of themselves. Surprisingly few studies have examined the mental health implications of membership in refugee CBOs or the role of CBOs in supporting community mental health. In the reminder of this chapter, I will draw on ethnographic fieldwork conducted among the Bhutanese refugees to offer some preliminary reflections on how refugee CBOs—even those with no explicit "mental health" agenda—may in fact function as invaluable psychosocial resources within the communities they serve. Building upon an existing literature on cultural concepts of mental health and illness, I will illustrate the ways in which several Bhutanese refugee CBOs with which I conducted fieldwork promoted both subjective and intersubjective dimensions of psychosocial well-being by, first, building the social capital of the most marginalized refugee individuals, and second, addressing major sources of distress.

BHUTANESE REFUGEE MENTAL HEALTH AND SOCIAL NETWORKS

The Bhutanese refugees represent a minority group of Nepali descent that fled Bhutan in the early 1990s (Hutt 2003). Almost all speak Nepali as a first language and consider themselves culturally Nepali. During the period of political oppression that precipitated the mass exodus of Bhutanese refugees from Bhutan, about 2 percent of the population directly experienced torture at the hands of the Bhutanese government, and many more experienced threats of violence and the repression of basic human rights (Mills et al. 2008). Most of the refugees traveled to Nepal, where despite their ancestral ties to the country, they were not granted citizenship, land, or the right to work. As a result, they were forced to reside in refugee camps, live in rudimentary bamboo shelters, and were dependent upon humanitarian agencies. Research conducted in the camp context revealed elevated rates of psychiatric distress, disorder, and disability across the population (van Ommeren et al. 2001; Mills et al. 2008; Thapa et al. 2003). Bhutanese refugee torture survivors, in particular, show a "dramatically high incidence of mental illness including depression, anxiety and post-traumatic stress disorder" (Mills et al. 2008, 5).

The permanent resettlement of Bhutanese refugees in host countries did not begin until 2008, and is likely to be ongoing today. Unexpectedly, the incidence of suicide among Bhutanese refugees increased substantially after resettlement began—to a rate roughly two to three times higher than that of host populations (Schinina et al. 2011). This trend has been linked in several studies to the degradation of social networks associated with resettlement. A report published by the International Organization of Migration identified "family conflicts and family separation, inability to fulfill responsibilities toward the family, and resulting social shame" as risk factors for suicide (Schinina et al. 2011, 16). Similarly, a study led by the US government's Centers for Disease Control (CDC) identified low perceived social support, increased family conflict, and difficulties sustaining cultural and religious traditions in the post-resettlement context as risk factors (Ao et al. 2012). Psychological autopsies conducted with families of suicide victims in the United States particularly highlighted the role of family separation and associated family restructuring as well as worry about family members back home (Hagaman et al. 2016).

A substantial literature on cultural concepts of mental health and illness in Nepali-speaking populations sheds further light on the role of social networks, and social capital more broadly, in Bhutanese refugee mental health. Kohrt and Harper's (2008) model of Nepali ethno-psychology identifies social status as one of five central elements of *self,* related to mental health and illness and suggests that both relationships and concerns about social status play a central role in shaping the ways people experience mental disorders and seek care. On one hand, high social status and strong relationships within the community may contribute to well-being and facilitate access to care resources. Kohrt and Hruschka (2010) have advocated for "social inclusion" activities as a pathway to improved mental health, and this approach has been successfully applied in intervention work with child soldiers in Nepal (Kohrt et al. 2010; Kohrt 2013; Kohrt et al. 2015). On the other hand, concerns about stigma and potential loss of social status may prevent the identification of suffering as a "mental health" problem and inhibit help-seeking in the mental health sector. In the context of Buddhist and Hindu[1] cosmological beliefs about karma, wherein present adversity is attributed to past misdeeds, forms of severe mental illness and even the experience of traumatic life events may confer stigma (Kohrt and Hruschka 2010). As a result, individuals suffering from pronounced mental distress or disorder may find themselves marginalized from social networks and unwilling to access formal care systems (Kohrt and Harper 2008).

DESCRIPTION OF THE FIELDWORK

This chapter draws from two ethnographic research projects focused on cultural and community pathways to psychosocial resilience in the context of Bhutanese refugee resettlement. During the summer of 2010 I conducted full-time ethnographic fieldwork in the resettled community of Burlington, Vermont (Chase 2011; Chase 2012). For a period of two months, I lived with a recently resettled Bhutanese refugee family, sharing a room with their two teenaged daughters, and participated fully in the family's daily life. With the support of Madhu Neupane, my host and a Bhutanese refugee community leader who wrote the commentary for this chapter, I also conducted twenty-two semi-structured interviews[2] with members of this community and participant observation at a number of community events and meetings.

In August 2011, I traveled to Nepal to conduct ten months of ethnographic fieldwork in the Bhutanese refugee camps. In this context I carried out extensive participant observation as well as semi-structured interviews with forty refugee individuals, including thirty randomly selected community members (a sample roughly representative of major demographic groups in the camps), and ten key informants in community leadership roles (for further information on participants, see Chase et al. 2013; Chase and Bhattarai 2013). With the help of two Bhutanese refugee assistants, I also translated, adapted, and administered the Brief COPE (Carver 1997) survey of coping behavior to nearly 200 refugees. Throughout this work, I received advice and technical support from my affiliate organization, the Transcultural Psychosocial

Organization-Nepal, an implementing partner of UNHCR and the main mental health and psychosocial care provider in the refugee camps at that time.

Over the course of both projects, I attended particularly closely to the language with which desired emotional, social, and mental states were described in order to sketch the contours of an emic conceptualization of psychosocial well-being among Bhutanese refugees (Chase and Bhattarai 2013). In line with the principles of ethnographic methodology, my research questions and focus shifted as I gained a better understanding of culturally salient indices of well-being as well as the factors and processes that contributed to and sustained well-being in the face of adversity. In both Vermont and the refugee camps, the relevance of the work of CBOs became clear early in the fieldwork period. In Vermont, I became interested in and carried out participant observation with two CBOs: a community farming project and a women's knitting group. I also conducted in-depth interviews with regular members of both groups. In Nepal, I interviewed representatives of a number of CBOs, including the Bhutanese Refugee Women's Forum (BRWF), the Youth Friendly Center, and the Camp Management Committee. I went on to engage in more extended participant observation in the meetings and activities of BRWF and to conduct two focus groups with BRWF members focused on their perceptions of community mental health needs and resources in the context of resettlement.

CBOs AND PSYCHOSOCIAL WELL-BEING IN THE CONTEXT OF RESETTLEMENT

Bhutanese refugees have a strong record of community organizing, which was recognized and reinforced over the years by the humanitarian agencies overseeing the refugee camps. As one observer commented: "The management of camps by the refugees is exemplary. The number of services carried out by refugees has increased steadily since their arrival. Since the mid-1990s, the Refugee Women's Forum and other Bhutanese refugee groups have developed an increasingly sophisticated network of activities" (Muggah 2005, 158).

Bhutanese refugee CBOs have now sprung up in numerous resettled communities in Western host countries. While none of the CBOs I encountered during fieldwork were explicitly linked with mental health or psychosocial well-being, I was drawn to these organizations early in both fieldwork periods by the language with which participants discussed them. Specifically, idioms or expressions of psychosocial well-being that I had identified as salient in other areas of my research were frequently mentioned in relation to participation in CBOs.

Many of these idioms centered on feelings in the *heart-mind*, or *man* in Nepali language, which has been described as the seat of emotion as well as some forms of thinking/cognition in Nepali ethno-psychology (Kohrt and Harper 2008). Feeling *light*, *fresh*, *happy*, or *relief/relaxation* in the heart-mind were common expressions used to describe states of health and well-being (Chase and Bhattarai 2013). Conversely, *thinking too much* and *tension* in the heart-mind were common idioms of distress (Kohrt and Hruschka 2010; Chase et al. 2013), and described states which could eventually lead to more serious disruptions in the *brain-mind*, or *dimaag* in Nepali—the seat of rational thinking and action which is implicated in most serious mental health problems (Kohrt and Harper 2008). CBO participants frequently invoked positive idioms related to the heart-mind when discussing their participation in organization activities, while also indicating that such participation reduced tension and prevented *thinking too much*.

Many participants also referenced a widespread belief that *remaining idle* was conducive to excessive thinking about or dwelling on one's problems, while keeping *active* or *engaged* could offer healthy distraction and promote positive feelings in the heart-mind (Chase 2012). Over the course of research, it became clear that one of the main goals of CBOs in both communities was to keep participants busy and pass the time. In the resettled community, participants emphasized the role of CBOs in *engaging* those who would otherwise be left at home alone, such as the elderly, the disabled, and non-English speakers, while other family members went out to earn. One resettled refugee explained: "These programs [CBOs] are important, especially to engage people who have stayed idle." Likewise, in the refugee camps, CBOs often targeted individuals who were otherwise unoccupied most of the day. This function became more important in the context of resettlement, wherein many had ceased working[3] to apply for resettlement and await the outcome. A representative of the Youth Friendly Center (YFC), a CBO run for and by camp youth, explained: "For youth . . . before the resettlement option they used to be engaged in earning, like as a teacher in local area. After, there is no personal income, which makes them free, and frustrated, also a kind of mental torture. . . . The main objective of YFC is to engage the youth generation." Thus, camp CBOs functioned to keep refugee individuals busy at a time when many described feeling suspended, waiting for their future to be decided through the resettlement process.

This YFC representative's description also gestures to an important link between mental health and financial stability. In line with the findings of another recent study in the Nepali cultural context (Bragin, Onta, and Nzeyimana 2014), my data suggested that the ability to meet basic needs was fundamental to Bhutanese refugee conceptions of psychosocial well-being. Unemployment and scarcity were frequently cited as sources of *tension* in the heart-mind. “Economic problems,” “low wages,” and rising costs were all named as possible causes of suicide. “Money problems” were also described as a source of social conflict (e.g., disputes among relatives). Conversely, earning and saving money, providing for one’s family, and obtaining material comfort and security were widely associated with health and well-being. When asked about appropriate forms of care for individuals suffering from distress or more serious mental health problems, many interviewees mentioned providing food, a loan, or support in finding work (Chase and Sapkota 2017). The value of such interventions was affirmed by a recent study among resettled Bhutanese refugees, which found that participation in a financial education program led to significant improvements in depression, anxiety, somatization, and PTSD symptoms (Mitschke, Aguirre, and Sharma 2013). Here, again, the support provided by CBOs in helping individuals to meet the needs of their families was clearly implicated in the alleviation of distress and promotion of well-being.

Finally, CBOs were also linked to intersubjective dimensions of well-being reflecting participants’ social health. Behaviors such as *sitting/staying alone* or *isolation* from others were described as highly maladaptive—both indicative of distress or more serious mental health problems and likely to contribute to them by leaving individuals susceptible to idleness and thinking too much. Some members of society were said to be particularly isolated from social support networks because the community “saw/took them negatively,” including those who had violated cultural taboos against, for example, divorce, remarriage, or alcohol use. Those who were involved in conflicts with their family or neighbors were also seen as vulnerable to isolation and associated emotional problems. Positive relationships with family members and neighbors, on the other hand, were associated with health and well-being. CBOs observed in this study created opportunities for social engagement and relationship building, and in some cases additionally worked to repair damaged relationships. As a member of a CBO in Vermont explained: “When people are home and jobless or lonely, it is good to be out and in a group . . . All young people are busy now so old people are lonely at home.” Thus, CBOs appeared to be particularly instrumental in engaging refugees who were otherwise isolated and idle.

Social status, reflected in expressions such as the “community taking/seeing [a person] positively,” was also integral to descriptions of desired states. One of the main ways in which CBOs facilitated improvements in social status was by engaging members in culturally sanctioned service and leadership roles. In particular, informants stressed the social value placed on community service in Nepali culture: “In Nepal our culture is to help each other. We have a good society.” Previous research in Nepal suggests charitable action is also religiously sanctioned, functioning as one method through which women, in particular, can accrue social status (Bennett 1983). As a result, many CBO members benefitted from the opportunity to occupy leadership and service roles in their community. Some additionally valued the chance to fulfill the role of financial provider within their families.

Overall, the link between CBOs and culturally salient manifestations of well-being (both subjective and intersubjective) was readily apparent in initial participant observation and interview data, prompting me to conduct more in-depth fieldwork with a handful of organizations in the camp and resettlement communities. In order to more fully illustrate the ways in which refugee CBOs contributed to and helped to sustain psychosocial well-being in the context of Bhutanese refugee resettlement, I turn now to ethnographic case studies of two such organizations: the Bhutanese Refugee Women's Forum in the refugee camps and a community farming project in the resettled community of Burlington, Vermont.

BHUTANESE REFUGEE WOMEN'S FORUM

The Bhutanese Refugee Women's Forum (BRWF) was launched in the refugee camps in eastern Nepal early in the 1990s with funds from an international aid agency. BRWF describes its mission as "campaigning to promote social and economic rights as well as literacy and skills-building for the most vulnerable and disadvantaged" in the camp population (Bhutanese Refugee Women Forum, n.d.). More specifically, BRWF programs target single mothers, divorcés, widows, and victims of rape, sex trafficking, and gender-based violence. By virtue of having broken with cultural norms, these women are often the subjects of stigma and thus are particularly marginalized from family and neighborhood social support.

At the time of fieldwork, BRWF was one of the largest CBOs in the camps. The organization's extensive leadership structure included representatives within each neighborhood who had myriad responsibilities, including the identification of vulnerable women, provision of information on and referrals to other camp resources, and monitoring of neighborhood cleanliness and hygiene. Leaders also organized awareness building activities such as marches and demonstrations to end violence against women. BRWF social networkers were active in neighborhoods throughout the camps. These women acted as mediators in resolving social conflicts, including in cases of gender-based violence, harassment, and marital disputes (or, commonly, disputes with in-laws). In some cases social networkers were also responsible for informing appropriate camp leaders or security services about an issue or connecting vulnerable individuals with other organizations.

Beyond these neighborhood-level leadership and mediation tasks, BRWF members participated in an ever-changing variety of income generation and vocational training programs such as rabbit breeding, beekeeping/honey production, baking, or micro-loan projects. The organization also hosted equipment for large-scale weaving which women used primarily to produce cloth sanitary napkins, which were then distributed to refugee women in the camps. Some also wove traditional shawls and bags that were sold locally. Most members were paid a small incentive for their participation in these activities (up to a few dollars per week) or received other practical support such as assistance transporting food rations to their homes.

In discussing valued aspects of the organization, many women associated positive feelings with participation in BRWF activities. One participant, for example explained: "When I go to the [BRWF] meetings and get to learn new things, I feel happy." Some women also connected such feelings with the financial support afforded by participation in BRWF. Another participant explained: "If I can provide something that is lacking in my family, that makes me happy. When my family is happy, that naturally makes me happy. [Having] no scarcity, no problems in my family is important for me." In this way, BRWF both alleviated distress associated with meeting basic needs and enabled women to occupy the valued role of financial provider within their families.

BRWF also contributed to social dimensions of well-being. At the community level, BRWF members worked to repair and strengthen social networks by mediating family disputes and other conflicts. In the context of resettlement, wherein families apply to resettle as a unit, within-family conflicts were common and the stakes ran high. BRWF members also provided mediation in cases of domestic abuse or underage, polygamous, or inter-caste marriage. One focus group participant explained: "There are also issues about discrimination within the family or within the community; in this situation people do not know where to go for help or justice. BRWF social members help them." Another member elaborated: "BRWF works for domestic violence, fights, quarrels, husbands that beat their wives after they drink. Victims can share their problems . . . so they can get a solution." At the most basic level, one participant explained that BRWF offices functioned as safe spaces for women suffering domestic abuse to spend the day, away from stressors at home.

BRWF representatives themselves also experienced social benefits as a result of their participation in the organization. Many of the women who went on to become mediators and neighborhood leaders in BRWF had experienced some level of social isolation or stigma themselves prior to engagement. At BRWF they found themselves embedded within a network of women who had had similar experiences. Participants described building friendships with other BRWF members and appreciated the opportunity to be out of the house and share with other women. There was also evidence that BRWF participants experienced improved social status. Working with BRWF afforded participants who had previously been *taken/seen negatively* by the community the opportunity to occupy a meaningful and socially valued role as leader and social service provider.

This transition from social vulnerability to social leadership, and the attendant psychosocial benefits, were most clearly illustrated in the account of Premila, a 50-year-old Hindu woman of the Chhetri caste. Premila was the first wife in a polygamous household in which her husband and her husband's second wife were abusive toward her children. After enduring this situation for a period, Premila made the decision to move into her own hut with her children and would no longer allow the couple into her home. In retaliation, Premila's husband spread rumors that damaged her reputation in the community: "He [husband] told other community people that I am a bad character woman. I was pregnant at that time but he refused to accept my child and blamed me, saying I had relations with another man."

At one point the stress induced by this situation led Premila to contemplate suicide:

> I tried to attempt suicide. But I thought about my child and decided not to commit . . . I was very frustrated. Nobody helped me. I felt ashamed to ask for help as my husband married twice. I used to cry most of the time. I had responsibility to take care of my children. I had no money. It was a very hard time. When I talk about these things my heart feels as if it is going to stop beating.

As a single mother who had rejected a traditional polygamous housing arrangement and been accused of adultery, Premila had transgressed important social norms and found herself marginalized from most forms of social support.

Eventually, a friend working with BRWF registered Premila for activities with the organization, despite Premila's insistence that she could not contribute because she was illiterate. Initially, BRWF provided Premila with support in learning to read and write. She then received training and participated in cleanliness and hygiene activities in her community. At the time of the interview, she had risen through the ranks to become head representative of her neighborhood in the camp. She recounted: "Slowly everything was going well and now I am happy with my children. . . . [At BRWF] I learned to speak. In the beginning, I had fear to face people. . . . Slowly I liked that work and I felt light." Thus, Premila's narrative reflects improvements in both subjective and intersubjective dimensions of well-being associated with her participation in BRWF.

On the other hand, Premila's initial reluctance to join the organization because she was illiterate suggests that BRWF's reach may be limited in some demographic groups. Women in our sample who were illiterate frequently described feeling that they did not "know how to speak" and were reluctant to become engaged in camp leadership roles. It is also noteworthy that despite her illiteracy, Premila comes from a high caste background (Chhetri occupy the second highest rung in the traditional social hierarchy in Nepal). At least one other informant in the camps expressed doubts about participating in CBO activities given his low caste background. Thus, it is conceivable that many women who were less educated and/or of a lower caste did not feel confident enough to seek membership in the organization.

BHUTANESE REFUGEE COMMUNITY FARMING PROJECT

In 2010, Madhu Neupane and Harka Kadhka, two prominent leaders in the Vermont Bhutanese refugee community, launched a community farming project in Sharon, Vermont. Together, they identified a plot of land on the property of a local restaurant and negotiated with its owner to have access to the space in exchange for providing fresh produce at a wholesale price. The men obtained loans from the USDA for buying tools and equipment to initiate the farm and attended trainings on the varieties of seeds grown in the short season in Vermont. Aside from this early assistance, the men ran the project independently of any outside support.

After spreading the word in the community about the project, Harka and Madhu identified five local families interested in participating, each of which agreed to send one family member to the farm three evenings a week. The final group was diverse, including two Hindu Brahmin families, a Hindu Chhetri family, a Buddhist Tamang family, and a Christian family. The group also included both experienced farmers and new enthusiastic learners. In describing the basis for selecting these families, Madhu elaborated, "we identified families who were idle, who were not easily employable and who were struggling to find engagement." With the exception of the leaders, all individuals who regularly participated in farming activities lacked basic skills needed to join the American labor market, such as proficiency in English. The group leaders, the only members of the group with driver's licenses, alternated days driving other participants to and from the farm.

Over the course of the summer, the community farm faced numerous challenges and participants developed creative ways of adapting their knowledge of farming to a new climate and growing season. For example, the religious beliefs of some members prohibited the killing of the insects that plagued the farm in its early days. In the end, members were forced to collect the insects by hand and release them into the surrounding wildlife. Yet despite these difficulties, the farm's first summer was a success. Altogether, the group produced thirty-eight different varieties of vegetables in a plot slightly greater than half an acre. They earned close to $8,000 from selling their produce and divided it equally among participating families. The project also encouraged a few other families to start similar farming projects.

Benefits cited by participants included, at the most basic level, improved physical health through regular exercise and access to fresh produce. The farm also spared families from having to purchase vegetables and contributed to family income. One participant explained: "It is important because we can eat our own produce, fresh vegetables." Others stressed benefits that were more obviously related to states of mind. For these individuals, farming combatted the conditions of *remaining idle*, by getting them *out of the house* and keeping the *mind busy* or engaged. As one elderly male farmer shared: "I love it. It keeps the mind busy, helps time pass."

Several interviewees described a sense of satisfaction arising from the fact that farming tapped previous knowledge and traditions from life in Bhutan. In this way, the farm enabled individuals who were not otherwise able to provide for their families to make a valuable contribution using their existing skillsets. The farm also afforded participants an opportunity to socialize with others, countering the tendency of the elderly and unemployed to *stay/sit alone*. One member summarized: "These [refugee farms] are important for the community. All these people have an agricultural background; because of this, getting involved in these projects, they get satisfied, because the get to do what they know, and get to chat. In this way, mental tension is reduced." Thus, as in the case of BRWF, participation in the community farm appeared to be linked to both subjective (e.g., reduction of tension) and intersubjective (e.g., social engagement) indicators of well-being.

DISCUSSION: COMMUNITY-BASED ORGANIZATIONS AND PSYCHOSOCIAL CARE

These ethnographic findings, interpreted through the lens of existing literature on cultural concepts of distress and well-being, provide compelling evidence that Bhutanese refugee CBOs often function to alleviate forms of suffering that fall within the purview of psychosocial care. They moreover suggest that CBOs play an especially important role in caring for those who slip through the cracks of traditional social support networks as well as, in the US context, resettlement policy. BRWF, for example, included women who had experienced social conflict or broken with cultural norms, and consequently suffered from stigma and isolation. In the post-resettlement context, the community farming project targeted individuals who were marginalized by the demands of adaptation in a society that values people through economic production: the unemployable. Unemployed refugees experienced both a loss of social support—left at home while their family members went out to earn—and a loss of social status, as they failed to provide for their families. Such individuals are largely overlooked by US resettlement policy, which prioritizes rapid economic integration. Given this orientation, refugee resettlement programs are forced to concentrate resources on supporting refugees likely to become family providers, rather than the community's most vulnerable.

One important way in which the CBOs described here facilitated positive psychosocial outcomes was by building the social capital of these vulnerable refugee individuals. At the most basic level, involvement in CBOs worked against social isolation to strengthen and expand social networks. By engaging individuals who were otherwise prone to staying alone at home in group settings, CBOs created invaluable opportunities to socialize and build relationships. The community farming project, for example, provided participants the occasion as well as the means (a ride) for meeting and getting to know others in the community, while the activities of BRWF extended even further to provide direct support in repairing and maintaining existing ties through conflict mediation. In the context of US resettlement, wherein many were resettled far from their relatives, friends, and former neighbors, CBOs offered some of the only opportunities to meet and share with others outside the immediate family.

These organizations also provided vulnerable individuals the opportunity to occupy a valued social role in their community, be it that of leader, volunteer, or financial provider. In the case of BRWF, women who had previously been the subjects of stigma and marginalization became neighborhood representatives and social networkers. Participants in the farming project found themselves able to contribute to their family's revenue for the first time since resettlement using their existing skills and expertise. Taken together, findings suggest that many CBO members accrued social capital through their involvement in these organizations, in some cases making a full transformation from social vulnerability to social leadership.

Another way in which CBOs contributed to psychosocial well-being was by directly addressing salient sources of distress. Economic hardship was identified as one of the primary causes of *tension* in both camp and resettled communities, associated with social conflict and suicide. Many of the CBOs I encountered foregrounded activities that promoted financial independence and stability. Community farm members, for example, received both monetary compensation and access to fresh produce in exchange for their participation. BRWF members often earned a small income through their work, gained skills or training that contributed to their employability, or received other practical assistance in meeting basic needs. BRWF's activities additionally addressed another important source of *tension*: social conflict within the family or neighborhood. During the fieldwork period, intra-family conflicts related to resettlement were common and could have serious implications for refugees' futures. In these ways, the CBOs discussed here helped to prevent and alleviate distress associated with some of the pressures introduced by resettlement.

The relationship between these forms of assistance and cultural concepts of psychosocial well-being was readily apparent in the language with which participants described their experiences in CBOs. At the subjective level, many CBO members recounted an increase in positive emotional states and decrease in maladaptive states and behaviors over the course of their participation. By keeping the mind busy and helping time to pass, participation in CBOs reduced tension and prevented idleness and thinking too much. Participants also attributed feelings of peace, happiness and lightness in the heart-mind to involvement in CBO activities, as well as to *speaking*, *sharing*, or *chatting* with others during activities. This is consistent with research on the broader Nepali cultural context highlighting the role of informal sharing activities within "youth clubs and women's gatherings" in mental health promotion (Tol et al. 2005).

In addition to facilitating these adaptive changes within the minds of refugee individuals, CBOs also worked at the interstices of the individual and the community to promote intersubjective dimensions of psychosocial well-being. Participants in CBOs developed new and stronger relationships, increasing their access to social support and protecting against social isolation. They also experienced improved social status in their community, as reflected in the *community taking/seeing [them] positively*. The centrality of relationships and social status to cultural concepts of mental health and well-being was evident in this study's findings, and has also been emphasized in previous research on Nepali ethno-psychology (Kohrt and Harper 2008).

Findings on the pathways from situational distress to more serious mental health problems in Nepali ethno-psychology (see Chase and Bhattarai 2013) further illuminate the link between the assistance provided by CBOs and mental health outcomes. First, CBOs can be understood to prevent the development of more serious mental health problems by promoting adaptive changes in the heart-mind early in the distress pathway; that is, by addressing important sources of distress, increasing positive emotions, and disrupting maladaptive states such as idleness and isolation, CBOs can prevent tension in the heart-mind from escalating to the point at which it disrupts the functioning of the brain-mind, resulting in more serious social, psychological, and behavioral problems (Kohrt and Harper 2008). Second, CBOs work against isolation and strengthen social networks such that individuals who do suffer from acute distress or mental health problems are more likely to be connected with the care they need.

Significantly, the ways in which the refugee CBOs described here enacted psychosocial care are largely consistent with current theory and best practice guidelines on early stage mental health intervention in refugee populations. The field of refugee mental health has seen a growing interest in interventions that recognize and develop the resilience of refugee communities by "building local capacities, supporting self-help and strengthening resources already present" (IASC 2007, 11). Scholars have also increasingly called for interventions that account for the social and ecological determinants of mental health problems (Miller and Rasco 2004; Ryan, Dooley, and Benson 2008) by strengthening social networks and addressing basic safety and survival needs (Psychosocial Working Group 2003; IASC 2007; Rousseau et al. 2011). By virtue of being refugee-led, refugee CBOs necessarily capitalize on the capacities and resources that exist within refugee communities and, through mechanisms elaborated above, help to further enhance these capacities. They also avoid pathologizing discourses on emotional suffering, working instead to resolve the environmental and social causes of distress such as financial hardship or family conflict. Finally, refugee CBOs not only account for, but also emerge from the cultural backgrounds of refugee communities, thus evading some of the issues of cultural insensitivity and misalignment that have been documented in other mental health intervention models (Tribe 2005).

Notably, the work of the CBOs described here is also congruent with recommendations on addressing the recent rise in suicide among Bhutanese refugees. A report from the refugee camps suggested that increased peer support could play an important role in suicide prevention (Schinina et al. 2011, 16). Directives from the CDC report on suicide include: "Strengthen community structures and expand programs for newly arrived persons that address post-resettlement isolation, non-clinical interventions in the context of Bhutanese culture, vocational training and community engagement" (Ao et al. 2012, 1). However, an analysis of psychological autopsies conducted by the CDC with suicide victims' families also highlights the limits of psychosocial intervention in the face of broader structural and policy-level problems contributing to suicide. These Bhutanese refugee families called mainly for modifications to the resettlement program to prevent or minimize family separation, as well as increased pragmatic assistance from resettlement agencies. Thus, while CBOs may provide a vital safety net for some individuals, there is an ongoing need to advocate for refugee resettlement policy that prioritizes the protection and promotion of psychosocial well-being.

Another important limitation of CBOs concerns their reach within refugee communities. There is evidence that CBO support may be less accessible to some demographic groups within Bhutanese refugee society, including uneducated and lower caste refugees. It is therefore important to remain mindful of issues of exclusion when partnering with or supporting CBOs in psychosocial health promotion efforts. Another contribution to this volume (Hoellerer) addresses the complex social politics of Bhutanese refugee CBOs in greater detail.

RECOGNIZING COMMUNITY PSYCHOSOCIAL RESOURCES: THE VALUE OF ETHNOGRAPHY

In addition to demonstrating the potential psychosocial benefits of participation in refugee CBOs, this analysis suggests that these important community resources may be easily overlooked or underestimated by host country mental health clinicians and researchers for several reasons. First, alleviating mental or emotional suffering is rarely a primary goal of refugee CBOs, even when it is a primary outcome. Neither of the CBOs described in the case studies above professed any explicit "mental health" orientation. Here, medical anthropology literature on the cultural construction of mental health—as a discipline and as a conceptual domain of human experience–is instructive. This work suggests that knowledge on the management of mental or emotional suffering in non-Western cultures may be organized around different conceptual categories, which do not problematize manifestations of suffering in the same ways or to the same extent as do biomedical psychiatric and psychological frameworks (Bracken, Giller, and Summerfield 1997). Without a developed understanding of these local systems of classification, it may be difficult to identify which individuals and organizations are implicated in addressing forms of suffering that fall within the purview of mental health and psychosocial care in non-Western refugee populations. For example, the ethnographic data presented above suggest that in the Bhutanese refugee cultural context, care for mental or emotional suffering is often embedded within broader care agendas that foreground the resolution of economic and social problems (Chase and Sapkota 2017).

Second, the particular manifestations of emotional suffering or distress that are addressed by refugee-led programs as well as the indices of well-being they promote may not be easily recognizable to host country mental health practitioners and researchers (Kleinman 1981; Kirmayer 1984; Nichter 1981). In the Bhutanese refugee context, salient idioms of distress included *tension* and *thinking too much* in the heart-mind, while desired states often referenced feelings of peace, happiness, relief, or lightness in the heart-mind. An examination of recruitment in CBOs further reflected a prevailing emphasis on inclusion on the basis of psychosocial vulnerability as indicated by the behaviors of *remaining idle* and *isolating* from others. Without a broader ethnographic understanding of the meaning and significance of these idioms, as well as their relationship to more serious forms of psychiatric disorder, the mental health implications of the refugee-led community initiatives described above may have been easily overlooked.

Finally, refugee CBOs engage diverse, culturally mediated logics of care—that is, beliefs and knowledge about what kinds of help are effective and why—that are not always commensurable with psychiatric, psychological, or even psychosocial frameworks for intervention. For example, one logic employed by many Bhutanese refugee CBOs revolved around the importance of *keeping busy*. As mentioned above, participants frequently described idleness as a source of vulnerability that could lead distress to escalate through the mechanism of *thinking too much*. As a result, efforts to care for individuals suffering from psychosocial problems often involved distracting them from these difficulties by engaging them in other work or activities. In this way, participants' perspectives on how CBOs contributed to well-being reflected particular culturally shaped understandings of the mechanisms of care, which do not resemble those underpinning mental health care in host countries.

In sum, this discussion points to a fundamental tension in emerging models of refugee mental health research and intervention: while international guidelines have increasingly advocated culturally grounded and community-based approaches to care, the efforts which most embody these principles may be difficult to recognize as mental health initiatives at all, as they derive therapeutic value from divergent understandings of suffering and are embedded within broader care agendas. Thus, some of the most important and appropriate mental health promotion activities taking place in refugee communities risk being overlooked by funding bodies, refugee assistance agencies, and mental health clinicians. This study offers one example of how open-ended ethnographic inquiry can help to reveal refugee community support systems with implications for mental health and psychosocial well-being. Specifically, this analysis points to the value of attending to emic concepts of distress, well-being, and care; employing a bottom-up approach to identifying psychosocial resources that suspends assumptions about how mental health care looks and functions; and exercising flexibility in adapting the research questions and focus in response to emergent findings.

CONCLUSIONS

In this chapter, I have argued that Bhutanese refugee CBOs often function as important sites of psychosocial care for those who have fallen through the cracks of traditional and post-resettlement support systems. The CBOs described here were directly linked with the promotion of culturally specific concepts of psychosocial well-being, including the reduction of tension and feelings of happiness and lightness in the *heart-mind*, as well as improved social support and social status. These organizations facilitated such positive outcomes first and foremost by building the social capital of the most marginalized refugee individuals, strengthening and expanding their social networks and engaging them in culturally sanctioned social roles. CBOs additionally addressed some of the main perceived causes of distress affecting Bhutanese refugees, including economic hardship and social conflict. These forms of assistance appeared particularly important in the context of resettlement, which has led to the degradation of social networks and introduced new social and economic pressures.

Taken together, these findings constitute preliminary evidence that supporting Bhutanese refugee CBOs may represent a cost-efficient, non-stigmatizing avenue to community mental health promotion and suicide prevention. Host-country stakeholders should consider partnering directly with CBOs in the development and implementation of interventions and the identification of at risk individuals. Given the high prevalence of mental health problems among refugees and the barriers to engaging this group in formal mental health services, there is an urgent need for further research on the potential and limitations of CBOs in mental health promotion in the context of refugee resettlement. At the same time, there is a need to recognize the limitations of these community support systems. This study found some evidence that certain demographics may experience reduced access to CBOs. Moreover, these organizations are not well positioned to address the deeper structural issues that contribute to distress and related mental health problems. For these reasons, there is an ongoing need to advocate for refugee resettlement policy that prioritizes fostering well-being beyond simple economic integration, and that better protects society's most vulnerable.

COMMENTARY

Madhu Neupane

Liana has worked hard to understand psychosocial care within the Bhutanese/Nepali community in the United States. She has done sufficient research to understand the psychology and the cultural norms of the Bhutanese community. Moreover, her involvement in community-based projects in Nepal provides her with a deep understanding of Nepali culture. There is need for research into understanding the importance of community-based organizations (CBOs) and their work within the community. I salute Liana Chase for her involvement in identifying the positive impact of community based programs and highlighting the work of the CBOs that promote the well-being of socially isolated people in the community, such as our community. When refugees from Nepal resettle, the separation from their immediate family members adds another layer of trauma to the preexisting traumatic past that each individual has faced in his or her life. The trauma could be due to leaving their home country, the difficult life in the refugee camps, or torture and other forms of violence they have suffered in their home country.

When people from within the community are involved in organizing the community, it is relatively easy to identify those who need immediate attention and assist them, all the while being sensitive to the cultural and social background of each person in the community. The western approach in treating the people with emotional or psychological problem is usually ineffective in the Bhutanese community because service providers and clinicians generally do not know how to adapt their services to the cultural values of community members. In my opinion, better results can be achieved when CBOs train these providers and clinicians aiming at designing culturally sensitive care that is tailored to individual communities and their values and traditions.

Liana's finding that keeping oneself busy can help to avoid mental distress is important within the Bhutanese community. Most members of the Bhutanese community are used to working hard and long hours. Most of them were farmers in their home countries and a few were business entrepreneurs. When unable to contribute to their family or society, they feel isolated, which worsens the impact of the traumatic experiences they have had in their home country. In other words, the inability to contribute to the well-being of others reinforces past trauma which results into mental health issues and tension in the *heart-mind*, which eventually translates into mental distress. Knowing the lifestyle, cultural background, and the caste of the person will help a service provider to adapt to the individual client and find the right intervention for that person.

The leaders of CBOs can easily identify the individuals who are experiencing the tension in the *heart-mind* through their change in behavior or change in the life styles. The work done by CBOs provides a platform for people to meet and socialize. Most importantly, the work done by CBOs allows people to talk among themselves which functions as a talk therapy since the people are meeting others, who are in similar situations, and thus realize that it is not only themselves who are facing this mental distress. This provides comfort and relief which translates into engagement and hence keeps the person away from isolation. For example, the people identified in the farming project were people who were prone to isolation because they found it difficult to find employment because of their difficulty to speak English and their skill level. That created a sense of isolation. The BRWF project is an example of the involvement of CBO leaders that can have a positive impact very quickly.

As Liana mentioned, the caste system is important to consider when service providers plan an intervention. The caste system is a very old traditional practice that cannot be abolished instantly. So, working closely with leaders of the CBOs is essential in identifying and providing needed support to individuals. It should also be understood that each person within the community is dissatisfied with the caste system and wants to change it. However, due to the complexity of our community, change does not come easily or quickly. It is important to train community leaders to facilitate a conversation in the community about the caste system.

Liana has learned the Nepali language and has been communicating with members of the community without having to use the services of interpreters. Her fluency in our language provides her with direct access to us and reduces the risk that meanings get lost in translation. While understanding the culture and caste system might be difficult for her, her involvement with our community is commendable. I wish Liana all the best in her future work and hope she can inspire other researchers to get involved in projects like her own, which benefits our community. I feel lucky to have worked with her and known her. I also thank her in highlighting the role of CBOs within their communities.

NOTES

1. At the time of my research, about two-thirds of the Bhutanese refugee population were Hindu and one-third were Buddhist.

2. All the interview quotes in this chapter have been translated from the original Nepali by Madhu Neupane or another research assistant. Although I studied and became proficient in Nepali over the course of this research and often posed questions myself during interviews, I consistently relied on the support of a native Nepali-speaker in interpreting participants' responses. All participant names included here are pseudonyms.

3. Although Bhutanese refugees do not have the right to work in Nepal, many did eventually find work illegally during their protracted stay in the country.

REFERENCES CITED

Ao, Trong, Eboni Taylor, Emily Lankau, Teresa Sivilli, Curtis Blanton, Sharmila Shetty, Barbara Lopes-Cardozo, Jennifer Cochran, Heidi Ellis, and Paul Geltman. 2012. "An Investigation into Suicides among Bhutanese Refugees in the US 2009–2012: Stakeholders Report." Atlanta: Centers for Disease Control and Prevention. Retrieved from http://philarefugeehealth.org/wp-content/uploads/2016/06/Bhutanese-Suicide-Stakeholder_Report_October_22_2012_Cleared_-For_Dissemination1-1.pdf.

Bennett, Lynn. 1983. *Dangerous Wives and Sacred Sisters: Social and Symbolic Roles of High-Caste Women in Nepal*. New York: Columbia University Press.

Bhutanese Refugee Women Forum. n.d. "About BRWF." Retrieved from https://sites.google.com/a/brwf.org/brwf-home/Home/about-brwf.

Bonanno, George A. 2004. "Loss, Trauma, and Human Resilience: Have We Underestimated the Human Capacity to Thrive after Extremely Aversive Events?" *The American Psychologist* 59 (1): 20–28.

Bracken, Patrick, Joan E. Giller, and Derek Summerfield. 1997. "Rethinking Mental Health Work with Survivors of Wartime Violence and Refugees." *Journal of Refugee Studies* 10 (4): 431–42.

Bragin, Martha, Karuna Onta, and Generose Nzeyimana. 2014. "To Be Well at Heart: Women's Perceptions of Psychosocial Well- Being in 3 Conflict-Affected Countries– Burundi, Nepal, and Uganda." *Intervention* 12 (2): 187–209.

Carver, Charles 1997. "You Want to Measure Coping But Your Protocol's Too Long: Consider the Brief COPE." *International Journal of Behavioral Medicine* 4 (1): 92–100.

Chase, Liana. 2011. "Coping, Healing, and Resilience: A Case Study of Bhutanese Refugees Living in Vermont." Unpublished paper. Hanover: Dartmouth College.

———. 2012. "Psychosocial Resilience among Resettled Bhutanese Refugees in the US." *Forced Migration Review* 40: 47.

Chase, Liana and Damayanti Bhattarai. 2013. "Making Peace In The Heart-Mind: Towards an Ethnopsychology of Resilience among Bhutanese Refugees." *European Bulletin of Himalayan Research* 43: 144–66.

Chase, Liana and Ram Sapkota. 2017. "'In Our Community, a Friend Is a Psychologist': An Ethnographic Study of Informal Care in Two Bhutanese Refugee Communities." *Transcultural Psychiatry* 54 (3): 400–422.

Chase, Liana, Courtney Welton-Mitchell, and Shaligram Bhattarai. 2013. "'Solving Tension:' Coping among Bhutanese Refugees in Nepal." *International Journal of Migration, Health and Social Care* 9 (2): 71–83.

Espinoza, Wilma and Claire Ferguson. 2006. *A Community Development Approach to Promoting Emotional Health and Wellbeing among Migrant Women: Review of Literature*. Syndey: Area Women's Health Unit.

Hagaman, Ashley, Teresa Sivilli, Trong Ao, Curtis Blanton, Heidi Ellis, Barbara Lopes Cardozo, and Sharmila Shetty. 2016. "An Investigation into Suicides Among Bhutanese Refugees Resettled in the United States Between 2008 and 2011." *Journal of Immigrant and Minority Health* 18 (4): 819–27.

Hutt, Michael. 2003. *Unbecoming Citizens: Culture, Nationhood, and the Flight of Refugees from Bhutan*. New Delhi: Oxford University Press.

Inter-Agency Standing Committee. 2007. *IASC Guidelines on Mental Health and Psychosocial Support in Emergency Settings*. Geneva: IASC.

Kirmayer, Lawrence J. 1984. "Culture, Affect and Somatization: Part I." *Transcultural Psychiatry* 21 (January): 159–88.

Kirmayer, Laurence J. 1989. "Cultural Variations in the Response to Psychiatric Disorders and Emotional Distress." *Social Science and Medicine* 29 (3): 327–39.

Kleinman, Arthur. 1981. *Patients and Healers in the Context of Culture: An Exploration of the Borderland Between Anthropology, Medicine, and Psychiatry*. Berkeley: University of California Press.

Kohrt, Brandon. 2013. "Social Ecology Interventions for Post-Traumatic Stress Disorder: What Can We Learn from Child Soldiers?" *The British Journal of Psychiatry: The Journal of Mental Science* 203 (3): 165–67.
Kohrt, Brandon and Ian Harper. 2008. "Navigating Diagnoses: Understanding Mind-Body Relations, Mental Health, and Stigma in Nepal." *Culture, Medicine and Psychiatry* 32 (4): 462–91.
Kohrt, Brandon and Daniel Hruschka. 2010. "Nepali Concepts of Psychological Trauma: The Role of Idioms of Distress, Ethnopsychology and Ethnophysiology in Alleviating Suffering and Preventing Stigma." *Culture, Medicine and Psychiatry* 34 (2): 322–52.
Kohrt, Brandon, Mark Jordans, Wietse Tol, Em Perera, Rohit Karki, Suraj Koirala, and Nawaraj Upadhaya. 2010. "Social Ecology of Child Soldiers: Child, Family, and Community Determinants of Mental Health, Psychosocial Well-Being, and Reintegration in Nepal." *Transcultural Psychiatry* 47 (5): 727–53.
Kohrt, Brandon, Mark Jordans, Suraj Koirala, and Carol Worthman. 2015. "Designing Mental Health Interventions Informed by Child Development and Human Biology Theory: A Social Ecology Intervention for Child Soldiers in Nepal." *American Journal of Human Biology* 27 (1): 27–40.
Lewis, Sara. 2011. "From Social Suffering to Social Resilience: Buddhism and Coping in the Tibetan Exile Community." Doctoral dissertation, Columbia University.
Miller, Kenneth 1999. "Rethinking a Familiar Model : Psychotherapy and the Mental Health of Refugees." *Journal of Contemporary Psychotherapy* 29 (4): 283–306.
Miller, Kenneth and Lisa Rasco. 2004. "An Ecological Framework for Addressing the Mental Health Needs of Refugee Communities." In *The Mental Health of Refugees: Ecological Approaches to Healing and Adaptation*, edited by Kenneth Miller and Lisa Rasco. Mahwah: Lawrence Erlbaum Associates.
Mills, Edward, Sonal Singh, Brenda Roach, and Stephanie Chong. 2008. "Prevalence of Mental Disorders and Torture among Bhutanese Refugees in Nepal: A Systemic Review and Its Policy Implications." *Medicine, Conflict, and Survival* 24 (1): 5–15.
Mitchell, Jenny, and Igacio Correa-Velez. 2009. "Community Development with Survivors of Torture and Trauma: An Evaluation Framework." *Community Development Journal* 45 (1): 90–110.
Mitschke, Diane, Regina Aguirre, and Bonita Sharma. 2013. "Common Threads: Improving the Mental Health of Bhutanese Refugee Women Through Shared Learning." *Social Work in Mental Health* 11 (3): 249–66.
Muggah, Robert. 2005. "Distinguishing Means and Ends: The Counterintuitive Effects of UNHCR's Community Development Approach in Nepal." *Journal of Refugee Studies* 18 (2): 151–64.
Nichter, Mark. 1981. "Idioms of Distress: Alternatives in the Expression of Psychosocial Distress: A Case Study from South India." *Culture, Medicine and Psychiatry* 5: 379–408.
Ommeren, Mark Van, B. Sharma, Komproe, B. Poudyal, G. Sharma, E. Cardeña, and J. De Jong. 2001. "Trauma and Loss as Determinants of Medically Unexplained Epidemic Illness in a Bhutanese Refugee Camp." *Psychological Medicine* 31 (7): 1259–67.

Psychosocial Working Group. 2003. *Psychosocial Intervention in Complex Emergencies : A Conceptual Framework*. Childhood A Global Journal Of Child Research. Edinburgh: Psychosocial Working Group.

Rousseau, Cécile, Taher Said, Marie-Josée Gagné, and Gilles Bibeau. 1998. "Resilience in Unaccompanied Minors from the North of Somalia." *Psychoanalytic Review* 85 (4): 615–37.

Rousseau, Cécile, Kevin Pottie, Brett Thombs, Marie Munoz, and Tomas Jurcik. 2011. "Appendix 11: Post Traumatic Stress Disorder: Evidence Review for Newly Arriving Immigrants and Refugees." In *Guidelines for Immigrant Health*, edited by the Canadian Collaboration for Immigrant and Refugee Health. Retrieved from http://www.cmaj.ca/content/suppl/2010/06/07/cmaj.090313.DC1/imm-ptsd-11-at.pdf.

Ryan, Dermot, Barbara Dooley, and Ciaran Benson. 2008. "Theoretical Perspectives on Post-Migration Adaptation and Psychological Well-Being among Refugees: Towards a Resource-Based Model." *Journal of Refugee Studies* 21 (1): 1–18.

Schininà, Guglielmo, Sonali Sharma, Olga Gorbacheva, and Anit Kumar Mishra. 2011. *Who Am I?* Assessment of Psychosocial Needs and Suicide Risk Factors Among Bhutanese Refugees in Nepal and After Third Country Resettlement. International Organization for Migration. Retrieved from https://www.iom.int/files/live/sites/iom/files/What-We-Do/docs/Mental-Health-Assessment-Nepal_Final_11March.pdf.

Summerfield, Derek. 1999. "A Critique of Seven Assumptions behind Psychological Trauma Programmes in War-Affected Areas." *Social Science & Medicine* 48 (10): 1449–62.

Thapa, Suraj Bahadur, Mark Van Ommeren, Bhogendra Sharma, Joop de Jong, and Edvard Hauff. 2003. "Psychiatric Disability among Tortured Bhutanese Refugees in Nepal." *The American Journal of Psychiatry* 160 (11): 2032–37.

Tol, Wietse, Mark Jordans, Sushama Regmi, and Bhogendra Sharma. 2005. "Cultural Challenges to Psychosocial Counselling in Nepal." *Transcultural Psychiatry* 42 (2): 317–33.

Tribe, Rachel. 2005. "The Mental Health Needs of Refugees and Asylum Seekers." *The Mental Health Review* 10 (4): 8–15.

Watters, Charles. 2001. "Emerging Paradigms in the Mental Health Care of Refugees." *Social Science & Medicine* 52 (11): 1709–18.

Woolcock, Michael. 1998. "Social Capital and Economic Development: Toward a Theoretical Synthesis and Policy Framework." *Theory and Society* 27: 151–208.

Part III

CITIZENSHIP AND BELONGING

Chapter 6

The Pitfalls of the Community Development Approach in Refugee Resettlement

Community Divisions among Bhutanese Refugees in Manchester, United Kingdom

Nicole Hoellerer, with commentary by Lance Rasbridge

RESETTLEMENT IN THE UNITED KINGDOM

In 2004, the United Kingdom (U.K.) initiated the Gateway Protection Programme (GPP), which facilities refugee resettlement from across the world to Great Britain. The GPP is funded by the British Home Office, and operated by the U.K. Border Agency (UKBA) in cooperation with various organizations, such as the United Nations High Commission for Refugees (UNHCR), the International Organization for Migration (IOM), Refugee Action (RA), Refugee Council (RC), and other governmental and voluntary organizations. Similar to other resettlement nations, the U.K. conducts interviews, as well as security and health screenings, prior to offering places to refugees. On arrival, resettled refugees received the Indefinite Leave to Remain (ILR) immigration status, which allows them to stay in the U.K. indefinitely, and bestows upon them the same rights to live, work and study in the U.K. as any other resident, as well as claim benefits and welfare payments.[1] Moreover, the ILR allows individuals to apply for citizenship after five years of permanent residence in the U.K. (Hoellerer 2013; Platts-Fowler and Robinson 2011, 4; UNHCR 2001, 2–3, 8–9; Wright, Ward, and Peach 2004, 13–15).

The first period of intensive support—including regular meetings with caseworkers, assistance with administrative and bureaucratic processes, and free English language classes—is followed by a second, forward-looking period of support, in order to address long-term needs, such as "integration"[2] into the host society. After approximately six months, service providers adopt an exit strategy, in which support is gradually outsourced to mainstream (public) services and local charitable organizations. The U.K. adopts a Front-End Loading (FEL) approach, which aims to provide support and resources only during the first stages of resettlement, "in the expectation that less support . . . would be needed in later stages as (economic) self-sufficiency is attained" (Duke, Sales, and Gregory 1999, 166). It is expected that after approximately six months, resettled refugees have obtained sufficient language and sociocultural skills in order to operate independently, seek employment or further education, and communicate with mainstream (public) services (Wright, Ward, and Peach 2004, 25).

COMMUNITY DEVELOPMENT IN RESETTLEMENT

One strategy of FEL is the implementation of the *Community Development Approach* (CDA),[3] that is, the formation of RCOs from within the refugee community, to which support can be outsourced once service providers exit, which is all the more important during a time in which governmental and NGO services in the U.K. are reduced due to a lack of public funds (Zetter and Pearl 2000, 682). Governmental services encourage the formation of RCOs with the help of professional community development workers, who advise refugees how to create an organization, what leadership structures have to be put in place, and what bureaucratic processes have to be completed (e.g., an RCO constitution and policies).

Policymakers in the U.K. define RCOs as the "ties to [the refugees'] ethnic social network" which serve as a "social buffer and informational translator," bridging "ethnic communities' public and private spheres by providing culturally tailored services" (Wright, Ward, and Peach 2004, 28). The overarching aim of the CDA approach in resettlement in the U.K. is to "develop a more cohesive community, where differences are accepted and there is respect, trust, cooperation and compassion between people in their daily interactions" (Mitchell and Correa-Velez 2010, 97–98). More importantly, service providers argue that RCOs run *for* and *by* refugees themselves have a better understanding of the refugees' needs, and are therefore able to provide more adequate support (Sales 200, 470; Griffiths, Sigona, and Zetter 2006, 884). Service providers acknowledge that refugees arriving in the U.K. suffer from various problems, such as a language gap, and a lack of access to the labor market, education, housing, child and elderly care, legal representation, and public facilities (RA and RC 2008; Spicer 2008, 493). In turn, self-support through RCOs may engender empowerment (Mitchell and Correa-Velez 2010, 104) which is one of the aims of refugee resettlement.

Once officially established through various bureaucratic processes (such as the development of a formal constitution, and the election of board members), these RCOs could provide free-of-charge support for resettled refugees. Service providers have the conviction that RCOs—by integrating formalized, bureaucratic organizational structures with informal networks (Sigona, Zetter and Griffiths 2004, 4)—are the most important tool, "providing advice and information for new arrivals, provide a safe meeting place where people can speak their own language and celebrate their own culture, provide formal or informal support to members seeking employment in local ethnic business and in gaining access to housing" (Zetter and Pearl 2000, 684).

In turn, engagement in and with RCOs is assumed to impede marginalization, as well as increase trust and social bonds with others.[4] As Heinemann et al. outline in this volume, communities foster both bonding and bridging capital, and therefore amplify the refugees' sense of certainty, safety, and self-sufficiency, easing the burden on governmental and nongovernmental services in the long term (Mitchell and Correa-Velez 2010).

My research showed that the shift of responsibility for refugee integration from governmental providers to local RCOs left Bhutanese refugees with a feeling of abandonment by the very agencies that brought them to the U.K. For example, new arrivals to the U.K. criticized the lack of empathy, as one of them stated: "[Social workers] do everything quick, like on an assembly line, ticking all the boxes 'yes, we have shown and explained all of this,' then they go home and get paid. . . . They don't care about us." It is the Bhutanese refugee community's responsibility to visit new arrivals to assist with translations and settling into their new homes. As a young refugee explained when picking up new arrivals at Manchester airport: "All of us, we are refugees, you know, we have to help [new arrivals]. You are scared when you come here; it's all new, and very big. Nobody speaks Nepali, only English. . . . 'No time, no time' [the social workers] say." Left to their own devices after governmental assistance ceases, fissions within the refugee community have become exaggerated and ultimately led to the division of Bhutanese RCOs in Manchester, which are divided not due to caste, gender or religious differences, but due to *othering* that is inherent in the creation of social networks.

Community is a "notoriously 'fuzzy'" concept, which in spite of being widely used and cited across the social sciences and in political and public discourses, resists precise definitions (Chatterjee 1998; Chatty 2010, 475; Rapport and Overing 2000, 60). It is the "most taken-for-granted and unexamined form as a unit of analysis, the location rather than the object of research" (Amit and Rapport 2002, 919). Similarly, U.K. policymakers do not critically reflect on the notion of community and its possible problematic features, leading to shortcomings of policy-intervention for refugees. My study puts into question the assumed positive attributes of community as a singular and permanent "rootedness, sense of locality, identity" (Shaw 2008, 25), and suggests that policymakers and service providers in the U.K. have to do more to address internal divisions by mediating between fractions within refugee communities.

THE PROBLEM WITH COMMUNITY: THE CREATION OF SIMILARITY AND DIFFERENCE

The CDA in the U.K.'s refugee resettlement program is based on the optimistic assumption that community is a "concept of always positive evaluation and evocation . . . to which people would expect, advocate, or wish to belong" (Rapport and Overing 2000, 65). Community in political, public, and even academic discourses appears as an ideal, and a possibility to create homogeneity and equality from *within* a social group (Shaw 2008, 27–28; 31). In public and political discourses in the U.K., community is a "warmly persuasive word" that unlike other forms of social relations and organizations (e.g., the nation state) is seldom "used unfavorably" (Baumann 1996, 15). Within these discourses, community is characterized by "mutuality, co-operation, identification" and loyalty, perpetuating the credulous stereotype of "uniform commonality" within communities, based on the conviction that refugees from a specific locality (e.g., Bhutanese refugees) automatically establish mutuality and solidarity with one another, and overcome difference in favor of the "good for all" (Spicer 2008, 493, 502).

For my informants, close personal relationships that are forged within a community are important elements of daily life in resettlement. As one of my informants stated:

> Community for me is a friendly and a fun environment where there are generous and helpful people, sharing their positive thoughts and feelings with each other, so that it will help the community to be developed. The people in the community should have a feeling of sharing, so that the community will never be left behind. It needs a unity of all the people to eradicate and eliminate problems, and this is how community is important. (Hoellerer's fieldnotes)

Their understanding of a Bhutanese refugee community is based on certain similarities, such as a shared history of life in and exile from Bhutan, life in the refugee camps in Nepal, and organized resettlement, as well as language, religions and sociocultural practices (e.g., Nepali New Year). Comments such as "we are only friends, but actually, we are family—we are the same people . . . we suffered together" are common when describing their intra-community relationships (also see Smith 2013, 176). This reflects

Appadurai's (1996) *community of sentiment*, in which a group of people share feelings, values and imaginations, arising within a specific discourse of ethnic categorizations. However, just because refugees have a shared language, country of birth and experience of displacement does not mean that they are one cohesive community (Mitchell and Correa-Velez 2010, 96). Thus, the term *refugee community* is difficult to pin down to one exact, coherent and all-encompassing interpretation.

Community is certainly reliant on commonality between its members. However, these shared traits, beliefs, and histories, may not be actual (socio-cultural, physical, historical) realities, but are located in the imagination of community members, who give meanings to these shared symbols or vocabularies (Anderson 2006; Cohen 1985, 98). These interpretations are not fixed, static, or homogenous, but depend on the context in which community takes place, allowing diverse, heterogeneous, and even contradictory communities to emerge (Rapport and Overing 2000, 62–63). The adaptation of the term community among Bhutanese refugees in the U.K. to denote social groups from close family to the global diaspora, is testament to this contextualization, as one of them stated: "Family is community, friends are community, we are all a community."

Social networks are sensitive to individuals' moods, values, personal preferences, and interactions (Amit and Rapport 2002, 508), as well as being influenced by external forces beyond the power of individuals. They are prone to mistrust and personal animosities, leading to disagreements between Bhutanese refugees in Manchester, and the split between three distinct RCOs, undermining the U.K. government's aim to outsource governmental support to formalized community organizations. These three Bhutanese RCOs do not work together, and some go as far as to cease any social interaction with members of "rival communities," as one of them stated: "When they are in the project, I don't want to be in [the project]. I don't work with [the rival community]." This also impacted on new arrivals, who were visited by RCO leaders, and were advised that if they do not join this particular RCO, they would not receive assistance—something an educated new arrival referred to as being "blackmailed into a community."

Several scholars working with forced migrations caution that although refugees may have common experiences, they may not perceive themselves to be part of one, all-encompassing community and culture, that is replicated in resettlement (see, for example, Mitchell and Correa-Velez 2010, 96). Baumann (1996, 17–18), for example, who worked in a diverse neighborhood in London (U.K.) comprised of migrants with South Asian background, criticizes the assumption that all those who share certain traits can be broadly defined as one community with shared interests, who naturally come together in one community organization, promoting the same social, cultural beliefs, and values.

Bhutanese refugee communities in the U.K. operate both through communality as well as through difference, or "othering." Community is often defined not only by what it *is*, but by what it is *not* (Amit and Rapport 2002, 985). Both Cohen (1985) and Anderson (2006) draw on Barth's (1998, 15) work on "othering" among ethnic groups, focusing on the boundaries that define social groups—that is, the "organization of culture difference"—and distinctions between *us* and *them* (Amit and Rapport 2002, 1307). Cohen (1985) highlights that unity is created through exclusion, and the imagination and consciousness of others beyond their boundaries (in Rapport and Overing 2000, 63; also see Hall 1996). As Bhabha (2004, 30) put it, a community "begins its presencing" exactly *because* of its consciousness of boundaries. Similarly, Bhutanese refugee communities are constructed along "two key axes" (Mohan 2002, 98): first, by shared sociocultural meanings, practices (or performances), histories, and experiences, and secondly by means of *othering*, defining themselves vis-à-vis others. Anderson (2006) highlights that this creation of similarity and difference is (akin to national identity) imagined by the individuals who employ it. That is, the criteria determining insider and outsider are not factual, but are negotiated, contested, and amended by the people themselves. It is this imagined *othering* that is important for the creation of community and the divisions between Bhutanese refugees in the U.K. Although a relatively small group of only about 200 individuals, Bhutanese refugees in Manchester founded three distinct RCOs, with about 50–60 members each, which are divided not due to caste or religious differences, but due to personal disagreements about who is a "legitimate Bhutanese refugee," how RCOs should be run and by whom, as well as on what funds should be spent.

As people move across boundaries, space, and time (as Bhutanese refugees have done), *othering* continues, although the means and definitions of boundaries may have changed (Amit and Rapport 2002, 367). Several scholars suggest that this is accentuated for forced migrants, whose previous notions of similarity and difference have been deconstructed, and who seek familiarity and stability in a time of transition (Boddy 1995, 18; Bromley 2000, 5; Colson 2003, 6; Shaw 2008, 28). Communities are created through and operate within interactions and experiences (Lovell 1998, 5), and are thus not an exact replica of the social networks individuals had before (forced) migration (Chatty 2010, 39; Malkki 1992, 35). Bhutanese refugees in the U.K. recognize that the values, meanings, and interpretations that are shared (with insiders) or not shared (with outsiders) are changing through migration (Barth 1998, 15). For example, my informants emphasized that in Bhutan, and initially in Nepal, boundaries based on gender-differentiations were common. However, due to aid intervention in UNHCR-led refugee camps, as well as through "awareness training" in resettlement in the U.K., gender relations have significantly shifted. Similar to caste divisions, many of my informants stated that these differentiations are simply "not practical anymore." For instance, as Bhutanese women became successful in education and access to the labor market, they demanded more power within their families and communities, leading to two young women becoming RCO board members (vice chairperson and treasurer) in two of the three refugee Bhutanese RCOs.

As old divisions fade, new boundaries emerge which determine with whom it *is* and is *not* appropriate to engage in social practice. The development of community and its inherent *othering* has the potential to produce and accentuate internal differences, leading to conflicts and factionalism, rather than unity (Shaw 2008, 29). My field site is an example of how a small social group is internally divided through the creation, negotiation, and contestation of imagined differences (Baumann 1996, 172), leading to the antagonistic assertion of insider versus outsider, and the "potentially violent expulsion of those who are not 'my blood, my family, my kin, my clan, my nation, my race'" (Voiscu 2013, 169; see also Rapport and Overing 2000, 64). The split between three different Bhutanese RCOs in Manchester is an outcome of this *othering*. On a small, local and face-to-face level, the intricate details of one's autobiography, affiliations, and relationships are of immense significance for others. For example, some Bhutanese refugees argue that what creates similarity is the shared experiences of refugee-ness, which includes the shared history of conflict in Bhutan, *life and struggle* in the refugee camps in Nepal, *and* organized resettlement to the U.K. That is, not all Bhutanese Nepalese who fled from Bhutan are considered Bhutanese refugees among my informants—some argue that those who arrived in the U.K. as asylum seekers rather than through the organized resettlement program, should not be part of Bhutanese RCOs in Manchester, as they lack the experience of resettlement, despite sharing a language and sociocultural traits. As several resettled refugees explained, refugees who left the refugee camps either to settle in Nepal or India, or who sought asylum in other countries such as the U.K., are portrayed as "traitors," who were "against the cause to be repatriated to Bhutan" and "left the camps for a better life abroad."

However, boundaries are not only created and maintained from *within* the community, but are also imposed from *outside* (Shaw 2008, 29–30). Aid intervention in refugee camps, and social policies and public discourses in the U.K. have an effect on Bhutanese refugees' communal identifications. For instance, refugee-ness is dependent on international definitions (such as the UN Refugee Convention) rather than on my informants' own definitions. Thus, formalized RCOs are constructed both by Bhutanese refugees *and* the social policies that underline the community development project (Shaw 2008, 30). Forced migrants consciously politicize their selves vis-à-vis other identities, and "reproduce a politicized version of an institutional category" (Zetter 2007, 187; see also Hall 1996, 15). That is, the development of community is a "professional . . . and a political practice" based on the relationship between individual agency, sociopolitical structures and power stratifications (Shaw 2008, 26–27). A community can expand or limit its boundaries depending on economic, political, and social advantages (Shaw 2008, 29), demonstrating both the agency of social groups and the adaptability of *othering*. For example, as stated above, within the Bhutanese refugee community questions arose as to whether someone is a refugee if they did not resettle via the GPP. In turn, this has adverse effects on the aims of the RCO project—that rather than being a durable solution to overcome uncertainty, new ambiguities are created, and therefore prevent the positive outcomes of the CDA for successful refugee resettlement.

CRITIQUE OF COMMUNITY DEVELOPMENT APPROACH

Communities too do not arise in a political, social, and cultural void, but are embedded in the context and prevalent power structures (Shaw 2008, 34). National governments, aid agencies, and service providers set "the parameters within which refugee groups may legitimately organize to represent their interests" (Sigona, Zetter, and Griffiths 2004, 8). Hence it is all the more important to understand the political, social, and cultural context in which these RCOs emerge (Sigona, Zetter, and Griffiths 2004, 7), and reflect critically on the prescribed aims of the CDA in refugee resettlement in the U.K.

Bhutanese refugees fashion old *and* new social relationships within formalized settings under the authority of external, Euro-American bodies (e.g., UNHCR, International Organization for Migration [IOM]), as well as national and international policy and funding regimes, who have their own agenda related to community development. Thus, communities are actively created and organized by policy (e.g., in the U.K.), rather than by the refugees themselves (Shaw 2008, 34). Community is imposed on my Bhutanese refugee informants *from above*: first, through the Bhutanese government's categorization of all Nepali-speaking Bhutanese as one homogenous community of *anti-nationals* (and therefore expelling them; see Hutt 2007 and Joseph 1999); secondly, through applying a participatory community development approach in the refugee camps in Nepal (see Muggah 2005 and Evans 2009); and thirdly, through British policymakers, who outsource support-provision to formalized RCOs, disregarding the power relations that come into play in any social group that bridge micro (i.e., individual concerns) with macro politics (i.e., public issues) (Shaw 2008, 31–32; Williams 2006, 870). RCOs operate within and are mediated by top-down British social policies,[5] funding regimes, and Euro-American definitions and values, which manage and control refugees arriving in the U.K. Bhutanese RCOs are symbolic constructs within the specific context of refugee resettlement and migration policy. The very structure, hierarchy, decision-making process, and aims of RCOs are in line with British bureaucratic requirements, rather than reflecting Bhutanese or Nepalese communities. Therefore, RCOs are not Bhutanese Nepalese organizations, but are highly formalized and bureaucratized British associations with non-British members, to which my informants (more or less successfully) comply. Official British government bodies (see, for example, Wright, Ward, and Peach 2004, 29) acknowledge that the "formation of constitutional organizations for social mobilization is a particular Western, if not British concept, which has been imposed on refugee communities in efforts to integrate them into the organizational structures of British civil societies."

RCOs are thus somewhere in between service providers, the host population and refugees, bridging the RCO/NGO nexus by linking informal and formal refugee groups with local communities, whilst establishing and maintaining relations with service providers and NGOs (Sigona, Zetter, and Griffiths 2004, 4). RCOs serve to help refugees integrate into the highly bureaucratized relationship between the citizen (or resident) and the state (Griffiths, Sigona, and Zetter 2006, 893). For example, RCOs are the main point of reference for service providers when attempting to enter a dialogue with a group of migrants. Rather than contacting individuals within the Bhutanese refugee community, it is more convenient to contact the RCOs' chairpersons, who then relay information to the rest of the community. Therefore, RCO leaders do not only serve as an authority in "dialogue with the state" (Kelly 2003, 39), but their role also strengthens their status within the community. Community leaders have the power over the dissemination of information, and to whom and how this information is presented. This personal status of leaders arises not only due to their RCO membership, but due to their claim to speak for the whole community (Baumann 1996, 64). Internal fights and criticism of leadership may lead to disunity, and therefore, in order to run a successful RCO, internal criticism has to be deliberately silenced in order to portray the RCO as one, cohesive social group to funding bodies and service providers (Amit and Rapport 2002, 1315). The division between two Bhutanese RCOs in Manchester is an example of this process: four Bhutanese refugee men sought leadership of one RCO, delaying the formalization of the RCO (such as opening a bank account, or ratifying the aims of the RCO). A young refugee onlooker, who witnessed the arguments during that time, argued that all individuals involved have a "big personality," and "want to be the boss." This would jeopardize the efficiency of an RCO, as my informants explained: "imagine—they would fight all the time, and nothing gets done." As no consensus could be found, Bhutanese refugees split in different RCOs, each with their own 'big personality' as a leader. One refugee informant suggested that although strong leadership is important, RCO leaders should "not have so much power over community members," especially when it comes to funding applications, and the planning of RCO events and projects. Several Bhutanese refugees remarked that decisions should be reached by involving "all of the community," rather than being limited to an RCO board. To prevent the accumulation of power amongst only a few individuals, U.K. service providers may choose to improve their quality control of RCOs beyond successful funding applications, and assure that RCO leadership is not only limited to a few, highly educated men.

Furthermore, rather than serving abstract interests of an ethnic group, or focus on the problems refugees experience (such as lack of employment and language classes), RCOs are formed because of "the inadequacy of existing [public] services to meet potential and material needs" (Zetter and Pearl 2000, 681). In a time in which service providers and NGOs in the U.K. had up to 80 percent of their government funding cut,[6] RCOs must take over the role of official support. RCOs have become "essentially 'defensive'—gap-filling and meeting essential needs—rather than being actively engaged in the development of individual and community resources" (Griffiths, Sigona, and Zetter 2006, 894). However, Bhutanese RCOs in the U.K. are unable to deliver support to refugees, as they lack both funding and know-how. For example, one of the main issues Bhutanese refugees experience is access to affordable housing and the labor market. RCOs and their board members have neither the knowledge nor resources to provide adequate assistance or information on how to access the housing market or employment, and are therefore powerless to prevent the marginalization of Bhutanese refugees from the labor and housing market. One RCO leader explained: "I don't have work since I arrived [two years ago]. I can't assist my community with jobs, because I don't know how to get [a] job. We don't have training, so what to tell people? I can only translate for them; I can't do more." Similarly, although Bhutanese RCOs did attempt to provide free English language training to their members who have no access to formal education in the U.K., the lack of funds and resources prevent any organized projects. Service providers in the U.K. have to acknowledge the limits of RCOs, and rather than outsource support to RCOs entirely, continue to offer assistance beyond a few months after arrival, in order to address the issues outlined above. Moreover, further training and education for refugees and RCO board members would benefit the effectiveness of RCOs in the long run.

Furthermore, the NGO and RCO sector is unbalanced: larger organizations are better mobilized than small RCOs and attract more public funding (Sigona, Zetter, and Griffiths 2004, 3). The three distinct Bhutanese RCOs in Manchester, with their approximately 50–60 members each, are unable to compete with larger RCOs with thousands of members (e.g., the Palestinian or Somali refugee communities). The treasurer of one Bhutanese RCO explained: "What can we do with £500 in the [RCO] bank account? We can't get funding, so we can't do anything. Events, projects—everything here is expensive! And we don't have jobs [yet], so how can [RCOs] pay for things for the community?" Due to these external factors, "RCOs, like the communities they serve, will remain on the margins" of official structures and networks, and thus are unable to serve their clients as intended by policymakers (Zetter and Pearl, 675–676, 682). Griffiths, Sigona, and Zetter (2006, 895) criticize that "far from promoting the integration of refugees, this [RCO] framework may rather perpetuate a condition of institutionalized marginality for refugee groups," and put into question the utility of RCOs in the mobilization and integration of migrant communities.

Contrary to the service providers' mission to outsource support, Bhutanese RCOs in Manchester do not provide the functions policymakers and service provider envision. Rather, it is informal social networks between refugees and non-refugees, who serve as a support network addressing these issues, regardless of their position within the RCOs. It was common for my informants to approach me for assistance, or, as a young refugee stated: "I better ask my British friends at school, or my teachers." In turn, this shifted authority and influence away from RCOs and their leaders. Furthermore, the investment of time in RCOs steadily decreased during my fieldwork, as more pragmatic issues, such as access to the labor market, education and childcare facilities, took center-stage, requiring solutions on an individual, rather than on a communal level. As RCO board members entered the labor market or full-time education, involvement in RCO matters declined, reducing the available support network on an RCO level.

This does not, however, deny the positive effects of community as providing "a sense of purpose, belonging [and] security" (Mitchell and Correa-Velez 2010, 94). Bhutanese refugees—as individuals in transition—assure continuity, rootedness, and a sense of "home" by belonging to a (more or less well-defined) community (see Rapport and Overing 2000, 63). But Bhutanese refugees do not reinvent "traditional notions of community" (Kelly 2003, 38) from Bhutan or Nepal. Rather, they form multiple new communities, influenced by migration and social policies. In a globalized world, the "very concepts of homogenous national cultures, the consensual or contiguous transmission of historical traditions, or 'organic' ethnic communities" (Bhabha 2004, 36) have to be examined and ultimately, abandoned. Migration (especially if involuntary) brings about drastic changes, which involve radical modifications of identities, communities, hierarchies, values, and lifestyles, which redefine the boundaries of cultures somewhere in between the past (and homelands) and the present (the host society), and requires a negotiation and transformation of relationships and hierarchical structures (Colson 2003, 1, 8; Mines and Lamb 2010).

Othering may be a key feature of community development and maintenance, but boundaries are adaptable, temporal (Grossberg 1996), imagined (Anderson 2006), and symbolic (Cohen 1985). Although Bhutanese refugees may be divided in several different RCOs in the U.K., their relationships are ever-changing and shifting. Community among Bhutanese refugees in the U.K. is not only about the bureaucratic, financial, and social advantages, but also about establishing mutuality, trust, and reciprocity within and outside of their Bhutanese refugee community, and community continues to be a vital element of everyday life among my informants, although not on a formalized level in RCOs. U.K. policymakers and service providers are called upon to re-evaluate their notions of homogenous refugee community, and the relevance and ability of RCOs to provide support to refugees. A focus on informal networks both within the refugee community and with external individuals may be more beneficial than the insistence on the RCO project.

CONCLUSION

Migration goes hand-in-hand with processes of "cultural translation" (Bhabha 2004, 40), which detach individuals from their past, in order to create *new persons* shaped by politics, history, and personal experiences. Bhutanese refugees are migratory individuals experiencing transition and change. They are in a continuous process of adapting to the context in which they find themselves, influenced by external forces, such as national and transnational policies, aid intervention (e.g., UNHCR, IOM), and nation states (Bhutan, Nepal, U.K.), while actively reworking their histories, identities, cultures, languages, sociocultural practices, and most importantly, their communities and social networks.

International and national policymakers, relief agencies and service providers employ the CDA and RCO project in order to provide a reliable support network for forced migrants. In political, public, and development discourses in the U.K., community becomes the solution for issues that arise due to forced migration (Baumann 1996, 20; Zetter and Pearl 2000, 681). In Zygmunt Bauman's (2000) words (Gemie 2010, 32), this conception of community seems to promise a "safe haven, the dream destination for sailors lost in a turbulent sea of constant, unpredictable and confusing change." Community has become an important linguistic tool (to describe various formations of social relationships) and symbolic referent (to create identity, belonging and emplacement, see Cohen 1985) in policymaking in the U.K. As a symbolic signifier, community is useful *because* it is vague, as it can be applied in various situations and social groups (Baumann 1996, 177). The notion of community continues to have "practical and ideological significance" (Amit and Rapport 2002, 323; Rapport and Overing 2000, 64), as it allows policymakers *and* the public to put people in (what they believe to be) easily identifiable categories of bounded, homogenous, and collaborative communities. They do so by means of stereotyping, by for example physical characteristics, religion, or ethnicity, such as the Asian, the Black, or the Muslim community.

U.K. policymakers and service providers are surely aware of internal conflicts among refugees, but expect that the positive functions of RCOs would transcend difference, and that the skills and resources RCO members possess (e.g., language skills for translations, social capital, or organizing social activities) would be shared equally within the community (Spicer 2008, 507; Zetter and Pearl 2000, 683). However, Bhutanese refugees do not recreate a coherent, all-encompassing community in resettlement. Rather, their social networks are characterized by heterogeneity, and their notion of community depends on individual circumstances, interpretations, and interactions (Amit and Rapport 2002, 253).

The RCOs they create are not Nepalese-Bhutanese communities, but are formalized British organizations with non-British members, which are created, controlled, and limited by international and national policies, service provisions, and infrastructures. Policies focused on forced migrants, such as the CDA and RCO project, intend to remind us of the well-known proverb "give a man a fish and you feed him for a day, teach a man to fish and you feed him for a lifetime." That is, refugees are encouraged to found RCOs in order to support themselves once governmental agencies reduce and cease their assistance. But as my own and many other studies with refugee and migrant communities in the U.K. has shown, RCOs often fall short of this commitment, and therefore put into question the very idea behind the Community Development Approach in refugee resettlement in the U.K.

Therefore, U.K. policymakers and service providers are called upon to revise the CDA and RCO-project in refugee resettlement, and address the complex processes in community development, that may impede the positive functions with which community is ascribed. The inherent *othering* in the formation of communities requires mediation by unaffiliated and external bodies (e.g., case workers or independent advisers), and the recognition that albeit sharing a common experience, communities may not come together naturally to form one cohesive and homogenous community serving the interests of all community members. This may require a better understanding of internal community dynamics, as well as analysis of prevalent power structures in refugee communities. This can only be achieved by long-term engagement and cooperation with refugees and their formalized communities beyond a few months after arrival, and continuous quality control of RCOs that take into consideration other factors than successful funding applications. U.K. policymakers and service providers have to address internal divisions (through mediation), or the RCO project is likely to fail. To conclude with a statement from a young Bhutanese refugee woman:

> If we put our heads together and co-operate we can become stronger, powerful. But if we are divided, we will fall (Hoellerer's fieldnotes).

COMMENTARY

Lance Rasbridge

As a medical anthropologist coordinating a refugee health clinic in Dallas, Texas, I am struck by the parallels in, but moreover the differences between, Hoellerer's description of the Bhutanese refugee community in Manchester and the counterpart in the Dallas-Fort Worth (DFW) area. Particularly striking is the fractiousness outlined by Hoellerer, to the extent that there are three competing refugee community organizations. In Dallas, I helped the first Bhutanese refugees connect with each other, early in 2010. As an informal advisor, I had a hand in setting up the Organization of Bhutanese Society, Dallas-Fort Worth (OBSDFW), the first and only mutual assistance association for Bhutanese refugees in the area, the eventual executive director being the very first area arrival, a young man with considerable education and good English skills. As hundreds more families were resettled over the next few years, the OBSDFW played a central role in the integration of the refugees into the larger society, until ultimately their financial support, mostly federal, began to dry up, as arrivals dropped off with the end of the federal resettlement program for Bhutanese.

While I see many similarities between the resettled Bhutanese community as described in Manchester and the community in Dallas-Fort Worth, there are most certainly some important differences as well that may explain the sharp contrast. For one, there are very few asylees as opposed to refugees in the US context, so virtually all share the same migration history, being resettled directly from UNHCR camps in Nepal to the United States through the United States Resettlement Program. However, there was already a sizeable Nepalese immigrant population already established in the DFW area, with many in the business and technology sectors. Furthermore, a Nepalese Hindu association was already established prior to the arrival of the refugees. These factors led to substantial assistance in welcoming and orienting the new arrivals, and ultimately led to the formation of the OBSDFW. So not only was there some existing seed funding readily available for a community organization to get rolling before the federal government specifically addressed the need, but there was already local expertise available and sympathetic to the Bhutanese.

And while not specifically mentioned for the U.K. setting, Bhutanese refugees were resettled by four different Voluntary Agencies (VOLAGS) in the DFW area, some with sub-offices in Dallas and Ft. Worth. Hence there were initially widespread disparities in the quality and quantity of resettlement services and even in the geographical distribution of apartment housing. The OBSDFW evolved as the singular representative body, and for a period of several years even had an office and meeting space, indeed a community center. This development was especially vital (and practical) for service providers like myself trying to reach the entire community. So, for example, rather than relying on each VOLAG to assist me in conducting health education workshops, the OBSDFW served as the centralized host in all the logistics: transportation, translation, and the like, borrowing caseworkers from all the different resettlement agencies. In other words, the OBSDFW served as the common umbrella over Bhutanese refugees who otherwise were spread across the various VOLAGS.

Of course, there is a great deal of intracultural variability, probably the most glaring being the marked educational-level discrepancy between many of the young adults who had had the opportunity for education in camps and even some in Nepali institutions, and those older generations who never had access to education in Bhutan, English fluency being the most obvious demarcation. Also, there is a high prevalence of multigenerational households resettled in DFW and a comparatively high number of elderly, much less common to other resettled refugees of the time such as the Karen and Chin Burmese, where the elderly and infirm were left behind in the arduous refugee flight. So, over time I saw that the function of the OBSDFW became one of literal and cultural translation, imparted from the officers and a host of young educated volunteers, to their largely elderly and less-educated compatriots.

I agree with Hoellerer's observation that over time, pragmatic issues take on more importance over more general communal concerns, and ideally a policymaker-led Community Development Approach should address both, but perhaps such breadth is unrealistic. This shortfall is perhaps best illustrated by my role as an educator on the Affordable Care Act rollout. Through the OBSDFW I could conveniently address the larger group on the basics of health insurance as well as the foundations of the Affordable Care Act. But when it came to questions on which type of plan would be best for particular individuals, I stressed that there was no one-size-fits-all solution, and factors like family composition, income, and preexisting health problems would all need to be considered at the individual level, and contacts outside the Bhutanese community, for example, with medical providers, workplace administrators, and the like, would need to be forged in order to best answer those types of questions. By any measure, integration is predicated on "informal networks both within the refugee community and with external individuals," but it is difficult to imagine how a community-based organization or even a government entity could facilitate all these networks; *integration* is ultimately not a community but rather a personal achievement.

NOTES

1. Most Bhutanese refugees in the U.K. are entitled to claim Job Seekers Allowance (JSA), a state-benefit for people who are out of work (but able to work), which in 2013 was a minimum of £56 per week. Working-age (18–64) British residents have the right to apply for JSA, but must demonstrate an active interest in looking for employment. If they miss an appointment at the Job Centre, refuse to take part in work programs and trainings and do not apply for the minimum number of jobs per week, they lose their benefits and are prevented to re-apply for benefits in between three months and three years (HM Department of Work and Pensions 2013, 4; 8–9).

2. The concept and definition of "integration" is widely debated in social sciences, and is referred to as "integration" (with inverted commas) in this work, to highlight the problematic nature of the term.

3. RCOs are enshrined in the U.K.'s Immigration Act of 1999 by giving them a major role in the support network provided for refugees (Zetter and Pearl 2000, 676). In the 1990s, the British Home Office placed emphasis on the development of social networks within a "co-ethnic" group in order to assure support, dissemination of information and "integration" (Cheung and Phillimore 2013, 520). However, in the 2000s, the political and public discourse shifted from a multicultural to an assimilationist approach in favor of networks between refugees, migrants, and local and host populations, reflecting critically on CDA as "anti-integrative", increasing segregation and extremism, and limiting access to employment (Cheung and Phillimore 2013, 521; Zetter and Pearl 2000). Successful "integration" is now measured by the social connections migrants have with their own community, other communities (both migrant and host), and "institutions of power and influence" (Cheung and Phillimore 2013, 520), such governmental and nongovernmental services.

4. Social bonds are defined as "a sense of belonging to a particular group or community" by service providers (RA and RC 2008, 1).

5. Anthropology defines policies as "classificatory devices with contextually-encoded meanings; as narratives that justify certain courses of action while disabling others; and as discursive formations that empower some voices, while silencing others" (Baba 2013, 3). That is, the laws and regulations governing refugees and their formalized organizations are not neutral tools functioning in the interests of migrants and their communities (Shaw 2008, 31).

6. Due to the economic downturn since 2008, resulting in a cut in government spending (private correspondence with NGOs and service providers in Manchester).

REFERENCES CITED

Amit, Vered and Nigel Rapport. 2002. *The Trouble with Community: Anthropological Reflections on Movement, Identity and Collectivity*. London: Pluto Press. Kindle edition.

Anderson, Benedict. 2006. *Imagined Communities*. London: Verso.

Appadurai, Arjun. 1996. *Modernity at Large: Cultural Dimensions of Globalization*. Minneapolis: University of Minnesota Press.

Azarya, Victor. 1996. "Community." In *The Social Science Encyclopedia* (2nd Edition), edited by Adam Kuper and Jessica Kuper, 114–115. London: Routledge.

Barth, Frederik. 1998. *Ethnic Groups and Boundaries: The Social Organization of Culture*. Long Grove: Waveland Press.

Baumann, Gerd. 1996. *Contesting Culture: Discourses of Identity in Multi-ethnic London*. Cambridge: Cambridge University Press.

Bhabha, Homi K. 2004. *The Location of Culture*. London and New York: Routledge.

Boddy, Janice. 1995. "Managing Tradition: Superstition and the Making of National Identity among Sudanese Women Refugees." In *The Pursuit of Certainty: Religious and Cultural Formulations,* edited by Wendy James, 17–44. London: Routledge.

Bromley, Roger. 2000. *Narratives for a New Belonging: Diasporic Cultural Fictions*. Edinburgh: Edinburgh University Press.

Butler, Judith. 2004. *Precarious Life: The Powers of Mourning and Violence*. New York: Verso.

Chatterjee, Partha. 1998. "Community in the East." *Economic and Political Weekly* 33 (6): 277–282.

Chatty, Dawn. 2010. *Dispossession and Forced Migration in the Middle East*. Cambridge: Cambridge University Press.

Cheung, Sin Yi and Jenny Phillimore. 2013. "Refugees, Social Capital, and Labour Market Integration in the UK." *Sociology* 48 (3): 518–536.

Cohen, Anthony. 1985. *The Symbolic Construction of Community*. London: Routledge.

Colson, Elizabeth. 2003. "Forced Migration and the Anthropological Response." *Journal of Refugee Studies* 16 (1): 1–18.

Duke, Karen, Rosemary Sales, and Jeanne Gregory. 1999. "Refugee Resettlement in Europe." In *Refugees, Citizenship and Social Policy in Europe*, edited by Alice Bloch and Carl Levy, 105–131. London: Macmillan Press.

Evans, Rosalind. 2009. "Inheriting the Past and Envisioning the Future: Young Bhutanese Refugees' Political Learning and Action." PhD dissertation, St. Antony's College, Oxford University.

Gemie, Sharif. 2010. "Re-defining Refugees: Nations, Borders and Globalization." *Eurolimes* 9: 28–37.

Griffiths, David, Nando Sigona, and Roger Zetter. 2006. "Integrative Paradigms, Marginal Reality: Refugee Community Organisations and Dispersal in Britain." *Journal of Ethnic and Migration Studies* 32 (5): 881–898.

Grossberg, Lawrence. 1996. "Identity and Cultural Studies: Is that all there is?" In *Questions of Cultural Identity,* edited by Stuart Hall and Paul Du Gay, 87–107. London: Sage Publications.

Hall, Stuart. 1996. "Introduction: Who Needs 'Identity'." In *Questions of Cultural Identity,* edited by Stuart Hall and Paul Du Gay, 1–17. London: Sage Publications.

Halsey, Albert. 1996. "Hierarchy." In *The Social Science Encyclopedia* (2nd Edition), edited by Adam Kuper and Jessica Kuper, 361–362. London: Routledge.

HM Department for Work and Pensions. 2013. *Jobseeker's Allowance: Help while You Look for Work.* London: HMDWP.

Hoellerer, Nicole. 2013. "Refugee Resettlement in the UK: Bhutanese Refugees in Greater Manchester." *European Bulletin of Himalayan Research* 43: 71–85.

Hutt, Michael. 2007. *Unbecoming Citizens: Culture, Nationhood and the Flight of Refugees from Bhutan.* New Delhi: Oxford University Press.

Joseph, Mathew. 1999. *Ethnic Conflict in Bhutan.* New Delhi: Nirala Publications.

Kelly, Lynnette. 2003. "Bosnian Refugees in Britain: Questioning Community." *Sociology* 37 (1): 35–49.

Lovell, Nadia. 1998. "Introduction: Belonging in Need of Emplacement." In *Locality and Belonging,* edited by Nadia Lovell, 1–24. London: Routledge.

Malkki, Liisa. 1992. "National Geographic: The Rooting of Peoples and the Territorialization of National Identity among Scholars and Refugees." *Cultural Anthropology* 7 (1): 24–44.

Mines, Diane and Sarah Lamb. 2010. "Introduction: Globalisation, Public Culture and South Asian Diaspora." In *Everyday Life in South Asia* (2nd Edition), edited by Diane Mines and Sarah Lamb, 399–405. Bloomington: Indiana University Press.

Mitchell, Jenny and Ignacio Correa-Velez. 2010. "Community Development with Survivors of Torture and Trauma: An Evaluation Framework." *Community Development Journal* 45 (1): 90–110.

Mohan, Giles. 2002. "Diaspora and Development." In *Development and Displacement,* edited by Jenny Robinson, 77–139. Oxford: Oxford University Press.

Muggah, Robert. 2005. "Distinguishing Means and Ends: The Counterintuitive Effects of UNHCR's Community Development Approach in Nepal." *Journal of Refugee Studies* 18 (2): 151–164.

Platts-Fowler, Deborah and David Robinson. 2011. *An Evaluation of the Gateway Protection Programme: A Report commissioned by the Home Office.* Sheffield: Centre for Regional Economic and Social Research.

Rapport, Nigel and Joanna Overing. 2000. *Social and Cultural Anthropology: The Key Concepts.* London: Routledge.

Refugee Action [RA] and Refugee Council [RC]. 2008. *Gateway Protection Programme: Good Practice Guide.* London: Refugee Action and Refugee Council.

Sales, Rosemary. 2002. "The Deserving and the Undeserving? Refugees, Asylum Seekers and Welfare in Britain." *Critical Social Policy* 22 (3): 456–478.

Shaw, Mae (2006). "Community Development and the Politics of Community." *Community Development Journal* 43 (1), 24–36.

Sigona, Nando, Roger Zetter, and David Griffiths. 2004. *Refugee Community Based Organisations in the UK: A Social Capital Analysis.* Retrieved from https://www.brookes.ac.uk/schools/planning/dfm/rco.htm.

Smith, Yda. 2013. "We All Bantu – We Have Each Other: Preservation of Social Capital Strengths during Forced Migration." *Journal of Occupational Science* 20 (2): 173–184.

Spicer, Neil. 2008. "Places of Exclusion and Inclusion: Asylum-Seeker and Refugee Experiences of Neighbourhoods in the UK." *Journal of Ethnic and Migration Studies* 34 (3): 491–510.

UNHCR. 2001. *Reinforcing a Community Development Approach*. Geneva: UNHCR. Retrieved from http://www.unhcr.org/en-us/excom/standcom/3ae68d330/reinforcing-community-development-approach.html.

Voiscu, *Cristina–Georgiana*. 2013. "Cultural Identity and Diaspora." *Philobiblon* 18 (1): 161–174.

Williams, Lucy. 2006. "Social Networks of Refugees in the United Kingdom: Tradition, Tactics and New Community Spaces." *Journal of Ethnic and Migration Studies* 32 (5): 865–879.

Wright, George, Kim Ward, and Esme Peach. 2004. *ICAR Navigation Guide to Key Issues: Resettlement Programmes and the UK*. London: ICAR.

Zetter, Roger. 2007. "More Labels, Fewer Refugees: Remaking the Refugee Label in an Era of Globalization." *Journal of Refugee Studies* 20 (2): 172–192.

Zetter, Roger and Martyn Pearl. 2000. "The Minority within the Minority: Refugee Community-Based Organisations in the UK and the Impact of Restrictionism on Asylum Seekers." *Journal of Ethnic and Migration Studies* 26 (4): 675–697.

Chapter 7

Refugee Perspectives on Social Networks and the Resettlement Information Landscape in the United States

Kathryn Stam, with commentary by Chris Sunderlin

Resettled refugees continue to experience shifts in their understandings of their sense of belonging to a new community long after they start their new lives in the United States. In this chapter, three different refugee groups living in Utica, a small city in upstate New York, are viewed through the lens of their information landscape, by which we mean the details of what, where, when, and how they get information about community news and events and through which social networks. The communities will be described here in order of their beginning arrival years: Somali-Bantu (2003), Karen ethnic group from Burma (2005), and Bhutanese-Nepali (2009). There is diversity in terms of religion, language, and culture between and within each group. Their behavioral and attitude differences manifest themselves in a variety of ways large and small, from house decorations and food choices to the naming of soccer teams and ethnic organizations. Through participation in a long-term ethnographic study and informal interviews with adults from each community, the author studied three refugee groups and their social networks, perspectives on their ethnic communities, and access to information. The study reveals the overall resettlement information landscape and compares features that affect their levels of social inclusion. I also address refugee policy related to group size, inclusion of disabled and elderly, poverty alleviation, and support for refugees beyond the first ninety days of arrival.

In terms of resettled refugees, community refers to the sense of connection with the people who came together from the same place, lived through the same conflict, and group themselves or have been grouped together due to ethnicity and culture. Community may refer to the entire group of refugees who were resettled from camps in the same country or to smaller groups such as families from a particular caste or religion, with whom a person feels a sense of belonging regardless of any internal conflicts that might be found. For example, within the 300 individuals from Somalia and Kenya who came to Utica, New York under the label Somali, the community itself marks differences between the Somali-speaking Somalis, the Somali-Bantu ethnic group that speaks Af Maay, and the Kizigua who do not consider themselves Somali. The Karen community is religiously diverse, with most affiliating with Christianity and Buddhism. Speaking different dialects of the Karen language, such as Sgaw and Poe, reflects ethnic differences as well. Salient for the Karen are relationships to the former military officers in Burma (respondents rejected the name Myanmar) who were involved in fighting for a Karen state. The Bhutanese-Nepali community is divided by three religions (Hinduism, Christianity, and Buddhism) and the vestiges of the strictly stratified Hindu caste system. There are also marked differences between those who identify as Bhutanese and those who identify as Bhutanese-Nepali or Nepali, which often depends on age and commitment to a desire to return to Bhutan someday, however unlikely that may be. Those who call themselves Bhutanese or Bhutanese-Nepali tend to be older, or in their twenties who tend more so than others to focus on the loss of their Bhutanese homes, positive memories of life in Bhutan, and wishes to return to Bhutan. Those who prefer to include Nepali in the name tend to be youth who do not remember Bhutan, do not hope to return to live in Bhutan, and consider themselves to have much in common with Nepali nationals.

These three groups are all now living in Utica, otherwise known as, "The Town that Loves Refugees" (UNHCR 2005), and have the advantage of being surrounded by people and languages of many different countries. There is a variety of perspectives about how welcoming the city is for certain underrepresented groups, but overall there is little racial or ethnic conflict compared to the bigger cities in the state. One particularly visible part of the community includes the English-as-a-Second-Language (ESL) students who learn together during the first months and years after arrival and continue to see and greet each other at appointments or around their neighborhoods. There have been approximately 15,000 individual refugees resettled through the Mohawk Valley Resource Center for Refugees from 1982 to 2015. Although the overall population numbers of each group have changed due to secondary migration, births, and deaths, refugees are estimated to make up approximately one quarter of the population of the city of 62,000. The refugees tend to live near each other in the eastern part of the city that is near the Resource Center and happens to be one of the poorest and cheapest areas of the city with few points of conflict with other groups except for a combined mistrust and underlying conflict with some of their African American neighbors.

Entering the new society brings about opportunities to reevaluate and redefine identity and community, and there are many aspects that go into where a person lands. First, individual identity and community are not easily separated for most people. Newly resettled continue to live and think communally, along with cultural tendencies, and refer to their group(s) when asked about themselves. Secondly, identity shifts for people when they come to the United States (Anthias 2008), and they may shift at different rates for different people and people playing different roles in the household. On a related note, multiple identities are recognized by respondents, who said on multiple occasions: "In the home there is one thing. Outside, another." Refugees manage their liminal status (Baird 2011) straddling between their previous lives and their new lives through careful management (Turner 1999; Williams 2005), and some find the period of liminality productive for changing and renegotiating unsatisfying relationships and resource streams (Suter and Magnusson 2015). For refugees, shifting identities after arrival is particularly complex due to the pressures for younger people to conform to the mainstream identity quickly and the vast differences between their traditional cultures and the mainstream American culture, as well as the reality that younger people have greater freedom and language skills that puts them into the position of interpreters and gatekeepers to the outside world for their own parents and grandparents. For minority groups in general, the presentation and explanation of that identity will be performed differently for outsiders or people with different roles (Barreto et al. 2003). Online, there is yet another set of rules for self-presentation for refugees that may be less conservative than in other circles. Naturalization complicates the matter of community identification further, because refugees are eligible to apply for naturalization after five years from their arrival. Many are happy to move from statelessness to citizenship regardless of the country, but for some, becoming American citizens is bittersweet because it symbolizes the end of a dream of a permanent and safe return to their birthplaces.

CONTEXT OF RESETTLEMENT FOR EACH GROUP

Refugees have been resettling to the small, former industrial city of Utica since the late 1970s, and it has become home to 15,000 refugees from Asia, Africa, and the Middle East who have helped stabilize a long declining population. Utica has a history of immigrant settlement, and relatively large populations originally from countries including Italy, Poland, Germany, Wales, Ireland, Lebanon, and Syria. With close to forty languages spoken in the school district, the city also boasts the fourth highest concentration of refugees of any US city. Although this diversity is mostly positive for refugees, there is also an element of resistance by some locals who think that refugees are using social services excessively and taking jobs away from Americans. These resisters, whose views are mostly visible on social media and not in public demonstration, do not recognize the role that the refugees have had in revitalizing the shrinking city. It is unlikely that the refugees have taken many of the available jobs, as the two largest employers of refugees are a Greek yogurt factory and a casino, both requiring a 40-minute commute for low-paying and night shift jobs that do not typically interest local people.

The three groups chosen for this study are similar because they are all relatively recent arrivals, have at least 300 members, and all were part of protracted refugee situations that meant many of the respondents lived in refugee camps for ten to twenty years. The conflicts were based on ethnic and religious differences, denial of citizenship, and the political tensions that resulted. Older members of the groups (over age 30 now) witnessed or were victims of violence and threats of violence, while the younger members under 25–30 years old have heard only stories of the past or were too young to remember what happened. However, there was occasional violence in the camps and the experience of living in a camp without much to do and limited freedom of movement shaped them as well. These three groups traveled through the same processes of resettlement, often starting their new lives in low-income housing and disinvested, sometimes dangerous urban neighborhoods. Their trauma of resettlement turned into further trauma for some and a golden opportunity for others, even within the same families. Disabilities, wartime injuries, and stress-related health problems are common in all three groups, exacerbated by inadequate medical care and long-term neglect in the camps, as well as inadequate health care and poor diet after resettlement. These factors have made it difficult for some to advance in the United States.

Managed by the United Nations High Commissioner for Refugees, the conditions of the camps in each country were similar in terms of rations and basic services offered, but different in terms of access to the outside. Many Somali-Bantu lived in Kenya's Dadaab, one of the largest and most dangerous refugee camps in the world, with violence, threat of rape, and chronic food scarcity. The Karen in Thai border refugee camps lived in jungle houses that looked much like those in any nearby Thai village, except that they were surrounded by barbed-wire fences and movement was very restricted. The Karen in exile had enough to eat but craved vegetables, for which they were willing to risk occasionally sneaking out of the camp. Bhutanese-Nepali refugees could travel freely but had little money to do so, and their camps were densely populated and lacked privacy. They were, additionally, victims of envy by the local Nepali population, who discriminated against them and stole from them. According to respondents, especially challenging for all groups was the extended length of time in the camps with little to no hope of political motion toward repatriation or resettlement.

Somali-Bantu refugees were resettled to the United States starting in 2003, after years in Kenyan refugee camps following civil war in Somalia in 1992 (UNHCR 2003). Their resettlement has been difficult for many reasons such as the timing of their arrival around the September 11 terrorist attacks in the United States, and the subsequent perception of their Muslim religious identity and darker skin, not to mention centuries of persecution that resulted in poor health and low educational levels (Smith 2012). An ethnic minority in Somalia made up of descendants of slaves from East Africa, the Muslim Somali Bantu ethnic group became farm laborers after slavery ended, but were continuously exploited and denied land ownership, and then were targets of attacks and looting when civil war broke out in 1991. Abused and traumatized as they were forced to flee from Somalia, they were further mistreated, assaulted, raped, and otherwise humiliated in the refugee camps because of their minority status and ethnicity. Resettlement to the United States was welcome but complicated and slow for Somali-Bantu in part due to their very large and, in many cases, polygamous families in which eight or more children were common. There were no additional resources devoted to helping this group resettle, even though it was clear that there would be additional obstacles in the way of adaptation and integration (Coughlan et al. 2016). Some of the teens are achieving academic success in high school and college, but the group continues to struggle with high rates of poverty, family upheaval, and mental and physical health problems remaining from their decades of abuse, vulnerability, and statelessness. Besteman (2013, 27) explained that "Somali Bantu refugees have quickly learned that refuge in the U.S. means poverty." The problem of food insecurity for the Somali Bantu was also noted in St. Louis, where Matsou et al. (2014) compared Bosnian and Somali experiences and found the Somalis faced more direct forms of discrimination due to the visible signs of their Muslim religion, skin color, and extended period of language and educational barriers. There are approximately 400 Somali-Bantu refugees in Utica.

The Karen conflict has also been a prolonged one, heightened by the independence of Burma in 1948 and subsequent civil war between ethnic groups that were fighting for land and power (Kenny and Lockwood-Kenny 2011). The Karen were forced into the eastern hilly jungle regions, where they ruled informally through the 1970s and 1980s, and then increasingly became the target of attacks by the Burmese military in the 1990s. The Karen people were caught between warring factions, and forced to alternately support whichever side threatened them, and occasionally fleeing as entire villages were burned. Fear of violence caused the Karen to move to Thailand, either settling illegally or moving into strictly controlled refugee camps in remote areas. The first large wave of resettlement occurred in 2004, and a second wave started after the 2006 waiver that allowed 9,000 Karen refugees into the United States. (CDC 2015). The Karen resettlement program closed after providing new homes in the United States for 73,000 refugees since 2005 (UNHCR 2015). Like most refugee groups, there is diversity in the ways that different Karen individuals experienced resettlement. From their own estimates, about half of them have become American citizens and in time, almost all of them will. This is consistent with statistics for the percentage of refugees naturalized (59 percent) versus other immigrants (44 percent) (Capps and Fix 2015). Current obstacles include misperceptions about the cost and difficulty passing the exam due to lack of English skills, although both of these obstacles can be overcome with help from the agencies processing the applications. There is both a high drop-out rate (30 percent) and a high rate (30 percent) of those who have gained a college degree (APIASF 2014). There are high rates of poverty, with 30 percent living below the poverty line. Karen cite their faith, in most cases Christian (Baptist or Seventh Day Adventist) or Buddhist, as being crucial to their ability to adjust and thrive in their new environment. Many Karen struggle with English language proficiency, even if they are working. The types of jobs available to the lower-level English speakers do not give them opportunities to improve their language skills or expand their social networks beyond the Karen speakers they already know. Community members' estimates point to a population of about 3,500 Karen in Utica in 2015.

The Bhutanese-Nepali refugee situation differs from the others because the ethnic conflict built up over time, but the expelling of the entire Nepali ethnic group from the country was brief and generally less violent than the other conflicts. Near the time of their expulsion, the ethnic Nepalis were invited to take a photograph of the entire family and then forced to sign a paper that declared their wishes to voluntarily leave the country. Initially invited as workers to Bhutan, the Nepalis had settled in southern Bhutan as early as the late nineteenth century (Hutt 2003) and did not want to leave nor did they have a place to go in Nepal or elsewhere. In 1990 over 100,000 individuals of Nepali origin were expelled against their will and fled to eastern Nepal, where seven refugee camps were created. It was not until almost eighteen years later that the first individuals began being resettled to third countries. Bhutanese-Nepali refugee resettlement and adaptation to the United States has been in the news quite a bit for the higher than normal rates of depression and suicide after resettlement (Glionna 2014; Adhikari et al. 2015). However, resettlement by the Bhutanese-Nepalis has been highly successful for many. The Bhutanese refugees have higher educational levels and English language literacy than the other groups, although their educational achievements and job history from Nepal were often not well documented or accepted by

United States institutions. While some families are isolated because of lack of transportation and difficulty adjusting to the cold weather, others have been financially successful and have been able to find a wider range of higher-skilled jobs than other refugee groups and they have found success in real estate and ownership of ethnic markets. Adept at "linking social capital" (Torezani, Colic-Peisker and Fozdar 2008), possibly due in part to confidence gained by higher-level language skills, the Bhutanese workers have been able to access information beyond their own community when they seek employment. This is consistent with Cheung and Phillimore's (2014) work on refugees in the U.K., and their findings that the length of residency in the new country and language competency play important roles in broadening refugees' social networks. The Bhutanese community claims that there are approximately 400 in Utica in 2016, as many have migrated to Ohio.

INFORMATION LANDSCAPE

The term, "information landscape" is a metaphor for a dynamic and complex information environment experienced by a set of social actors (Lloyd et al. 2013). Much like a geographic landscape, a newcomer might need some guidance in navigating the information landscape at first. The landscape may include social and spatial aspects of communication or other aspects such as organizations, types of information, and information channels. The information landscape has aspects that are specific to characteristics such as culture, gender, and age (Lloyd et al. 2013). The information landscape approach that was adapted for this study helped identify the content, contexts, social networks, spatial aspects of the resettlement information landscape, and community identity issues for each group.

Central to the concerns of this study are the concepts of information poverty and information abundance. Refugee communities experience information poverty of many kinds; for example, lack of consistent access to electronic devices, resources to pay for Internet access, links to organized and high-quality information about the things they need, as well as inadequate language support, and the ability to make sense of the information they do receive. Although some argue that the "digital divide" might be an outdated concept, there remains inequality in the amount, quality, and access to information for marginalized groups such as refugees. Britz (2004, 194) defines this phenomenon as information poverty, describing a context in which the relevant people "do not have the requisite skills, abilities or material means to obtain efficient access to information, interpret it and apply it appropriately." Within the resettlement community, there are some refugee individuals with adequate technology access and others without.

Data were collected as part of a long-term ethnographic study and included field notes about participant-observation sessions, home visits, and informal interviews done with approximately fifteen families and countless individuals over a period of months between 2012 and 2015. In some cases, contacts were established through local interpreting agencies, although interpreters were only necessary in less than half of the interviews. Other families were acquaintances through students or members of a local community center that serves refugees where the author volunteers ten hours per week. The author knew some of the respondents through her long-term ethnographic study and chose to interview some who were able to converse fluently in English about their experiences and others who required interpreters. Other community members were part of a performing arts group called International Artists of Utica that was organized by the author and gave her frequent access to informal conversation while driving and invitations for tea or meals in the homes of refugees. In addition, the author is a Thai and Lao language interpreter and is well known to the refugee community for helping at appointments. The main limitation of the sample is that the data is more focused on adults, and the author notes that the younger generation has a radically different experience and sense of what makes up the salient features of their community issues due to the timing and age at which they resettled. Analysis was based on basic questions about features of the information landscape, approached through prompts and described by members of each ethnic group.

The resettlement information landscape is dynamic and shifts according to age, gender, and other social characteristics within the refugee groups (e.g., disability, English literacy, poverty), but the results show that the overall view of the landscape was found to be identifiable. The results are presented first in terms of the general characteristics of the information landscape of the refugee community and then specifics are given for each of the three ethnic groups (Somali-Bantu, Karen, and Bhutanese-Nepali). Five main topics were revealed about the community aspects of the information landscape described by respondents: the content of cultural information, the contexts of its distribution, the social networks, the spatial aspects of the information sharing, and issues of community identity. Examples of information abundance and poverty were sought and summarized below.

CONTENT OF CULTURAL INFORMATION

Community information relates to cultural or community events of interest to refugees, news about refugee groups, local services, and resources that could possibly affect a particular community, and major news events that might affect all refugee groups. From field notes of long-term observation, community information can be grouped as including content about the following: 1) religious rituals, festivals, events, or news (e.g., a Hindu festival), 2) life events (e.g., birthdays, weddings), 3) local news about refugee community members (e.g., car accidents, arrests), 4) local news about the city that also affects refugees (e.g., upcoming storm, daylight savings), 5) community compliance information requiring behavioral responses from refugees (e.g., lead poisoning prevention, fire alarm batteries), 6) local opportunities for refugees (e.g., job fairs, bicycle giveaway), and 7) news related to the diasporic community (e.g., news about suicides of group members living in other states, famous musicians on tour). Certain types or individual nuggets of information were found to be particularly relevant and thus were shared rapidly and widely within the group (e.g., a specific workplace accident, rules for social services eligibility status), and spread rapidly and accurately. However, compliance-related information (e.g., driving-while-impaired awareness, smoking cessation) that was disseminated through the refugee center or social services did not get the same attention and did not reach all community members. In terms of the ethnic groups, there were several key differences. The Somali-Bantu focused on the sharing of scarce resources with their friends and relatives (including conflict over not sharing), and information about donations, social services, and the specific price of everyday items took priority. The Karen's community information revolved around church and temple topics, celebrating successes, sharing clothing or food, and helping others in hardship. Strong bonding ties like those developed in the church setting for the Karen were also noted by Suter and Magnuson (2015). Most of the Karen are Christian and most attend three different churches, but there is a Buddhist group as well, and there is very little tension between community members of different religions. They describe a fluid connection between community members that is not characterized by tension. The Bhutanese-Nepalis, the newest group, tended to discuss community information surrounding Christian versus non-Christian events, news, and people, and emphasized diasporic community information and national and international news items (e.g., the April 2015 earthquake in Nepal) more than the other groups. Both groups explain that there is conflict and tension related to religious differences that were not as much of a concern in Nepal but have become salient in recent years and rapidly changing role of caste.

CONTEXT OF INFORMATION SHARING

For the resettled refugee groups in general, community information was shared during social visits to each other's homes, but the frequency of these encounters was different for each group. Somali-Bantu tend to gather occasionally and seasonally more often for weddings, at which time the women over about thirty years-old get together for several days to cook and prepare. Living in extreme poverty, the respondents reported spending most of their time working or at home taking care of children rather than socializing. They reported that much of their interaction with others in their community occurred either at work (e.g., housekeeping) or during the 45-minute commute to work at the casino or hotel. Fatuma explained her situation this way: "The ride to work is like a vacation for me. We talk. We share. No kids. . . . We laugh a lot." The Karen ate meals together with friends and neighbors on a regular basis, saw each other while out doing errands, and shared community information during weekly visits to church or the temple. Other important occasions were Christmas caroling, gratitude dinners, and Karen New Year, which always included the Don Dance, a Karen New Year traditional dance and song performance highlighting the unity of the Karen people worldwide. Amoo (aged 40) described the Karen style of information as: "Talkative. You can see even gossipy sometimes. We are busy working and taking care of family but Sunday is not like that. After church, we all eat together and catch up." The Bhutanese-Nepalis spent a great deal of time together and visited other homes very frequently alone or in small groups. They celebrated birthday parties and baby naming ceremonies, which was also frequently because they have a young population with many new babies every year. Bishnu (aged 24) explained: "Birthday parties are busy with going to grocery to buy cake, making momos or kheer [rice pudding]. But we see each other every day anyway so it doesn't matter. All we do is talk together (laughs)."

For all of the groups, face-to-face communication was preferred to other forms of communication. Written brochures, handouts, and posters were described by all three groups as mostly not helpful, or a waste of paper and time. Bhutanese-Nepali ESL student Bikash (aged 36) explained: "They put up so many things on bulletin boards but we cannot read them. We don't know what that's about. The only ones I know are at the Nepali market because they are in Nepali." Facebook was important for information sharing about the communities for some, but not everyone had the access, skills, or interest in online media. Eh Soe, a Karen man in his early 20s explained: "We younger generation use social media but our parents don't even know how to turn on a phone. They speak into the wrong side and we have to press the numbers for them." Reactions to different types of communication and media also differed across groups. Somali-Bantu language is not a written language so efforts to communicate using an anglicized version of their language were widely considered useless by respondents even though many agencies tried to use that method. They spent quite a bit of time on the phone with family members in Africa, either in refugee camps or in Somalia. One respondent, Ahmed, said that he talked on the phone for two to three hours a day, with family members within the United States, in Kenya, and in Somalia. He said, "Most of the time they are asking for money, but I still answer them and tell them I can't help them." Another Somali-Bantu, Hamida, reported that she had to watch the children in the evenings for hours because her mother was on the phone with "everyone and her sister. They can't wait for weddings when they really get together to gossip. They have to prepare ahead with small gossip. They talk about every single family member and then go through the whole list again." For Karen, written materials were considered more effective and "normal." They regularly received a newsletter in the Karen language from church, and read posters at ethnic markets and the local refugee center. They saw other Karen around town and received community information about the same topics in a variety of different ways throughout their day. Laynaw explained: "Sometimes I see the same people in social services and then the Burmese grocery, and again at Bible study that same night. Everyone Karen knows everything about the Karen. No secrets in Karen [community]. We even know what happened in Thailand." Bhutanese-Nepalis, on the other hand, reported not seeing any information about their community or culture in the United States except for on Nepali radio and television news stations accessed online, specifically Facebook. They did not receive much information in their language, aside from an occasional "welcome" sign or translated form, and could find a family member to help translate as needed. They did not always read or respond due to information overload and lack of understanding that was not related to the language barrier, but to larger questions about the systems in question. There was widespread attitude that older Bhutanese-Nepalis knew nothing about American systems such as social services, banking, or taxes, and that no amount of effort would lead to a greater understanding. Mon described his situation with the elders in his life: "Oh, the moms and dads don't know nothing. They depend on us for everything except school [ESL class]. They can handle that. But anything that requires English, we must be there for them." Bhutanese-Nepalis in general prefer to have at least one person accompany them whenever possible and interpret for them when needed. This was an extension of a cultural practice in Nepal and other Asian countries where people do not like to go places alone and family members regularly go places in large groups.

Decisions about how and what information is worth sharing was done differently based on the sources of the information, and can be grouped into three main sources—from outside agencies, other community members living locally, and group members living in the United States and the home country. From refugees' perspectives, the compliance-type information they received from local agencies was overwhelming, seemed irrelevant, and was often impossible to follow through on. One example is fire prevention, which suggested the use of smoke alarms and removal of all tapestries for

Somali-Bantus. Refugees had trouble imagining these scenarios and have different cultural expectations about acceptable risk levels. For example, the required smoke alarms were frequently sounding due to improper placement and cultural cooking techniques, and so fire alarms were almost always disabled. Frequent fires in their neighborhoods did not change their behavior. The messages and materials were sometimes culturally-specific and in their own language, and even simplified for them, but did not come in forms that they enjoyed or could remember. Salima (aged 33) reported: "When the teachers talk to me, sometimes I just look out the window and daydream about Africa. I never went to school so I don't know about writing and listening. I do not remember anything." While top-down information from agencies was difficult to spread, respondents from every group said that people in their cultures do not have trouble sharing community information with each other. In fact, they found that information got around too quickly sometimes, particularly in terms of the types and accuracy of gossip that could get people in trouble with family members. Zaynab (aged 21) expressed this about her community: "Somali-Bantu, they snitches. They see you do something and by the time your mother hears about it, you robbed a bank." Somali-Bantu illiteracy and lack of education was common in their community and respondents often relied on their school-aged children to translate or confirm any correspondence they received. Fortunate to have a larger community, the Karen could ask neighbors for help and said that it was difficult for other Karen to refuse to help because of their communitarian values. Pawser (aged 27) explained: "Karen have always had to live together and help each other. Our villages were burned down. That connects us. We can't say no to each other now." Much of the community information they had access to was in Karen language, making it more accessible for the women and older people who are sometimes left out. Pawser continued, "It's going to be easy for the next generation. But the elders struggle every day. We just leave them that way. We speak for them and help them. They love us and cook for us." Bhutanese-Nepalis, on the other hand, described feeling marginalized because of the small size of their community, the divisions within it, and their lack of access to community information in Nepali language. They identified closely with other Bhutanese-Nepali refugees in other cities, drove to see them relatively often, and considered moving to the larger cities (e.g., Cincinnati, Pittsburgh) where their friends and relatives were living. Subash (aged 22) explained the perceptions of the Bhutanese-Nepalis about Ohio: "Anyone can get job there. Here, you need English to pass the test. There, there are so many Nepalis in every factory. There are interpreters. It's easier there." In fact, over one hundred members of the community of less than 500 migrated to Ohio in the summer of 2016.

Priorities of refugee groups and subgroups in terms of information is deeply cultural and at times unexpected. Where to find halal goats for sale, fresh marigolds for ceremonies, or children's traditional clothing poses information problems that are considered urgent and important but are not issues that social service agencies or neighbors would learn about or normally know where to find. Respondents also explained that some types of information, for example about where to get pork (for some Bhutanese-Nepalis) or what stores sell inexpensive brand-name makeup (for some Somali-Bantu teens) is not meant to be shared widely because those activities are considered taboo by their families.

SOCIAL NETWORKS AND KEY ACTORS

The resettlement information landscape relies heavily upon networks of refugees, mostly from the same groups of origin but also other refugee and non-refugee groups who talk to each other on a regular basis. It is a small city where the refugees are concentrated closely together and work in a small number of workplaces (e.g., casino and yogurt factory), where their coworkers are often their relatives and close friends. Some community information came from supervisors, social services employees, refugee center staff, and staff from other agencies (e.g., the Department of Motor Vehicles, the tuberculosis clinic). More relevant for community information were friends and relatives, ESL teachers, pastors, "American" teachers and friends, mentors, and other acquaintances they encounter while shopping or at the doctor's office. Friends on Facebook are another source of information for Karen and Bhutanese-Nepalis, but less so for Somali-Bantu, for whom it was often a source of conflict and initiation point of community gossip. Somali-Bantu who were home with children looked to their fathers and older brothers for community information, because they tended to be out during the day. Amina (aged 23) explained: "I don't let my brother see my Facebook, but somehow he finds out everything. He is out in the car talking to people and somehow he knows right away whatever I do. It's very annoying." For Karen, main sources were Karen staff of the local refugee center, Karen teaching assistants/liaisons at school, pastors, and other religious leaders, and former village heads and respected elders who continue to serve as community leaders. Laynaw (aged 32) described the Karen social situation this way: "There are only so many families. Everyone is pretty much related. We see them in all of the places we go. There is no hiding nothing from them." The Bhutanese-Nepali group spent much of their time with their extended families, and relied mostly on the young men (aged 25–35) with the best English language skills to relay the most accurate information. San (aged 28) explained: "My family is everything to me. But they can't do anything without me. My uncle can walk from house to house to visit people, but they ask me about every little thing. I am so exhausted sometimes. I sleep in the driveway in my car when I am too tired to answer their questions."

For the Bhutanese-Nepali Christians, social lives and information sharing revolved around the two churches and their pastors. Hindu community members worshipped at home but had access to one Hindu priest from within the Bhutanese-Nepali community for special occasions. However, this was considered less than ideal because he was related to most of the high-caste community members and therefore an inappropriate religious leader for them.

Within the landscape, group-specific approaches to perceptions of and use of previously formed social networks varied considerably. The three groups were similar in that they all managed ways to negotiate social networks that were formed in their home countries and refugee camps. However, some subgroups and individuals worked hard to maintain their former social networks while others found it advantageous to distance themselves from former social networks that they viewed as oppressive. The Bhutanese-Nepali community, for example, was split by both caste and religion, and reported that information resources related to job opportunities, donations, and events tended to remain within caste and religious boundaries.

SPATIAL ASPECTS OF INFORMATION SHARING

For sharing information about American life, systems, and settings most commonly noted for information sharing were home, worksite, commute to work, walking around town, grocery stores, ethnic grocery stores, social and human services offices, laundromats, places of worship, ESL classes, medical clinics, and hospitals. The main differences between the groups centered around their places of worship and the associated behavior there in terms of information sharing. Somali-Bantu only attended mosque on special occasions, usually a Bosnian one, and there they were expected to pray and not talk. Fatuma (aged 24) explained: "Mosque is for praying. My mom is gonna yell at me when I get home if I talk there. You get nothing from praying if you are busy gossiping." Karen information-sharing happened at church or temple and ethnic markets, where meeting for lunch after church and talking together was expected. Saywa (aged 47) said: "We meet together and have noodles every week, every week, all year. We ask about everything and we see everyone. If someone is missing, we ask about them and send noodles or chicken home for them too." Bhutanese-Nepali respondents lived near each other and were usually together so they explained that sharing information is never a problem. Kalpana (aged 22) described the information sharing in her community this way: "Oh my God. We know everything. We are always together. No one can go anywhere alone. Even you want to go alone, my father isn't going to let us. We don't have to talk about it. We see what everyone is doing with our eyes."

Access to a vehicle or transportation through relatives and friends affected information access as well, as newer arrivals and poorer groups are restricted in their movements and contact with others. More men tended to own vehicles than women, and they usually control access. Members of newly arrived groups with language obstacles take longer to complete the process of becoming legal drivers, but this did not always stop them from driving vehicles. Teenaged students from the Bhutanese-Nepali and Karen groups had more access to vehicles than the Somali-Bantu. New mothers, of which there are many in all of the groups, were more obstructed in terms of their access to community information because of not knowing how to drive or not having access to a vehicle. Somali-Bantu families are typically too large to transport in one vehicle so they tend to stay home more, further limiting their access to community information that can be found while out of the home.

Refugee groups in small cities such as Utica are isolated from the larger society, and certain subgroups are more isolated than others. Families without working members, including disabled families, or those without working-aged adult family members, are especially isolated. While they may not feel lonely or deprived because they are near family and neighbors from their group, they are not able to access many of the opportunities that are available to others who speak English better or have more points of meaningful contact with the host city's residents. There are many points of contact that involve the delivery of services, for example schools, workplaces, and health clinics. However, these types of interactions can be characterized as weak ties (Williams 2006) and have practical and tactical benefits but do not typically go deep or personal and cannot be trusted for enduring informational or emotional support. There are many members of households who are involved in caregiving or for other reasons have very little opportunity to improve their English skills or get to know more about American culture in general. For some refugee women, their isolation persists because they have many children and do not get a chance to attend school or work outside the home. Others attend English classes but improve very slowly because they have trauma issues, learning disabilities, or are illiterate in their own language, which obstructs the speed of their learning. These individuals do not answer the telephone or go to appointments without interpreters or family members. Bhutanese-Nepali San (aged 29), whose grandfather is disabled, explained: "Grandpa and Grandma need us. What happens if there is a fire? Or if they fall? Or if someone comes to the door? They are old and they cannot speak [English]. It is our job to keep them safe. That means all day every day. That is my duty." These sentiments were echoed by many respondents who felt an urgent responsibility to protect their vulnerable family members from harm.

Online "places" used by refugees included Facebook, video chat services (e.g., Skype, Viber), Nepali, Indian, Karen, and Thai television news shows on YouTube, and Internet and cable television and radio. While Karen youth accessed the Internet and used social media, the older generations tended to feel uncomfortable with English and use only the resources that include Karen or Thai language, or were video-based such as Skype. Somali-Bantu had very limited access to the Internet because of lack of funds to purchase devices and wifi access, depending instead on cable television to receive much of their news. This meant it is more available to individuals with English comprehension, which in their community meant men and teens. Somali-Bantu expressed a preference for talking on the phone, and explained that the home country and refugee camps did not have reliable television or resources to provide current news so they got news from each other. For older Bhutanese-Nepalis, many learned about world news and relatively local information (e.g., snow storms) from Nepali-based online television and radio stations such as Kanitpur FM, Canada Nepal, and BBC Nepal. Younger members of all groups found Facebook a welcome and comfortable way to access news.

COMMUNITY IDENTITY AND INFORMATION LANDSCAPE

Fears about community identity were expressed by all three of the groups with marked differences between older (aged 30 and over) versus younger people (aged under 30). Somali-Bantu refugees experienced a prolonged period of oppression and experience in urban areas that was characterized by mistrust. Many talked about their community as being closed-minded, gossipy, and unpleasant, with some of that aimed at women and girls' behavior while outside of the home. Information about the behaviors and specifically women's dress observed in public were at the forefront of their minds, because it reflected on family honor and adherence to Muslim religious expectations. Teens actively managed the flow of information about themselves and their peers when with parents. Mohammed (aged 22) said: "My sisters, they are good. But if they dress inappropriately, it's not good for the family. I have to tell them if someone sees them wearing pants. They can't do that except for gym class." The Karen, on the other hand, expressed more interest in fitting into their new home, while at the same time the older generations felt anxiety about the rapid pace of culture change they observed in their children and grandchildren, particularly surrounding respect for elders. Younger people expressed negative emotions about the difficulty of negotiating their new identities and lifestyles with their conservative parents, who know enough

English and have enough contacts in the schools that they can easily keep tabs on their children. Isabel (aged 23) explained: "My mom is cool but she measures my skirt. It has to be near my knees. No one can see my bra strap. She is joking but also not joking. In Thailand, we could not dress like this so she has those ideas. But we don't really listen." For the Bhutanese-Nepalis, the conflict that turned them into refugees was one identifiable event. The Bhutanese-Nepalis experienced the same specific conflict event when they were expelled from Bhutan, but became deeply divided since resettlement due to caste conflict, religious changes, and identity struggles that differ by generation as well. The younger people tend to be more empowered within and beyond the family context because they speak English and many of their parents do not. Monisha (aged 29) explains: "When I grew up in the camps, I had to obey. My brothers, they don't care. They are the boss now. They write their own notes to school. It's not the same." The elders tend to communicate by telephone and personal visits, and tend to know more news about Nepal and extended family, while the younger people (aged under 40) have more access to resettlement community information and information about issues related to various American systems with which they interact. The political implications of identity choices and naming were salient for the older Bhutanese-Nepalis who preferred to identify as Bhutanese, even when it was unlikely that local naming and identity choices would affect future opportunities for repatriation. Identification as Bhutanese versus Bhutanese-Nepali or Nepali had implications for access to local information and opportunities because families felt so strongly divided emotionally by the preferences of affiliation, regardless of the fact there were few practical implications resulting from these preferences.

The context of information sharing for refugees must also be seen in terms of their relationship with the other residents of the city and organizations with which they interacted. For all three groups, the non-refugee or majority "white" community (as referred to by the refugee respondents and includes non-white Americans) was perceived as both supportive (teachers, neighbors, some social services staff) and negative (e.g., drug dealers, noisy neighbors who have parties, rude people on the street). There was overwhelming positive experience with and admiration of teachers, including ESL teachers and the teachers of their children. Some people in the wider community, from all walks of life, were kind to them and brought them gifts, offered them help, and got to know their names and family members. However, all of the groups described some harassment by African American or "black" neighbors who have called them names, stolen bikes or cell phones from them or their children, and destroyed their gardens or flowers. They are referring specifically to the people in their immediate neighborhood who have been inconsiderate toward them, intimidate, or harass them, smoke marijuana and sell drugs near their homes. It is also this group that tends to have loud late-night house parties and be held responsible for the not uncommon shooting incidents.

DIFFERENCES IN INFORMATION ABUNDANCE BY GROUP

The information landscapes of each group appear to have different characteristics because of the lifestyles, cultures, and economic situations common to each group. The contexts of community information sharing and the other details in the information landscape have some commonalities across groups, such as the ease with which certain types of information flow rapidly and similar situations present in which community members meet regularly and talk face-to-face. It is interesting to see that each group has areas of information poverty as well as abundance. All three of the refugee groups spend quite a bit of time and energy staying in touch with friends and family in their home countries and in other cities, regardless of their economic status and very limited income. Along with group size and year of arrival, each group had particular historical characteristics and cultures that played a part in their current perspectives on community information and the information landscape. One might expect that the longer the group has stayed in the United States, the more access they would have to information and varied ways of receiving it, but this was not the case.

The Somali-Bantu were in the United States longest and experienced many gaps in information flow. Their landscape includes both material poverty and profound information poverty, especially for women and elderly. Although they are abundant in social networks and communication with these networks by phone, their social isolation is compounded by their physical isolation and continuing poverty. Their small group size (a little more than 300) is one factor in limiting access to information because subgroups end up being prohibitively small. It is also difficult for them because they came to the United States with virtually no economic resources or formal education, a high level of trauma, poor health care, and many disabled family members. Their precarious economic situation was perpetuated by their large family sizes and continuing discrimination because of their race and religion. These problems subsequently present additional challenges for accessing community information, due not only to limited access to mobile devices and the Internet but also an overall orientation toward staying at home and being wary of outsiders. With little access to cash or vehicles, they do not shop frequently and do not have the luxury of frequent visiting because their vehicles cannot carry all family members and they do not have much money to pay for gas other than to get to work. Living in municipal housing or inexpensive rentals on the edge of the city, the small Somali-Bantu community members tend to live further away from the urban center and commercial areas due to the timing of their arrival and their continued poverty. Somali-Bantu older women, most of whom are illiterate, are in situations that severely limit their access to community information that comes from the outside. Efforts to make information available to Somali-Bantu have been relatively ineffective because they do not use knowledge of the cultural context adequately.

The highest level of information abundance was found in the Karen group to which they view their larger population (about 3,500) and their length of stay as a cause, as well as the presence of many working members in their families who are bringing home paychecks. This is consistent with Suter and Magnuson (2015) who found that strong bonding ties of Karen with people they knew in the refugee camps that they maintained and reformed in resettlement helped their integration process as a group. They tended to have access to vehicles, lived in the center of the city near many other Karen, and had access to mobile devices and Internet. Information was printed in their language and there were many family members available to help translate or interpret. The younger generations are advancing their education and becoming fluent in English, so they are helpful as well. Information abundance was found in their cultural practices, of which gossip was not the most prevalent type. Most of the Karen are members of religious communities that helped provide information sharing. Their information poverty was noticeable in problems with the language barriers and slow adjustment of older community members, but they were not particularly isolated. Beaman's (2012) work shows that an increase in network size (new arrivals from the same group in the same year or two) can be both negative, because it causes short-term competition, and positive because a previously established group increases the chances that a new arrival can find work and at a higher wage. In addition, previous social disadvantage such as caste may reproduce itself in the new setting, as seen with the Bhutanese-Nepali refugees.

The Karen situation appeared better than that of the Bhutanese-Nepalis, who were isolated due to the small size of their community (about 400), the lack of information available in their language, and their self-identified community divides. However, higher educational achievement, good English language skills because of strong English education programs in the refugee camps, and a culture that values frequent visiting within the city and in other states allowed them to thrive in terms of information access and its rewards. Many of them have been able to overcome group isolation geographically because of strong social network ties with Bhutanese-Nepalis in other cities, states, Nepal, and their home country of Bhutan. The young people have used their strong English skills to learn about jobs in a nearby casino and yogurt factory, have maintained good relationships with their supervisors, and have been able to save money and purchase reliable vehicles and other material goods. On the other hand, the women and elderly family members at home continue to be relatively isolated and very dependent on the English-speaking and working members of each household.

POLICY AND PRACTICE RECOMMENDATIONS

The findings of this study have implications on refugee policy in several ways, as determined by the results that show widespread isolation of groups and subgroups, problems with the communication of information from non-refugee population to refugees, and the inadequacy of current efforts to target information toward specific cultural groups and other vulnerable subgroups such as mothers, disabled, and elderly. Adoption of an information abundance approach in which internal skills and communication strengths are highlighted is preferable to an approach that maximizes inabilities and cultural dysfunction. Other problems suggest that poverty alleviation overall is an urgent need.

First, spreading refugees out across the country has been a main aim of US refugee policy for many decades. In the case of smaller cities such as the one in this study, the populations are sometimes so small that their social networks are ineffective and even dysfunctional. Refugee groups that have more members have more ways of communicating, increased diversity of ideas, and less of a danger of creating isolated members and subgroups. While a specific number is not suggested by this study, it appears that the Karen population with 3,500 members in this city has reached a tipping point, enhancing the possibility that most community members feel included and can find people to talk to and help them. The two smaller groups reported struggling with a greater sense of isolation as well as tension, arguments, and identity crises.

Refugee policy in the US requires that new refugees receive support for ninety days after arrival, at which time they should be set up with the services they need and moving toward self-sufficiency. The problems shared by the respondents show that this short period of time is woefully inadequate. The groups studied including one that was resettled thirteen years earlier and another which began to arrive nine years earlier, were still feeling isolated and very unaware of what residents would consider the most basic information about obtaining health care, transportation, local events and venues, and how to accomplish normal tasks such as shopping and banking. The importance of providing long-term case management (Smith 2013) and providing resources for extensive language competency cannot be underestimated, as it has positive outcomes for accessing work opportunities and housing (Chueng and Phillimore 2014).

From a service provider perspective, this study shows that increased knowledge about and sensitivity to the specific cultures and needs of each group is important (Smith 2013). It is common to try to spread information through flyers and other printed materials and all of the groups found this relatively ineffective. Another common pitfall is to distribute printed information to ESL students who are the newest arrivals and least equipped to understand and make decisions about that information.

Learning about the resettlement information landscape has implications for improving the ways cultural and community information are delivered and spread effectively to each of the groups. This work suggests that a more nuanced understanding and culturally tailored approach would be more successful than a generalized one-for-all policy. One common attitude toward refugees stems from a cultural deprivation paradigm in which refugees are considered deficient in the skills and cultural knowledge it takes to be successful in the new environment, and does not recognize that the problem is that their vast skills and cultural knowledge are not understood or acknowledged as relevant in the new context. In contrast, this study not only points to the existence of information abundance in each group, but also the presence of sophisticated cultural methods and practices for sharing information that may be different from the ones typically at work in the new land.

There are many opportunities within the information landscapes of each group and overall. For example, the people within all three of the landscapes communicate frequently and accurately with the community information to which they have access. The refugees live and work near each other, in relatively small groups that are easily identifiable. The Somali-Bantu are very interested in each other's lives and when they do meet, they can share information effectively. They rely on each other to help navigate American social and human service systems that can be very difficult for them (Smith 2013). The Karen have a larger community and the strength of strong religious communities where information is shared. The Bhutanese-Nepalis visit each other frequently and are very close, even though there is one large religious divide and several caste conflicts that divide them. The strength of the face-to-face form of communication in all of the groups is especially promising for contributing to information resilience, which combats the uncertainty of the refugees' past and helps them learn in a grounded way (Lloyd 2014). Information literacy training may be helpful for helping refugees use outsider information more effectively, as long as it is done in a culturally sensitive manner, using their native language and avoiding formal workshops. This study and others point to the importance of improvements in English language competency for both job seeking and overall integration and expansion of social networks (Cheung and Philllimore 2014) that can help alleviate some of the problems for newer arrivals.

In some ways, the refugee information landscape in this especially diverse small city may be more effective than the typical non-refugee situation in the United States because a variety of cultural groups interact with each other frequently and share a great deal of information. Unfortunately, there is also an abundance of community information in the landscape that does not get spread to all members due more to structural reasons and poverty than anything else. Many of the barriers to community information access would be improved through alleviation of poverty, but discussion of that is beyond the scope of this chapter. Building information resilience is one solution that has been suggested (Lloyd 2014), which entails learning more about how resettled refugees seek and make use of information.

CONCLUSION

It is possible to identify and describe refugee perspectives of the resettlement information landscape and how it is compares across different resettled groups. The landscape is characterized by an abundance of community information but inconsistent in the reach of that information to the more vulnerable and isolated members. The features of the landscape were studied and summarized for the following features: content and context of information sharing, social networks and key actors, spatial aspects of information landscape, and community identity as it related to the information landscape. There was diversity among and between the ethnic groups in terms of their information landscapes because of the cultures, skills, economic status, and a variety of other elements of their information use. In summary, the Somali-Bantu focus on religious identity as Muslims, their minority status in American life, and their material poverty when they discussed community information and lack of access to opportunities that could improve their lives. Online forms of communication for Somali-Bantu were not reliable, but telephone was. Karen refer to their large and supportive ethnic community and their faith communities, Christian and Buddhist, as contributing to their sense of community awareness, well-being, and access to information and opportunities to function well in their new land. Struggles with learning English were negated by widespread translation and interpreting availability, due in part to the larger group size and length of stay. Karen used Skype to communicate with other Karen in other cities and in Thailand. Bhutanese-Nepalis perceived their small community as being further divided due to religious differences (primarily Christian vs. Hindu), remnants of the Hindu caste system that was still very much alive for the older generation (over 50 years old), and individual affiliation with or against Bhutan. Information that was available to these refugee groups was filtered through these cultural attachments and tendencies, bringing new dimensions to their community identity choices. There were pockets of isolation for mothers, elders, and disabled people. Even though they were the newest group of arrivals for whom one might expect language to present a problem, relatively strong English language skills helped many of them overcome limited information access and take advantage of somewhat limited job opportunities. Bhutanese-Nepalis use social media frequently but have limited information literacy in general. There was an abundance of community information present in the information landscapes of all three groups, but the types of information gaps were found to be group specific. Recommendations include changes in information practice by agencies toward culturally responsive services that take into account the particular contexts of information landscapes of each group. Language support is important but should be done alongside redesigned cultural competency support.

Further study on the refugee resettlement information landscape for these groups and others will be important next steps for determining the best ways to enhance information flow in culturally appropriate and specific ways, and thereby improve adaptation and integration. More detailed study of social networks and key actors, including refugee and non-refugee actors local and dispersed, is promising because those actors are mentioned frequently and appear to have an effect on the adaptation process for families and groups in myriad ways (see Smith 2013). Prioritizing the nuances of information abundance rather than poverty is a positive way of addressing the issue and seeking creative solutions. Studying the diversity within each group is promising for answering broader questions about adaptation and cultural change.

COMMENTARY

Chris Sunderlin

As a person who spends most of my time with the refugee community in Utica, New York, I consider Stam's chapter intriguing and humorous. I could picture the respondents commenting in that way, and even heard their voices as I read. I have spent the past eight years teaching English-as-a-Second-Language (ESL) and have gotten to know refugees from many different war-torn countries including Thailand and Burma, Nepal and Bhutan, Kenya and Somalia, Sudan, Cambodia, Laos, Iraq, Yemen, Russia, and Vietnam. Often times, the outside community refers to the refugee community as a whole, and can be insensitive about the religious, ethnic, cultural, and linguistic differences between the many groups that have called Utica their new home. This article is effective in showing the similarities and differences between several of the more recent arrivals. All of the groups struggle with various aspects of adaptation and learning about the new system, but they bring their cultural viewpoints and histories to each new challenge. The quotes in this article rang true to each of the cultures that Dr. Stam mentioned. In order to get a cultural response, I asked three individuals from the Midtown Utica Community Center to read through the article and share their reactions. There were approximately twelve other people in the room, working on an unrelated art project, and they chimed in as appropriate.

In response to the sections and quotes directly related to the Somali-Bantu, Nerto (who has lived in Utica for thirteen years) chose to focus on the quotes about information sharing in her community and requests for help from relatives in Africa:

> They [my parents] wait until people from Africa call them. They usually say they are having a difficult time, and they ask for money to help their families buy food. They say they don't even have beds to sleep on, and it's true. Our parents feel very concerned when their parents are sick, and ask for money for the medicine and the doctor, and they don't have money for food and clothing. The refugees here understand all of the details so they don't mind. They send small money, like $30 or $50, to help out. They wish they could send more. The older people stayed in Kenya and they don't want to lose their houses or their country.

Another topic that she found salient in the article was that of gossip. She said the following about gossip by people from her "tribe":

> Somali-Bantu are very, very gossipy. They talk about each other. They don't care what anyone else is doing but only Somali-Bantu. The main thing is they criticize each other for being greedy. They talk about how the high schoolers dress and talk, and how they try too hard to fit in. The children are supposed to be a reflection of their parents or something. Some people who don't talk much stay out of trouble. Like me, I don't talk much so no one talks about me much. Somali-Bantu parents believe what other people say. People embellish and go back to the past for things that happened a year ago, and then the kids get in trouble all over again. Parents don't understand what we are going through in life. It's [gossip is] entertainment to them, both their own and others. It's harder if you have an older brother. Some people fight back now and say they do whatever they want. Our older brothers say we have changed. He wants to go back to Africa together. They also control what we wear. Wearing pants is okay at work and JROTC [Junior Reserve Officers' Training Corps]. The hardest thing about being Somali-Bantu refugees is women not having a say. Last year in American history the teacher was saying how wonderful and free we are and I said to myself, I don't have freedom. I can barely step outside my house without my parents giving me a hard time. My brother can go anywhere. The gender equality issue is major for us. There are many men who beat their wives but they tell us to keep it on the hush-hush. Being Somali-Bantu, we don't have money. All we have is our honor. You don't want to be shaming. They always blame it on the women.

It is interesting that the topic of women's equality came out as particularly difficult, while the topic of poverty was not mentioned as the most difficult issue for Nerto. Switching to the Karen concerns, Karen community member Lay Htoo responded in this way to the article:

> It is human nature to gossip. Everybody does it. Yeah (laughs). They do it at church. It is true that everyone knows everything. There are no secrets for Karen. Our parents don't like it when I come home late from friends' houses. They want us to be home all the time doing our housework and helping them, cooking and whatever. Out of the house, we try to help each other. About information, how much people know about it depends on what kind of problem it is. We know what is happening in the refugee camps because our relatives are still there. We share news with them too because we have Internet and they don't always have good phones or online stuff. Our parents never talk to us about this. I want to be the army too.

Finally, the Bhutanese-Nepali perspective of Monisha focused on the community in general:

> A lot of Nepali from all over the country are there. Here there are not any Nepali stores. Our parents don't need very much except our attention. They can do most things on their own. They stay home most of the time and take care of the grandchildren. Everything related to English, we do for them. Some of them are getting better in English now, but some of them do not speak it at all. We get information by talking, not reading. Even the posters in Nepali I don't read. I agree with most of what the article says. But there are still some gender differences. Our brothers can go wherever they want but I always need to report to mom and dad. They want me home by the time it's dark. That's fine in summer but in winter, it's already dark when I get home from school.

In summary, I would say that the article is accurate for the middle generation, not the elders and not the youth. The responses I describe here are from relatively young people who view their parents' situation with a mix of empathy and exasperation. The younger people in the community have a different experience with being refugees, distant from some of the traumatic experiences of war but still struggling with adjustment issues, freedom, and family.

REFERENCES CITED

Adhikari, Surendra Bir, Kelly Yotebieng, Jhuma Acharya, and Jaclyn Kirsch. 2015. *Epidemiology of Mental Health, Suicide and Post-Traumatic Stress Disorder among Bhutanese Refugees in Ohio, 2014*. Columbus: Ohio Department of Mental Health and Addiction Services, Community Refugee and Immigration Services.

Anthias, Floya. 2008. "Thinking through the Lens of Translocational Positionality: An Intersectionality Frame for Understanding Identity and Belonging." *Translocations: Migration and Social Change* 4 (1): 5–20.

Asian and Pacific Islander American Scholarship Fund (APIASF) 2014. *Invisible Newcomers: Refugees from Burma/Myanmar and Bhutan in the United States.* Retrieved from http://apiasf.org/research/APIASF_Burma_Bhutan_Report.pdf.

Baird, Martha and Joyceen S. Boyle. 2011. "Wellbeing in Dinka Refugee Women of South Sudan." *Journal of Transcultural Nursing* 23 (1): 14–21.

Barreto, Manuela, Russell Spears, Naomi Ellemers, and Khosrow Shahinper. 2003. "Who Wants to Know? The Effect of Audience on Identity Expression among Minority Group Members." *British Journal of Social Psychology* 42: 299–318.

Beaman, Lori. 2012. "Social Networks and the Dynamics of Labour Market Outcomes: Evidence from Refugees Resettled in the U.S." *Review of Economic Studies* 79: 128–161.

Besteman, Catherine. 2013. "Somali Bantus in a State of Refuge." *Bildhaan: An International Journal of Somali Studies* 12 (8): 11–33.

Britz, Johannes. 2004. "To Know or Not to Know: A Moral Reflection on Information Poverty." *Journal of Information Science 30* (3): 192–204.

Capps, Randy and Michael Fix. 2015. "Ten Facts about U.S. Refugee Resettlement." Washington, DC: Migration Policy Institute.

CDC, Centers for Disease Control and Prevention. 2015. "Promoting Cultural Sensitivity: Karen Guide." Retrieved from http://www.cdc.gov/tb/publications/guidestoolkits/ethnographicguides/burma/chapters/chapter1.pdf.

Cheung, Sin Yi and Jenny Phillimore. 2014. "Refugees, Social Capital, and Labour Market Integrations in the UK." *Sociology* 48 (3): 518–536.

Coughlan, Reed, Kathryn Stam ,and Lindsey Kingston. 2016. "Struggling to Start Over: Human Rights Challenges for Somali-Bantu Refugees in the United States." *The International Journal of Human Rights* 20 (1): 123–137.

Glionna, John. 2014. "Immigrant Keeps Suicide Watch Over Fellow Refugees from Bhutan," Los Angeles Times, October 8. Retrieved from http://www.latimes.com/nation/la-na-c1-bhutanese-suicides-20141008-story.html.

Kennan, Mary Anne, Annemaree Lloyd, Asim Qayyum, and Kim Thompson. 2011. "Settling In: The Relationship between Information and Social Inclusion." *Australian Academic & Research Libraries* 42 (3): 191–210.

Kenny, Paul and Kate Lockwood-Kenny. 2011. "A Mixed Blessing: Karen Resettlement to the United States." *Journal of Refugee Studies* 24 (2): 217–238.

Lloyd, Annemaree, Mary Anne Kennan, Kim Thompson, and Asim Qayyum. 2013. "Connecting with New Information Landscapes: Information Literacy Practices of Refugees. *Journal of Documentation* 69 (1): 121–144.

Lloyd, Anne Maree. 2014. "Building Information Resilience: How Do Resettling Refugees Connect with Health Information in Regional Landscapes- Implications for Health Literacy." *American Academic & Research Libraries* 45 (1): 48–66.

Matsuo, Hisako, Kathryn Kuhn, Emmanuel Uwalaka, Cynthia Wessel, Thu Do, Wala Almostadi, and Candace Ruocco. 2014. "Refugee Resettlement in St. Louis, Missouri: Race, Religion, and Identity." *International Journal of Humanities and Social Science* 4 (11–1): 207–216.

Qayyum, Asim, Kim Thompson, Mary Anne Kennan, and A. Lloyd. 2014. "The Provision and Sharing of Information between Service Providers and Settling Refugees." *Information Research* 19 (2): 57–73.

Smith, Yda. 2012. "Resettlement of Somali Bantu Refugees in an Era of Economic Globalization." *Journal of Refugee Studies* 26 (3): 477–494.

———. 2013. "We All Bantu- We Have Each Other: Preservation of Social Capital Strengths during Forced Migration." *Journal of Occupational Science* 20 (2): 173–184.

Suter, Brigitte and Karin Magnusson. 2015. "Before and After: New Perspectives on Resettled Refugees' Integration Process." In *Resettled and Connected: Social Networks in the Integration Process of Resettled Refugees,* edited by Brigitte Suter and Karin Magnusson, 55–144. Malmö: Malmö University.

Torezani, Silvia, Val Colic-Peisker, and Farida Fozdar. 2008. "Looking for a "Missing Link": Formal Employment Services and Social Networks in Refugees' Job Search." *Journal of Intercultural Studies* 29 (2): 135–152.

Turner, Stuart. 1995. "Torture, Refuge and Trust." In *Mistrusting Refugees,* edited by Valentine Daniel and John Knudsen, 56–7. Berkeley: University of CA Press.

UNHCR. 2003. "Somali Bantus leave for America with hope for a new life." Retrieved from http://www.unhcr.org/3eccda802.html.

———. 2005. "The Town that Loves Refugees." Complete Journal Issue. *Refugees* 1(138). Retrieved from http://www.unhcr.org/426f4c772.html.

———. 2015. "US Wraps up Group Resettlement for Myanmar Refugees in Thailand." Retrieved from http://www.unhcr.org/52e90f8f6.html.

Williams, Lucy. 2005. "Social Networks of Refugees in the United Kingdom: Tradition, Tactics and New Community Spaces." *Journal of Ethnic and Migration Studies* 32 (5): 865–879.

Chapter 8

The (Re)Generation of Life in Resettlement

Birth and Social Connectedness for Central African Refugee Women in Australia

Georgina Ramsay, with commentary by Kiri Hata

Weaving my way through fluorescent corridors, I make my way to the maternity ward of a large hospital in a regional Australian city.[1] From the reception desk I am directed to a birthing suite down another hall. Justine sits in a large chair beside the bed that she gave birth in. Apart from her new baby in a plastic bassinet, Justine is alone.[2] She smiles, wanly. I offer my congratulations.

Sitting beside her, I coo at the infant. She encourages me to pick him up and hold him, so I do, whilst she sits beside me and fixes her make-up. Alongside the smell of new baby and hospital sterility, Justine's perfume lingers throughout the room. She is wearing a brightly colored *kitenge* skirt with a matching blouse. Justine appears to be preparing herself for a day of greeting visitors. It is hard to reconcile her polished appearance with the notion that she gave birth only hours ago.

Still cradling the baby in the crook of an elbow, I ask Justine how she feels. "I am tired," she says. Then, gazing down at the tiny baby in my arms, she adds: "But I am happy." Before she can say more her phone vibrates beside us, receiving a text message, and interrupts our conversation.

"Today," she says, reaching for the phone, "many, many people will come here to visit." She sighs. The phone vibrates again. Probably a potential visitor. We both laugh, until the baby begins to stir.

More quietly now, I observe: "It is a big celebration." "Yes," Justine nods: "Since I have come here, I have wanted to bring a baby. Trying, trying for three years. Now, it is good. All of my family and friends; they are all so happy." There is a pause, before she adds: "Life here is good." I clarify: "In Australia?" "Yes," she says, then repeats: "the life here is good."

The above encounter occurred hours after the birth of Justine's sixth child, and first baby born in Australia. Justine was resettled in Australia with her husband and five children in 2009, after living in a refugee camp in Kenya for seven years previously and having fled the Democratic Republic of Congo prior to that. As she emphasizes in the above epigraph, since being resettled in Australia Justine had actively sought to conceive another baby. Although she was already mother to her other five children, Justine wanted, specifically, to bear and raise an infant in Australia. Doing so would, as she suggests above, confirm that the "life is good" in Australia. For Justine and other Central African women, as I witnessed during fieldwork with refugees resettled in Australia, bearing a child is a way to definitively transcend a sense of displacement through the expanding of social connectedness to family, friends, and others. Birth and reproduction are social processes through which these women regenerate connections to, and emplacement within, settings of resettlement.

The United Nations High Commissioner for Refugees (UNHCR) (2011) outlines three "durable solutions" to refugee displacement, including: repatriation to the origin country; integration within the host nation of asylum; and resettlement to a third country. Within settings of protracted displacement—in which refugees cannot be repatriated, integrated, or resettled—refugees represent a "problem" to established logics in which global relations are organized according to a "national order of things" (Malkki 1992, 33). The solutions to displacement that are put forward by the UNHCR aim to re-locate refugees within a recognizable nation-state framework, as either citizens in their origin country; or identified permanent residents within the host country of asylum or country of tertiary resettlement. Conflating the re-locating of refugees within a nation-state system as thereby constituting a "solution" to their displacement can, however, ignore the social and political contexts through which a subjective sense of belonging and emplacement is developed (Souter 2014).

Community, locality, and emplacement are subjective experiences that cannot be reduced to, or conflated with, geographic location and national identification (Appadurai 1988; Malkki 1992, 1995b; Gupta and Ferguson 1997, 6). Whilst providing refugees with physical safety, resettlement does not automatically result in a sense of belonging (Fozdar and Hartley 2014). In a way, this lack of an immediate sense of inclusion is to be expected. For migrants, belonging to a new country of settlement is generally a negotiated process of layered cultural identifications (Coutin 2003; Ong 1996). Indeed, resettled refugees often maintain salient transnational connections to friends and family in other parts of the world, including in their country of origin. Yet, enduring connectedness to the peoples, places, and cultural beliefs of their pre-settlement lives does not annul the possibility of social belonging to the nation of migrant settlement. In Australia, however, refugees resettled from Africa report that they do not feel that they belong because, despite themselves trying to fit into the cultures of everyday life that surround them, they continue to be confronted with experiences of discrimination. Still, these transnational relations that endure between resettled refugees and their country of origin unsettle the idea that resettlement is an automatic process of emplacement through reterritorialization (Lems 2014; Lindley 2009, 2010; Horst 2007, 2008; McMichael and Manderson 2004). Such characteristically transnational experiences of refugee subjects complicate conventions of the 'natural' relatedness between persons and geographic place (Malkki 1992, 1995b), which has been a central problematic in anthropology over past decades.

The *spatial turn* in anthropology that emerged in the late 1980s served to recognize and emphasize that the localization of lived experiences within distinct ethnographic settings does not mean that there exists a "natural" link between people and place (Warf and Arias 2009, 2). Instead, anthropologists like Appadurai (1988) and others (Rosaldo 1988; Rodman 1992) became concerned with the assumption of cultural cohesion implied in ethnographic field sites bounded by place; a concern that was to be expanded on in work by Gupta and Ferguson (1992, 1997), in which anthropology conducted on the basis of a bounded geographic location was critiqued as reproducing relations of power. These works imply that relation to place is shifting, dynamic, and unable to be automatically conflated to a subject's physical positioning within a geographic space. Instead, "social and political processes of place making" are formed through those "embodied practices that shape identities and enable resistance" (Gupta and Ferguson 1997, 6). Drawing from these conceptualizations of feeling in *place* as subjectively constituted, processual, and embodied, I consider in this chapter that the resettled Central African women I conducted fieldwork with are, subsequently, never reducible to refugees who are resettled in a particular "place." Rather, these women negotiate a sense of *emplacement* through engaging in "cultural processes and practices through which places are rendered meaningful" (Feld and Basso 1996, 7). It is especially through practices of reproduction, and the kinds of beliefs about regeneration and potentiality that are attached to the birth of children, that this sense of finally feeling secure, and of being emplaced, is experienced by these women. In this chapter, I follow Ginsburg and Rapp (1995) in considering that reproduction is not simply a biological experience to which cultural meanings are attached, but is itself an experiential platform through personal subjectivities and political interventions are mediated. Applying this idea to the context of refugee resettlement, I consider that it is through reproduction that women, in particular, negotiate belonging: birth can, at once, be a way to signal connectedness to the host nation of resettlement and an opportunity to create social networks with others within it. In this chapter, I explore how these women experience being a mother as a practice of social expansion through which their sense of displacement can be transcended.

CENTRAL AFRICAN REFUGEES IN AUSTRALIA

Approximately 13,500 refugees are resettled in Australia every year (Department of Immigration and Border Protection 2013, 3). The Australian government delivers an extensive program of settlement support to refugees. Upon their resettlement, refugees resettled in Australia are provided with *permanent residency status* which guarantees them the majority of rights afforded to naturalized citizens, including payments for the unemployed and social welfare services to access housing, education, and basic necessities. The provision of these civil rights to refugees upon resettlement does not, however, address the social, cultural, and political dimensions of their lives following resettlement in Australia (Fozdar and Hartley 2014). Despite this problematic that emerges in contexts of refugee settlement in Australia, the resettlement process as lived and experienced by refugees in Australia remains uncritically explored and largely unchallenged in academic research (Nuemann, Gifford, Lems, and Scherr 2014, 13). As suggested by Jackson (2013, 92–93), there is a need to re-position the subjectivities of refugees themselves within academic research in contexts of resettlement. This includes avoiding assumptions that the protection offered to refugees through resettlement mechanistically resolves their sense of displacement. When conducting ethnographic fieldwork with a group of Central African refugee women resettled in Australia between August 2012 and March 2014, I sought to avoid attaching such assumptions of resettlement as an automatic solution to displacement. By spending time with the women in their everyday lives by travelling with them, living among them periodically, and becoming involved in community events, I was able, instead, to witness the understandings and practices through which they themselves experience resettlement in Australia.

The most recent 2011 census in Australia estimates that 2,576 refugees that originate from the Democratic Republic of Congo have, specifically, been resettled in Australia, with lesser numbers of Burundian and Rwandan refugees (DIBP 2014, 3). At the time I conducted this research, approximately 250 Central African refugees were living in the regional town in which the majority of fieldwork was undertaken. In this context, regional refers to cities outside of those that are the capital for each state. I focused specifically on the experiences of women within this cohort and over the 18-month period of research I developed informant relationships with thirty-five participants. Prior to their resettlement, the women had lived for years in refugee camps in Africa. They migrated to Australia with members of their immediate family, including husbands and children, but had left behind other close kin who were not recognized as family through the resettlement process (Wilmsen 2011). Most were married, and the majority had already had children prior to being resettled. As I experienced it, the rhythm of everyday life in these settings encompassed caring for children, preparing meals for the family, watching television with family and friends, grocery shopping at local stores or at markets, church and religious observation, and participating in education or, for some, employment. Interwoven among these daily activities the women maintained an active social life, despite living dispersed from friends across different suburban neighborhoods. The women's closest social relations were with other Central African refugees, yet they had also developed friendships with refugees from other cultural backgrounds and with white Australians. Visiting each other at home was the typical way in which these friendships were maintained, so it was not unusual for me to conduct fieldwork in one home but in the presence of three or four Central African women. On average, the women had been resettled in Australia for approximately five years.

My lack of children, in combination with my younger age and unmarried marital status, meant that the women I came to know in the field incorporated me into their lives through the role of a "daughter." Apart from cooking and service responsibilities encompassed in my status as a "daughter," I had a concurrent obligation to adhere to the advice of the women whom I lived amongst. Most often, their guidance focused on assumptions about my future reproductive trajectory. Particularly, I was most privy to advice from the women to bear as many children as possible. To do so would, in their perspective, bring a sense of fundamental purpose to my existence. It was from this methodological standpoint as a "daughter" that I thus began to understand how these women experience a sense of existential purpose as intimately interwoven with reproductive potentiality. Within the context of refugee resettlement, however, bearing and rearing a child is not a politically neutral phenomenon. Motherhood and reproduction can become, for refugee women, a site of contestation between state expectations and local understandings of childrearing. At the same time, rearing a child in a new context of resettlement can also bring opportunities to expand social networks. Through the birth of children, refugee women can rebuild the social contexts of their lives in resettlement. The social networks that they constitute through motherhood are, for them, a central basis of emplacement.

HISTORICAL RUPTURES AND CONTEMPORARY CONTINUITIES

The contemporary lives of Central African refugees resettled in Australia cannot be detached from the contexts of their forced migration. This is not to say that women are "incarcerated" within the spaces of their past (Appadurai

1988, 37). Their contemporary sense of emplacement in Australia as a resettled refugee is informed by both their immediate settings and the landscapes of their past. Their lives in resettlement are not inherently "rooted" to one specific space or place but are shaped within dynamic intersections of their lived historicities and their contemporary contexts of everyday life (Malkki 1992, 26).

Whilst the women's prior experiences of conflict, exodus, and protracted exile cannot be homogenized, there are, nonetheless, commonalities of experience threaded throughout the conflicts in Central Africa from which they fled that similarly shape their contemporary understandings. In periods of intensified civil war in Central Africa over the past three decades, the destruction of family lineage has emerged as a primary aim of the violence utilized during the conflicts. Malkki (1995a) describes how, in Burundi, militarists specifically targeted the reproductive organs of victims when committing violence. Similarly, Taylor (1999) recounts how the forms of violence enacted during the exodus of refugees from Rwanda in the 1994 genocide were intended to target systems of metabolic and reproductive flow in the body. In Congo, the use of rape as a weapon of war has been characterized as a way for militarists to physically occupy and dominate the bodies of women by impregnating them with children that share their genetic heritage (Bosmans 2007). In Central African conflicts, forms of violence were frequently leveled at obliterating the familial and social continuity of those targeted.

When conducting fieldwork, I did not assume that the women I came to know had direct experience of such atrocities. Yet, their status as refugees suggests that, within those contexts of conflict, the women fled persecution and, possibly, violence. For them, experiences of refugee displacement that stem from contexts of conflict in Central Africa cannot be singularly reduced to shifts in politico-legal status or sociospatial location. Instead, displacement for these women also encompasses an existential sense of insecurity through the ways in which the violence utilized in Central African conflicts often targeted the continuity of family and social relatedness, particularly. This sense of displacement is not mechanistically resolved upon resettlement in Australia but is mediated there through acts of reproduction.

For Central African refugees, bearing and rearing children in settlement symbolizes and affirms continuity following experiences of displacement, in which a sense of social continuity may have been ruptured through acts of violence in Central African conflicts specifically intended to obliterate forms of social relatedness and the expansion of familial lineage (Apter 2012). For the Central African women I conducted fieldwork with, the birth of a child in resettlement is, therefore, a significant event that not only manifests the corporeal presence of a baby, but which also affirms a sense of existential continuity that has been potentially threatened through their prior experiences of forced migration. Echoing the sentiments of Justine, described in the introductory epigraph, another of my informants, Beatrice, described how it is through experiences of birth that a sense of life in Australia as "good" is expressed:

> Over pots of simmering food on the top of her stove, Beatrice tells me that she suspects one of her friends—another Congolese refugee woman–is pregnant.[3] After confiding to me about suspicions of her friend's pregnancy, I make an offhand comment to Beatrice about the burgeoning number of Central African women who have given birth to children in recent months. Beatrice smiles and directs her attention to the pot of simmering food on the stove in front of her, stirring it gently. "That is our way," she says, eventually. "Being here, in Australia, it is good to bring another one."

This is a practice I have observed on multiple occasions, in which newly arrived Central African women that resettle in Australia within a family group with their husbands will conceive and bear a child as soon as possible following their migration. The majority of women that I conducted fieldwork with had given birth to child within two years of resettling in Australia; even those women who had already borne up to ten children. "Why do women want to give birth when they come to Australia?" I ask Beatrice. "The life is good here," she responds.

REPRODUCTION AND SOCIAL REBUILDING

While research in the field of migration studies emphasizes that a sense of belonging in settings of settlement is forged for migrants through the development of social networks, the ways in which these networks can also constitute a locus of anxiety is less understood (Menjivar 2000). For refugees in particular, the re-establishing of social networks in settlement can be especially tense. In Australia, resettling refugees mostly arrive in the country as isolated family groups with few or no direct contacts in the community. Subsequently, the Australian government usually relocates them into contexts where there is an existing community of other resettled refugees who share their cultural or ethnic background. The purpose of resettling newly arrived refugees within a community of established refugees is to provide them with a familiar cultural context through which they can readily rebuild social connections. It cannot be assumed, however, that shared background constitutes an immediate basis of social connectedness. Past experiences of war, displacement, and life in camps or other settings of insecurity can erode "social reciprocity, trust, and social cohesion" meaning that social networks are, regardless of cultural context, not "readily reformed upon resettlement" (McMichael and Manderson 2004, 89).

In a study exploring how Somali refugee women experience and re-establish social connectedness in Melbourne, McMichael and Manderson (2004) describe how intergroup gossip, financial hardship, distance from extended family, and lack of physical proximity to other Somalis in Australia can lead to a sense of social isolation. The re-establishing of social networks of trust is not, subsequently, a mechanistic process for the Somali women in McMichael and Manderson's (2004) study. Rather, their social networks are incrementally developed over time through the establishment of informal friendship relationships as well as participation in formal events.

Religious practice, in particular, is drawn on by the Somalis to not only establish a personal sense of connectedness to place in resettlement, but to also establish connectedness to others (McMichael 2002). Also working with resettled refugees in Melbourne, Lems (2013, 2014) discusses how emplacement is forged for them through connectedness to the "everyday." Once familiarity is developed with the people, practices, and places of resettlement for refugees, this "centrality of activity growing an attachment" is a platform of social and existential trust from which broader relations of communality can develop (Lems 2014, 14–15). What these works point to is that social networks for refugees in resettlement are not mechanistically reducible to shared ethnic or cultural background, but are cumulatively constituted over extended periods of time as refugees become familiarized with, and trusting of, their social surroundings. For the Central African women I conducted fieldwork with, this incremental process of developing a sense of attachment, trust, and social expansion becomes cemented through the birth of a child in resettlement. For them, the newborn infant is a powerful symbol of continuity. Birth represents a locus through which networks of social relatedness can be expanded, rebuilt, and regenerated.

Despite anthropological scholarship increasingly recognizing the significance of non-biological formations of kinship (Howell 2009; Levine 2008), becoming a mother through childbirth remains, across many global contexts, a salient "social practice and kinship category" (Ginsburg and Rapp 1991, 329). For many women in sub-Saharan Africa, motherhood continues to be significant aspect of social recognition, even though discourses around childbearing have changed in recent years due to an increasing focus on educational attainment (Johnson-Hanks 2006). Indeed, in Central Africa, motherhood is often interwoven with personhood: it is through bearing a child that a woman becomes finally emplaced in her familial context because of the filial lineage and social continuity that a child represents (Feldman-Savelsberg 1999). However, although a body of research focuses on how perceptions and practices of kinship and motherhood are experiences in contexts of migration, broadly, (Yarris 2014; Horton 2008; Liamputtong 2006; Parreñas, 2001, 2005), few studies explore how women who experience forced migration and refugee resettlement experience motherhood (Lenette 2014; McMichael 2013; Madziva and Zontini 2012; Shandy 2008).

For the women I conducted fieldwork with bearing a child is an experience through which to rebuild and regenerate the social context of their lives in resettlement. As part of affirming a sense of continuity for them, being mother to an infant in Australia is a way to regenerate relatedness through the dissolving of boundaries between themselves and others in their local community. Attention to the newborn, and the special status of being mother to an infant, provides the Central African women I encountered with a social role through which they can more deeply embed themselves within the local settings of their resettlement, as emerges in the vignette below:

> Since having her baby a month previously, I have not been out with Louise in public.[4] Today, we are going to shops to buy groceries. At the local shopping center we strap her month-old son into a stroller and make our way toward the grocery store. As we negotiate the stroller around other shoppers, I notice that we are receiving furtive glances from people around us as we pass. Conducting fieldwork in a largely mono cultural Anglo-Australian city in regional Australia, this tendency for the women I conduct fieldwork with to be the subject of undue attention when in public is not unusual. Normally, the attention is limited to overlong glances; although I have occasionally witnessed the women being subjected to disparaging comments and even verbal abuse from the people they encounter in public. On one occasion previously when out with Louise, a car drove past us whilst the passenger leaned out of the vehicle to yell: "Go back to Sudan!" Louise had turned to me and said, impassively: 'I am not even from Sudan.'
>
> Subsequently, neither Louise nor I am perturbed by the subtle glances we attract in the shopping center. That is, until our progress along the aisles of the grocery store is obstructed by a woman who stands directly in front of the stroller. Louise's expression hardens, at first, until the woman leans toward the stroller and smiles at the baby.
>
> "Oh," she says: "he's so gorgeous. Absolutely gorgeous!" She glances up at Louise and smiles again. "And so small! How old is he?" "One month," Louise responds, then adds: "his name is Richard." "Oh, he's beautiful," the woman before us says, repeating her earlier sentiments. In the stroller, Richard stirs but does not wake.
>
> "Thank you," Louise says, now smiling warmly. We continue talking in the aisle of the grocery store for another five minutes. The conversation between Louise and this new acquaintance centers entirely on their shared experience of having children.

For Louise, the experience of being a mother to an infant has changed the ways in which she connects to the social surroundings of her resettlement. Rather than being labeled as, and reduced to, the category of a "refugee"—and thus silenced by assumptions of difference—having her baby by her side identifies Louise, first, as a mother. Being a mother with an infant child is, as I observed in the field, a basis of social expansion that collapses boundaries between Central African women and the people they encounter in their daily lives.

FOSTERING SOCIAL NETWORKS IN INSTITUTIONAL SPACES

In addition to being treated differently in public spaces, I also observed how being mother to an infant in the regional setting conducive to the women developing friendships with other mothers from refugee backgrounds. This expansion and strengthening of social relatedness to others in resettlement as a result of having a baby is in contrast to other research that identifies refugee mothers as more likely to be socially isolated in their communities, due to responsibilities to stay at home and care for the child (McMichael 2013; Morantz et al. 2013). In a study of teenage mothers with a Sudanese refugee background living in Melbourne, McMichael (2013, 671) describes how her informants became isolated from both their broader Australian and Sudanese-specific communities after having a baby, due to the "loss of freedom and increased social isolation" entailed in rearing an infant. However, little other research explores the impact of bearing a child on everyday life for refugee women within an Australian context of resettlement. In contrast to McMichael's (2013) research, the women I conducted fieldwork with were mostly married and the majority had given birth to children prior to their resettlement. As such, they were familiarized with the responsibilities of caring for an infant; although most identified their lack of extended family and friends in resettlement as a difficult adjustment to make in the context of giving birth to a child in Australia. This was mostly because they still had family who remained in Africa, but who were unable to join them because the program of refugee resettlement to Australia, as elsewhere, privileges the settlement of families who fit a *nuclear* definition of kinship—that is, parents and directly descended biological children (Wilmsen 2011). This absence of extended family led to an often acute sense of isolation.

One way in which this potential for social isolation in resettlement was mediated for the women was through their participation in an English language class at a local vocational education institution. This particular class was reserved entirely for mothers with infants and young children. The intended purpose of this class was to provide an educational environment in which mothers could freely attend to the breastfeeding of their children without impacting on other students without the same responsibilities. Yet, the inadvertent effect of this grouping of refugee mothers was the development of relationships and friendships between the attending women, as implied in the vignette below:

> I ask Lisa how her English lessons at the college are coming along.[5] Excitedly, she begins telling me about how the large number of women who have given birth in the past year from the mainstream language class prompted the college to open up a class specifically to new mothers with babies under the age of two years. Lisa is now enrolled in this class, along with other refugee mothers from backgrounds as diverse as Iraq, Afghanistan, Sudan, Congo, and Ethiopia. She had, she says, not spoken to these women very much before the class was opened. Now, they are friends. Since the class began, the women have bonded over their shared experiences of raising an infant in Australia.

Providing an English tuition class that is exclusively administered to women from a refugee background with young children has created a space for social inclusion and the expansion of social connectedness. Indeed, the diverse national, ethnic, and social backgrounds of the mothers involved in the class appeared to be a basis from which to develop social networks among women who would not ordinarily have an opportunity to mix in similar social circles, and without the intra-group tension that can sometimes accompany the settlement of refugees who share a nationality. Although intended primarily to address the pragmatic needs entailed in concurrently caring for a child and being a student, the class also fostered inclusion through the inadvertent recognition of the social and cultural significance attached, for them, to being a mother. The outcome, for the women, was the development of new friendships as well as an increased investment in regularly attending the language class. By providing an environment that fosters social recognition of motherhood, this language class represents an innovative approach to fostering social integration for resettling refugee women. While developed unintentionally in that context, this model of recognizing and addressing the priorities of resettling refugee women, such as caring for children, could be applied to other practices of settlement support more broadly.

The birth and raising of a child in Australia emerges in the above accounts as an act of shared experience that connects Central African women to other mothers within their surrounding social milieu. Bearing a child serves to emphasize their identity as a mother rather than as a refugee, and also represents a shared experience and source of bonding with other women from both refugee and non-refugee backgrounds. Through reproducing a child in this setting of refugee settlement, the women expand, regenerate, and rebuild the social contexts of their everyday life in Australia. The significant social and cultural meanings that are interwoven within experiences of reproduction for the Central African women are not, however, recognized in the formal government bureaucracies through which their resettlement and daily lives in Australia are organized. Whilst reproduction is central to the constituting of social life for Central African women, the bearing and rearing of children is never neutral but is shaped within the politicized contexts of their resettlement (see also Ginsburg and Rapp 1995; Shandy 2008; Unnithan-Kumar and Khanna 2015).

BUREAUCRATIC INDIFFERENCE AND SOCIAL EXCLUSION

African mothers and their babies can be perceived by some as a distinct threat to the countries in which they are settled as migrants, refugees, and asylum seekers, with their presence sometimes being drawn on in political discourse as symbolizing the erosion of citizenship norms and conventions of the mainstream populace of a nation (Shandy 2008). Exploring how African asylum seekers in Ireland experience pregnancy and mothering, Shandy (2008) describes how, when citizenship to African asylum seeker women became contested in that context, childbirth subsequently emerged as an arena of in which rights to citizenship were lived and played out through the lived bodies of asylum seeker women and their children. In the context of resettlement in Australia, however, Central African women are purposefully resettled in the nation as permanent residents whose presence in the country is supported by the state. However, despite their access to civil rights in Australia, the Central African refugee women I conducted fieldwork with were still confronted with instances of disempowerment. In particular, the bureaucratic institutions that deliver settlement and welfare support to refugees operate in ways that can challenge their cultural and social logics. During fieldwork, I witnessed how such experiences of cultural discordance were frequently leveled at the women's assumptions of social connectedness through motherhood, as demonstrated in the vignette below:

> At the Centrelink office, Sima and I wait 20 minutes to be called up to a desk to meet with a worker.[6,7] Sima's welfare payments have been cancelled because she could not declare her income to the agency over a two-week period. Today, we are trying to rectify the situation so that Sima can have her payments reinstated. Without the welfare money, she will be unable to afford the rent for the coming fortnight. This could potentially lead her to be evicted from her house. Eventually, our number is called.
>
> We are directed to two seats at a cubicle desk. Opposite us sits the Centrelink worker. Sima explains the current dilemma. The worker nods, and then explains that the problem can be fixed. Sima turns to me with a smile that belies visible

relief. However, the worker adds that the processing period for the documents may take up to fourteen days. It will be another two weeks until her payment is available. Sima tells the worker that she requires the payments earlier; otherwise, she will be unable to pay her rent. The worker repeats that there is no way of negotiating the payment lapse.

Trying to reign in her increasing panic, Sima says: "You are a mother, yes?" Her eyes flicker to the one photo pinned to the worker's cubicle wall, which depicts two school-age children. "That is not a concern," the worker replies. "Are you a mother?" Sima repeats. "Well," the worker concedes: "well, yes, I am." Sima's gaze intensifies. "So," she says, firmly: "you cannot do this. You are a mother. I am a mother, too. I have children. I have to keep the house . . . you are a mother." Sima says this as if there is an expectation of social connectedness implied through the shared act of bearing children. It seems that, for her, bearing children directly corresponds to a form of social obligation to ensure that children of others do not suffer.

The worker appears to be genuinely apologetic, but says: "I am very sorry. There is nothing I can do from here." Sima interrupts. "But you are a mother," she repeats, emphasizing the last word. "If you go back to the front counter you could use the phones and try to arrange an emergency payment," the worker says; all business, once again. "I cannot do that from here. You will need to make the call. But it is late in the afternoon and the branch will shut in the next hour. You should come back tomorrow to organize the payment."

We leave, unable to solve Sima's problem. Although Sima is upset about the impending financial crisis, that is not the focus of her shock as we leave the Centrelink branch together. As we walk out the door, she turns to me and says: "These Australians are bad people. They pretend to be mothers, but they are not."

Australia administers one of the most extensive programs of refugee resettlement in the world. Newly arrived refugees are provided with permanent residency rights, as well as access to welfare payments, temporary housing, English language tuition, universal health care, and social support services through which to access long-term housing and general casework. Their children are provided with automatic citizenship, but this is a social and symbolic, rather than wholly political or legal, anchor to Australia, since the permanent residency rights that are provided to resettled refugees ensure mean that they remain legal residents of Australia for their rest of their lives, and can themselves claim citizenship after five years of residency. The provision of permanent residency rights to resettled refugees and the services which that status provides does not, however, mean that refugees will automatically experience a subjective sense of inclusion as a result of their civic belonging. The processes of refugee resettlement in Australia are, as Fozdar and Hartly (2014) suggest, designed to provide them with civic recognition but not social or cultural belonging. As the vignette above implies, the workers within, and bureaucratic cultures of, the institutions through which experiences of settlement are organized for Central African women intersect with, but often fail to recognize validity of, their cultural understandings about the imperative of motherhood to connect with social others. These institutions that structure experiences of settlement in Australia can, unintentionally, reproduce forms of displacement for Central African women by undermining the cultural significance of motherhood for them.

While birth is an act that embodies social expansion and familial continuity for these Central African women, experiences of hardship in resettlement are also expressed through reproductive symbolisms. Like Sima, who contextualizes the bureaucratic indifference she experiences in the welfare agency as undermining the cultural logics of social connectedness that she attaches to motherhood, Beatrice describes to me, in the vignette below, how her contemporary struggle to gain employment is interwoven with a concurrent struggle to conceive another child:

> "It is very hard here, without a job.[8] I want to have a baby, but we will see." Beatrice frowns. "No more are coming. And no work is coming. It is hard. People do not want a refugee. . . . Still, I will keep trying," she says, then smiles at me slyly: "For both."

CONCLUSION

Two decades ago, Ginsburg and Rapp (1995) problematized reproduction as more than just a biological process to which specific cultural understandings are attached. Instead, they locate reproduction as itself a platform of social theory and political intervention; as a site of experience through which the lived realities of ethnographic subjects are constituted and expressed. Reproduction does not simply represent a corporeal means of establishing social, cultural, and familial continuity. Rather, "reproduction also provides a terrain for imagining new cultural futures and transformations, through personal struggle, generational mobility, social movements, and the contested claims of powerful religious and political ideologies" (Ginsburg and Rapp 1995, 2). The Central African women with whom I conducted fieldwork do not perceive or experience the reproduction and rearing of children in a vacuum of cultural, social, or political conventions, but live reproduction as transformative process of rebuilding such *new cultural futures* through emplacement within the settings of their resettlement.

Refugee settlement cannot be reduced to a simplistic process of resolving refugee displacement through reterritorialization (Malkki 1992, 1995b). As first impressions of resettlement can be vastly disorienting at a subjective and existential level, a sense of being *displaced* is not mechanistically solved by physical relocation to a setting of resettlement. It is through living in the spaces of their settlement as cultural and social beings that refugees are able to develop a sense of being subjectively *emplaced* (Lems 2013, 2014). As I have described in this chapter, such processes of *place making* are oriented for Central African women resettled as refugees in Australia through acts of reproduction. The continuity of social regeneration that is implied for them through acts of reproduction means that the experience of bearing and rearing a child is a way to rebuild the social contexts of their lives following resettlement to Australia. Through bearing a child in resettlement, the women are affirming and expressing that the "life is good." Reproduction is an embodied act of place making through social expansion that therefore affirms, for them, the potential for "new culture futures" (Ginsburg and Rapp 1995, 2).

The sense of place that is developed for Central African women through reproduction is not, however, deterministic; but emerges in this chapter as temporal and shaped within the social and cultural particularities of the resettlement context. While the women actively seek to regenerate a sense of belonging and emplacement in resettlement through acts of bearing children, the social connectedness they attach to motherhood is not similarly recognized or reciprocated in their encounters with the bureaucratic institutions through which resettlement in Australia is organized. It has been suggested that academic research pertaining to refugee resettlement in Australia often overlooks the subjectivities of settlement experiences by focusing instead on the policy agendas of the government and non-government organizations that provide settlement support (Gifford, Nuemman, Lems, and Scherr 2014, 13). My encounters with Central African refugee women suggest, additionally, that this tendency to overlook resettlement as a lived experience that unfolds within a socially, culturally, and politically loaded context is similarly discounted by the institutions that organize and administer refugee settlement support.

Providing refugees with access to settlement support services, even those that are so extensively administered in Australian contexts of resettlement, does not automatically produce for them a subsequent sense of inclusion, belonging, and connectedness to settings of refugee settlement. However, settlement structures that recognize and validate the subjective cultural understandings through which resettlement is lived and understood by refugees can, as implied above, develop forms of support that foster their sense of belonging by focusing on broader scopes of social inclusion; such as, in the context of this chapter, providing services that address the significance of bearing and rearing children for Central African refugee women. Recognizing the subjectivities through which refugees understand and experience their resettlement can be a way for organizations that provide settlement support to broaden the scope of opportunities through which social integration is fostered for resettling refugees. Anthropologists who come to know and work with communities of resettled refugees are, subsequently, positioned to have their insights hold salience beyond the academy. Through ethnographic engagement with these communities, anthropologists become familiarized with the subjective understandings that refugees attach to their experiences of settlement. Anthropologists can usefully apply such insights to the policy fields and organizations that support refugee settlement in order to contribute to the development of settlement services that recognize, foster, and regenerate social networks for resettling refugees.

COMMENTARY

Kiri Hata

After eleven years of working with the Central African community in regional refugee resettlement in Australia, I see in my own experience some resonance of the themes of overlapping spheres of influence impacting the lives and cultural practices of women who have resettled here. There are significant differences in how we arrived in Australia, but some common themes are also evident. We carry with us our own understanding of life and meaning; we arrive having our own culture but quickly realize that some aspects of our culture have little or no meaning here. Even in the everyday interaction within a community, an experience is relayed through the chosen words of a teller, while the listeners try to understand what is being said. The age, sex, and life-stage of the tellers give context to their words and story, which is further defined by the same set of circumstances of the listener.

I heard many African women speak on arrival in Australia of their desire to have a baby. Some even spoke of the fortunate few who were already carrying a child when they arrived. The pride on the face of the new mother—whether she had multiple children already or this was her first—indicates her positive experience of being the center of attention among the women of her community and explains her basking in the positive affirmation surrounding her newly minted belonging by bringing a new baby into her new home. The importance of having a baby in the new country gave the whole family a greater sense of belonging. I have seen women assume higher relevance and authority within their community by that act of birth. Giving birth confers greater connectedness with the wider community. She has been to many places—often alone, without the benefit of the traditional support of her community—and has managed the process of birthing with limited (if any) fluency in English and little understanding of the sterile, shiny, quiet, and enclosed private space of birth in a modern hospital unit. The importance of her achievement is underscored by and evident in the quick arrival of female family members and community friends, with herself and her baby being the center of attention. However, this sense of belonging to a wider community is often short-lived. The community expects certain things, while doctors want something else; and the government demands compliance in so many ways that the women feel like shouting out, "stop asking me how I feel or what I think; just tell me what to do." And those of them who arrived with their children, having succeeded to keep them alive and as safe as possible, feel that the way we parent in Australia does not make any sense at all. When, God forbid, they come to the attention of authorities for their parenting practices or even for fulfilling some obligations they have to their community, the whole experience of dispossession and loss comes slamming back as them as they are questioned and accused. It is almost unbearable for some of them. They are told about counseling, training, and support services and rules. They meet with a panel of "human services" workers and interpreters, if they are lucky, the interpreter is present in person not a distant and hard to understand anonymous individual on the phone. They fear that their children will be taken away, particularly when police are present. These are just some of the experiences and conversations around birth in Australia by recently arrived refugees from anywhere, really.

"Yes, we need to have babies, so we have a future in this country," the men and women say. But does this mean these communities have truly settled in Australia? They tell me they live here and are grateful. They talk of the few with whom they have a close relationship. They tell me of their children and what they are up to. But they also say, "Resettlement, what is that?" Resettlement is the word the government uses to talk about a process, which they fund and private and nonprofit organizations. It sets the agenda and the outcomes. It tells them what to do. But something else is missing. They feel the need to have a friend, an ally, and advocate. And, there is also the "me"; they want to be recognized and taken seriously as individuals. And wouldn't you think, after all this time, that we would have finally had the wit to ask those who are offered safety on our shores and under our sun, "what do you think and how I can help you feel at home, because we are both in this together."

NOTES

1. Vignette taken from the author's field notes: 10/15/2013.
2. Names and identifying details of the participants have been changed.
3. Vignette taken from the author's field notes: 11/02/2013.
4. Vignette taken from the author's field notes: 05/01/2013.

5. Vignette taken from the author's field notes: 09/04/2013.

6. "Centrelink" is a federally operated branch of the Department of Human Services in Australia that coordinates the provision of welfare payments to citizens and permanent residents.

7. Vignette taken from the author's field notes: 05/29/2013.

8. Vignette taken from the author's field notes: 09/20/2013.

REFERENCES CITED

Appadurai, Arjun. 1988. "Putting Hierarchy in its Place." *Cultural Anthropology* 3 (1): 36–49.

Apter, Andrew. 2012. "Matrilineal Motives: Kinship, Witchcraft, and Repatriation among Congolese Refugees." *Journal of the Royal Anthropological Institute* 18 (1): 22–44.

Bosmans, Marleen. 2007. "Challenges in Aid to Rape Victims: The Case of the Democratic Republic of the Congo." *Essex Human Rights Review* 4 (1): 1–12.

Coutin, Susan. 2003. "Cultural Logics of Belonging and Movement: Transnationalism, Naturalization, and U.S. Immigration Politics." *American Ethnologist* 30 (4): 508–526.

Department of Immigration and Border Protection (DIBP). 2013. "Humanitarian Program Information Paper." Retrieved from http://www.immi.gov.au/media/publications/refugee/ref-hum-issues/pdf/humanitarian-program-information-paper-14-15.pdf.

———. (2014). "The People of Australia: Statistics from the 2011 Census." Retrieved from https://www.immi.gov.au/media/publications/statistics/immigration-update/people-australia-2013-statistics.pdf.

Feld, Steven and Keith Basso. 1996. *Senses of Place.* Santa Fe: School of American Research Press.

Feldman-Savelsberg, Pamela. 1999. *Plundered Kitchens, Empty Wombs: Threatened Reproduction and Identity in the Cameroon Grasslands.* Michigan: The University of Michigan Press.

Fozdar, Farida and Lisa Hartley. 2014. "Civic and Ethno Belonging among Recent Refugees to Australia." *Journal of Refugee Studies* 27 (1): 126–144.

Ginsburg, Faye and Rayna Rapp. 1995. *Conceiving the New World Order: The Global Politics of Reproduction.* Berkeley and Los Angeles: University of California Press.

Gupta, Akhil and James Ferguson. 1992. "Beyond 'Culture': Space, Identity, and the Politics of Difference." *Cultural Anthropology* 7 (1): 6–23.

Gupta, Akhil and James Ferguson. 1997. *Anthropological Locations: Boundaries and Grounds of a Field Science.* Berkeley: University of California Press.

Horst, Cindy. 2007. *Transnational Nomads: How Somalis Cope with Refugee Life in the Dadaab Camps of Kenya.* New York: Berghahn Books.

———. 2008. "The Transnational Political Engagements of Refugees: Remittance Sending Practice Amongst Somalis in Norway." *Conflict, Security & Development* 8 (3): 317–339.

Horton, Sarah. 2004. "Different Subjects: The Health Care System's Participation in the Differential Construction of the Cultural Citizenship of Cuban Refugees and Mexican Immigrants." *Medical Anthropology Quarterly* 18 (4): 472–489.

Howell, Signe. 2009. "Adoption of the Unrelated Child: Some Challenges to the Anthropological Study of Kinship." *Annual Review of Anthropology* 38: 149–166.

Jackson, Michael. 2013. *The Politics of Storytelling: Variations on a Theme by Hannah Arendt. 2nd Edition.* Copenhagen: Museum Tusculanum Press.

Johnson-Hanks, Jennifer. 2006. *Uncertain Honor: Modern Motherhood in an African Crisis.* Chicago; London: University of Chicago Press.

Lems, Annika. 2013. "Being Here: Emplacement and Displacement in the Life Stories of Two Somali-Australians." Doctoral Dissertation, Swinburne University of Technology.

———. 2014. "Placing Displacement: Place-making in a World of Movement." *Ethnos: Journal of Anthropology* 81 (2): 315–337.

Lenette, Caroline. 2014. "'I Am a Widow, Mother, and Refugee': Narratives of Two Refugee Widows Resettled to Australia." *Journal of Refugee Studies* 27 (3): 403–421.

Levine, Nancy. 2008. "Alternative Kinship, Marriage, and Reproduction." *Annual Review of Anthropology* 37: 375–389.

Liamputtong, Pranee. 2006. "Motherhood and 'Moral Career': Discourses of Good Motherhood among Southeast Asian Immigrant Women in Australia." *Qualitative Sociology* 29 (1): 25–53.

Lindley, Anna. 2009. "The Early-Morning Phonecall: Remittances from a Refugee Diaspora Perspective." *Ethnic and Migration Studies* 34 (2): 1315–1334.

———. 2010. *The Early Morning Phonecall: Somali Refugee Remittances.* Oxford: Berghahn Books.

Madziva, Roda and Elisabetta Zontini. 2012. "Transnational Mothering and Forced Migration: Understanding the Experiences of Zimbabwean Mothers in the UK." *European Journal of Women's Studies* 19 (4): 428–443.

Malkki, Liisa. 1992. "National Geographic: The Rooting of Peoples and the Territorialization of National Identity among Scholars and Refugees." *Cultural Anthropology* 7 (1): 24–44.

———. 1995a. *Purity and Exile: Violence, Memory, and National Cosmology among Hutu Refugees in Tanzania.* Chicago: University of Chicago Press.

———. 1995b. "Refugees and Exile: From 'Refugee Studies' to the National Order of Things." *Annual Review of Anthropology* 24: 495–523.

McMichael, Celia. 2002. "'Everywhere is Allah's Place': Islam and the Everyday Life of Somali Women in Melbourne, Australia." *Journal of Refugee Studies* 15 (2): 171–188.

———. 2013. "Unplanned but not Unwanted? Teen Pregnancy and Parenthood among Young People with Refugee Backgrounds." *Journal of Youth Studies* 16 (5): 663–678.

McMichael, Celia and Lenore Manderson. 2004. "Somali Women and Well-Being: Social Networks and Social Capital among Immigrant Women in Australia." *Human Organization* 63 (1): 88–99.

Menjivar, Cecilia. 2000. *Fragmented Ties: Salvadoran Immigrant Networks in America.* Berkeley: University of California Press.

Morantz, Gillian, Cécile Rousseau, Anna Banerji, Carolina Martin, and Jody Heymann. 2013. "Resettlement Challenges Faced by Refugee Claimant Families in Montreal: Lack of Access to Childcare." *Child & Family Social Work* 18 (3): 318–328.

Neumann, Klaus, Sandar Gifford, Annika Lems, and Stefanie Scherr. 2014. "Refugee Settlement in Australia: Policy, Scholarship and the Production of Knowledge, 1952-2013." *Journal of Intercultural Studies* 35 (1): 1–17.

Ong, Aihwa. 1996. "Cultural Citizenship as Subject-Making: Immigrants Negotiate Racial and Cultural Boundaries in the United States." *Current Anthropology* 37 (5): 737–762.

Parreñas, Rhacel. 2001. "Mothering from a Distance: Emotions, Gender, and Intergenerational Relations in Filipino Transnational Families." *Feminist Studies* 27 (2): 361–390.

———. 2005. *Children of Global Migration.* Stanford: Stanford University Press.

Rodman, Margaret. 1992. "Empowering Place: Multilocality and Multivocality." *American Anthropologist* 94 (3): 640–656.

Rosaldo, Renato. 1988. "Ideology, Place, and People without Culture." *Cultural Anthropology* 3 (1): 77–87.

Shandy, Dianna. 2008. "Irish Babies, African Mothers: Rites of Passage and Rights in Citizenship in Post-Millennial Ireland." *Anthropological Quarterly* 81 (4): 803–831.

Souter, James. 2014. "Durable Solutions as Reparation for the Unjust Harms of Displacement: Who Owes What to Refugees?" *Journal of Refugee Studies* 27 (2): 171–190.

Taylor, Christopher. 1999. *Sacrifice As Terror: The Rwandan Genocide of 1994.* Oxford: Berghahn Books.

United Nations High Commissioner for Refugees (UNHCR). 2011. "UNHCR Resettlement Handbook." Retrieved from http://www.unhcr.org/46f7c0ee2.html.

Unnithan-Kumar, Maya and Sunil Khanna. 2015. *The Cultural Politics of Reproduction: Migration, Health, and Family Making.* Oxford: Berghahn Books.

Warf, Barney and Santa Arias. 2009. *The Spatial Turn: Interdisciplinary Perspectives.* London: Routledge.

Wilmsen, Brooke. 2011. "Family Separation: The Policies, Procedures, and Consequences for Refugee Background Families." *Refugee Survey Quarterly* 30 (1): 44–64.

Yarris, Kristin Elizabeth. 2014. "'Pensando Mucho' ('Thinking Too Much'): Embodied Distress Among Grandmothers in Nicaraguan Transnational Families." *Culture, Medicine, and Psychiatry* 38 (3): 473–498.

Chapter 9

The School Socialization of Young Nepali Women Refugees in a Medium-Sized Town in Québec, Canada

Béatrice Halsouet, with commentary by Bimala Bastola

Around 250,000 legal migrants per year are settling in Canada. The younger generation's integration takes place mostly at school, the first context for their daily interactions and confrontations with local social codes (TCRI, 2011). Their relationship to school is often studied only in the light of school achievement (McAndrew, 2015) and accomplishments in big urban centers. In contrast, my study focused on school socialization in medium-sized cities with first-generation young refugees, specifically children of Bhutanese refugees. They are children of Bhutanese refugees, born and raised in camps in Nepal after their parents' generation fled Bhutan in the early 1990s due to the homogenizing effects of the "One Nation, One People" policy. Despite their Bhutanese heritage, these teenagers tend to call themselves "Nepali" in their post-migration context. They were resettled in eight different countries in 2008, including Canada. In the French-speaking province of Quebec, they were welcomed in four regional and medium-sized cities.

In this chapter, I will first introduce some details of school socialization policies specific to the Canadian context. I will then present characteristics of the methodological choices of this five-year-long qualitative study. Finally, I will end with a discussion of the limits and possibilities of the young women's experiences in Quebec regional schools with the aim of suggesting recommendations for the socialization policy to be more effective.

SOCIALIZATION: THE CENTRALITY OF A COMPLEX CONCEPT

As a preliminary remark, the term *socialization* is chosen here rather than school integration, even if this latter term may be more commonly used in the literature. The concept of school integration refers to a wide range of subjects, including dimensions of psycho-sociology and identity, or political involvement and aspects of participation in the host society (Castellotti 2007), that are not relevant to our concerns in this chapter. Moreover, some authors consider integration to be a bi-directional process that depends on both migrants and the receiving society (Berry 1999; Li 2004; Winnemore and Biles 2006), and it was not possible to circumscribe this aspect here.

Socialization was understood in the 1950s and 1960s according to a functionalist perspective. It included three dimensions: acquiring the common culture of a society, integrating these values within the personality of the child, and acquiring the sense of belonging to the collectivity (Robert and Tondreau 1997). But this definition was often used toward ideological purposes that tended to ignore the complexity and diversity of societies. Socialization had another sense in the Marxist perspective that predominated at the end of the 1960s and beginning of the 1970s. In this model, socialization is explained by the deterministic relations between the dominant and the dominated persons, where social mobility is impossible. This vision was countered by numerous authors such as Bourdieu and Passeron (1964) with their theory on social inheritance and reproduction. School socialization is considered a system of negotiation and interactions for persons who share the same type of situations to which they are adapting (Tondreau and Robert 2011). In this perspective, the person as an actor is in constant negotiation with his/her personal means and limits, rationality, and cultural habits. According to Ritzer (2011), a person may make sense of his/her reality through this type of socialization, which is a dynamic and mutual social process between an individual, those who surround him/her, and the entire society. This definition is particularly appropriate for my study as I examine how young women deal with their environment and their opportunities for socialization.

Socialization at School: A Priority?

As education is a provincial jurisdiction in Canada, the Quebec school system has declared socialization to be one of its three official missions, along with instruction and qualification of pupils with adequate diplomas. This is not the case in other provinces. For instance, in 2014, the Ontario Ministry of Education did not include socialization in its priorities even though they referred to the importance of socialization in the children's well-being: "Developing child and student well-being means supporting the whole child—not only the child's academic achievement but also his or her cognitive, emotional, social and physical well-being" (OMoE 2014, 13). In other countries like France, the programs for primary and secondary schools privilege competencies and knowledge over social issues. In 2013, a policy which promoted a *common base of knowledge, skills, and culture* instructed French Primary school teachers on how to teach languages and various academic skills while favoring the development of the *autonomy and initiative* of the students. In 2015, the secondary school program had focused on many of these aspects, but no particular emphasis was paid to socialization. Thus, is socialization so implicit that it does not need to appear in a school curriculum? Do students develop it without needing any help or academic support?

In the Quebec Education programs, socialization as a policy is directed toward migrants for whom French is not their mother tongue. In this "Linguistic, School and Social Integration" program, the students are prepared to develop a fourth skill for Primary school "to adapt to the culture of its environment" and, for the secondary school, "to integrate to school environment and Quebec society" (Gouvernement du Québec 2003). In those skills, social rules in the daily school life have to be learned; however, they are not evaluated as other skills are, such as language skills, which beg the question how to assess socialization.

The problem with promoting and assessing socialization is that every school exercises a "hidden curriculum" (Forquin 1989; Hohl and Normand 1996): "those things that are acquired at school (knowledge, skills, representations, rules, values) without ever appearing in the official or explicit programs" (Forquin 1989, 23). The hidden curriculum, which has a great impact on socialization and the interactions between the students and between them and teachers, is implicitly learned by each person from the beginning of his or her school life. But, it may be very different from one country to another, especially between a post-migration country and the country of first schooling. These implicit differences in rules and expectations may create disparities between students, particularly for migrants.

Indicators for School Integration

To evaluate school socialization for migrants, we might start by determining its main indicators. McAndrew (1994) has established three principal types of potential indicators of school integration: individual or collective participation in various structures and activities; the potential contact between members of the host group and those of the original group, and the quality of inter-ethnic relations. Each of these indicators measures the spectrum of social relations from internal or bonding networks to external or bridging networks (Putnam 2000).

The indicators of contact concern the relationships within the ethnic group itself, between the ethnic groups and those of the host society, and between the members of different ethno-cultural groups. They allow us to examine the structure of the network (number, diversity of persons attended, quality of the strong or weak links), the dynamic of the relations (frequency and reciprocity), and the nature of the exchanges (emotional, affective, material, and instrumental resources circulating in the network) (Bouchard, Roy, and Van Kemenade 2006).

The indicators of participation evaluate the level of participation young people exhibit in the activities of their original group and host group; that is, the curricular and extracurricular activities, such as leisure, associations, feasts, and cultural events. Nevertheless, time is a major problem for this indicator and, according to McAndrew, it is necessary to consider a period as long as ten or fifteen years to evaluate it. I took this into account as my young study participants were first-generation migrants and were already socialized in refugee camps, and my research focused on activities they were continuing from the camps.

The indicators of quality in inter-ethnic relations seek to measure how people live and appreciate different types of relationships. In the context of my study, a medium-sized city north of Montreal, it is important to note that only a few ethnic groups are present at school, as explained in the following section.

School Socialization: Peculiarities of the Social Context

The migrants' school integration (McAndrew et al. 1999) has mostly been studied in urban multiethnic areas (Anisef et al. 2010), and less frequently in regional areas. The difference is obvious in terms of the proportion of migrants in the classrooms: migrants represent 57.8 percent of the pupils in Montreal and less than 5 percent in nine other regions (McAndrew 2013); as many as 237 languages can be heard on Montreal playgrounds (de Koninck and Armand 2012, 7) as opposed to just twenty in the area of the study. Moreover, in Quebec's regional areas, residents tend to perceive the social environment as mono-ethnic despite the resettlement of refugees in thirteen regional cities since 1992. Migrants, thus, remain treated as exceptions in spite of the pro-migration policies of the province and greater nation. As a potential consequence, some regional secondary schools might breed animosity between teenagers (Steinbach 2010) and prejudice, racism, lack of communication and create barriers to intercultural exchanges as observed by Steinbach and Lussier (2013) in Quebec secondary schools.

Another peculiarity of schools in this regional context is the mode of school integration: whereas in Montreal migrants are welcomed in specific classes to learn French intensively, in the less populated regions they are immediately integrated into regular classrooms and are provided with linguistic support given by a specialized teacher during certain periods of the week. Even if conditions of linguistic support are very different according to the schools, it should be included if certain conditions are respected, such as a high frequency of French-speaking courses and collaboration between all the teachers (de Koninck and Armand 2012).

Finally, the last important point to note in this context is the active role of the Non-Governmental Organization (NGO) which the Ministry of Immigration delegates the responsibility to welcome and accompany the social insertion of migrants, particularly refugees, during their first five years in the country. Each of the thirteen cities selected by the government has a specific NGO. In Saint-Jérôme, the city where this study takes place, the NGO's name is Le COFFRET (Centre of Orientation and Training to Promote Traditional Multiethnic Relations). Its role as an interface between school and family is essential (Kanouté et al. 2008) and the Ministry of Education supports it through financing a specific person, the Intercultural Community School contributor (ICSI), who mediates between school and family. Given these structural and place-specific concerns, how do young first-generation migrants negotiate their socialization at school in the regional areas?

RESEARCH METHODOLOGY

The methodology of this research draws upon five years of fieldwork (from June 2010 to June 2015) and semi-directed interviews (in summer and autumn 2014). I will now elucidate the methodological approach I adopted as a researcher.

An Engaged Approach to Research

My field involvement was regular and took the form of helping with learning French for a family (seven young adults from ages 16 to 30 and two parents around 60 years old) from June 2010 (two months after their arrival in Quebec) to June 2015 (when the family moved to Ontario). I also helped two young women with their homework in the 2012/2013 school year. These exchanges were an excellent opportunity for regular and often novel observations. Moreover, I organized bi-weekly tutoring classes between students of an international program and the Nepali students in a secondary school of the city. My position as researcher can be described as an engaged position in reference to Charest (2005) as it contributed to the process of adaptation of some refugees in their new context of life. As Charest (2005) suggests, certain aspects of my position can also be considered as applied: some of the data collected served for a training session for teachers about cultural diversity during winter 2015.

My methodological position is inspired by an interactionist model where subjectivity is not an obstacle but rather facilitates unique insights (Jaccoud and Mayer 1997; Cefaï 2003) as it may give better access to understanding the life of those being studied (Vatz Laaroussi 2007). Being close to study participants is even considered a strength and a guarantee of validity in the data collected as familiarity with actors legitimates the opportunity to assess them (Le Breton 2008). The anthropologist becomes a partner in some significant situations and may be reflexive to his or her own analysis as the research process is realized over quite a long period (five years, as was already mentioned). This type of approach needs nevertheless to be questioned in four dimensions as Fassin (2008) suggests: authority, loyalty (to whom?), responsibility (and how to assume it?), and legitimacy (for whom, for what?). The *right distance* (Bensa 1995) is always a delicate balance to seek. I will now present my choices in terms of methodological tools.

Methodological Tools: Field Observation and Semi-Directed Interviews

My five years of fieldwork were based on ethnographic methods (Laplantine 2005). In spring and autumn 2014, thirty interviews were conducted. First, nine 14–21-year-old young women living in the city were interviewed because they were the only ones corresponding to the selected criteria: being born in the refugee camps, attending a French-speaking school system (as it is compulsory in Quebec for Primary and secondary schools) and being members of a Hindu family. Five mothers, who were all born in Bhutan, ages 37 to 58, were also interviewed. Whereas in Nepal, they never or rarely attended school, they all went to French-speaking training courses in Canada.

Additionally, I interviewed thirteen teachers, three men and ten women, who work in two secondary schools and one adult education center where the respondents participated. Two interviews were conducted with community stakeholders, one being the mediator between school and family, or ICSI as mentioned previously. The interviews were all conducted in French with the exception of two mothers whose mastery of the language was tenuous. For those interviews, a female family member translated from Nepali to French. Finally, a thematic analysis of content (Paillé and Mucchielli 2012) was carried out with a focus on the sense of the discourse rather than on linguistic signs. I will now present the results that emerged from this analysis and then discuss them in the final part of the chapter.

RESULTS

The young women and their mothers perceive the goal of going to school in the same way. They viewed school as allowing them to learn about new subjects, specifically a new language. It will also allow them to obtain their high school diploma and get a good job in the future. Hence, they referred directly to two of the three missions of Quebec schools to instruct and qualify. However, no study participants mentioned the third goal of socialization. Considering this omission, it is necessary to analyze why and how school socialization is not mentioned.

Partial Socialization at School

To better understand the socialization of Nepali young women at school, I directed questions and observations around the three indicators as mentioned above: contact, participation, and quality (McAndrew, 1994).

In their classrooms, the young women had classmates who identified origins in Quebec, Africa or Colombia. But, the young Nepali women rarely associated with non-Nepali peers. In fact, during breaks, they usually joined their friends of the same ethno-cultural origin or stayed with the teacher to finish their work. During lunchtime, for instance, they mostly stayed with each other or returned home. A few women mentioned some occasional contacts with friends from other ethnic groups outside of the classroom. For one of them, several factors helped her: her mastery of French language due to coming to Canada very young and immediately attending primary school, and her outgoing nature, an attribute that her teachers confirmed.

The mothers affirmed the scarcity of such interactions with non-Nepalis; all of them except one had never observed non-Nepali friends at home. The exception was one girl going to the adult education center whose teachers also insisted on her ability to create contacts with a lot of people, including boys. She brought a boyfriend home and her family accepted him because he was coming to help her with homework. Nevertheless, these relationships remained fragile: they stopped as the person changed schools, class groups or moved to another city.

Thus, for all respondents, interactions with individuals from other ethnic groups tended to be limited to the classroom. In the classroom, however, some classmates have helped them in their personal or teamwork. The respondents seemed to appreciate this help and some of them also shared their skills, for example in English (as they learned English in the refugee camps). Their progression in mastering French helped them to build contacts. More so than language, it was the social environment of the classroom that decreased some of the young women's willingness to interact with classmates. One participant in particular mentioned that it was her own timidity which prevented her from socializing much outside of her own ethnic group. This has been an obstacle to her socialization since childhood. This perception was reinforced by the assertion of one of her teachers that she was a "non-integrated pupil." In conclusion, regarding their contacts, the peer relationships they succeeded in building at school were mostly confined to academic help found in the classroom.

Regarding the second indicator of participation, the young Nepali women I interviewed were happy to go on every field trip and mentioned various destinations. In fact, they greatly appreciated the new locales they had discovered. Nevertheless, these experiences did not afford many opportunities to join with their peers: most of them mentioned that they felt isolated in such situations, as their classmates did not include them in their groups. According to them, the interactions were easier with the teachers in these occasions. Another school activity that might engender better prospects was a Christmas celebration, for example, when the respondent who regarded her shyness as an obstacle had experienced pleasant interactions with her peers for the first time. These moments of interaction seem uncommon according to the analysis of these refugee young women's experiences and it may reveal either attitudes of indifference from their peers or an absence of active participation on the part of the young women. Regarding extracurricular activities, the study participants tended to not engage in them except for two who played soccer. They all participated in school activities, such as field trips in which the entire classroom visited a museum or an interesting site, but in these occasions interaction remained limited.

Toward the third indicator, quality of inter-ethnic relations, all of the young women described their classmates as very nice and helpful in the classroom. However, their descriptions of their classmates were not very elaborate as contacts with their peers remained infrequent outside the classroom. At the very least, there was no mention of discrimination or racism at school. Only one mother mentioned racism, believing that it played a role in her daughter's experience.

The NGO mediator provided a different perspective, maintaining that the young adults she accompanies after their secondary school may have experienced intimidation due to racism, even if this phenomenon was mostly emerging from other migrant groups, such as Congolese refugees. One instance of racism toward Bhutanese refugees occurred in August 2010 when forty-eight cases of aggression (verbal and physical ones) were identified in a part of the city where they reside in large numbers. The situation was quickly managed and addressed through meetings and consultations between the NGO, the police, and other neighborhood associations. As a result, the police increased their visits to the area, an offender was arrested, and people living in the area were trained for effective means to resolve future incidents.

Parallel to these three indicators, another phenomenon emerged from the interviews; that is, a lack of relationships with boys. The mothers recommended that their daughters keep far from male friends or "dangerous" friends, as one described such interactions. In fact, the mothers themselves did not have any male friends before getting married. Only one mother tolerated a male friend of her daughter, but only in terms of academic support. Teachers also identified gender issues as a source of potential social difficulty. They noticed that Nepali students did not socialize with the opposite gender. Additionally, they identified the young Nepali women's tendency to hold hands with each other as a possible reason for prejudice.

As opposed to these observations, two respondents declared they had some boys as friends at school and reported sharing time with them. But they also insisted on the fact that they would never date them or have sexual relations before marriage. This position reveals the influence of cultural norms, such as the notion that the Hindu *vivahā* (marriage) unites a virgin girl with her chosen bridegroom (chosen by love, family arrangement, or semi-arrangement). According to one teacher, one of them did publicly declare her loyalty to premarital sexual abstinence even though it caused her to be considered silly by her peers. As a conclusion, we might regard the young women's socialization at school as relatively weak and limited to academic help in the classroom, an outcome that is emphasized in social relations in the sparse interactions with the opposite gender.

The Teachers as Essential Agents of Socialization

The teachers perceive the Nepali teenagers to be very dedicated to their work but also very shy and introverted. Most of them affirmed that they did not know much about the Nepali migration route or conditions of life prior to resettlement (culture and religion, for example). In fact, this type of information is not documented in student records and would require personal investigation or direct questions to the student, which is rarely done.

The teachers' role in the evolution of the young women's socialization might be critical. For one teacher, he never attempted to intervene on the young women's behalf. For example, he remained silent when the students had to choose their classmates for teamwork and nobody wanted to pair with a Nepali. His reasoning was based on the respect for a teenagers' freedom and the offer of different modalities of work, in team or alone. This reasoning nevertheless forgets the third mission of the Quebec school programs, the role of peers in addressing the disparity of students' needs. Fortunately, this attitude was quite infrequently reported.

Some teachers chose to be more vigilant within the classroom. For instance, they demonstrated respect for the pronunciation of 'exotic' first names and liked to ask direct questions to involve the shy students. Such interventions can also take the form of specific encouragements. For example, when an English teacher delivered a certificate of excellence to her Nepali student, she noticed that her classmates did not even know the student's first name. Two other instructors appealed to students they knew as good at leading and cooperating to explain to the other students how important it would be to be on a team with the Nepali classmate. These examples may seem to be small gestures within the daily life of a classroom, but make quite a difference in the socialization of a young refugee young woman.

While describing these situations, the teachers criticized their lack of training in respect to how to welcome migrant students in their classes. Three teachers did have some training—one specialized in French linguistic support and attended several training sessions on working with migrant students; the other two were instructors at the adult education center and had attended a conference on Bhutanese refugees. Apart from these three, however, the remaining teachers reported they felt helpless and solely dependent on their personal strengths of resourcefulness, absence of prejudice, and compassion. One teacher said: "I try to put myself in their shoes because if one looks at the situation from their view, one may finally understand." Some of them could also rely on their initial training, in Orto-pedagogy or school adaptation. But few of them appealed for support from the NGO, Le COFFRET. Although a few of them knew about this resource and personally knew its mediator, only two of them used its services. In fact, as one confessed: "There is no problem of attitude and generally, the lessons are studied. So, I did not feel the need to contact Le COFFRET." Here an important insight has emerged; since teachers are forced to give significant attention to disruptive students for their behavior (rowdiness, absenteeism, missing homework), they are left with little time and energy to address the comprehension and inclusion of migrant young women who tend to be quiet and less outwardly demanding. As one mediator admitted: "There was a lot of absenteeism to solve, but not for these young women. They are working very hard . . . I rarely intervened in their activities for the entire year."

Learning about the cultural specifics of the migrant students should be part of the training policy for teachers as well as requiring them to collaborate with community partners to give students additional support. In fact, for the moment, the collaboration with Le COFFRET is in its infancy and this might be due to the historic relationships between this organization and the school board. The NGO's role has been evolving for three years but still appears to be lacking in some situations. Its mediator is aware of this situation and affirms that she is better known by secondary school directors than by their teachers, and even more so in primary schools. Let us now turn to this mediator's analysis of the situation and role.

The Role of the NGO in Young Refugee Women's Socialization

The NGO mediator, or ICSI, between family and school is a social worker employed by Le COFFRET but also funded by the Education Ministry. She has had little influence on the Nepali young women's socialization partly because of the number of schools she supervises (fourteen primary and secondary schools) and the dispersion of the migrants over a wide geography. The settlement of refugees and migrants in the less urban parts of the region (far from Montreal and its concentration of migrants) raises many types of challenges that should be addressed. Moreover, the quality and nature of the relationships she has with schools are uneven. While it is easy and efficient in some contexts, she faces difficulties in communication in others, particularly in secondary schools. She had to establish priorities due to the large amount of schools covered and the heterogeneity of the schools. Of her 54 long-term cases, only one concerned a Nepali girl. As she explained, these teenagers now have less need than more recent migrants and do not manifest the problems of absenteeism or disruptive behavior as other students might. The one case of a Nepali student requiring more attention was a result of the girl's lower ranking in a pre-vocational training school.

In the least, the NGO mediator remained a reference person in weekly activities where she could meet the young women and continue to observe their experiences. In fact, Le COFFRET organized homework assistance for migrants with students who benevolently help them each Saturday, and the respondents' attendance at this activity was appreciated by the mediator. For two of the women, this involvement had extended beyond academic help: it had been an opportunity to socialize with teenagers and to join in activities outside of homework help, such as planning trips to other provinces. These types of activities refer to what Bautier and Rayou (2009) call non-school forms of socialization that build on social events of companies, churches and associations.

The role of Le COFFRET also encouraged the non-school form of socialization in which volunteer families are matched with a newly arrived family to help them adjust to life in Canada. These matches led to increased academic support and social outings for some of the Nepali women, such as going to the movies, engaging in winter activities or accessing better conditions for studying.

Difficult Periods of School Socialization

The young refugee women's process of socialization in this regional context is not linear. One of them specifically told me how difficult her first day had been at school when she could not understand her timetable and how to reach her classroom in the large secondary school. When she arrived in a French class on this first day of arrival, the teacher gave her an exercise where students had to find orthographical errors and simply told her: "Try, try . . ." She could laugh at this memory during the interview, four years later, but affirmed: "I will never forget this in my life." With regard to an analytic point of view, this situation reveals a total lack of comprehension toward non-French speaking students and a lack of differentiation in teaching, which harms students with specific needs.

Other difficult moments were experienced while a transition was occurring (to another level, to another classroom). One of the young Nepali women spoke of one such move as a moment of feeling targeted. As she was the only Nepali in the group, she felt as if her classmates were always laughing at her and did not feel supported by her teacher. Ultimately, her situation gradually improved as she changed her sitting area and met other students, leading her to be more active with her classmates and to interact with them as often as possible.

The point of view from a second social worker, who worked on raising young women's self-esteem, is also relevant. While she met with six of them for six sessions in a qualitative program named "Go, girls," she measured their awareness of concepts such as self-esteem or personal qualities. The basics of child education and well-being had to be explained and illustrated by many examples to be transferred to their reality and self-perception.

Despite the difficult early phases, the young women could identify significant advances achieved during their three to five years of socialization in Quebec. The first one became more outgoing: "Now, I am less afraid to talk. I don't know why." Although some of their timidity might be due to the social norms of Hindu women or cultural norms of the Nepali classroom, it is clear that many of the young women were experiencing an increase in self-confidence. One asserted: "I never thought I could be someone. I thought it was not possible. . . . If you are interested you can do everything." Their teachers also noticed these changes when comparing the beginning and end of the school year. Talking about one Nepali girl, one teacher commented: "When I am greeting her, she now answers back. It is a great sign and I think it is also due to herself, to her school results."

In conclusion, the school socialization of refugee first-generation young women is a gradual process. While they benefit from supportive teachers and other avenues of development such as the nonprofit organization, they must struggle with consistent barriers, which leaves their socialization in constant flux.

POLICY RECOMMENDATIONS

Rather than in-class instruction, the general socialization of young Nepali women in the three schools observed here is gradually developing through the less formal instruction of the "hidden curriculum" (Forquin 1989; Hohl and Normand 1996) that students absorb in the classroom, and through extracurricular activities and field trips. However, the official policy of socialization has yet to make a dramatic effect on the experience of the Nepali young women as bonding networks remain much stronger than bridging networks. Below, I outline how the socialization policy falls short and suggest several recommendations in terms of peer relations, teacher involvement and training, and the role of the NGO.

Based on my assessment of their socialization according to the social integration indicators (McAndrew 1994), I identified a large role for peers of the same ethno-cultural group, but there remains a lack of consistent connection with their Quebecer peers. The Quebecer tend to be mostly indifferent, which is unfortunate given the importance of host country peers to break the isolation of first-generation migrants (Fiset 2009). Despite the lack of connection with host country peers, both the young women and their mothers reflect on school positively and all of them consider school to be a means for learning and advancing (Kanouté et al. 2008).

The strength of bonding social networks within the Nepali community also extends to a transnational level through new communication technologies and networks. In fact, the influence of the internet on social networks is tremendous, allowing them to maintain relationships with a diaspora that is dispersed in eight countries around the world. On the other hand, the internet is used less frequently to create new social links (Nadeau-Cossette 2013), a finding that is consistent with the social interactions at school.

The teachers may have an important role to facilitate socialization but many remain too distracted or busy to seize it. Furthermore, all of the teachers called attention to their lack of training on the subject. This point is underlined in recent research (Larochelle-Audet et al. 2013) that proved that the progress Montreal universities made in training is impactful but also quite new, not even one decade old. This would not concern the teachers interviewed in the experiment who were trained more than one decade prior. Bakhshaei (2015) also identifies the lack of expertise developed in regional school contexts as they have far less experience welcoming migrants than in Montreal schools. Nevertheless, this case provides us with a strong recommendation for future educational policy to prioritize and recognize the need for increased training of teachers. Training is essential for teachers to understand the subtleties of action and comprehension of the cultural diversity of students (Sanchez-Mazas and Fernandez-Iglesias 2011; Gajardo and Leanza 2011). According to Guilbert (2005), effective training efforts must also include the school principals. Finally, training should be supplemented by intercultural teaching and activities in the classroom as well and opportunities for interactive exchanges between schools, students, and families.

The introduction of the NGO mediator could also support and benefit the efforts of teachers to more effectively welcome and instruct migrant students. Moreover, as I have shown, the mediator and NGO structure holds immense potential for facilitating socialization beyond the strict confines of the school with family matches and planned social outings. However, the mediators' extensive case load and geographic distance between schools greatly diminishes their ability to play an effective role. Thus, it is necessary for the NGO to hire more mediators or reduce the limitations on the mediator for this role to be more productive.

A Complex Socialization

The socialization of migrants at school in a regional *mono-ethnic* context falls on the shared responsibility of multiple actors and social networks. It extends beyond the school to interconnect with other spheres of socialization, such as NGOs, family, and peers. Despite the parent-children conflicts that Banerjee and Coward (2005) anticipated, the young respondents affirmed that their socialization between school and family was going fluidly. We could question if this stance is due to their high sense of loyalty or to the lack of confrontations between the values of their home and those of their peers at school. As Tyyskä (2008, 82) underlines: "There are patterns of both continuity and change in family relations and hierarchies upon immigration and settlement. Some traditional patterns prevail while others change significantly." In fact, they described their socialization as a dual process akin to "compartmentalization" (Singer 1972; Ramanujan 1990), or "seamless compartmentalization" (Beyer 2007), in which school and home are conceived as separate social worlds. As such, they can conform to expectations of being the studious student at school, and the "good girl" at home without contradiction. However, considering a third sphere through interactions with their peers, at both a local and transnational level, complicates the binary of home and school. Although most of their social worlds are quite exclusively composed of young women originating from their ethno-cultural group, their social horizon is slowly opening to interactions with young men that might challenge gender norms at home. Finally, the nonprofit organization might also represent a fourth sphere of socialization in which they may widen their social context to include non-school forms of socialization that may lead to strong and durable relationships outside of the co-ethnic bonding relations (Bautier and Rayou 2009).

These multiple sites of socialization have not surfaced in academic literature but can be an important key for comprehending the processes of incorporation for refugee groups. My analysis demonstrates that systemic support is necessary for first-generation refugees and/or migrants to attain social integration and achievement. Furthermore, we must consider the local relations of school and home in relation to trans-local and transnational contacts.

COMMENTARY

Bimala Bastola

I am one of the participants included in this study and I do agree with its analysis. Béatrice Halsouet discussed her findings and conclusions with me last summer and I was surprised to see how much she could understand from our reality as young migrant girls recently arrived from Nepali refugee camps.

Nevertheless, her analysis differs from my current situation that reflects some changes in my life. For example, thanks to my teacher in the French linguistic support class, I now meet every two weeks with two young Quebec girls, who are in secondary school. The meetings with them are such important moments for me! Thanks to soccer, an extracurricular activity I started last year, I can share some leisure time with the team during evenings and weekends, which has been a great experience for me. At the same time, locally and through the Internet, my contacts have broadened to include people outside of my community as many friends of my background have moved to other provinces in the last few months.

My efforts at school have given me a good mastery of the French language and set me up to pass the final exams of high school in June, 2017. For me, it was an important victory as I arrived here just five years ago and went directly to the secondary school system. My possibilities for continuing my education after high school are now open and attractive. I will finish with the poem I wrote last winter in my French class, inspired by the motto of the province of Quebec: "I remember."

I remember
Nepal is my country
My identity, my language, my life
Nepal is not my country
Without papers, a refugee only
My life in the camp was cheerful and joyful
With my extended family, and all my friends, full
My life in the camp taught me daily
To endure so many difficulties
Here the climate is freezing
In Nepal, summer all year long.
When it was raining, water was coming in
In the hut everything became wet
Hindu Festivals were great moments
With new clothes and shimmering saris
With lots of people dancing
Music, flowers, incense fumes floating
Here teachers are just like friends
But they were frightening to me in Nepal
I was an obedient pupil
But could not have dreams
And how is it that I live here and now?
I still dream in Nepali
I grow up in French
And I come out of my shell slowly

REFERENCES CITED

Anisef, Paul, Robert Brown, Kelli Phythian, Robert Sweet, and David Walters. 2010. "Early School Leaving among Immigrants in Toronto Secondary Schools." *Canadian Review of Sociology* 47 (2): 103–128.

Bakhshaei, Mahsa. 2015. "La Scolarisation des Jeunes Québécois Issus de l'Immigration: Un Diagnostic." Research report for the Lucie et André Chagnon Foundation. Retrieved from https://www.fondationchagnon.org/media/107917/rapport_recherche_diagnostic_enfants_issus_immigration_version_finale.pdf.

Banerjee, Sikata and Harold Coward. 2009. "Hindus in Canada: Negotiating Identity in a 'Different' Homeland." In *Religion and Ethnicity in Canada,* edited by Paul Bramadat and David Seljak, 30–51. Toronto Buffalo London: University of Toronto Press.

Barth, Frederick. 1969. *Ethnic Groups and Boundaries: The Social Organization of Culture Differences.* Boston: Little, Brown and Company.

Bautier, Élisabeth and Patrick Rayou. 2009. *Les Inégalités d'Apprentissage. Programmes, Pratiques et Malentendus Scolaire*s. Paris: PUF.

Bensa, Alban. 2009. "Remarques sur les Politiques de l'Intersubjectivité." In *Politiques de l'Enquête: Épreuves Ethnographiques,* edited by Daniel Fassin and Alban Bensa, 323–328. Paris: La Découverte.

Berry, John. 1999. "Intercultural Relations in Plural Societies," *Canadian Psychology* 40 (1): 12–21.

Beyer, Peter. 2007. "Can the Tail Wag the Dog? Diaspora Reconstructions of Religions in a Globalized Society." *Nordic Journal of Religion and Society* 19 (1): 41–63.

Bouchard, Louise, Jean-François Roy, and Solange Van Kemenade. 2006. "What Impact does Social Capital have on the Health of Canadians." *Policy Research Initiative*. Ottawa: Government of Canada.

Bourdieu, Pierre and Jean-Claude Passeron. 1964. *Les héritiers: les étudiants et la culture*. Paris, France: Les éditions de minuit.

Castellotti, Véronique. 2008. "Vers la Construction d'une École et d'une Société Plurielles: Des Notions en Débat, des Orientations à Construire." *Revue Sociolinguistique en Ligne* 11: 2–12.

Cefaï, Daniel. 2003. *L'enquête de Terrain.* Paris: La Découverte.

Charest, Paul. 2005. "Les Assistants de Recherche en Tant que Médiateurs Culturels." *Études/Inuit/Studies* 29 (1–2): 115–129.

De Koninck, Zita and Françoise Armand. 2012. *Portrait des Services d'Accueil et d'Intégration Scolaire des Élèves Issus de l'Immigration*. Report for Quebec Education Ministry.

Edwards, John. 1992. "Language in Group and Individual Identity." In *Social Psychology of Identity and the Self Concept,* edited by Glynis Marie Breakwell, 147–186. London: Surrey University Press.

Fassin, Didier. 2008. "Répondre de sa Recherche. L'Anthropologue Face à ses 'Autres'." In *Politiques de l'Enquête: Épreuves Ethnographiques,* edited by Didier Fassin and Alban Bensa, 299–319. Paris: La Découverte.

Fiset, Monika. 2009. "L'Expérience de Socialisation Scolaire des Élèves Issus de l'Immigration. Étude Phénoménologique Menée Auprès d'Élèves du Primaire de la Ville de Québec." Master thesis, Université Laval.

Forquin, Jean-Claude. 1989. *École et Culture. Le Point de Vue des Sociologues Britanniques*. Bruxelles: De Boeck Université.

Gajardo, Anahy and Yvan Leanza. 2011. "De l'Interculturel de Valeurs à l'Interculturel de Faits, Entretien Croisé Avec Tania Ogay et Jacques Proulx." *Alterstice* 1 (1): 69–80.

Gohier, Christiane. 2004. "Le Cadre Théorique." In: *La Recherche en Éducation: Étapes et Approches,* edited by Karsenti Thierry and Lorraine Savoie-Zajc, 81–107. Sherbrooke: Éditions du CRP.

Goulet, Jean-Guy. 2010. "Trois Manières d'être sur le Terrain. Une Brève Histoire des Conceptions de l'Intersubjectivité." *Anthropologie et Sociétés* 35 (3): 107–125.

Gouvernement du Québec. 2003. *Integrating the Cultural Dimension into School.* Reference document for Teachers. Quebec: Bibliothèque nationale du Québec.

Guilbert, Lucille. 2005. "La Ville de Québec: Un Laboratoire Pour la Mise en Oeuvre de Médiations Avec les Réfugiés." *Canadian Ethnic Studies* 37 (3): 59–75.

Hohl, Janine and Michèle Normand. 1996. "Construction et Stratégies Identitaires des Enfants et des Adolescents en Contexte Migratoire: le Rôle des Intervenants Scolaires." *Revue Française de Pédagogie* 117: 39–52.

Isajiw, Wsevolod. 1993. "Definition and Dimensions of Ethnicity: A Theoretical Framework." In *Challenges of Measuring an Ethnic World: Science, Politics and Reality: Proceedings of the Joint Canada-United States Conference on the Measurement of Ethnicity, April 1-3, 1992*, edited by the Statistics Canada and U.S. Bureau of the Census, 407–427. Washington, DC: Government Printing Office.

Jaccoud, Mylène and Robert Mayer. 1997. "L'Observation en Situation et la Recherche Qualitative." In *La Recherche Qualitative: Enjeux Épistémologiques et Méthodologiques,* edited by Jean Poupart, Jean-Pierre Deslauriers, Lionel Groulx, Anne Laperrière, Robert Mayer, and Alvaro Pires, 211–249. Montréal: Gaëtan Morin.

Juteau, Danielle.1999. *L'Ethnicité et ses Frontières*. Montréal: Presses de l'Université de Montréal.

Kanouté, Fasal, Michèle Vatz Laaroussi, Lilyane Rachédi, and Madeleine Tchimou. 2008. "Familles et Réussite Scolaire d'Élèves Immigrants du Secondaire." *Revue des Sciences de l'Éducation* 34 (2): 265–289.

Laplantine, François. 2005. *Le Social et le Sensible: Introduction à une Anthropologie Modale*. Paris: Tétraèdre.

Larochelle-Audet, Julie, Corina Borri-Anadon, Marie Mc Andrew, and Maryse Potvin. 2013. *La Formation Initiale du Personnel Scolaire sur la Diversité Ethnoculturelle, Religieuse et Linguistique dans les Universités Québécoises: Portrait Quantitatif et Qualitatif*. Research Report. Montreal: Université de Montréal.

Le Breton, David. 2008. *L'interactionnisme symbolique*. Paris: Presses Universitaires de France.

Li, Peter. 2004. "Social Capital and Economic Outcomes for Immigrants and Ethnic Minorities." *Journal of International Migration and Integration* 5 (2): 171–190.

Mc Andrew, Marie and GRIÉS. 2015. *La Réussite Éducative des Élèves Issus de l'Immigration. Dix ans de Recherche et d'Intervention au Québec*." Montréal: Presses de l'Université de Montréal.

Mc Andrew, Marie, Michel Pagé, Mathieu Jodoin, and Francine Lemire. 1999. "Densité Ethnique et Intégration Sociale des Élèves d'Origine Immigrante au Québec." *Canadian Ethnic Studies/Etudes Ethniques au Canada* 31 (1): 8–25.

Mc Andrew, Marie. 1994. "Pertinence et Limites des Indicateurs Socioculturels dans la Mesure de l'Intégration Scolaire." In *Actes du Séminaire sur les Indicateurs d'Intégration des Immigrants*, edited by Centre d'Etudes Ethniques de l'Université de Montréal, 279–295. Québec: Gouvernement du Québec.

———. 2013. *Les 50 Ans du Rapport Parent. L'école et la Diversité Ethnoculturelle.* [Unpublished manuscript].

Nadeau-Cossette, Anaïs. 2013. *L'Intégration Socio-Scolaire des Adolescents Immigrants: Facteurs Influents*. Research Report. Québec: Université Laval.

Ontario Ministry of Education . 2009. *Ontario's Equity and Inclusive Education Strategy*. Ontario: Government of Canada.

———. (2014). *Achieving Excellence. A Renewed Vision for Education in Ontario.* Ontario: Government of Canada.

Ramanujan, Attipat Krishnaswami. 1990. “Is There an Indian Way of Thinking? An Informal Essay.” In *India through Hindu Categories,* edited by McKim Marriott, 41–77. Delhi: Sage.

Ritzer, George. 2011. *Sociological Theory* (9th edition). New York, NY: McGraw-Hill.

Robert, Marcel and Jac Tondreau. 1997. *L’École Québécoise. Débats, Enjeux et Pratiques Sociales: Une Analyse Sociale de l’Éducation Pour la Formation des Maitres*. Anjou: Éditions CEC.

Ruddick, Elizabeth. 2003. “Immigrant Economic Performance: A New Paradigm in Changing Labour Market.” *Canadian Issues* 5: 16–17.

Sanchez-Mazas, Margarita and Raquel Fernandez-Iglesias. 2011. “L’Interculturel à l’Épreuve de l’Action: Comment Équiper les Enseignants Face au Public Scolaire Fétérogène.” *Alterstice* 1(1): 35–46.

Singer, Milton. 1972. *When a Great Tradition Modernizes. An Anthropological Approach to Indian Civilization.* NewYork: Praeger Publishers.

Steinbach, Marilyn and Sylvain Lussier. 2013. “L’Intégration Sociale des Élèves Issus de l’Immigration dans une Région du Québec.” In *Les Collectivités Locales au Coeur de l’Intégration des Immigrants: Questions Identitaires et Stratégies Regionals,* edited by Michèle Vatz Laaroussi, Estelle Bernier, and Lucille Guilbert, 29–47. Québec: Presses de l’Université Laval.

Steinbach, Marilyn. 2010. “Eux Autres Versus Nous Autres: Adolescent Students’ Views on the Integration of Newcomers.” *Intercultural Education* 21 (6): 535–547.

Table de Concertation des Organismes au Service des Personnes Réfugiées et Immigrantes. (2011). *L’Intégration des Enfants et des Jeunes Immigrants de Première Génération au Québec. Perspective des Organismes Communautaires au Service des Nouveaux Arrivants*. Rapport d’Enquête.

Tyyskä, Varkaus. 2008. “Parents and Teens in Immigrant Families: Cultural Influences and Material Pressures.” *Canadian Diversity* 6 (2): 79–82.

Vatz Laaroussi, Michèle. 2007. “La Recherche Qualitative Interculturelle: Une Recherche Engagée?” *Recherches Qualitatives, Hors Série* 4: 2–13.

Winnemore, Lara and John Biles. 2006. “Canada’s Two-Way Street Integration Model: Not without Its Stains, Strains and Growing Pains.” *Canadian Diversity – Diversité canadienne* 5 (1): 23–30.

Part IV

SPACE AND PLACE

Chapter 10

"There Will Never Be a Foreclosure in Our Community"

Networks of Dependence in the Secondary Relocation of Nepali-Bhutanese Refugees

Andrew Nelson, with commentary
by Khada Bhandari

Since late 2007, more than 90,000 Nepali-Bhutanese refugees have resettled in the United States.[1] Over 5,000 have resettled in the Dallas-Fort Worth (DFW) metroplex, initially placed by resettlement agencies in neighborhoods of Dallas and Fort Worth consisting of apartment complexes with lower rents. Many of these refugees, however, have relocated to other states, cities, or neighborhoods. Commonly called secondary migration, scholars explain this process as a response to the resettlement policies of dispersal in which states scatter refugees all over the country in nuclear family houses separated from extended families (Simich 2003). Among refugees in DFW, a perception exists that refugees initially settled in the southern and hotter parts of the United States are moving toward the northern states of Ohio and Pennsylvania where large communities of Nepali-Bhutanese are developing in the Pittsburgh and Columbus areas, among other cities. However, in DFW, many are also relocating to the northern suburbs of Fort Worth where they are buying new houses. For example, in one revealing case, more than seventy-five Nepali-Bhutanese families have purchased and moved into houses in Lanewood, a suburban subdivision ten miles to the north of downtown Fort Worth.[2] In moving to the suburbs, they have traded the high population density of apartment complexes in southeastern Fort Worth and northeastern Dallas for neighborhoods of detached single-family houses consisting of uniform architecture, cul-de-sac streets, brick walls, and Homeowner Associations (HOA). Rather than the long-distance shift of secondary migration, then, the short-distance move between urban apartments in Fort Worth and Dallas to suburban houses in Fort Worth is better represented by what I call secondary relocation.

ENTRY POINT

This chapter is based on seven years of interactions with Nepali-Bhutanese refugees resettled in the United States. Recently returned from my dissertation research in Kathmandu, Nepal, in 2009, I was hired as an English-Nepali interpreter by the International Rescue Committee (IRC) in Charlottesville, Virginia to help the agency address the language needs of its incoming Nepali-Bhutanese. Over the next two years, I met many refugees who expressed a consistent complaint that resettlement spread their family all over the country, and in some cases, the world. When I relocated to Denton, Texas in 2012, I connected with the Nepali-Bhutanese community in Dallas and Fort Worth as an English/Civics teacher and ethnographer. During the academic year of 2013–2014, I made weekly visits to the Vickery Meadow neighborhood of Dallas where I taught classes and conducted interviews. For many of these refugees, now having been in the country for several years, the main problem was living in the crowded apartments of the lower-income areas. They complained of not having enough space to accommodate family members or grow gardens, and lamented "throwing away" money every month on rent to an unknown landlord. Quickly adopting American racial prejudices, they also disliked living among African Americans and Spanish-speaking Latinos, who they associated with crime and poverty.

In the fall of 2015, as I learned of families moving from the urban apartments to suburban houses, I started conducting research in one of the most popular neighborhoods of relocation, Lanewood. Since this time, I have been conducting interviews, attending *garage pujas* and other rituals and festivals, teaching a weekly citizenship class, and following one of the community's real estate agents. Interestingly, when my own family moved to Texas and bought a house, my entry into the world of owning real estate provided a reflexive source of contrast to how Nepali-Bhutanese conceived of their new houses. I understood home ownership as a sign of economic independence in spite of the fact that buying the house was made possible by a family member's financial support and an FHA loan. The Nepali-Bhutanese home-buyers with whom I spoke, conversely, emphasized the cooperation and dependence on family members and close friends in describing their route to home ownership. While valuing the economic advantages of ownership, they also highlighted the more collectivist meaning of the house over the individualism often embedded within American ideologies of private property. Listening to the narratives of new refugee home-owners influenced me to reconsider the value of dependence that comes with economic support from kin, community and institutions.

SECONDARY RELOCATION AS EMPLACEMENT

The Nepali-Bhutanese are just the most recent in a line of DFW-resettled refugees to establish enclaves in suburban neighborhoods. In the 1980s and 1990s, the southeast Asian refugees of Cambodian, Vietnamese, and Laotian origins established presences in localities on the outskirts of Dallas and Fort Worth. More recently, Kurds have relocated to rural parts of Mesquite on the eastern periphery of Dallas County, while Burmese have resettled in large numbers in Lewisville, a suburb to the north of Dallas. These movements of secondary relocation dispel the image often expressed of refugees as stuck in a permanent state of displacement—not attached to any place or people. As Malkki (1992, 1995) has identified, refugees have often been imagined as passive victims, a notion she attributes to the sedentarist bias of scholarship. The bias implies that the condition of displacement renders refugees not only without the rights of citizenship, but also lacking agency and even morality. In opposition to the territorially fixed citizen, the refugee is rendered abnormal, even a "pathological condition" to be fixed (Malkki 1992, 33). Amid the process of displacement, however, refugees do maintain and remake a sense of place (Korac 2009; Hammond 2004; Lems 2014). Lems (2014), in particular, argues that emplacement is not about creating ties to fixed and stable built environments, but instead a process of being-in-place, something that is always occurring. She states, "place does not cease to exist, even if it is experienced as a sense of deep and utter disruption (or displacement). It is always there, where we are" (2014, 6). The sense of place that refugees create is active regardless of the uncertainty or improvisation in which it is made (Korac 2009, 9). Thus, while displacement is something that has happened to them, it is emplacement that they *do*. Nowhere is the active process of emplacement more apparent than in the making and remaking of one's sense of home (Brun and Fábos 2015; Hammond 2004; Smith 2016).

Few groups in the world understand emplacement-amid-displacement better than the Nepali-Bhutanese who have spent more than the last century making a home in a "foreign" territory. Their ancestors left Nepal starting in the late nineteenth century and early twentieth century to be laborers in the development of Bhutan's southern regions. In Bhutan, they were considered outsiders, or *Lhotshampa* (Dzongkha term for "southerner"), Nepali-speaking and predominantly Hindu in a Buddhist state dominated by the Dzongkha-speaking ethnic majority of Drukpa.[3] Nonetheless, they established a vibrant diaspora and contributed to Bhutan's development of its southern plains and infrastructure (Hutt 2005, 82–84). When they "returned" to Nepal as refugees starting in 1990, despite being of the same linguistic and cultural heritage of Nepalis, they were again labelled outsiders, this time as "Bhutani" and were accused of taking advantage of Nepal's hospitality. For instance, in the Prajwal Parajuly short story, "No Land is Her Land," a refugee woman is told by a Nepali to "'Go back to your damn country.' Another voice, shriller than the rest, brought applause and hoots from the crew. 'Go to Bhutan. No one wants you in Nepal.'" In a similar vein, Dil, a 72-year-old man living in Fort Worth, recalled how Nepalis were treated as inferiors: "When we had nothing, begging for water, food, they said go drink from the well. They called us *kalo luga manchhe* ['black clothes wearing people' implying their poverty] and looked down upon us. They would never give their daughters to our sons. Now that we have come to America, they respect us. They want to marry their daughters to our sons." Now, in the United States (as well as in Canada, Australia, and four European countries), the Nepali-Bhutanese are again remaking a home in geographic context where they are considered minorities. As I will show, the ability to purchase houses within the first decade of resettlement is a testament to their strategies of emplacement and effective social networks of dependence.

SECONDARY RELOCATION AS NETWORKS OF DEPENDENCE AND EXCLUSION

The emplacement processes of house-buying challenge the dominant ideology guiding the resettlement agencies and wider society that welcomes them to the United States. Contrary to the emphasis on self-sufficiency and economic independence in the policies and programs of the agencies, it is an alternative logic of social dependence on networks that informs their emplacement strategies. In the era of neoliberalism, dependence is often conceived as a barrier to freedom or progress, but the case of Nepali-Bhutanese secondary relocation urges us to consider the social benefits of it as well as the costs of independence. Although far from the context of US refugee resettlement, Ferguson's (2013) insights on the neoliberal labor regimes in southern Africa provide a lesson in how the promotion of economic and social independence produces considerable asocial effects and can be quite destructive to a people-centric society in which personhood is constituted through relations of dependence. Freedom, as such, is not to liberate one's self from social structures of hierarchy and obligation, but rather to have access to a "plurality of opportunities for dependence" (2013, 226).

After several years in the United States, Nepali-Bhutanese refugees often fear that their "plurality of opportunities for dependence" is shrinking. As I discuss later, after six to eight months in the country, they are effectively cut off from financial and (most forms) social support from the agencies, leaving many with bitter feelings toward the very institutions that facilitated their arrival in the United States. While they can, and often do, transition from agency support to a dependence on government programs, public aid also becomes threatened if refugees do not attain citizenship. They become eligible to apply for citizenship after five years, but then have just two years to obtain it or else lose access to governmental benefits. Ideally, they will have gained employment by that point and are able to secure the benefits of retirement and health insurance through employers for themselves and dependents. Unfortunately, however, the majority of Nepali-Bhutanese in North Texas are employed in the service and light manufacturing industries, which tend to be reluctant to provide benefit packages to workers.

With the precariousness of relations with agencies, government and employer, Nepali-Bhutanese in DFW turn to the bonding social capital of their own networks to provide the sort of mutual dependence they seek. In considering how the process of secondary relocation is built on networks, it is necessary to examine how the Nepali notion of "home" encapsulates notions of social dependence. Rather than a sign of economic independence as the ownership of one's residence is often framed in the United States (Perin 1977), the production of a Nepali *home* (*ghar*) is constituted through social relations of place, memory, territory, and networks. As the Nepali geographer Bhim Prasad Subedi (1999, 138) suggests, "*ghar* is neither limited to physical structure nor a physical space to carry on livelihood. It captures broader networks, intimate relations with the land and environment, a place of rooted memory." Thus, any economic understanding of the physical house must be grounded in a more holistic notion of the home as a social process embedded within networks of dependence.

The social meaning of the home requires thinking beyond it as a bounded or solely local entity. Home rather becomes part of, as Massey (1994, 156) argues, a "global sense of place" that is "constructed by linking [a] place to places beyond." Place is thus a social process dependent on the myriad interactions of people here *and* there. The physical house may be limited to a certain number of inhabitants, but its social context extends from them outwards to a translocal and transnational sense of place. Making a home in the suburbs is, thus, contingent on relations between the social ties with the apartments, other cities and countries of refugees, as well as Nepal, India, and Bhutan. Building on Massey, Gielis (2009) demonstrates that an analysis of migrant social networks is the best articulation of a global sense of place for how networks connect multiple places and scales. Specifically, he argues for a study of "migrant places" as both the physical places where migrant networks meet and extend to social processes beyond them and as translocalities (Appadurai 1995)—the deterritorialized networks of virtual communication and linkage.

Although the networks of the house are expansive, open, and spatially flexible, they are also limited by the social exclusions of a group of people's particular history and society. As I will demonstrate, the formation of a Nepali-Bhutanese community in the Fort Worth suburbs consists only of a particular sub-section of high-caste Hindus within the larger Nepali-Bhutanese refugee population. Networks of dependence, thus, enable as well as disable the processes of home- and place-making to occur. To frame our discussion of how these networks function, I will now turn to a case of when they failed. I then attribute this failure to the short-term policies and economic ideologies of the agencies, and contrast them with the alternative practices of dependence that serve as the foundation of home-buying in the Lanewood neighborhood.

THE CASE OF FAILED SECONDARY RELOCATION: "THEY BOUGHT A HOUSE, BUT NO ONE FOLLOWED"

When I ask Nepali-Bhutanese in DFW about the advantages and disadvantages of buying houses, the story of Harka's family is told as a precautionary tale. They are referred to as "the family who bought a house, but no one followed." Harka is the oldest male son of one of the first families to arrive in Dallas in 2008. Even before arriving in the United States, his family was often on the periphery of Nepali-Bhutanese society. In Bhutan, unlike most Nepali who were farmers, his father was a merchant who had a 'modern' cement house in a market town as well as a more traditional mud and stone house in a village area. Consequently, Harka grew up in between village and town with the ability to attend school full-time, a privilege to which few other Nepali in Bhutan had access. Because of his father's trading connections and his political activism on behalf of Nepali in the 1980s, the family received considerable persecution from the Bhutanese state. His father was one of the first Nepali to be arrested and tortured in the 1980s. Soon after he was released from detention, the family left Bhutan for Nepal, resettling in the cities of Nepal's southeastern corridor of the Tarai prior to the mass entry of Nepalis from Bhutan in the early 1990s.

As the refugee camps in Nepal were forming in the early 1990s, Harka's family maintained a hut inside the camps, but also lived outside of the camps in Nepal and India in order for Harka and his siblings to pursue degrees and employment opportunities. All of the family's children—three sons and two daughters—received a Bachelor's degree or higher. Harka, in particular, earned a master's degree in Physics from an Indian university where he stayed and became a secondary school teacher. Inside the camps, however, resentment against his father grew due to his advocacy for third-country resettlement, which irritated the refugee activists in favor of repatriation to Bhutan. Due to repeated threats against his father, the family had to permanently leave the camps and stay in hiding, constantly moving in between cities in southeastern Nepal. The father's advocacy for resettlement, however, did put the family high on the list of families to be resettled. When the family received notification of their acceptance to be resettled, Harka immediately returned from his teaching job in India to enter the resettlement process with his immediate family in 2007.

Thanks to his education and English language fluency, Harka found employment with one of Dallas' resettlement agencies. They were placed in the Chimney Hill area which had fewer refugees, and was separated by a major highway in between it and central Dallas. In 2010, three years after arrival, Harka married and convinced his family to move out of the apartments and buy a house. With the help of an Indian real estate agent, Harka, his wife, two brothers, and parents (his sisters had married and moved in with their spouses' families) chose a large five-bedroom house in Garland, a suburb six miles to the east of Chimney Hill. However, after four years in the house, his brothers got married and found jobs as computer engineers in Pennsylvania and North Carolina, leaving just Harka, his wife and parents in their large suburban house. It was at that point that his parents started urging Harka to sell the house and move back to the apartments in Chimney Hill. The reason was not necessarily that the house was too large, but rather that it was geographically disconnected from other Nepalis. He explained: "My parents needed community, needed to be near other Nepalis. They were frustrated from being alone." Harka went on to explain that his mistake was to buy a house that was "too expensive for other Nepalis" (in the $200,000–300,000 range), and that the area, built in 2010, was already full with no room for new construction. Instead of Dallas, the majority of Nepali-Bhutanese buying houses elected to move to the suburbs of Fort Worth, where real estate tends to be cheaper.

In addition to being the reason for early resettlement, one must also wonder if the peripheral social position of Harka's father, as a bazaar merchant and resettlement advocate, contributed to the absence of fellow refugees following them to Garland. In other words, could there be social reasons for this case of failed secondary relocation? Coincidently, as part of his job, Harka now runs seminars for refugees and others in which he discourages people from buying houses. He explained that "If you make more than $100,000 a year that is enough, but for everyone making nine or ten dollars per hour, there is no way." He mentioned the ignorance of many who do not consider the cost of insurance, house maintenance, utilities, HOA fees, and property taxes—"the expenses that don't exist in Nepal. What will happen if you get hurt or sick and can't work?" He elaborated on his cynical opinion of home ownership: "In the U.S., you never truly own your house. Even if you have paid off the loan, it is just a business center for the government to make tax money to pay for schools and public hospitals."

It is interesting to contrast Harka's advice against house buying with his own experience of selling his house. Whereas Harka advises other refugees against home-buying based on financial grounds, in his own account he attributed his personal failure to social reasons, specifically his parents' lack of a community in the new neighborhood. It very well could be that the price of the neighborhood kept other families from joining them, but his narrative suggests that there is more to successful home-buying than just finances.

THE IDEOLOGICAL FOUNDATIONS OF REFUGEE RESETTLEMENT IN THE UNITED STATES

Harka's description of relocation differed immensely from the narratives of relocation I heard from folks living in the suburban Lanewood. The contrast paralleled a larger discrepancy between the descriptions of success by refugees and by the resettlement agencies that oversee and guide their entry to American society. Much like how Harka advises potential home-buyers, resettlement agencies define success in terms of economic indicators of financial self-sufficiency and independence. On the other hand, the refugees of Lanewood define success according to a longer-term more holistic notion of "home" that is based on family and community relations of dependence.

Initial Resettlement

First, and foremost, the goal of agencies is to remove refugees from harm and place them in a safe environment; and, to provide them with basic necessities of shelter, food, care services, legal representation, and social integration. They meet these needs with financial support from the US State Department which provide agencies with a one-time $1,100 per refugee "Reception and Placement" (RnP) fund to cover one to two months of rent, furniture, and spending money. This small budget, in addition to the fact that refugees have no rental or credit history, greatly limits rental options. Furthermore, agencies look for neighborhoods that are within walking distance from their offices.[4] The only variable, one agency representative explained to me, is the "employability" of a given family. The more family members that are able to work, the more likely the agency is willing to place them in more expensive apartments. In a city as economically segregated as Dallas, rental prices can make a large difference in the sort of neighborhood one can afford. Housing options in Fort Worth are a bit more limited. In fact, the largest resettlement agency in the city, Catholic Charities, tends to place refugees in just four apartment complexes located in the southern edges of the city. The most common sites of refugee resettlement in both cities—Vickery Meadow area in Dallas or

Ladera Palms Apartments in Fort Worth—reflect the impoverished economic environments in which most refugees enter the country. They consist of few employment possibilities within close proximity, which leads refugees to learn the public transit system quickly and endure long commutes or purchase private vehicles to reach jobs. Thus, while the placement of refugees in Vickery Meadow and Ladera Palms is an outcome of the agency's struggles to find secure housing on limited budgets in a short period of time, the lower socioeconomic position of both places become structural obstacles to the longer-term goals of the agencies to make refugees self-sufficient.

Labor

After the need for housing is met, the longer-term goal of economic self-sufficiency is communicated to refugees through the emphasis on securing employment. After the initial Reception and Placement check, financial support for refugees is linked to finding work. First, there is a federal match grant program in which the government will match the agency's contribution to provide rent and cash stipends to refugees enrolled in job training and English-as-Second-Language (ESL) programs for four to eight months. The support is further contingent on enrollees accepting the first job offered. A second Texas state program—Refugee Cash Assistance—offers a bit more flexibility to recipients, but still requires enrolling in at least one job training program, and only lasts for a maximum of eight months.

Both during and after this initial four to eight-month period of funding attached to employment or training, the compulsion to earn an income takes precedence over the other needs of refugees, such as learning English. Obtaining a decent job is often dependent on English fluency. For some of the Nepali-Bhutanese refugees, this is not a problem. In fact, many of the first lot of resettled were English teachers in Nepali and Indian schools. For the less fluent, however, improving their English often becomes structurally impossible as the pressure for earning an income becomes a priority over taking ESL classes. Thus, they often remain in a cycle of low-paying and unskilled positions from which it is difficult to impossible to escape. The pressure to secure an income is compounded by the fact that refugees arrive already in debt due to IOM loans that covered their travel expenses to the United States.[5] For instance, a family of five could easily face over $10,000 of debt upon immediate entry to their new life.

Long-term Integration

After the initial four- to eight-month period, the agency has no additional funding opportunities to offer refugees and essentially closes its services.

It might offer some mental and physical health programs, and perhaps be able to lobby on behalf of a client's job situation (for better hours or second job, for example), but it is not able to offer any financial support. For this reason, agencies understand their role as purely 'transitional'. Unfortunately, as one agency representative admitted to me, the transition is too often from the agency to government social services and a continued life in poverty. However, the transitional period does at least provide refugees with the documentation—credit and rental history—that will help them move into better neighborhoods in the future.

In addition to providing the basic tools for securing future housing, the main emphasis of agencies is to make refugees self-sufficient. Foremost, self-sufficiency means economic independence that is predicated on the obligation of labor production. The overwhelming message to refugees is that more than language acquisition, educational opportunities or cultural adjustment, the agency-assisted integration to United States society depends on contributing to the pool of low-skilled labor. Beyond employment, the idea of self-sufficiency represents other ideological consequences that have immense cultural effects for refugees. For example, agencies agree on the need to discourage refugees from sending earned money home to family members. One agency uses the airplane example of securing your own oxygen mask before helping others to teach this point. As an informant from one agency frames it: "If you can't help yourself first, you can't help anyone else."

In terms of government support, the notion of self-sufficiency is a bit more ambiguous. According to one agency I spoke with, self-sufficiency does not necessarily preclude state assistance. As long as refugees have one dollar saved after using their pay checks and government assistance to pay their bills, they are considered self-sufficient. For others, however, they feel the need to emphasize that self-sufficiency means independence from government support, especially not living in public housing. As several agency representatives explained to me, the Nepali-Bhutanese, in particular, have gained a reputation for seeking out disability benefits, which is framed as an obstacle to self-sufficiency.

Despite the four- to eight-month limit to financial help and the ideological insistence on self-sufficiency, agencies do offer some longer-term support systems for a select few. For instance, they facilitate Individual Development Accounts (IDA) in which banks or government programs match clients' saving accounts up to $8,000 toward buying a house or starting a business. Additionally, agencies often pair refugee families with mentors, volunteers from the community who offer assistance after the initial period. Although offering support, even these select exceptions reproduce the ideology of self-sufficiency in which an individual's contribution to society is measured purely in terms of economic production. Not only does the economic focus neglect the complexity of refugee lives, it often clashes with the adaptation strategies that refugees have cultivated through years of persecution and displacement (Keles 2009). In the remainder of this chapter, I contrast the agencies' model of self-sufficiency with the social networks of dependence demonstrated in the narratives of relocation told by refugees who have bought and moved into suburban houses.

SOCIAL NETWORKS OF DEPENDENCE: THE PRACTICES OF SUCCESSFUL SECONDARY RELOCATION

In the narratives of relocation to the suburbs for Lanewood residents, the economics of house buying is articulated through social terms. In contrast to the relocation of Harka's family, the recent house buyers to Lanewood have, in large part, moved together. The appeal of Lanewood developments were their newness, as they were started as recently as 2010, which allowed many Nepali-Bhutanese to buy brand new houses relatively close together. And although few families were able to get houses next door to each other, they were able to find houses on the same block. Often, the clusters of Nepali-Bhutanese on the same blocks are related to each other or come from the same village in Bhutan or same camp in Nepal. While the first few houses were independently secured with the help of American real estate agents, when a member of the community, Arun, gained his real estate license in 2012, the number of Nepali-Bhutanese in the subdivisions started to exponentially grow.

As a result of this concentration of Nepali-Bhutanese moving from the apartments and other cities to these two subdivisions, social interaction is relaxed with doors rarely locked as visitors enter and leave houses as they please. Residents view their new houses in terms of a certain social and economic freedom that they did not enjoy in the apartments. As tenants, they were unable paint their houses during major Hindu festivals of Dashain and Tihar, keep gardens or dry their vegetables in the yard, or invite over many guests to their residence. This lack of control over their domestic space reminded most of their time in Nepali camps where they were not allowed to own land or work outside of the camps. When residents reflect on their time living in the apartment complexes, it is the monthly payment of rent that they disliked the most. Rent was a monthly "headache," I am told. It was "like throwing money into the trash" one resident explained. Owning a house, in turn, connects families, at least metaphorically, to their life in Bhutan. For Surendra, a 42-year-old father of two, living in Lanewood, house ownership is important for his mother. Since she had to leave property behind in Bhutan, he was "relieved to finally give her a place to rest in America. Our father we couldn't bring, but at least mother can have a house to die in. It's a chance to give back to her what she abandoned in Bhutan." In Bhutan and now in the United States, refugees have property to pass on to children, the only difference, as the real estate agent Arun, put it, was that: "We have shifted our logic from that of giving land to the next generation (in Bhutan) to giving houses." However, the social processes of giving have remained the same.

Translocal Networks of Financial Support

The gift of the house to future generations is made possible by money exchanged between family members—exactly the sort of kin support that the agencies discourage. The case of the Bhattarai family demonstrates the impact of maintaining transnational economic support networks in their relocation process. The Bhattarai family consists of a mother, father, four sons and five daughters-in-law (one case of polygyny), two daughters, one son-in-law, and twelve grandchildren. When they resettled to the United States in 2010, they were unable to bring their oldest son, Jetho and family, and oldest daughter, Jethi, due to legal problems in Nepal and Bhutan. While Jetho was burdened with legal fees and prosecution resulting from a car accident in Nepal, Jethi's husband was arrested in Bhutan, leaving her solely responsible for raising four children.[6] To each, the Bhattarai family would send several hundred dollars on a monthly basis.

In spite of sending money to Jetho and Jethi in Nepal and Bhutan, the family was able to buy a $195,000 two-story, five-bedroom house in late 2014 in Lanewood. The three brothers in the United States and their wives had each contributed over $21,000 to the down payment. The contribution of each son's family, however, was supported by donations from other family and friends all over the United States. However, in order to circumvent United States mortgage regulations, the money contributed to the sons was not given directly to Mailo or Kancho, the second and fourth sons who applied for the mortgage, but rather to the third son, Sailo, who lives in Alabama. If given to Mailo or Kancho, the gifts would have needed to have been documented with letters verifying that they were gifts rather than loans in need of repayment. However, since they were given to Sailo, the only documented gift was from him, a family member, to his brothers. Thus, although the house title is written in Mailo and Kancho's names, the family does not conceive of them as the owners. The father of the family, Dil, stated "The house belongs to everyone in the family" and adds, "to even Jetho and Sailo, too," thus implying that the four sons share ownership.[7]

In order to avoid mortgage insurance fees, families aim to pay at least 20 percent of the house cost in the down payment, which ranges between 30 and 50 thousand dollars in Lanewood. Since few families have this much capital saved, community members organize financial pooling schemes in which down payment support is gifted with expectations of delayed balanced reciprocity. According to Texas law, any monetary gifts given toward paying down payments must come only from family members, but the loophole is that non-family can give money to the family gift-givers, who in turn, can give up to $14,000 tax deductible. Oftentimes, non-family will contribute between $1,000 and $5,000 which they understand to be part of a pool that each giver can later access when it is their turn to buy a house. Arun, the real estate agent, calls this system an "informal *sahakari*." *Sahakari* refers to a common form of community financing found in Nepal, in which small collectives will pool funds into savings accounts from which individual members can then draw money from the interest turn by turn.[8] However, since interest rates tend to be much higher in Nepal than in the United States (often between 10 and 15 percent), people are less likely to wait in the United States for the interest to accrue in order to take their "turn." Rather, when someone gives to a family member or friend to help pay the house down payment, they expect the balanced reciprocity of equal repayment, which is usually given after the home-buyers receive their tax returns in the spring.

In the narratives of relocation to Lanewood, the raising of funds for down payments reflects an alternative practice that functions within the American mortgage system to reduce interest rates and insurance payments. Families conceive of bank mortgages much like house rent—as an evil to be avoided as much as possible. Just as they conceive of losing each month's rent in the apartments, they also speak of losing any additional interest or insurance paid on mortgages. Thus, families strive to (a) give as high a down payment as possible; at least 20 percent to avoid paying mortgage insurance payments; and (b) pay off mortgage debt as soon as possible. Although most families take out 30-year loans to keep monthly payments lower, several have already paid off their loans in just a few years.

As the house makeup changes with marriages, births, and relocations, the dynamics of paying monthly mortgage payments can become more difficult. Since moving into the Lanewood house, the inhabitants of the Bhattarai house have changed several times. Jetho, his second wife and child, finally resettled to the United States in 2015, but had to live separate from the family of his first wife. Consequently, they could not join the larger family in the Lanewood house, but had to stay in the apartments as an independent family. One year later, as of writing, Jetho and his two wives and children moved into an apartment complex one mile from the Lanewood subdivision—close both to family and to their place of employment—Walmart and a cell phone repair shop. Additionally, Mailo, his wife and child have since moved to New

York where he is pursuing a graduate degree and his wife works as a nurse. With both Jetho and Mailo's families gone, the Bhattarais have lost the regular contributions of the three incomes to the monthly mortgage payment of $1175. Now, payment is the main responsibility of Kancho, his wife, and the social security and disability checks to the family's father, Dil and his wife, Shova. To make matters more challenging, Dil failed his first two attempts to gain citizenship, but was given a special conversation test after the second failure (which he did pass in early 2016). If he had not gained citizenship by 2017, at the end of his seven years in the United States, he would have lost his social security benefits and been forced to wait another two years before he could retake the exam.

Even if Dil had failed his exam and was forced to go two years without social security, the Bhattarais were not overly concerned about their ability to maintain mortgage payments. As seen in previous generations of refugees resettled in the United States such as the Vietnamese, households will pool material resources, share information, and offer assistance to ensure the survival of co-ethnics (Gold and Kibria 1993). From Arun and several other residents, I have repeatedly heard the phrase: "there will never be a foreclosure in our community." Kumar, a carpenter and tailor, claimed to me that: "We won't let anyone lose their house. If you get hurt or sick or anything, the community will help you." While this promise had not yet been tested to my knowledge, its sentiment is reflected in how community members share rides to reach grocery stores and workplaces. Since many of the employed residents of Lanewood work in cell phone repair shops and textile manufacturers that are located outside of the city where public transportation does not serve, they also set up car share systems in which a driver will take three to four passengers who each give the driver $50 for a month of transportation.

Impersonal Debt Bad, Personal Debt Good

The particular economic arrangements of Nepali-Bhutanese house-buying practices reflect a preference for the balanced reciprocity of the bonding social networks of co-ethnics, and a distrust in accruing debt from the bridging capital of impersonal and external institutions. Such economic practices demonstrate an interesting comparison to other migrant communities that have established alternative debt practices. Maurer (2006) has shown how, like the Nepali-Bhutanese, Muslim migrants in the United States prefer to leave rented housing as soon as possible for purchased homes. Furthermore, they have sought alternative debt arrangements in accordance with cultural practices. However, unlike the Nepali-Bhutanese, Muslim migrants avoid the conventional interest-bearing mortgages that violate the Islamic prohibition on *riba* (interest or usury). Interestingly, however, Maurer notes that many Muslims, particularly of more conservative leanings, prefer the more professional and impersonal types of loans that meet Islamic criteria over ones involving personal relations. Conversely, Nepali-Bhutanese accept the conventional interest-bearing mortgages, but attempt to reduce their dependence on the impersonal and professional distance of the financial institutions. Rather they prefer a greater reliance on friends and family to reduce the extent to which they are dependent on the bank. Thus, instead of debt owed to impersonal outsiders, whether it be the landlord in the form of rent or the bank in the form of insurance and interest, it is the personal debt to kin and close others that this group prefers to purchase houses.

Arun attributed the preference for personal relations of dependence to the group's many years in refugee camps in which they were unable to accumulate capital and property, and thus, forced to depend on the informal networks of cash transactions. While I have no doubt that the restrictions of camp life contributed to and helped shape current practices, I believe that it is also a consequence of a social preference for community-based forms of debt that are socially regulated. As the promise to stop any members from losing houses to foreclosure goes, community members provide economic insurance for each other. As such, personal debt within the community becomes not just expected, but generative of social solidarity (Mauss 1954; Munn 1986). In addition to the contrast with the house buying practices of American Muslims, the emphasis on economic dependence embedded within community social networks differs with the larger ideology of self-sufficiency and economic independence they encounter in the United States. Instead of striving to remove themselves from relations of dependence with the government, family members, or friends—as is recommended by the resettlement agencies, the goal is to remove themselves from the impersonal rent or debt to landlords and banks with whom they have no preexisting relationship.

Exclusionary Limit of Social Networks

While the personal debt relations within the community allow many Nepali-Bhutanese refugees to buy detached houses in the suburbs, it also exposes the limits and exclusiveness of social networks. The sociality referenced above is contingent on a social homogeneity of the Nepali-Bhutanese who are found in the suburbs. With the exception of just one house in Lanewood, all of the families in the two subdivisions are upper-caste Hindus belonging to *Bahun* or *Chhetri* castes. Moreover, the majority of the neighborhoods' families were landowning farmers in Bhutan and English-educated teachers in Nepal. Missing from this group are the diversity of lower-caste groups of historically

Buddhist and Tibeto-Burman language–speaking *Janajati* groups, the Nepali-speaking lower castes, as well as the groups of Christians that one finds in the apartments.

The caste, ethnic, and religious divide demonstrates that it is the networks of land-owning, English-educated, upper-caste Hindus that have tended to produce economic structures that support house ownership, while the networks of other social groups have not. Cheung and Phillimore (2014) have documented how the factors of language competency and pre-migration qualifications and occupations are telling of which refugees can access the bridging or linking social capital to find quality employment. In the Nepali-Bhutanese refugee community, an investigation of group religion reveals such a divide. The question of segregation plays a central role in the neighborhoods' discussions of raising money to build a local temple. On the eighth night of Dashain, one of the most celebrated of Nepali Hindu festivals, many in the two subdivisions gathered at the house of the community *purohit* (priest) for what they called a *samaj puja*—society worship. The goal was to raise money for a future temple in the area. After the worship, conversation turned to who would be included in the religious space. Would it only house Hindu gods, or also include Buddhists and Kirati groups—in what Stadler (2016) has referenced as the "Omkar family" of Himalayan religions? One person spoke for the concern of lower castes from "below"—meaning the apartments of southeastern Fort Worth—"they must also be welcomed."

This discussion raised a stark contrast between the residents of the suburbs and those in the apartments. Although it is clear that the upper-caste Hindus of Lanewood entered the United States with much greater access to social capital and labor opportunities, it is unclear why. The real estate agent Arun claimed that the upper-caste homogeneity of home owners is not a result of discrimination, but merely a consequence of these individuals being processed for resettlement before others, and thus, able to gain access to bank financing faster. But, his explanation begs the question of why were the upper castes processed first? While the temple-building group was willing to consider reaching out to Buddhists, Kirats, lower castes—even to the universalist religious group called Manav Dharma—there was no talk of including Christians. In fact, there exists some resentment among upper-caste Nepali-Bhutanese for the fact that they have not been able to build a temple, while the Christians have established a church. This result, many tell me, is due to the greater support that the Christians receive from "outsiders," meaning American Christians. While US-based Hindu groups, such as *Sewa International*, have contributed to efforts of Hindu Nepali-Bhutanese, this support is not perceived to be of the same level as the Christians. The support of American Christians is beyond the scope of this chapter, but this claim reveals an interesting perception of upper-caste Hindus and social networks. They perceive that the Christians have used religion to form bridging networks with American society which reduces their need to be included in the predominantly Hindu-Omkar group more dependent on bonding networks.

While the Nepali-Bhutanese Christians have established a place of worship before their Hindu compatriots, the former tend to stay more in the apartments, whereas Hindus have bought houses. The different outcomes of the bridging social capital of Christians and bonding social capital of Hindus suggest a counter-example to the prevailing claim that migrants are more likely to succeed if they establish networks with external communities and institutions. As Putnam's famous statement claims: one *gets by* with bonding capital, but *gets ahead* with bridging capital (Lamba and Krahn 2003). But, as the case of Lanewood shows, the dependent networks of bonding relations have helped Hindus establish their own upper-caste enclave in the suburbs. This outcome contrasts with the typical perception of bonding capital as isolating (Morrice 2007, 166). The Lanewood case demonstrates that bonding social capital is not necessarily disadvantageous (Cheung and Phillimore 2014; Bloch 2004) nor necessary just for survival (Gold and Kibria 1993), but can actually be advantageous if linked with an ideology of economic cooperation and solidarity, albeit in exclusive ways.

CONCLUSION

The secondary relocation of Nepali-Bhutanese refugees from urban apartment complexes of the DFW Metroplex to the detached houses of suburban Fort Worth reflects the centrality of social factors in emplacement processes. Although buying a house requires immense material capital for a recently arrived refugee family, it also requires considerable social capital. As demonstrated by Harka's narrative of buying into a neighborhood where no one followed, the agencies' focus on economic independence and self-sufficiency misses a more holistic conception of home and place. The growing Nepali-Bhutanese presence in Lanewood illuminates that the bonding networks of dependence, reciprocity, and obligation are not impediments to home ownership, but rather integral to it. In the case of these two particular subdivisions, however, those networks have been limited to one particular sub-section of the Nepali-Bhutanese refugees in the United States, namely upper-caste Hindus. As the Nepali-Bhutanese enter their second decade of resettlement in the United States, it will be necessary to assess whether the secondary relocation and house-buying patterns become more or less inclusive.

COMMENTARY

Khada Bhandari

I was born in Sallary, Chirang, Bhutan in 1975 and lived there until I moved to Nepal in 1992 due to political persecution by the Bhutanese government against us Nepali speakers. We lived in refugee camps in Nepal for sixteen years until finally being resettled in the United States in 2008. Along with my grandmother, mother, father, wife, daughter, sister, and brother, we settled in the Vickery Meadow area of Dallas. In 2013, we were one of the first families to move to Centex in suburban Fort Worth. Since then, over 120 families have moved into the suburbs of north Fort Worth.

As Andrew Nelson has written, the move to the suburbs means many things for us Nepali-Bhutanese. As refugees in Nepal, we had no value and were seen as the lowest grade of people in the world. Now that the United States has given us status, we want to succeed in America and in adopting the country's lifestyle. Owning a house is part of that success, especially in areas where the schools are better and more job opportunities exist.

Owning a house also represents our integration into American society. It gives us a chance to intermingle with Americans and for our children to learn how to succeed in this country. Our community is new in the United States, so, many people do not know us. But, we are good people who respect all religions and all kinds of people.

Owning a house also brings certain challenges, but we must struggle to succeed in a growing city. If someone is in financial trouble with his or her house or experiences an accident or death in the family, we will help this individual by offering financial contributions and providing other supports. For us, it is important to solve our problems within the community. Since our new houses are outside the city, the older generation, those who do not have a formal education and are without citizenship, can become homebound. We are working to get them citizenship and connect them better with the larger community. But, for the first time since they left Bhutan, they are at least now in their own houses.

NOTES

1. This group is called by many different names. In Bhutan they were known as "Lhotshampa," which meant "Southerner" in the national language of Dzongkha, but most refugees interpret this term as derogatory. Despite their Nepali heritage, they were called "Bhutani" while living in Nepali refugee camps by Nepali nationals. In the United States, some groups prefer to be called "Bhutanese" to emphasize their

unity and difference from other Nepalis in the States, whereas some go by "Nepali-Bhutanese" or "Bhutanese-Nepali" to reflect their multiple nationalities. A few are starting to say "Bhutanese-American" to reference their growing incorporation within the United States.

2. I have assigned the pseudonym of Lanewood to maintain the confidentiality of the neighborhood and research participants.

3. It must be noted that many Nepali-Bhutanese are Buddhist and speak Tibeto-Burman ethnic languages. Nevertheless, the Bhutanese state tended to lump them as one group of Hindus and Nepali-speakers (see Hutt 2005).

4. It is interesting to note that the moves of the Dallas International Rescue Committee (IRC) office reflect the shifts of refugee locations as well as gentrification patterns in Dallas over the past forty years. Originally located in East Dallas, the IRC welcomed Southeast Asian refugees to that part of town in the 1980s and 1990s. When rents started to rise there, the office shifted to the western side of Oak Lawn, which was historically the center of "Little Mexico" and heavily Latino, but now home to some of the trendiest developments in the city. One now sees a similar process in the office's current Vickery Meadow location in which the more expensive developments of the Lower Greenville neighborhood are spreading northward toward Vickery Meadow. I suspect the office's next move will be further north toward I–635 where the most recent refugees are being placed.

5. IOM, or International Office of Migration, manages the travel and resettlement processes for refugees, but the loan is issued by the government of the accepting country.

6. In 2008, as Jethi and her husband were considering leaving Bhutan for Nepal in an attempt to resettle with her parents to the United States, the husband was sentenced to fifteen years in prison for "assisting an anti-national," which meant he gave shelter to a Nepali-Bhutanese who had entered Bhutan without authorization.

7. The male-specific designation of house ownership is partially reflective of virilocal marriage practices in Nepali society in which daughters will move into their husbands' houses, but also a consequence of patriarchal property laws. Although the state of Nepal has recently changed inheritance laws to encourage female ownership of land, inheritance remains heavily gendered in favor of male ownership (see Kunreuther 2009).

8. See Fisher (2001, 90–104) for further discussion of rotating credit associations in Nepal. Specifically, Fisher addresses the Thakali ethnic group's rotating credit system of *dhikur*, which he describes as both economic and social for how it serves mutual assistance and community harmony, and is understood to be less impersonal than banks.

REFERENCES CITED

Appadurai, Arjun. 1995. "The Production of Locality." In *Counterworks: Managing the Diversity of Knowledge,* edited by Richard Fardon, 204–225. London: Routledge.

Bloch, Alice. 2004. "Labour Market Participation and Conditions of Employment: A Comparison of Minority Ethnic Groups and Refugees in Britain." *Sociological Research Online* 9 (2): 1–19.

Brun, Cathrine and Anita Fábos. 2015. "Making Homes in Limbo? A Conceptual Framework." *Refuge* 31 (1): 5–19.

Cheung, Sin Yi and Jenny Phillimore. 2014. "Refugees, Social Capital, and Labour Market Integration in the UK." *Sociology* 48 (3): 518–536.

Ferguson, James. 2013. "Declarations of Dependence: Labour, personhood, and welfare in Southern Africa." *Journal of the Royal Anthropological Institute* 19: 223–242.

Fisher, William. 2001. *Fluid Boundaries: Forming and Transforming Identity in Nepal*. New York: Columbia University Press.

Gielis, Ruben. 2009. "A Global Sense of Migrant Places: Towards a Place Perspective in the Study of Migrant Transnationalism." *Global Networks* 9 (2): 271–287.

Gold, Steve and Nazli Kibria. 1993. "Vietnamese Refugees and Blocked Mobility." *Asian and Pacific Migration Journal* 2 (1): 27–56.

Hammond, Laura. 2004. *This Place Will Become Home: Refugee Repatriation to Ethiopia*. Ithaca and London: Cornell University Press.

Hutt, Michael. 2005. *Unbecoming Citizens: Culture, Nationhood, and the Flight of Refugees from Bhutan*. New Delhi: Oxford University Press.

Keles, Fethi. 2008. "The Structural Negligence of US Refugee Resettlement Policy." *Anthropology News* 49 (5): 6.

Korac, Maja. 2009. *Remaking Home: Reconstructing Life, Place and Identity in Rome and Amsterdam*. New York and Oxford: Berghahn Books.

Kunreuther, Laura. 2009. "Between Love and Property: Voice, Subject, and Subjectivity in the Reform of Daughter's Inheritance in Nepal." *American Ethnologist* 36 (3): 545–562.

Lamba, Navjot and Harvey Krahn. 2003. "Social Capital and Refugee Resettlement: The Social Networks of Refugees in Canada." *Journal of International Migration and Integration* 4 (3): 335–360.

Lems, Annika. 2014. "Placing Displacement: Place-Making in a World of Movement." *Ethnos* 81: 1–23.

Malkki, Liisa. 1992. "National Geographic: The Rooting of Peoples and the Territorialization of National Identity among Scholars and Refugees." *Cultural Anthropology* 7 (1): 24–44.

———. 1995. "Refugees and Exile: From 'Refugee Studies' to the National Order of Things." *Annual Review of Anthropology* 24: 495–523.

Massey, Doreen. 1994. *Space, Place and Gender. Minneapolis: University of Minnesota Press.*

Maurer, Bill. 2006. *Pious Property: Islamic Mortgages in the United States*. New York: Russell Sage Foundation.

Mauss, Marcel. 1990 [1954]. *The Gift: The Form and Reason for Exchange in Archaic Societies*. London: Routledge.

Morrice, Linda. 2007. "Lifelong Learning and the Social Integration of Refugees in the UK: the Significance of Social Capital." *International Journal of Lifelong Learning* 26 (2): 155–172.

Munn, Nancy. 1986. *The Fame of Gawa: A Symbolic Study of Value Transformation in Massim (Papua New Guinea) Society*. Cambridge, UK: Cambridge University Press.

Parajuly, Prajwal. 2013. "No Land is Her Land." In *The Gurkha's Daughter,* edited by Prajwal Parajuly. New York and London: Quercus.

Perin, Constance. 1977. *Everything in its Place: Social Order and Land Use in America*. Princeton.: Princeton University Press.

Simich, Laura. 2003. "Negotiating Boundaries of Refugee Resettlement: A Study of Settlement Patterns and Social Support." *Canadian Review of Sociology* 4 (5): 575–591.

Smith, Ei Phyu. 2016. "To Build a Home: the Material Cultural Practices of Karen Refugees across Borders." *Area* 48 (3): 278–284.

Stadler, Joseph. 2016. "Review of 'Buffalo Conference.'" *Himalaya* 35 (2): 165–167.

Subedi, Bhim Prasad. 1999. "An Anthropo-Geographic Approach to Territorial Mobility: Examples from inside a Rural Nepali Community." In *Anthropology and Sociology of Nepal: Cultures, Societies, Ecology and Development,* edited by Ram Chhetri and Om Gurung, 122–150. Kathmandu: Sociological and Anthropological Society of Nepal.

Chapter 11

Refugee Resettlements Divergent Outcomes

The Role of the Social Network in Housing Type and Location

Audrey Lumley-Sapanski, with commentary by Dave Thatcher

It is well established that social networks impact the adaptation pathways of refugees and immigrants (Beaman 2012; Cheung and Phillimore 2013, 2014; Edin et al. 2003; Gold and Kibria 1993; Lamba and Krahn 2003; Simich 2003; Yu et al. 2007; Zhou 1992); however, there are several competing hypotheses concerning how. Research has primarily focused on understanding whether immigrant participation in or use of social networks affects the speed of adaptation as measured by language acquisition, employment, or residential attainment. Findings exist that support both the speeding up and slowing down hypotheses, suggesting that use of social networks may work differently depending on the socioeconomic and demographic characteristics, as well as length of residence of the populations in question (Beaman 2012; Edin et al. 2003; Kibria 1994; Logan, Zhang, and Alba 2002; Lamba and Krahn 2003; Yu et al. 2007; Zhou 1992).

The purpose of this chapter is to explore how the use of social networks affects one measurement of adaptation—housing quality. Relying on eight years of work in the field of refugee resettlement combined with semi-structured interviews conducted during 2013–2014, this chapter examines the residential type and location of refugee groups resettled between 2008 and 2012. My research indicates that while refugees who are resettled within Chicago receive fairly similar services, there are startlingly different long-term socioeconomic and residential outcomes. This is particularly true for the Burmese and Iraqi populations, the two largest groups resettled during the study period. In general, Iraqis have moved into improved housing and often relocate outside the city limits. Meanwhile, the Burmese remain in agency-located housing and employment on Chicago's Northside. Iraqi housing quality improved post-resettlement while Burmese housing quality stagnated or declined. These differences can be explained in part by differences in human capital, as well as access to financial resources, but there are also differences in how ethnic groups engage with their respective ethnic communities. Specifically, Iraqis expressed a disinclination to use ethnic social networks while the Burmese relied on ethnic ties for support related to housing, family, and employment needs. This difference contributed to the observed housing quality variation between the two populations. Socioeconomic status clearly plays a role in differentiating these two groups; however, it is clear that the use of social networks contributes to long-term outcomes particularly in the form of housing location and type.

SOCIAL NETWORKS, REFUGEE HOUSING, AND ADAPTATION

Both housing quality and social network participation have been connected directly to adaptation outcomes for immigrant and refugee households. However, most research treats social networks and housing attainment as separate mechanisms shaping immigrant outcomes. In contrast, I examine housing as a measure of adaptation given the use of social networks and socioeconomic attributes. Further, I identify the reciprocal effects of social networks on housing and vice versa, demonstrating that these two mechanisms are strongly linked in shaping one another.

Previous research has shown social networks can both hinder and speed up the adaptation process for refugees in a new country (Beaman 2011, 2012; Cheung and Phillimore 2013, 2014; Lamba and Krahn 2003). The rate of adaptation is affected by the individual attributes of the social network members. Participation in social networks with good labor market information and members who have been in the host country for longer periods of time may speed up the rate of adaptation of new members, increasing employment rate and earnings (Beaman, 2011; Correa-Velez et al. 2013; Edin et al. 2003; Lamba 2003; Mamgain and Collins 2003). For those social networks whose members have been in country for less time, social networks have the opposite effect, decreasing labor market participation and acquisition of host country skills like language (Beaman 2011). The impact of social network participation on adaptation has as much to do with the individual skills of the participants and length of residency as it does existence and use of a social network.

A smaller body of research has explored the relationship of refugee housing quality to adaptation. Carter and Osbourne (2009) demonstrate that adequate housing is the primary need in positive adaptation; refugees housed in an urban area experiencing decline made adaptation more difficult. Darboe (2003) and Shio's (2003) research suggests that housing refugees in highly concentrated pockets may lead to ethnic clusters and present challenges to long-term integration. Francis and Hiebert (2013) link housing to integration outcomes demonstrating that refugees in adequate housing were healthier, better able to find and maintain work, pursue education, and engage with their communities. Conversely, those poorly housed experienced difficulties locating work, experienced more stress and had a longer integration period overall. Though limited in scope, available research indicates a strong relationship between housing quality and adaptation measures.

While the use of social networks and housing conditions each affect immigrant adaptation outcomes, scholarship has identified an independent bidirectional relationship between the use of social networks and housing location. The presence of co-ethnics in close proximity encourages use of social networks and can work against mobility, encouraging clustering. The location of the cluster dictates the type of housing available to members as well as its location (Cutler, Glaeser, and Vigdor 2008; Logan, Zhang, and Alba 2002; Zhou 1992). This in turn affects the growth of the social network; the presence of co-ethnics often leads to further clustering and expansion of the social network (Massey 1990; Simich 2003).

RESEARCH SITE, PARTICIPANT SELECTION, AND METHODOLOGY

Research for this chapter was conducted in the city of Chicago. Chicago has a long history as a resettlement site; historically, it is the third largest metropolitan resettlement site after New York and Los Angeles (Singer and Wilson 2006). I worked for eight years at Heartland Alliance in Chicago as a case worker, employment specialist, and program director. In this role, I served hundreds of refugees, many of whom were interviewed for this chapter.

Heartland Alliance provided data for this study and its staff referred participants. Heartland is responsible for the resettlement of between 150 and 500 refugees per year, about one-third to one-quarter of the approximately 2,000 refugees who come to Chicago annually. Over the last ten years, Heartland has resettled predominately Iraqi, Burmese, and Bhutanese refugees with fewer refugees and asylees receiving services who arrived from the Horn of Africa, Latin America, the Middle East, and other parts of Asia. The populations Heartland resettles are generally reflective of the groups resettled to the Chicago area and nationally.

Heartland Alliance provided anonymized housing records for all refugees resettled during the study period. The data file contained the initial, agency provided name-redacted addresses of all refugees (725 individuals) resettled between 2008 and 2012 as well as basic demographic and arrival data (race, ethnicity, date of arrival, language). I geocoded this information to determine where these households were initially housed and where they chose to move later. I used American Community Survey Five Year Data to build a picture of the neighborhood context. I compared the first and final neighborhoods of residence compositionally, focusing on socioeconomic and demographic differences. I also explored the spatial distribution of ethno-cultural groups over time comparing differences in trajectory by country of origin, time of arrival, and original neighborhood.

Through Heartland I arranged for interviews with refugees and asylees. I conducted sixty-two semi-structured interviews with refugees and asylees who received services at Heartland. I also interviewed fifty-five stakeholders who I identified through my previous role as an employee of the agency. These individuals provided services to or worked with refugees resettled during the period (i.e., landlords, caseworkers, government employees, and employers). Snowball sampling (i.e., referrals by interviewees) enlarged my interview pool. I met with refugees in their homes or in public places as they preferred. Interviews ranged from between 15 minutes and six hours, on average lasting an hour. I recorded and transcribed interviews with permission of the participants.

Although I interviewed refugees from eleven nation-states, I interviewed the most refugees from Burma and Iraq, the largest two groups resettled in Chicago over the last ten years. The group of Burmese refugees I interviewed included individuals from the Karen, Karenni, and Chin ethnic groups.[1] The Iraqi refugees I interviewed were predominately Arabic-speaking[2] and Assyrian refugees, but also included Catholics and Chaldeans. I focus here on findings from thirteen interviews with Arabic-speaking Iraqis and twelve with Karen Burmese as they were the primary interview participants.

HOUSING: PARAMETERS, CONSTRAINTS, AND APPROACH

Refugees resettled to Chicago are secured housing by the refugee resettlement agency prior to arrival.[3] Agencies find an apartment within the City of Chicago and sign a lease on behalf of the arriving refugee. The agency pays the majority of the rent for ninety days at which point refugees become responsible for paying their own rent.

Locating housing for refugees prior to their arrival is a difficult endeavor. Resettlement agency workers must find housing on short notice (typically, ten days to one month prior to a refugee's arrival). Within this time constraint, case managers must find housing that refugees will be able to afford on a single minimum wage salary, and, that is accessible to cultural amenities, public transit, the refugee resettlement agency, and, if possible, family or community members willing to assist in the resettlement process. These constraints limit the possible location of housing to just a few neighborhoods within the city.

The lack of refugee documentation makes the process of housing location more difficult. Refugees lack background information and documentation typically used to establish suitability for renting an apartment. Landlords must agree to lease to a new family without social security numbers or American references. Perhaps most significantly, refugees are unemployed at arrival with no guarantee of employability. Landlords must trust that the agency will find work for the refugee so that they are able to pay rent.

In order to ensure that case workers can find housing that meets these criteria, refugee resettlement workers rely on established relationships with brokers and landlords. These landlords understand the resettlement system and are (more) willing to take the risks associated with housing unemployed refugees with limited employment prospects. Importantly, these landlords also own or manage multiple units. This saves agency case workers time and money while guaranteeing a unit is available. Rather than form new relationships each time an apartment is needed, the case worker can reach out to a partner with a ready, available unit. In exchange, landlords are guaranteed demand.

Initial Housing Location

The parameters facing case managers responsible for finding housing contribute to a tendency to cluster refugees in a relatively small area in the Northeast quadrant of Chicago. Refugees who arrived during the study period were overwhelmingly provided housing in the neighborhoods of Edgewater, Rogers Park, and West Ridge (or West Rogers Park). Of all refugees 70.9 percent were provided housing in one of these contiguous community areas. An additional ten percent of resettled refugees were provided housing in Uptown and Lincoln Square. Rogers Park was by far the most common site of resettlement, accounting for 39 percent of all homes provided to refugees.

Social Ties and Housing after Initial Placement

Though the resettlement agency typically signs a yearlong lease on behalf of the refugee, refugees may choose to stay in agency-provided units or to relocate at any time. As refugees move into self-selected housing, differences in preferences for housing type and proximity to peers begin to emerge between ethno-cultural groups. Refugees arriving with strong social ties have a tendency to rely on one another for assistance, increasing their proximity to one another residentially and through employment. Refugee groups without strong social ties within Chicago demonstrate the opposite effect—out-migrating to other cities, or scattering apart.

These differences in residential behavior are partially explained by pre-arrival conditions. The Karen Burmese, for example, arrive in Chicago with large, complex social networks established over a long period of time in refugee camps. These social networks are the basis for their post-resettlement community once they arrive in Chicago. Conversely, urban refugees—those who fled their homes not to a camp but to another city and arrive in singular family units like first-wave Iraqis—are more likely to lack these strong ties. Findings suggest that within the first five years, post-resettlement Iraqis distribute widely, predominately throughout the suburbs. These moves are made possible by socioeconomic resources that the Iraqi community possessed at entry that the Karen Burmese community in general lack.

The Iraqi Experience

The Iraqis who spoke to me for interviews were the first in a wave of Iraqis who began arriving in 2008. This group was distinct from other refugee groups arriving concurrently for a number of reasons. Iraqis resettled in this wave differed in family structure, level of education, work experience, and access to human and financial capital. Specifically, most Iraqis entered with some financial assets, which gave them more flexibility in choosing housing. Further, Iraqis believed their educational credentials and previous professional work experience promised greater future earnings. Thus, choosing more expensive housing was perceived as less risky. These differences help explain why Iraqi refugees were able to act on a desire to move from apartments within Chicago into single-family homes in the suburbs.

This wave of Iraqis also differed from other interviewees in their use of and engagement with their ethnic community. Individuals within the community had fewer social ties within Chicago than other groups because of the nature of Iraqi resettlement, and, the community lacked social cohesion overall. In general, proximity to peers was not a stated rationale for housing location. At times interviewees expressed outright animosity toward one another. Without the desire for a co-ethnic support network or the promise of shared resources an enclave offers, there was little incentive to cluster residentially. Iraqis chose dispersed housing instead based on lifestyle preferences over community proximity.

The group of Iraqis resettled during the study period (2008–2012) were members of the professional class in Iraq and had lifestyles commensurate with their positions and income. This wave of Iraqis was composed of academics, engineers, and physicians, as well as entrepreneurs and translators. Only three had not completed their postsecondary degrees; they had been in the process of finishing when they were forced to relocate, all other Arabic-speaking Iraqis had postsecondary degrees. Iraqi families were resettled directly from major urban centers—Amman, Jordan and Damascus, Syria—rather than camps. There they lived in self-located housing and many of the adults had continued to work professionally albeit illegally or with restrictions. Each family had owned property (a home) in Baghdad and most still did.

In the five years after arrival, this group of Iraqi families moved from the initial resettlement site on the Northside of Chicago, where they were provided apartments, to the suburbs. I interviewed thirteen non-Assyrian Iraqi family groups in 2014. Only five of these families remained in Chicago. Of the others, five families were in the suburbs of Skokie and Evanston, which border Chicago. The other three were in distant suburbs of Hainesville, Joliet, and Niles, which are approximately forty-five minutes from Chicago by car. These families had moved from their initial agency-provided housing and neighborhoods; the mean distance between their first apartments and their current apartments for all thirteen families was 10.34 miles. Several had moved even farther, the longest distance a family had moved was 45.9 miles. The overall trend was to move away from the city and into less dense, more homogenous suburban landscapes. Many had the resources to move into single-family houses or townhouses in the suburbs. Four families now lived in standalone homes, five in townhomes or condos, and four in apartments.

One explanation Iraqis offered for their move to the suburbs was the desire for single-family homes, which they saw as symbolic of a return to their previous lifestyle. Interviewees expressed a strong preference for single-family homes and had negative associations with apartments. Prior to arrival, these interviewees had lived in houses that they had owned. Rarely had any of the Iraqi families previously lived in an apartment, even during displacement. The trajectory of interviewed Iraqis was to live in ones' childhood home with ones' parents until marriage, at which point young couples moved into new houses. Interviewees reported that after receiving citizenship, Iraqi families were selling their Baghdad homes and purchasing homes in the U.S.

In addition to the desire for a particular lifestyle, early arriving Iraqis lacked strong ties to keep them in the city. Only three had family members in Chicago when they arrived, none of the others possessed a family sponsor. Five Iraqi interviewees still had no family members in Chicago at the time of interviews five years later. Their ethnic social networks were restricted to the members of their nuclear family units with whom they had arrived.

One explanation for the lack of strong ties within the Iraqi community is the social conditions of displacement. This wave of Iraqis did not live with or necessarily near their fellow Iraqi refugees in Jordan or Syria, as they would have done in refugee camps. Instead, they lived in housing in large urban centers that they self-selected and were financially responsible for. This engendered more self-reliance than community dependency observed in refugees arriving in later waves and from camps.

Beyond lacking connection to one another, many interviewees expressed a lack of trust, antipathy, and negative feelings for their Iraqi peers. Many Iraqis expressed this as a result of the sectarian violence, which occurred in the years preceding their departure from Iraq. Iraqis did not arrive as one community; they arrived as a fractured community and a product of their previous experiences. As explained by an Iraqi mother and social worker:

> Unfortunately, because there was sectarian plan [violence in Iraq], when they [Iraqis] come here they have these fears. They don't interact with each other because what happened in Iraq. I saw an Assyrian woman, I asked her how she was doing in her ESL class and she said: "We are not going." I said: "Why you are not going to ESL classes?" And she said that because at the centers in this area, there are now many communities coming from Iraq, different from them and they don't want to be together. They said: "We flew Iraq for this reason, we can't be with them." Unfortunately. So they left.

Others did not necessarily feel fear or antipathy for their fellow Iraqis, but they felt intentional separation fostered integration. Many interviewees wanted to integrate and felt Iraqis should be intentionally separated to accomplish this. For these reasons, some Iraqis had moved away from the resettlement community in Chicago. Said one interviewee:

> Spread them. They need to learn how deal with the rules here. How to live, how to shop, how to take the train. If you separate a person and they want to visit their neighbor, that person has to take this bus or this train or drive here or do this. They have to learn what to do. If you put them all together, they are not going to learn English, learn how to shop, learn how to take the train and they need that.

Another woman reiterated the need to "learn the rules," emphasizing that moving people away from one another helps to ensure new families receive good information: "[separate them] they will learn the rules, they will learn from somebody that is right. If they're all Iraqi then if somebody makes a mistake, they will all make the mistake. Don't listen to other people, other Iraqis. It is better to isolate yourself from this." These comments underscore a commonly vocalized desire to integrate beyond the ethnic community and into the larger community. This manifested itself socially and physically in terms of residential locus. People spread to other communities within the city and moved to the suburbs.

Overall, Iraqis lacked many strong ties within their community and lacked a desire to form new ties within their refugee community. The lack of extended family or social networks generally freed them from obligations and left the benefits of social ties unrealized. After their agency-arranged leases expired, most of the families moved quite far from where they were initially resettled. The housing quality improved. New neighborhoods were perceived as quieter with more space, access to open space, and increased safety. These new locations returned them to a standard of living they preferred. The lack of strong social ties allowed their individual socioeconomic characteristics and individual preferences to dominate in making decisions about where to live. As one interviewee said: "They're not into reunification, becoming a community. . . . They expanded and everybody went their separate ways."

The Burmese Experience

The Burmese resettlement experiences within Chicago varied greatly from that of the Iraqis both spatially, by housing quality and type, and in the use of community networks. The Karen I interviewed remained in neighborhoods where resettlement agencies initially provided housing. Those who had moved had moved into buildings that contained kin or co-ethnic peers. Interviews indicated that the Burmese chose to cluster together, unlike the Iraqis. This was in part because of a stated reliance on and need for support from co-ethnic peers. It was also because the Karen arrived with fewer economic resources and less transferrable human capital. As a result, the Burmese were more restricted in where they could afford to live.

The Burmese interviewed for this project were in the first waves of Burmese refugees to come to Chicago; however, unlike the Iraqis, they tended to be members of larger family units. All but one family had a sibling or parent in Chicago and many had more; most of the interviewees joined other members of their family units when they were resettled. One interviewee was related to four other households in the city, two others were related to three households, and the remainder had at least one or two other households containing relatives in the city. Unlike the Iraqis, the Burmese had familial anchors—family members previously resettled—who assisted in their resettlement.

Not only did the Burmese tend to have family in Chicago, they chose to live with or near to one another often sponsoring or housing relatives. According to agency records, approximately 20 percent of Burmese families were resettled by the agency into just one census tract; the majority of them were split between just two streets. This formed an inadvertent cluster that was exaggerated by the tendency of the Burmese to cohabitate in the period after arrival. Of those larger families interviewed, seven of nine had lived in the same apartment with extended family members. All but three families reported living in the same building as other families of their same ethnicity. Two families reported living in the same building or complex with over five families of their same ethnicity. This contributed to the formation of a small ethnic enclave.

This Karen enclave was located within the same general area that housing was provided by the agency. Two families—sisters with their husbands and children—had moved outside the city, but all other Karen I spoke with were still in Chicago's Northeast quadrant. The average distance between their initial apartment and their apartment at the time of the interview was only 0.77 miles. Of the factors which motivated housing location decisions, the Karen showed a preference for living near to peers above others (like location, size, or quality).

Interviewees chose to live together for support from people who had had similar life experiences. A single mother who moved into a building with other Karen families described the importance of living within this community: "I think it is better for me because sometimes if you need help, sometimes the people are from my country, if you're out of socks you can borrow them. It's a community. Yeah, I like that." Further, they needed the support of people who spoke their language and came from a similar background. It validated advice given when they first arrived. One young woman said:

> We're new to the country and a lot of people who come to this country come as adults. . . . It is very difficult for a lot of the people to adapt, as compared to kids. One of the ways they stay connected is to bond . . . [they can] depend on and to ask for help from people with the same background. They will not be able to ask for help from people who have no idea where they're from. The connection is stronger. I think it is because of the experience, what they've gone through . . . especially if they're from the same area, speak the same languages. We tend to stay close.

Interviewees mentioned using their ethnic group peers for help with transportation, childcare, finding work, going to church, translating paperwork, and reading the mail. Proximity mattered because for ongoing daily needs as well as bigger requests, like childcare. No one suggested dispersion to help with adaptation; rather, most Karen Burmese felt clustering families would help them adapt more quickly.

The resettled Karen Burmese refugees had strong social networks they had established in refugee camps prior to arrival and imported to Chicago. This fostered community inter-reliance. The majority of those refugees interviewed from Burma were Karen refugees who arrived via camps in Thailand. Most had lived in refugee camps on the Thai-Burma border for 20–30 years. Karen Burmese resettled to Chicago came from the two or three same camps. Thus, in addition to their family members, many arrived with larger social networks. One single mother described her experience: "In my building, I know friends from the same camp. Then some, not the same camp but they're from refugee camps, in the building. Not just one family, I think 1, 2, 3, 4, 5, 6 . . . Yeah. All Karen. My sister lives in the building and my brother lives in the building. If I need someone to watch my kid, my sister-in-law, my brother's wife would do it."

The Burmese tendency to stay in these neighborhoods is largely because of familial support, but interviewees also lacked the financial assets or human capital that would allow them to move elsewhere. Of those interviewed, only two individuals had any secondary education, which limited their employment opportunities. These two received their education after arriving to Chicago. Interviewees also arrived lacking basic spoken English language or literacy skills. Additionally, most interviewees arrived with work experience in a limited number of fields—primarily agriculture. The lack of English and their non-transferrable labor experience limited the work opportunities available to them.

The Burmese who moved to Chicago between 2008 and 2012 were housed in Northside neighborhoods, where they remain as of writing. The lack of financial assets meant that the support of the institutions and individuals from their communities was doubly important. Interviewees expressed the same dissatisfaction with housing as Iraqis; the presence of bedbugs, poor relationships with landlords, and feelings of lack of safety. However, these factors did not precipitate moves elsewhere because the interviewees had supports to help them navigate their day-to-day lives. Further, they had strong initial ties within their ethnic communities, which they built on.

POLICY RECOMMENDATIONS REGARDING HOUSING QUALITY

Both the Iraqis and Burmese believe housing quality could be improved. There are two ways federal governmental policy could improve this. The first is on the supply side. If the government could guarantee arrival dates and numbers further in advance, agencies would have more time to secure housing. This would improve the available stock of housing and the number of available units. As it is now, refugees arrive over the course of the year, but the majority come in September in a rush at the end of the federal fiscal year. If this were more predictable, it would make availability and quality of housing better. The second is on the demand side. Landlords willing to rent to refugees are few and far between, in part, because refugees lack standard identity documentation and some lack financial resources. Most landlords simply turn away refugees given they lack social security numbers. If the federal government was able to educate landlords, either through formal communication or some form of training, it might increase the willingness of landlords to engage with resettlement agencies. If it were the government, rather than resettlement workers, that assured the extensive background checks of refugees, it could improve the number of landlords willing to rent to refugees. Further, were agencies able to assume the financial risk on behalf of the landlord and refugees—for instance, guaranteed rent—it would greatly open doors.

POLICY RECOMMENDATIONS REGARDING USE OF SOCIAL NETWORKS

Refugees exhibit different strategies for utilizing their social networks. Resettlement agencies could improve refugee satisfaction with the resettlement process and adaptation outcomes if the use of social networks was considered explicitly in assigning housing. Since particular groups, like the Karen Burmese, rely on their co-ethnic peers for support with adaptation, it makes sense to intentionally house these groups together or near to one another. However, it is difficult to alter distribution patterns of refugees consciously and doing so could be a violation of federal housing law. Thus, despite tendencies of groups to behave in certain ways it is not as easy to recommend policy that would affect distribution at the city level.

One possible alternative suggestion is to consider trends in preferences for housing type by group that would allow refugees to actualize their preferences for engaging with their social networks. Those country of origin groups typified by large extended familial or social networks, like the Karen Burmese, tend to cohabitate and could be provided housing in apartment buildings with larger apartment sizes or rented homes in which multiple family units could cohabitate. Those groups, like Iraqis, who prefer standalone housing in the suburbs could be assigned housing there with the caveat that that housing be affordable and public transit be accessible. Resettlement agencies would need to expand their available housing types consciously to reflect the array of housing types groups preferred. Currently, all groups are provided similar housing which is contributing to relocation post resettlement and further disrupting adaptation.

CONCLUSION

The Iraqis and Burmese use their communities in very different ways. The Iraqis did not necessarily identify with fellow countrymen, and lacked social ties to bind them together. They saw continued reliance on the enclave as a barrier to integration and adaptation. Even for those that remained housed near to other Iraqis, the desire to utilize these connections for assistance was minimal, particularly after the initial resettlement. The Burmese saw continued residence in the enclave as beneficial to adaptation. They had peers to rely on for assistance with daily tasks and help them interpret their new surroundings. These mind-sets concerning their social networks combined with different entering financial situations contributed to the distinct differences in housing type and location by country of origin. Though the time period since arrival is relatively short, between 4 and 8 years, it suggests that the Burmese are staying in agency-provided housing and moved closer to one another. They are building on a network of familial and peer support that they formed prior to arrival, which forms the foundation for the community and community institutions here. The Iraqi population, conversely, shows a return to their previous lifestyle. Rather than cluster together with their same ethnic group peers, they have moved from the city, distributing themselves in suburbs. They live in single-family houses or townhomes with only members of their nuclear family.

These two refugee group experiences offer insight for case workers and policy makers who design housing strategies for refugees. Neighborhood selection for Burmese refugees is significant because it is more likely to be long term and should be considered as such. Consequently, factors such as housing quality, school quality, and amenities are also important in resettling groups that are more immobile or show a preference to form an enclave. Education levels, English proficiency, financial resources, preexisting refugee social networks, and pre-resettlement conditions (i.e., urban resettlement vs. camps), can all be used to some extent in determining the relative permanency of initial resettlement locations.

Conversely, knowing that the Iraqis are less likely to stay in the initial housing provided by resettlement agencies for long, it might be advisable to develop an alternative housing strategy. One idea floated during interviews included the option of the master lease. If agencies were to sign the master lease for buildings, or alternatively were able to purchase buildings, they could provide temporary housing for refugees who were more likely to move out. This would also protect landlords from refugees who vacate apartments on short notice.

COMMENTARY

Dave Thatcher

Having worked in refugee resettlement now, both directly and indirectly for the past ten years, I have experienced firsthand the contrasting adaptation pathways different refugee populations use to integrate and adapt to their new homes in the United States. I have seen similar trends in both Chicago where I first started working as an Employment Specialist and later in Denver where I worked on supplemental social programming for new refugees.

I strongly agree with Lumley-Sapanski's findings in the difference between Iraqi and Burmese refugee populations in terms of how they value and use social networks for integration and in how they prioritize housing choices. Additionally, I saw this impact their employment trajectories.

I found that the Burmese often replicated clustering in employment placement leveraging their close-knit community and familial relations. As Lumley-Sapanski effectively pointed out, due to lower levels of human and financial capital and the limited scope of their work experience in the refugee camps, employment opportunities were restricted in the United States. We tended to place Burmese in entry-level manual labor positions with a heavy concentration in the meat-packing industry as well as cleaning positions at the airport.

Placement for the Burmese often happened in large-scale hiring events where employers would hire anywhere from five to ten Burmese at a time. Collective placement of Burmese meant they would commute to work in groups. At times the community would pool money together to purchase vans or other vehicles to facilitate transportation. Also, those individuals in the group with greater English language skills would often become advocates for the other workers. Employers who hired groups of Burmese would often promote those individuals with higher English fluency to supervisor positions where they help act as translators and interlocutors with non-Burmese management. The use of social networks and community resources to help facilitate employment integration and sustainability in turn created further incentives for Burmese to stay in cultural enclaves.

In contrast employment strategies for Iraqis were much different. We worked with Iraqis on a more individual basis. We saw them less frequently than the Burmese in terms of employment interaction. Due to higher levels of financial resources and English fluency than the Burmese, Iraqis bought cars with greater frequency and much sooner than many of the Burmese. This gave them greater mobility, independence, and led to an ability to seek out employment opportunities on their own. Additionally, due to higher education levels and a greater diversity in employment backgrounds Iraqis often came to the United States with more transferable work skills and resources like resumes and interview skills.

For the Iraqis, we saw a greater number of out-migrations from their initial resettlement housing and, as Lumley-Sapanski's findings suggest, often to the suburbs. We had a harder time convincing Iraqis to take entry-level manual-level positions, which sometimes meant longer placement times for initial employment for Iraqis as compared to the Burmese. This again was possible for many of the Iraqis due to financial resources brought with them to the United States. Overall Iraqis tended to prioritize independence over community resourcing, which translated into less time spent at the resettlement agency in comparison with the Burmese. Iraqis also tended to experience higher rates of job mobility such as more frequent raises and promotions. This in turn helped to facilitate moves to neighborhoods they found more desirable and as Lumley-Sapanski demonstrates, aligns more closely with their housing experiences in Iraq.

Housing plays a huge impact on refugee's ability to both obtain and maintain employment. For the Burmese housing located close to public transportation and other community members is critical to making it through the first ninety days of employment at any new job. For the Iraqis, this is not necessarily the case. Our Iraqi clients often found initial resettlement housing to be inadequate to their standards, which often created stressors that would impede the initial employment search.

NOTES

1. I chose to use the name Burma throughout as the refugees I worked with refer to their former home country as Burma. The name was officially changed to Myanmar by the ruling military junta in 1989 following the violent repression of widespread democratic protests in 1988. Many refugees chose not to recognize the name Myanmar.
2. I use Arab speaking to denote non-Christian and non-Assyrian refugees for lack of a better term. This group was predominately Muslim, and mostly comprised of Baghdadis.
3. Refugees are occasionally provided housing with a family member or peer in which case the agency does not assist in locating housing. This occurs rarely.

REFERENCES CITED

Beaman, Lucy. 2012. "Social Networks and the Dynamics of Labour Market Outcomes: Evidence from Refugees Resettled in the U.S." *The Review of Economic Studies* 79 (1): 128–161.

Borjas, George. 1998. "To Ghetto or Not to Ghetto: Ethnicity and Residential Segregation." *Journal of Urban Economics* 44 (2): 228–253.

Carter, Thomas and John Osborne. 2009. "Housing and Neighbourhood Challenges of Refugee Resettlement in 'lining Inner City Neighbourhoods: A Winnipeg Case Study." *Journal of Immigrant and Refugee Studies* 7 (3): 308–327.

Cheung, Sin Yi and Jenny Phillimore. 2013. *Social Networks, Social Capital and Refugee Integration*. Research Report. Retrieved from http://www.birmingham.ac.

uk/Documents/college-social-sciences/social-policy/iris/2013/nuffield-refugees-integration-research-report.pdf.

———. 2014. "Refugees, Social Capital, and Labour Market Integration in the UK." *Sociology* 48 (3): 518–536.

Correa-Velez, Ignacio, Adrian Barnett, and Sandra Gifford. 2015. "Working for a Better Life: Longitudinal Evidence on the Predictors of Employment Among Recently Arrived Refugee Migrant Men Living in Australia." *International Migration* 53 (2): 321–337.

Cutler, David, Edward Glaeser, and Jacob Vigdor. 2008. "When are ghettos bad? Lessons from Immigrant Segregation in the United States." *Journal of Urban Economics* 63 (3): 759–774.

Darboe, Kebba. 2003. "New Immigrants in Minnesota: The Somali Immigration and Assimilation." *Journal of Developing Societies* 19 (4): 458–472.

Edin, Per-Anders, Peter Fredriksson, and Olof Åslund. 2003. "Ethnic Enclaves and the Economic Success of Immigrants-Evidence from a Natural Experiment." *The Quarterly Journal of Economics* 118 (1): 329–357.

Francis, Jenny and Daniel Hiebert. 2014. "Shaky Foundations: Refugees in Vancouver's Housing Market." *The Canadian Geographer / Le Géographe Canadien* 58 (1): 63–78.

Gold, Steve and Nazli Kibria. 1993. "Vietnamese Refugees and Blocked Mobility." *Asian and Pacific Migration Journal* 2 (1): 27–56.

Hagström, Mirjam. 2009. "Winners and Losers? The Outcome of the Dispersal Policy in Sweden." In *Resettled and Included? The Employment Integration of Resettled Refugees in Sweden,* edited by Bevelander, Peter, Mirjam Hagström, and Sofia Rönnqvist, 159–190. Malmö: Malmö University.

Kibria, Nazli. 1994. "Household Structure and Family Ideologies: The Dynamics of Immigrant Economic Adaptation among Vietnamese Refugees." *Social Problems* 41 (1): 81–96.

Lamba, Navjot and Harvey Krahn. 2003. "Social capital and refugee resettlement: The Social Networks of Refugees in Canada." *Journal of International Migration and Integration / Revue de L'integration et de La Migration Internationale* 4 (3): 335–360.

Logan, John, Wenquan Zhanga, and Richard Alba. 2002. "Immigrant Enclaves and Ethnic Communities in New York and Los Angeles." *American Sociological Review* 67 (2): 299–322.

Mamgain, Vaishali and Karen Collins. 2003. "Off the boat, Now Off to Work: Refugees in the Labour Market in Portland, Maine." *Journal of Refugee Studies* 16 (2): 113–146.

Massey, Douglas. 1990. "Social Structure, Household Strategies, and the Cumulative Causation of Migration." *Population Index* 56 (1): 3–26.

Simich, Laura. 2003. "Negotiating Boundaries of Refugee Resettlement: A Study of Settlement Patterns and Social Support." *Canadian Review of Sociology/Revue Canadienne de Sociologie* 40 (5): 575–591.

Singer, Audrey and Jill Wilson. 2006. *From 'There' to 'Here': Refugee Resettlement in Metropolitan America.* Washington, DC: Brookings Institute.

Shio, Thadeus Joseph. 2006. *Housing Experiences of Somali Immigrants in the Twin Cities, Minnesota-A Housing Careers Perspective.* PhD dissertation, University of Minnesota.

Smith, Yda. 2013. "We All Bantu – We Have Each Other: Preservation of Social Capital Strengths during Forced Migration." *Journal of Occupational Science* 20 (2): 173–184.

United States Census Bureau. 2013. *2008 – 2012 American Community Survey.* Washington, DC: U.S. Census Bureau's American Community Survey Office. Retrieved from http://ftp2.census.gov.

Yu, Soonjin, Estelle Ouellet, and Angelyn Warmington. 2007. "Refugee Integration in Canada: A Survey of Empirical Evidence and Existing Services." *Refuge* 24 (2): 17–34.

Zhou, Min. 1992. *Chinatown: The Socioeconomic Potential of an Urban Enclave.* Philadelphia: Temple University Press.

Chapter 12

Emplacing Bhutanese Refugees in the Rust Belt

Work, Networks, and Mobility in Resettlement

Joseph R. Stadler, with commentary by Jay Breneman

This chapter examines strategies through which Nepali-Bhutanese refugees seek emplacement (Malkki 1995) within and across the dichotomously racialized urban spaces of the "rust belt" city of Erie, Pennsylvania. Since 2008, around 5,000 Nepali-Bhutanese refugees have resettled mostly into Erie's dilapidated east side. This mostly residential neighborhood is, socio-economically, the poorest in the city and exists in the popular imagination as a "blackened space" (Jackson 2001) of violence and danger. Historically, this was also the case, as the east side was the locus in which the city's large populations of European immigrants were concentrated. These immigrants, followed by migrations of African Americans from the southern United States, came to work mostly as unskilled labor in Erie's formerly booming factories, of which most have now long ceased to operate. Depleted by Erie's deindustrialization and loss of population, the neighborhood is now home to a new burgeoning population of refugee immigrants. The segregated space, on top of which Nepali-Bhutanese attempt to build their community, while it provides cheap, readily available housing, is also marked by its social, political, and economic exclusion. By paying attention to their negotiations of uneven local spaces and the ways in which they orient themselves within "multiple frameworks of meaning" (Narayan 2002, 425), I interrogate the co-production of "good citizenship" (Brettell and Reed-Danahay 2012) in Erie by Bhutanese refugees, caseworkers, and other neighborhood residents as well as nonprofit and non-governmental "shadow state" (Wolch 1990) organizations.

I find that the Bhutanese Community Association of Erie (BCAE)—a representative body for Erie's Nepali-Bhutanese refugee community—negotiates racialized and neoliberal modes of belonging to fashion community members into "good citizens." This chapter looks at how Bhutanese community leaders creatively rework the networks and knowledge gained "on the job" and in everyday life to support the needs of their community. Through their work, they seek the recognition that will bring incorporation for not only their co-ethnics but, crucially, for their neighborhood, or place in the city, as well. This research suggests that resettled refugees, though they are often perceived simply as burdens on the local economy, can positively contribute to the restructuring of downscaled cities. Thus, I propose that not only their economic capabilities, but also the social, cultural, and political contributions of refugee communities need to be recognized and integrated into the urban revitalization efforts of what Glick Schiller and Caglar (2011) call "downscaled cities."

While the transnational practices of Nepali-Bhutanese refugees are certainly of great interest, their efforts at emplacement (Malkki 1995)—in the face of rapid global dispersion and the emergence of their population as a new diaspora—warrant scholarly attention. Here, I join Bugg (2013) in countering Tololyan's (2003, 67) claim that, in diaspora studies, "routedness is more interesting than rootedness." Thus, my focus in this chapter is on how Nepali-Bhutanese refugees negotiate local belonging, or emplacement, through everyday spatial practice. They connect workplace with neighborhood—a constructed place (Martin 2003) shaped by social and political-economic relations (Escobar 2001) "where everyday life is *situated*" (Merrifield 1993, 522, emphasis in original)—by creatively reworking networks and skill sets that allow them to subsist within these underprivileged spaces by working across post-industrial Erie's uneven geography. Nepali-Bhutanese refugees, displaced for so long, seek to "(re-)make place," or inscribe their belonging into the city and feel "at home" in resettlement.

NEPALI-BHUTANESE REFUGEES

In 2008—following the 2006 announcement by UNHCR and a group of member states, including the United States, Canada, New Zealand, Australia, Denmark, Norway, and the Netherlands, to launch a third-country resettlement program—Nepali-Bhutanese refugees began their rapid global dispersion (Hutt 2013, 5). The United States, with the vast majority, at more than 84,000, has far surpassed its original agreement to resettle 60,000 Nepali-Bhutanese refugees (Das Shrestha 2015). Several other countries have similarly exceeded their quotas. At present, nearly all of the estimated 108,000 Nepali-Bhutanese refugees have been resettled.

Nepali-Bhutanese refugee subjectivities have been produced in the context of a protracted refugee situation. Most Nepali-Bhutanese refugees spent approximately two decades in UNHCR-administered refugee camps. Within this context of protracted limbo, two generations of Nepali-Bhutanese refugees came of age. However, this time of limbo was not time of liminality. For Nepali-Bhutanese refugees, being without legal, political, social, and cultural rights was a fact of life. But, rather than being a period marked by an absence of activity, refugee living was, for many Bhutanese refugees in Nepal, characterized by a practical education in neoliberal governance, as they had to "make do" (de Certeau 1984) in a national context shaped by agents of Western economic development and humanitarian aid (Rankin 2004). Today's Bhutanese community leaders—most of whom became refugees during their childhoods—learned lessons of self-determination, flexibility, personal responsibility, and how to maximize their "human capital" as refugees. They utilized pre-existing skill sets—like knowledge of the English language attained through an English-medium education system in Bhutan—and cultivated new skill sets, through the work of international and camp-based NGOs seeking to "empower" refugees, in order to ameliorate the difficulties of surviving in an unstable political-economic environment (Evans 2009, 7–8). For instance, many of the men who appear in this chapter worked illegally throughout Nepal as teachers in private "English boarding schools," with some even bringing their children to live with them. They developed networks to guide other Bhutanese refugees into other English boarding schools, creating what amounted to a development-driven market niche, albeit a technically illegal one. These networks approximate a form of what Putnam (2000) has referred to as "bonding social capital." Although this "bonding" form of social capital remains more prevalent than the "bridging" form among Bhutanese in resettlement, I should note that these bonds often fracture along the fault lines of caste, ethnicity, and religion, reflecting internal divisions in the Bhutanese community, which is anything but homogenous. The neoliberal survival skills these former refugees learned in Nepal—and which they continue to learn through Erie's refugee resettlement agencies and service providers—have been crucial in shaping their subjectivities and modes of adaptation to Erie's hollowed-out service and light manufacturing economy.

NGO "CONTACT ZONES" AND THE BCAE

What "kinds of subjectivity" (Rankin 2001, 22) do resettlement agencies aim to produce among refugees? What modes of self-regulation do they attempt to inculcate? And, what purpose does this serve? Pratt (1992, 4) defined what she calls the "contact zone" as "social spaces where disparate cultures meet, clash, and grapple with each other, often in highly asymmetrical relations of domination and subordination." I find the contact zone "good to think with" (Levi-Strauss 1963), as it emphasizes the agency of the subordinated subject within an order imposed from without. In the case I explore here, "contact zones" are found in the form of resettlement agencies and the BCAE. The grappling BCAE leaders engage in with a range of actors at the workplace in resettlement—shaped by NGO missions and federal policies—produces particular *truths* about life in America and a particular knowledge of the *good citizen*. And, this grappling has led them to see particular kinds of "apolitical" and "technical" solutions for the "problems" they encounter in resettlement (Ferguson 1990).

There is something specifically "neoliberal" in the structuring of the problems and solutions of resettlement. Putting it bluntly, a senior representative of a local resettlement agency said: "The goals of the resettlement program, as set by the Department of State, are self-sufficiency and integration." Self-sufficiency, in this staff member's words, is "an American value" defined as "reducing or stopping reliance on public benefits." Further, as this individual explained:

> The resettlement program is a humanitarian effort, but it's also a program that shouldn't take from communities. It should also contribute back to them, which means people becoming self-sufficient, paying taxes, buying homes, cars, so-on-and-so-forth. I think it goes back to what we value as Americans. It's pretty basic. What we value are people who go to work and work hard. Period. It doesn't matter where you come from. So, it would make sense that a federal program would have those outcomes.

Economic self-sufficiency, hard work, property ownership, and consumerism are identified here as valued dimensions of social and political belonging in America. They are given as solutions to the problem of welfare dependency. Thus, resettled refugees are constructed as subjects in need of neoliberal intervention, which aims to integrate them as, and shape them into, "deserving citizens" (Ong 2003) in American society. Their role, thus, is to actively produce value and to foster the flow of capital through self-reliance rather than passively receiving benefits. To put it simply, their social value lies in their economic productivity. As Thomas Lemke (2001, 203) acknowledges of neoliberalism, it is "a political rationality that tries to render the social domain economic and to link a reduction in (welfare) state services and security systems to the increasing call for 'personal responsibility' and 'self-care.'"

The BCAE, registered as a 501(c)(3) nonprofit in Pennsylvania, takes a two-pronged approach to the emplacement of their community in resettlement, with social integration and cultural preservation as its primary aspirations. In both form and content, it creatively borrows from the NGOs that served and educated them as refugees in Nepalese refugee camps, and the refugee resettlement agencies at which many community leaders are employed as caseworkers and job developers. However, the BCAE deploys this programming exclusively in the service of Erie's Bhutanese community, thereby offering a vehicle for the cultivation of bonding social capital. Erie's resettlement agencies employ dozens of Bhutanese refugees variously as caseworkers, job developers, instructors, and interpreters, among other positions. Most of these agency employees have become community leaders who, in their work within and alongside these local contact zones, fashion particular understandings of what it means to be an American or Bhutanese American citizen. The BCAE allows these men to apply their practical, on-the-job knowledge in innovative ways that are responsive to what they understand to be the needs of their community. This is critical, as the US refugee resettlement policy of "front loading"—also called "front-end loading" in the U.K. (Hoellerer 2013)—sees Refugee Cash Assistance and Refugee Medical Assistance dry up within a matter of months, and the Office of Refugee Resettlement's Matching Grant funding to agencies pushes them to become self-sufficient within 120 to 180 days (ORR 2014, 7). After this, refugees' only options for survival are employment, TANF (Temporary Assistance for Needy Families; also known as "workfare"), or Supplemental Security Income—administered through the Social Security Administration—for disabled and elderly refugees).

As the nonprofit sector has taken on some of the state's integrative functions over the past four decades of state restructuring—what Wolch (1990) referred to as the constitution of the "shadow state"—service-providing organizations have been furnished with new rules and responsibilities as well as material resources that affect the construction of citizenship (Brown 1997; Mitchell 2001; Lake and Newman 2002; Fyfe and Milligan 2003). The state's decreasing involvement in service provision, however, does not mean that it is absent from governing processes. Nonprofits have become spaces in which particular definitions of citizenship are enacted (Milligan and Fyfe 2005). Mitchell (2001) argues that shadow state organizations, by implementing state-sponsored workfare agendas, produce a notion of neoliberal citizenship in which standing as a full member of society is contingent upon labor market participation. In taking responsibility for welfare service provision from the state, nonprofits can influence citizenship by working to address issues of societal belonging and, sometimes, by providing individuals with state-sponsored social welfare services, which can affect perceptions of social groups' status in the polity (Bloemraad 2005). For Gramsci (1971), a "volunteerist" (Kearns 1995) civil society organization like the BCAE should be where substantive, counter-hegemonic social change takes root. But, as

Perkins (2009, 397) has pointed out volunteerism often "provides consent [to neoliberal hegemony] through governance" because ideology within these organizations "links volunteerism with active forms of citizenship."

Because the state has rolled back responsibility for service provision, Bhutanese community leaders are obliged to take responsibility for their community's future. In the case of the BCAE, as we will see, Bhutanese community leaders use the networks and skills they have developed at their shadow state employers to supply for their community what the state often fails to provide. Because they are subject to less regulatory oversight than their employers, they are able to weave together novel ways of coordinating this work. And, they are able to tailor their initiatives directly to their community's localized sociocultural and economic needs. Yet, because the state essentially outsources responsibility for social support to bonding networks of the BCAE, their efforts to reorganize and support the community come with a cost. Namely, they are unable to focus their minimal resources on building broader bridging networks. Additionally, the creative emplacement practices through which they bond community members by getting them to work must take place within and across unequal spaces.

RACE, MIGRATION, AND UPWARD MOBILITY

Erie's population, according to the 2010 US census, is approximately 75 percent White and 18 percent Black (U.S. Census Bureau 2010). Although Erie has long been a site for refugee resettlement, the city has only recently begun to show glimpses of cosmopolitanism. The sense of "Americanness" or "Whiteness" that the Bhutanese encountered upon arrival appeared quite monolithic. However, Erie's rich history of migration belies this experience. With as many as 5,000 Bhutanese currently residing in the city, they may now make up nearly 5 percent of the city's population. At the time of the 2010 census, however, the city's total Asian population was only 1,515 or 1.5 percent of the total population (U.S. Census Bureau 2010). The rapidly growing Bhutanese community has not only surpassed the statistical representation of any other Asian population in the city, they are quite literally the most visible population, and many Erie locals note their ubiquitous presence on the streets of the east side of town. But, the east side is imagined locally as a "blackened space" (Jackson 2001), and a "racist common sense" among Erie residents enforces what Philippe Bourgois (2003) has called "inner city apartheid" by convincing locals that this place is dangerous, violent, and home to morally deficient people.

The "good citizens" the members of Bhutanese Community Association of Erie (BCAE) look to cultivate must be nurtured in Erie's east side neighborhoods. The city of Erie currently boasts a poverty rate (27.4 percent) nearly double that of the national poverty rate (14.5 percent). While more than 40 percent of Erie's black population and more than 50 percent of Erie's Hispanic population live below the federal poverty line, this is true for only about 20 percent of the white population (U.S. Census Bureau 2014a). The story is different for Erie's immediate suburbs. Millcreek, a township that borders Erie to its south and west and has a population more than half of Erie's size, has a poverty level of just 10 percent. Millcreek is approximately 93 percent white and only 2 percent black (U.S. Census Bureau 2014b). Viewed on a map, the geography of poverty in Erie is overwhelmingly found to be the worst in the east side neighborhoods where Bhutanese and other refugee populations have been resettling. As one east side neighborhood watch organizer related to me: "Even here in the 21st century in Erie, it still ranks very high in terms of being disproportionately impoverished." By this, he means that Erie's poverty is concentrated along racial lines. On top of that, this area of the city and its inhabitants are often blamed for the city's ills. Indeed, in a quick online perusal of Erie's *Craigslist* "Rants & Raves," one can find local citizens' fears of a coming "Nigerie" or "Little Detroit"—this coming from the regular assertion that Erie's growing drug crime problem has been facilitated by drug dealers from Detroit. However, the discursive construction of this space as *other* is not a recent development, nor is it one historically tied exclusively to the black community.

The east side of Erie has always been home to the "huddled masses." Before this part of town came to be thought of as a place of black crime—extensive black migration to Erie did not take place until the first half of the 1900s in the "Great Migration"—waves of European immigrants arrived, hoping to work their way up and out. Many of these former immigrants and their institutions, however, remained in the neighborhood and continue to shape it in the present. Due to the nature of immigration, the national, and racialized origins of the immigrants (Jacobson 1998) and the roles immigrants have historically played in the development of Erie's economy, this area has always been derided as backward and "other." And, as two local historians (Kelly and Rossi 1993) noted, this area has always been home to low-paying jobs, high rates of worker turnover, and unemployment. With a few exceptions, the residents of Erie's east side have been socially, culturally, economically, and politically excluded from the local mainstream for nearly the entirety of the city's history. However, while ethnic succession was a reasonable expectation for the neighborhood's earliest residents, it has become progressively more difficult over time for newcomers to "make it."

While Erie was a site of economic growth for much of its history, post–World War II economic globalization, technological shifts, corporate mergers, headquarter relocations, outsourcing, and a transition from heavy to light industry and services have hollowed out the local economy, leaving each subsequent group of newcomers with the increasingly more difficult task of working their way out of poverty. Throughout the twentieth century, ethnic and racial clustering (Massey 1985; Massey and Denton 1987) and segmentation (Waldinger 1996; Zhou 1992; Portes and Zhou 1993) came to characterize, respectively, Erie's housing and labor markets. A negative result of this, as it played out spatially, was disinvestment along with mounting stigmatization and discrimination by those more powerful local actors who shaped where resources and opportunities went (Wacquant 1993). Locals know where in the city poverty is to be found, and they have a cultural understanding of who lives there and what their lives are like. Erie's east side neighborhoods are, today, envisaged as "no-go areas . . . where only the rejects of society could bear to dwell" (Wacquant 2008, 29). Locals make "culturalist" assumptions (Bayart 2005; Alexander 2004) about the people and place. And, the state of life within these neighborhoods is most often presumed to be a "manifestation of cultural difference and dysfunction" rather than an outcome of structural conditions of economic marginalization, segregation, racial stigma, and alienation from institutions (Rhodes 2012, 685; Bourgois 2003; Anderson 1999).

In their first months and years, Bhutanese refugees are eligible to participate in several government welfare programs. As Schneider (1999) and Bourgois (2003) have noted, white, middle-class ideology, hegemonic in public perceptions of poverty and welfare, is often internalized by inner-city residents who reproduce its race and class-based stereotypes within their own neighborhoods and among their own ethnic and racial groups. In Robert Castel's words: "the politics of welfare [in the United States] centers around the management of individual deficiencies" (1978, 47), and these "deficiencies" have historically been tied to race (Wilson 1996). Suspicion and a need for supervision have historically driven American attitudes about welfare recipients. This is at least as old as the New Deal division between "welfare" and "entitlement" programs, but clearly the roots are deeper than that (Reich 1966). And, as Marchevsky and Theoharis (2000, 251) note, the workfare reforms of the 1990s "played on the racial antagonism of (imagined white) workers toward (imagined colored) welfare recipients to distract workers . . . and to prevent any alliances between recipients and workers."

The racial logics that infuse discourses about welfare and "deserving citizenship" (Ong 2003, 74) combine to produce a distrustful and sometimes violent relationship between Erie's native black and refugee populations. The structural conditions of inner-city poverty in Erie weaken the potential for bridging relations and seemingly preclude any possibility of local solidarity, as many Bhutanese and native-born residents feel they are locked into a zero-sum game. Assaults against Bhutanese refugees have been somewhat commonplace on the east side, yet many Bhutanese have been reluctant to report these crimes. On the one hand, this is due to a feeling of mistrust toward the authorities, which is likely a byproduct of their experiences in Bhutan and in Nepal, where they were variously treated with suspicion or specifically discriminated against by the police and military. On the other hand, they harbor a fear of violent retaliation from their black neighbors. Although they live side-by-side, neighborly relationships are relatively rare. The mistrust in the neighborhood is mutual among all residents, it seems.

This mistrust works also work their way into neighborhood sentiments about "who deserves what" and illusions about how residents come by the resources they have attained. Bhutanese refugees are often looked at as getting a "free ride." As Aihwa Ong (2003, 4) has pointed out, anti-immigrant views in the United States often seek to deny ethnic succession to new immigrants. Feeling that new immigrants are moving up the socioeconomic ladder can be particularly painful for Erie's impoverished black citizens. There is a great sense of injustice within Erie's impoverished neighborhoods, with many residents understanding that they have been subjected to generations of continued hardship. And, this sense of injustice plays a major role in shaping the lens through which longtime residents consider the arrival of new immigrants and, especially, refugees. As Carl, a black, middle-aged neighborhood watch coordinator, said to me: "That animosity has been going on long before the Bhutanese came. With the migration of the Bosnians, then the Iraqis . . . that was a major issue with the Americanized citizens." With the workfare "reforms" of the 1990s and the accompanying "onerous and humiliating bureaucratic obligations" (Wacquant 2009, 59) they place upon the east side's poor, who now have to "earn" their food stamps and cash assistance, Carl notes a mentality among residents: "We have to struggle for what we have, and sometimes we find it very difficult to keep what we have." On the other hand, residents find that refugees "get jobs," "get cars," and "get housing; not just apartments, but housing!" This, he feels: "automatically draws a line of separation of human compassion. Because, there is an oppression that they feel, as citizens that are from these 'great' United States—from the All-American City, as it was designated years ago, called Erie." There is a feeling that "everything that we have, we have had to fight hard for."

As I have discussed elsewhere (Stadler 2013), the local media along with representatives from resettlement NGOs attempt to ameliorate local residents' suspicions and fears of refugee welfare abuse by framing the city as a home for refugees and framing Erie's refugees as worthy of belonging. An Erie Times News article from 2009, written by the then-president of a local resettlement NGO (Grode 2009, 3B), tells us: "The U.S. State Department has stated that Erie has proved over and over again that it is the most welcoming community in America for refugee resettlement. The entire Erie community should be proud of this fact." In the past fifteen to twenty years, the city certainly has embraced a large number of refugees, many of whom came in the 1990s from the Balkans and, now, overwhelmingly from Asia and Africa. Reporters and resettlement NGO representatives also draw historical connections between today's refugee population and the immigrants who built Erie's golden age in the early twentieth century, ensconcing refugees in a larger, powerful narrative about Erie as a city of immigrants. Bhutanese refugees are represented as victims, passive, gentle people, and as vital new blood that injects new life into the city. And, it is recognized that it is not simply the refugees who benefit from resettlement in Erie, but the city itself. It is clear that the local press and the resettlement agencies are working to ensconce refugees as deserving citizens in the local imaginary. However, the narratives they utilize to accomplish this task are noticeably silent about Erie's black community.

GETTING TO WORK

The restructuring (or rescaling) of the welfare state has not only produced new ideological forms, it has mobilized new technologies of power. What we witness in the BCAE are the effects of a biopolitical project of post-welfare state neoliberal governance, which, through "technologies of citizenship" (Cruikshank 1999) enacted in refugee resettlement NGO programming, seeks to create "engaged" and "compassionate" citizens who take personal responsibility for the welfare of their community (Fyfe 2005; Muehlebach 2011). Bhutanese community leaders are, in this sense, "effects" and "instruments" of political power exercised "in the material, learned, and habitual ways" they have learned to "embody citizenship" (Cruikshank 1999, 5, 124). Rather than looking to the state as a benefactor or interrogating larger structural causes for their hardships, the BCAE looks to harness their community's human and social capital to ameliorate the severe inequalities members of their community must confront in Erie. This reducing of their burden on society expresses itself in BCAE leaders' work as compassionate caretakers and gatekeepers (Barrow and Jennings 2001) for their community, and much of this work revolves around creating a community of good, productive, neoliberal citizens.

Khem, situating the BCAE as just another refugee resettlement NGO, tells me: "Like all other agencies . . . who are helping refugees, [our] job is to make each and every person self-sufficient. The BCAE is the organization for the people who are from Bhutan." Referencing the BCAE's two-pronged approach, Khem notes that the main objectives of the BCAE, are, "in general, protecting our culture and our identity. Besides that, making our community's people self-sufficient. . . . So, we always encourage each and every person in our community to find a job, to 'go for' a job." Learning about the importance of working is very important for learning one's duties as a citizen, according to Khem. Some of BCAE's organizational efforts at crafting "good citizens" include: developing relationships with employers who find the Bhutanese to be "good workers"; teaching community members how to find their way to work on the bus; organizing carpools for community members who work at the same site; teaching English-language classes to women and the elderly; doing "PR work" to represent the community as economic contributors in local media. In addition, community leaders tell other Bhutanese to "go for a job," and that dependence on welfare is not a suitable option.

Notably, however, Erie's Bhutanese community does not consider all forms of welfare as unhealthy signs of dependence. Increasingly, Bhutanese households are moving into subsidized public housing. And, considering the traumas faced by elders and other adults and the difficulties many have with transitioning into the labor market, Bhutanese increasingly see mental health diagnoses and their corresponding benefits as important resources for full citizenship. Being diagnosed means acquiring a disability waiver that allows the most vulnerable to forego civics and language testing to gain legal citizenship. Additionally, it means crucial access to Social Security benefits for people who are less easily able to adapt to the local and national mandate to labor. The community generally views this as a moral and honorable way to take care of the disabled and elders who suffer from "loneliness" and other issues caused by the major upheavals in their lifeways in exile and in resettlement. However, Bhutanese community leaders and resettlement agencies—with the backing of federal policy—exert moral pressure on "able-bodied" refugees by connecting citizenship to employment and self-sufficiency and actively encouraging those who can work to work.

The US State Department and the Department of Health and Human Services' Office of Refugee Resettlement (ORR) set refugee resettlement policy at the federal level. To reduce "dependency," ORR advocates what is called "front loading," describing it as something that "empowers" refugees "through early employment"; helps them "reach self-sufficiency as soon as possible"; and helps them to "become active, contributing participants in their communities" (ORR 2010, 1). While "self-sufficiency" seems at first glance a relatively benign term, it has been used in US policy as a means of regulating those populations defined by their presumed dependency. In a 2005 address, J. Kelly Ryan (the then Deputy Assistant Secretary for Population, Refugees and Migration in the US Department of State) explained: "An important U.S. Government priority is to promote economic self-sufficiency as quickly as possible, so as to limit the need for public assistance" (Ryan 2005). Refugee programs and general welfare programs have gone through similar localizing and privatizing processes of "destatization" (Jessop 2002). These are often justified, as Trudeau and Cope (2003, 780) note, in terms of citizenship: "the squeeze on services is cast as a way of placing greater 'personal responsibility' on the individual in a shift toward obligation and away from entitlement."

Although the Bhutanese community is varied in terms of caste, class, religion, language skills, job skills, and education, the kinds of employment they are prepared for and funneled into by resettlement NGOs suggest that they are being prepared to join their neighbors as members of the working poor (Ong 2003, 83–4). While general welfare recipients are "aggressively encouraged to join the paid labor force regardless of how dead-end or poorly paid the job is" (Trudeau and Cope 2003, 780), Bhutanese refugees in Erie are enrolled in job preparation classes upon arrival through resettlement agencies who, in order to satisfy government contracts and secure future funding streams, must meet self-sufficiency benchmarks for their clients within an ever-diminishing timeframe. These resettlement agencies must also compete for additional discretionary grants to sustain their operations. By meeting certain standards of job placement and keeping refugees off of welfare, they can compete for grants such as ORR's "Preferred Communities" program, which can increase refugee placements and, thus, funding to the local affiliate. Preferred Communities are defined as places with "a history of low welfare utilization and a favorable earned income potential relative to the cost of living" (ORR 2003, 33). While it is difficult to see how Erie fits the first part of this definition, the second part surely rings true. While it may be advantageous to many struggling localities—like Erie—who can use the labor supply boost, an unfortunate effect of this policy for many refugees is that their host communities are ill-equipped to handle them, in terms of infrastructure, social services, and viable employment (Singer and Wilson 2006; Barkdull et al. 2012).

Erie, however, has sent several delegations, consisting of mayors, US representatives, prominent figures from the local business community, and representatives from local resettlement agencies, to Washington, D.C., to lobby the State Department for more refugee placements. A local news story reprinted by a State Department newsletter in 2005, quotes then-mayor Rick Filippi as saying: "For us, [resettlement] really gives us a pool of immigrants that can help revitalize the city" (Bureau of Population, Refugees and Migration 2005). The delegation, which met with then-Assistant Secretary of State Arthur E. Dewey, spoke of the positive impact refugees have had on Erie's population, economy, and urban renewal, by making the city more ethnically diverse, being motivated to take on jobs and start businesses, and renting, buying, and renovating blighted properties.

While this is not a fabrication, the lived reality of their positive impact on Erie, for the refugees themselves, is hardly as rosy as the picture the former mayor painted in Washington. Bhutanese refugees' livelihoods in Erie depend largely upon their ability to navigate the city's unstable labor market and "make do" with its low-paying, precarious jobs. For Bhutanese women, this means working as housekeepers, cleaners, food workers, office assistants, and caregivers. For Bhutanese men, this means finding employment as non-union factory workers, dealers at a local casino, cleaners, food workers, and truck drivers. A few Bhutanese families have been able to pool resources and open several small grocery stores and one clothing store.

Through their attention to inculcating the virtues of self-sufficiency, the BCAE also takes a vital role in constructing a new social network for Erie's Bhutanese community. There is an important spatial dimension at work here, as well. As I discussed previously, the neighborhoods in which the Bhutanese reside provide a constant source of fear. Many Bhutanese rely upon public transportation to get to their jobs, as most of the factories, hotels, and hospitals in which they work are located well outside of their neighborhood. Through experiences and stories of racialized harassment and violence described earlier, as well as the negative racial stereotypes they have absorbed through Hollywood movies and local media outlets, they have developed a fear of the racial other with whom they share space in the city. Sharing the bus with their African American neighbors can be a scary experience for many Bhutanese. Many Bhutanese youths have had issues with bullying on their school busses, and many adults are hesitant to be alone on the street, fearing that they could also be targeted. To ameliorate this, Khem says the BCAE tells people: "If they find a job and . . . are having problems with transportation, [the BCAE] can also help them connect with other people in the community who are going to the same sites. [The BCAE] can help them understand the bus routes and all those things, so that they can catch the bus and go for the job."

Many Bhutanese, on the other hand, are unable to reach their jobs by public transportation. Changes in industrial technology, the simultaneous growth of the trucking industry and the interstate highway system, and increased global competition had, decades earlier, accelerated Erie's post–World War II sprawl. Manufacturers began leaving the city for more advantageous locations. Many of the businesses that chose not to relocate to the "Sunbelt" or overseas moved in significant numbers to Erie's surrounding suburbs, along with scores of white residents—a trend that continues to this day. Several of the largest employers for Bhutanese refugees are located in Lake City, a town some eighteen miles west of the east side neighborhoods in which the Bhutanese live. Public transportation routes end roughly eight miles from this town. The BCAE, utilizing networks built through community leaders' positions in local resettlement and social service agencies, steps in to assist community members in accessing these jobs. Aditya, who works in the employment department at a resettlement agency, has "contact with the employers." The employers will call him saying, "I need five people." Aditya will then "look for somebody who has a car in the community and is looking for a job" and "offer the job to that guy," telling him, "Please help these guys." Aditya sees his role as "assisting both people": "The people who have cars get a job to work every day, and they will not mind to take two people with them." For people who live in the same area this is simple enough, according to Aditya. If they cannot meet at someone's home, the driver will pick them up at location they know well. These locations tend to be the resettlement and social service agencies: "If people live around one agency, they will just meet in front of that agency. Or, if they live around another agency, they will meet in the parking lot." Aditya essentially sees himself serving as a "compassionate" (Muehlebach 2011) labor broker for the people of the Bhutanese community, helping people reach their workplaces. And, he sees his work as providing them with the security that comes with employment, self-sufficiency, and mobility: "I will make sure that, after they are hired, they will have transportation to get to their job every day."

Through this work, the BCAE sets itself up as a co-ethnic mediator that further passes the proverbial buck of the shadow state workfare project and takes an active role in organizing the community. Though they also pursue community organization through cultural strategies, the BCAE, here, distinctly rebuilds the community's social networks through connecting neighborhood and workplace by working through an uneven geography. Their daily negotiations of their neighborhood's spaces are turned into social events through carpooling and a "buddy system" approach to public transportation. This effort also works to bridge their neighborhood with workplaces unreachable by means other than automobile. Rather than looking toward the suburbs for housing near their jobs, they seek creative ways to labor for and emplace themselves within a Bhutanese community space on the east side, even if they cannot earn a wage within it. The act of connecting fellow Bhutanese to work and to one another through common transportation constitutes one new foundation on which they may begin (re)building their community. It is also an event that reinforces a neoliberal notion of self-sufficiency, which prevails in federal policies, resettlement agency practices, and Nepali-Bhutanese conceptions of American citizenship. Learned through the work of community leaders at local NGOs and bolstered for community members through the organizing of the BCAE, this notion of citizenship facilitates Nepali-Bhutanese claims of belonging in the United States, in general, and Erie, in particular. By traversing the city in solidarity while working to reduce the burden they place on society and contribute their labor to the economy, Bhutanese refugees stake their claim to a neoliberalized citizenship. However, this has the negative consequence of mutually justifying and reinforcing their fears and misunderstandings of their African American neighbors, who are further "othered" through Bhutanese refugees' engagement with this necessarily racialized modality of citizenship. And, this spatial practice leaves unquestioned Erie's "racialized mobility regime" and the "cultural mechanisms of white privilege and racial fear" that shape it (Sheller 2015, 71–2).

On the other hand, this spatial practice also allows Nepali-Bhutanese refugees to resist the long-entrenched patterns of spatial racialization and ghettoization that have made suburban "white dominance and privilege" seem "natural" in the region's "social and technological organization" (Zylstra 2011, 685). Crucially, the Bhutanese are not trying to escape Erie's east side. They are not only opening grocery stores that serve their community; those community members who have found some economic success are buying homes on the east side. The Bhutanese are not only investing in this neighborhood economically, but at a human level as well. And, they are working to reshape it along with their community to carve out a place in which they can make 'home.'

CONCLUSION

As we conversed at a Martin Luther King Jr. Day celebration in 2016, a local black politician told me he likes to call the Bhutanese "the saviors of Erie." Echoing what has become a local trend, he explained their redeeming value in terms of their economic impact: buying houses and opening businesses. But, the Bhutanese and other refugee immigrants also have the ability to begin to do the symbolic work of decoupling their east side neighborhood from its "territorial stigmatization" (Wacquant 2007; Wacquant 2008). This stigmatization, as Wacquant has pointed out, furthers processes of disinvestment and fuels powerful actors' structural violence, which materializes, for instance, in institutional withdrawal and increased surveillance. The ultimate effects of this tend to be the demoralization and disunification of residents and a diminution in their potential for social mobility (Wacquant 2008). In essence, this is a self-reproducing situation in which structural forces continually combine with discourses of poverty, race, and morality to produce ever more "undeserving poor" (Katz 1989) in spaces increasingly framed as undeserving of resources. This self-reinforcing process, buttressed by dominant ideologies of "dependency" and the "culture of poverty," helped to justify the so-called 'welfare reform' of the 1990s, which further stripped away the social safety net for people in poverty or at risk of entering into poverty (Wilson 1996).

Welfare reform, or "workfare" as it is colloquially known in the United States, has been criticized for forcing inner-city residents into jobs at the bottom of the labor market and, thus, further ensuring the reproduction of their poverty (Trudeau and Cope 2003). As I noted earlier, a similar neoliberal policy exists in the form of 'front loading' for refugees. While I have outlined above a strategy of resilience among Bhutanese refugees—where, through the process of building bonding social capital, they bridge the spatial mismatch between neighborhood and workplace—it is important to recognize that they and their neighbors face important structural, social, cultural, economic, and spatial barriers to their full incorporation as deserving, local citizens. While resettled refugees like the Bhutanese are crafting innovative strategies for achieving economic self-sufficiency in resettlement, these strategies are produced under relatively coercive conditions that push members of the community into the lowest levels of the labor market. This is done under the moralizing pressure of 'good citizenship,' where resettled refugees' social value is determined by their economic productivity.

With BCAE leaders taking on responsibility for the provision of social support in the community—which has its own history and internal dynamics—within a particular city and through particular neighborhoods—each of which has their own histories and social dynamics that structure what Bourdieu (1983) would call their "space of available possibilities"—Bhutanese refugees' possibilities for building bridging social capital are severely curtailed. Social capital, for Erie's Bhutanese refugees, would therefore appear to be of the more exclusionary 'bonding' type in Putnam's (2000) typology. Yet, the Bhutanese community is anything but a homogenous community with reference to race, ethnicity, class, education, and access to resources (see Hoellerer, this volume). The networks created by BCAE leaders are rife with their own internal conflicts and are constructed on an ad hoc basis. Some in the community feel as though they cannot trust the BCAE leadership. Rumors circulate that they ration their care and only help their friends. This may point to a need for a more comprehensive understanding of how resettled refugees' social capital is contingent upon broader structural forces, local histories, and group-specific factors. And, it suggests that the differential social-structural positioning of groups—not to mention the internal dynamics of groups—structures the space of available possibilities for the development and deployment of group strategies for generating social capital. Applying Putnam's typology too strictly may restrict our field of vision to surface-level relationships, while missing the deeper dynamics that shape the very possibility of those relationships and, especially, the subjective experiences of the actors that put them into place.

Erie, as a "downscaled city" (Glick Schiller and Caglar 2011) that has suffered losses of population and capital, is seeking revitalization through transitions to more and more flexible forms of manufacturing and to "new economy" industries, which produce services rather than goods. This has created a plethora of low-paying jobs at the bottom of the labor market. The city has shown support for refugee resettlement efforts, as the refugees fill a market demand for an inexpensive labor force in a city that does not attract great deals of economic migrants. These refugees—among whom the

Bhutanese are but one population—are bolstering the local economy and the city's competitiveness as laborers, consumers, taxpayers, and, increasingly, as property owners. This dimension of their value is appreciated by local resettlement agencies, business owners, and city officials, even if it has yet to take root among the general public.

However, their social and cultural values as members of the community and parts of the local landscape have been mostly neglected. I propose that their raison d'être in the city extends beyond their economic value, as great as that may in fact be. The Bhutanese, other resettled refugee populations, and the poor, working-class, and minority populations with whom they share space in the city should be recognized as integral parts of the community. Rather than considering how it might attract middle-class suburbanites, I suggest the city should shift its focus from outside to within should it be looking to revitalize. The city might benefit most by asking those who have stayed why they remain and how it can work better toward making them feel "at home." It is my hope that the ethnographic material presented here will, at the very least, help to humanize Erie's resettled refugees and other inner-city immigrants and contribute to their recognition as citizens deserving of full social, cultural, political, and, yes, economic rights.

COMMENTARY

Jay Breneman

Erie is very much a city in contraction, as demonstrated in the city's newly adopted (and first) comprehensive plan which speaks of "right-sizing" housing stock and infrastructure to meet the reality of a population unlikely to rebound much beyond the 100,000 people currently living here.

What goes underreported—or undervalued—is that, if it were not for the recent and significant migrations of Bhutanese and other peoples, particularly in the urban core where whites have all but fled and seemingly avoid, Erie's disproportion of people and structure would be considerably more apparent. Further urban decay has been ostensibly held at bay by the relocations and investments made by these new Erieites.

Erie is going through a phase of deindustrialization like many other rust-belt cities, but it will be intriguing to watch and see what patterns develop, locally, as the Bhutanese do not come from a heavily industrialized country. We might see further tensions, with the "whitened" Erie continuing to lament the decline of manufacturing. But, the emergence of an entirely new segment of the population, which will join with the most recent generation of native Erieites in being separated from any visceral connection to Erie's heavy manufacturing past, could open up entirely new pathways for the city, looking forward.

Will the Bhutanese chart a new course and bring Erie with them? Their location (made both by necessity and choice) serves as a human-element experiment on city revitalization. The unintended and challenging hardships the Bhutanese faced as refugees perhaps gave them a surprising readiness for the task of tackling the hardest hit neighborhoods in this shrinking rust belt city.

Perhaps, though, that is not the "American Dream" they envisioned upon their arrival. Does Erie present a land of opportunity where they can build a strong future for themselves and their families while simultaneously rebuilding Erie? Or, are these hardships of fragmentation, segregation, cultural barriers, and urban decay presenting challenges too large for the city to expect that such a vulnerable group will overcome them?

While the mass migration of Bhutanese into Erie's core fits near perfectly within Erie's history of previous migrant influxes, their predecessors were filling in relatively stable neighborhoods, while the more established Erieites moved ever further outward in the midst of a (mostly) growing economy and region. Here, the Bhutanese people are placed within an urban core that has the greatest need for renewal, while they represent a group who are, themselves, seeking to renew and re-establish the foundations of their own culture and community.

The city needs to rectify the political, social, and economic differences and inequities faced by the Bhutanese as well as the additional burdens they face in adapting to a new society. If the city refuses to dedicate itself to working toward these goals, perhaps the arrival of the Bhutanese will only temporarily staunch the downturn facing Erie as they find new opportunities and move on to better circumstances elsewhere in Anytown, United States.

The true test will inhere in the business, civic, and political leaders of their newfound home developing the foresight, mustering the willingness, and facilitating the engagement that can ensure the welcome and inclusion of the Bhutanese while we collectively learn what tools and opportunities we need to grow together as one larger Erie community.

The potential outcome of this written work is that the established Erie community, along with Erie's new Bhutanese community, can begin the task of asking those necessary questions and start fervently working to answer them.

REFERENCES CITED

Alexander, Claire. 2004. "Imagining the Asian Gang: Ethnicity, Masculinity and Youth after 'the Riots.'" *Critical Social Policy* 24 (4): 526–49.

Anderson, Elijah. 1999. *Code of the Street: Decency, Violence, and the Moral Life of the Inner City*. New York: W. W. Norton & Company.

Barkdull, Christine, Bret Weber, Amy Swart, and Amy Phillips. 2012. "The Changing Context of Refugee Resettlement Policy and Programs in the United States." *Journal of International Social Issues* 1 (1): 107–119.

Barrow, Ondine and Michael Jennings, eds. 2001. *The Charitable Impulse: NGOs and Development in East and North-East Africa*. Oxford: James Currey Publishing.

Bayart, Jean-Francois. 2005. *The Illusion of Cultural Identity*. Translated by Steven Rendall, Janet Roitman, Cynthia Schoch and Jonathan Derrick. Chicago: University of Chicago Press.

Bloemraad, Irene. 2005. "The Limits of de Tocqueville: How Government Facilitates Organizational Capacity in Newcomer Communities." *Journal of Ethnic and Migration Studies* 31: 865–887.

Bourdieu, Pierre. 1983. "The Field of Cultural Production, or: The Economic World Reversed." *Poetics* 12 (4–5): 311–356.

Bourgois, Philippe. 2003. *In Search of Respect: Selling Crack in El Barrio*. 2nd Edition. Cambridge: Cambridge University Press.

Brettell, Caroline and Deborah Reed-Danahay. 2012. *Civic Engagements: The Citizenship Practices of Indian and Vietnamese Immigrants*. Stanford, CA: Stanford University Press.

Brown, Michael. 1997. *Replacing Citizenship: AIDS Activism and Radical Democracy*. New York: Guilford Press.

Bugg, Laura Beth. 2013. "Citizenship and Belonging in the Rural Fringe: A Case Study of a Hindu Temple in Sydney, Australia." *Antipode* 45 (5): 1148–1166.

Bureau of Population, Refugees and Migration. 2005. "Resettlement Success in Pennsylvania." *U.S. Refugee Program News* 3 (1).

Castel, Robert. 1978. "La 'guerre à la pauvreté' aux États-Unis: le statut de la misère dans une société d'abondance." ["The 'War on Poverty' in the United States: The Status of Poverty in an Affluent Society"]. *Actes de la echerché en science sociale* 19: 47–60.

Cruikshank, Barbara. 1999. *The Will to Empower: Democratic Citizens and Other Subjects*. Ithaca, NY: Cornell University Press.

Das Shrestha, Deepesh. 2015. "Resettlement of Bhutanese Refugees Surpasses 100,000 Mark." *UNHCR*, November 19. Retrieved from http://www.unhcr.org/en-us/news/latest/2015/11/564dded46/resettlement-bhutanese-refugees-surpasses-100000-mark.html.

de Certeau, Michel. 1984. *The Practice of Everyday Life*. Translated by Steven Rendall. Berkeley, CA: University of California Press.

Escobar, Arturo. 2001. "Culture Sits in Places: Reflections on Globalism and Subaltern Strategies of Localization." *Political Geography* 20: 139–174.

Evans, Rosalind. 2009. "Inheriting the Past and Envisioning the Future: Young Bhutanese Refugees' Political Learning and Action." PhD Dissertation, Oxford University.

Ferguson, James. 1990. *The Anti-Politics Machine: 'Development,' Depoliticization and Bureaucratic Power in Lesotho*. Cambridge: Cambridge University Press.

Fyfe, Nicholas. 2005. "Making Space for 'Neo-communitarianism'? The Third Sector, State and Civil Society in the UK." *Antipode* 37 (3): 536–557.

Fyfe, Nicholas and Christine Milligan. 2003. "Out of the Shadows: Exploring Contemporary Geographies of Voluntarism." *Progress in Human Geography* 27 (4): 397–413.

Glick Schiller, Nina and Ayse Caglar. 2011. "Downscaled Cities and Migrant Pathways: Locality and Agency without an Ethnic Lens." In: *Locating Migration: Rescaling Cities and Migrants*, edited by Nina Glick Schiller and Ayse Caglar, 190–212. Ithaca, NY: Cornell University Press.

Gramsci, Antonio. 1971. *Selections from the Prison Notebooks*. Translated and edited by Quintin Hoare and Geoffrey Nowell Smith. New York: International Publishers.

Grode, Ed. 2009. "Honor Refugees in Erie Today." *Erie Times News* June 20: 3B.

Hoellerer, Nicole. 2013. "Refugee Resettlement in the UK: Bhutanese Refugees in Greater Manchester." *European Bulletin of Himalayan Research* 43: 71–85.

Hutt, Michael. 2013. "Editorial." *European Bulletin of Himalayan Research* 43: 5–6.

Jacobson, Matthew Frye. 1998. *Whiteness of a Different Color: European Immigrants and the Alchemy of Race*. Cambridge, MA: Harvard University Press.

Jackson, John. 2001. *Harlemworld: Doing Race and Class in Contemporary Black America*. Chicago: University of Chicago Press.

Jessop, Bob. 2002. *The Future of the Capitalist State*. Oxford, UK: Blackwell.

Katz, Michael. 1989. *The Undeserving Poor: From the War on Poverty to the War on Welfare*. New York: Pantheon.

Kearns, Adrian. 1995. "Active Citizenship and Local Governance: Political and Geographical Dimensions." *Political Geography* 14 (2): 155–175.

Kelly, Michael and John Rossi. 1993. "Nagle Machinists and the American Dream, 1890-1910." *The Journal of Erie Studies* 22 (1): 2–22.

Lake, Robert and Kathe Newman. 2002. "Differential Citizenship in the Shadow State." *GeoJournal* 58: 109–120.

Lemke, Thomas. 2001. "'The Birth of Bio-politics': Michel Foucault's Lecture at the College de France on Neo-liberal Governmentality." *Economy and Society* 30 (2): 190–207.

Levi-Strauss, Claude. 1963 [1962]. *Totemism*. Translated by Rodney Needham. Boston: Beacon Press.

Malkki, Liisa. 1995. "Refugees and Exile: From 'Refugee Studies' to the National Order of Things." *Annual Review of Anthropology* 24: 495–523.

Marchevsky, Alejandra and Jeanne Theoharis. 2000. "Welfare Reform, Globalization, and the Racialization of Entitlement." *American Studies* 41 (2/3): 235–265.

Martin, Deborah. 2003. "Enacting Neighborhood." *Urban Geography* 24 (5): 361–385.

Massey, Douglas. 1985. "Ethnic Residential Segregation: A Theoretical Synthesis and Empirical Review." *Sociology and Social Research* 69 (3): 315–350.

Massey, Douglas and Nancy Denton. 1987. "Trends in the Residential Segregation of Blacks, Hispanics and Asians: 1970-1980." *American Sociological Review* 52: 802–825.

Merrifield, Andrew. 1993. "Place and Space: A Lefebvrian Reconciliation." *Transactions of the Institute of British Geographers* 18(4): 516–531.

Milligan, Christine and Nicholas Fyfe. 2005. "Preserving Space for Volunteers: Exploring the Links Between Voluntary Welfare Organizations, Volunteering, and Citizenship." *Urban Studies* 42: 417–433.

Mitchell, Katharyne. 2001. "Transnationalism, Neo-liberalism, and the Rise of the Shadow State." *Economy and Society* 30 (2): 165–189.

Muehlebach, Andrea. 2011. "On Affective Labor in Post-Fordist Italy." *Cultural Anthropology* 26 (1): 59–82.

Narayan, Kirin. 2002. "Placing Lives Through Stories: Second-Generation South Asian Americans." In: *Everyday Life in South Asia*, edited by Dian P. Mines and Sarah Lamb, 425–439. Bloomington: Indiana University Press.

Office of Refugee Resettlement (ORR). 2003. "Annual Report to Congress 2003."

———. 2010. "Annual Report to Congress 2010."

———. 2014. "Voluntary Agencies Matching Grant Program: FY 2014 Program Guidelines."

Ong, Aihwa. 2003. *Buddha is Hiding: Refugees, Citizenship, The New America*. Berkeley, CA: University of California Press.

Perkins, Harold. 2009. "Out from the (Green) Shadow? Neoliberal Hegemony through the Market Logic of Shared Urban Environmental Governance." *Political Geography* 28: 395–405.

Portes, Alejandro and Min Zhou. 1993. "The New Second Generation: Segmented Assimilation and Its Variants." *The Annals of the American Academy of Political and Social Science* 530: 74–96.

Pratt, Mary Louise. 1992. *Imperial Eyes: Travel Writing and Transculturation*. London and New York: Routledge.

Putnam, Robert. 2000. *Bowling Alone: Collapse and Revival of American Community*. New York: Simon & Schuster.

Rankin, Katharine. 2001. "Governing Development: Neoliberalism, Microcredit, and Rational Economic Woman." *Economy and Society* 30(1): 18–37.

———. 2004. *The Cultural Politics of Markets: Economic Liberalization and Social Change in Nepal*. Toronto: University of Toronto Press.

Reich, Charles. 1966. "Social Welfare in the Public-Private State." *University of Pennsylvania Law Review* 114: 487–493.

Rhodes, James. 2012. "Stigmatization, Space, and Boundaries in De-industrial Burnley." *Ethnic and Racial Studies* 35 (4): 684–703.

Ryan, Kelly. 2005. "Refugee Resettlement and Integration." Address given to the Tenth Regional Conference on Migration, Vancouver, Canada, March 2005. Retrieved from http://2001-2009.state.gov/g/prm/rls/44154.htm.

Schneider, Jo Anne. 1999. "And How Are We Supposed to Pay for Health Care? Views of the Poor and the Near Poor on Welfare Reform." *American Anthropologist* 101 (4): 761–782.

Sheller, Mimi. 2015. "Racialized Mobility Transitions in Philadelphia: Connecting Urban Sustainability and Transport Justice." *City & Society* 27 (1): 70–91.

Singer, Audrey and Jill Wilson. 2006. "From 'There' to 'Here': Refugee Resettlement in Metropolitan America." Living Cities Census Series, Metropolitan Policy Program. The Brookings Institution. Washington, D.C.: The Brookings Institution.

Stadler, Joseph. 2013. "Refugees and Advocates: Bhutanese Refugees, Resettlement NGOs and the Co-construction of a Social Memory of Victimhood." *European Bulletin of Himalayan Research* 43: 86–102.

Tololyan, Khachig. 2003. "The American Model of Diasporic Discourse." In: *Diasporas and Ethnic Migrants: Germany, Israel and Post-Soviet Successor States in Comparative Perspective*, edited by Munz R. and R. Ohlinger, 50–66. London: Frank Cass Publishers.

Trudeau, Daniel and Meghan Cope. 2003. "Labor and Housing Markets as Public Spaces: 'Personal Responsibility' and the Contradictions of Welfare-Reform Policies." *Environment and Planning* 35 (5): 779–798.

U.S. Census Bureau. 2010. "Profile of General Population and Housing Characteristics." 2010 U.S. Census, Erie, City, PA.

———. 2014a. "Poverty Status in the Past 12 Months." 2010–2014 American Community Survey 5-Year Estimates, Erie, City, PA.

———. 2014b. "Poverty Status in the Past 12 Months." 2010–2014 American Community Survey 5-Year Estimates, Millcreek Township, Erie County, PA.

Wacquant, Loic. 1993. "Urban Outcasts: Stigma and Division in the Black American Ghetto and the French Urban Periphery." *International Journal of Urban and Regional Research* 17(3): 366–383.

———. 2007. "Territorial Stigmatization in the Age of Advanced Marginality." *Thesis Eleven* 91 (1): 66–77.

———. 2008. *Urban Outcasts: A Comparative Sociology of Advanced Marginality*. Cambridge, UK: Polity Press.

———. 2009. *Punishing the Poor: The Neoliberal Government of Social Insecurity*. Durham and London: Duke University Press.

Waldinger, Roger. 1996. *Still the Promised City? African Americans and New Immigrants in Post-Industrial New York*. Cambridge, MA: Harvard University Press.

Wilson, William Julius. 1996. *When Work Disappears: The World of the New Urban Poor*. New York: Alfred A. Knopf.

Wolch, Jennifer. 1990. *The Shadow State: Government and Voluntary Sector in Transition*. New York: The Foundation Center.

Zhou, Min. 1992. *Chinatown: The Socioeconomic Potential of an Urban Enclave*. Philadelphia: Temple University Press.

Zylstra, Geoff. 2011. "Whiteness, Freedom and Technology: The Racial Struggle Over Philadelphia's Streetcars, 1859-1867." *Technology and Culture* 52 (4): 678–702.

Conclusion

Toward a More Humane Resettlement Policy—A View from Europe

Roos Willems

A lot of water has passed under the bridge since the three editors of this volume organized a panel at the 75th annual meeting of the Society for Applied Anthropology in Pittsburgh, United States (March 24–28, 2015) on the theme *The Crux of Refugee Resettlement: Rebuilding Social Networks*, which included sixteen paper presentations (Society for Applied Anthropology, 2015). For most of us this was when we met for the first time and learned about each other's research.

At that time, Europe was confronted with its worst refugee crisis since World War II. More than a million refugees, mostly from Syria but also from other countries such as Afghanistan, Iraq and others, crossed the Mediterranean Sea or made their way to Central and Northern Europe via the Balkan routes, more than four times the number of refugees arriving there in 2014. Tensions between European Union (EU) member states rose because of the disproportionate burden faced by the countries where the majority of migrants had been arriving, namely Greece and Italy. Emphasizing solidarity among EU member states, each country agreed to relocate each a certain number of refugees, from the arrivals in Greece and Italy, yet eventually only 33,400 had actually been relocated outside Greece (33 percent) and 11,180 outside Italy (28 percent) leaving the remainder of refugees in overcrowded refugee camps in these two countries (UNHCR 2018, 4). The number of arrivals into Europe decreased however by 53 percent in 2017, to "only" 172,300, compared to 2016 (Ibid.,1).

Regarding *direct resettlement* from third countries outside of the EU, it was agreed in 2015 to resettle a little over 22,000 refugees directly from refugee camps outside Europe (mostly Syrian refugees from Turkey). Moreover, in addition to finalizing a common asylum system, EU countries have been discussing since mid-2016 a European Union Resettlement Framework.

With the goal of streamlining European resettlement efforts in the future, this framework would establish a common set of standard procedures for the selection of resettlement candidates and a common protection status for persons resettled to the EU. As EU member states continued debating,[1] the President of the EU Commission Jean-Claude Juncker in his State of the Union Address 2017 urged them to nearly double the original number of refugees to be resettled to 40,000 and to not focus exclusively on Syria, but to also include Egypt, Libya, Niger, Ethiopia, and Sudan (EC 2017b). In 2017, 25 European countries did resettle around 26,400 refugees, up from the 17,100 by 23 countries in 2016 (UNHCR 2018, 4), yet despite the significant increase these numbers are still a far cry from Juncker's ambition.

Before these recent EU initiatives, resettlement in the individual EU member states were either a combination of national or multilateral programmes, or organized in an ad-hoc way and concerned far lower numbers. Between 2011 and 2015, the total number of resettled refugees in the EU annually was around 5,000–6,000. Before the Syrian crisis, even fewer refugees were resettled in even fewer European countries in comparison with other resettlement countries. In 2013, for example, Europe received 6,800 refugees for resettlement (less than 7 percent of the total) compared to 66,200 by the United States (two-thirds of the total number of resettled refugees), 13,200 in Australia, and 12,200 in Canada (UNHCR 2014: 20). Within Europe, Norway and Sweden took in almost half of all refugees resettled. Together with Finland, Denmark, the Netherlands, and the U.K., Norway and Sweden admitted 83 percent of all resettled refugees between 2011 and 2015. Of the remaining European countries, six did not even resettle a single refugee in the same period (EMN 2016: 13).

This global picture changed completely in the 2016–2017 period; whereas in 2016, the United States still resettled more refugees than the rest of the world combined (97,000 versus 92,000, respectively) trends reversed dramatically in 2017 with the United states resettling only 33,000 refugees, less than half the number of all other countries combined, namely 69,000.[2] Overall, however, the number of refugees resettled in 2017 was barely half of the numbers of 2016 (103,000 vs. 189,000). The United States still resettled more refugees than any other one country; following were Canada (27,000), Australia (15,000), and the U.K. (6,000) while Sweden, Germany, France, and Norway each settled around 3,000[3] (Pew Research Center 2018).

Notwithstanding the very recent developments, it remains safe to say that contrary to the United States, Canada, and Australia, who have been resettling refugees since several decades past, most European countries have limited experience with regard to refugee resettlement. This observation not only explains the preponderance of US-based research in this volume, but also the relevance of these experiences for preparing Europe for the successful integration of increasing numbers of refugees resettling there in the near future. The 2016 European Migration Network report comparing resettlement policies across twenty-four European countries is a useful first step in this direction. However, its top-down focus on policy analysis largely foregoes the point of view of the resettled refugees themselves. Indeed, apart from a number of studies from the U.K., we could find only a single (!) European research publication that includes a more refugee-centric approach with regard to the resettlement of refugees (Suter and Magnusson 2015). This study focuses mainly on Sweden, which has for decades been accepting the largest number of resettled refugees in comparison with other European countries, and, unsurprisingly to the editors of this edited volume, focuses on the role of social networks in the integration of resettled refugees.

The contributions in this volume illustrate through a variety of case studies that resettlement is more than a change of place. Rather it is a lived experience unfolding in a socially, culturally, and politically laden context. These particularities of context(s), unfortunately, are often not sufficiently taken into account by the institutions that organize and administer refugee resettlement support. They often overlook the fact that resettlement not only includes an initial loss of social networks and familiar surroundings in their countries of origin, but also a "second" loss of social networks and familiar surroundings due to the prolonged stay in refugee camps before resettlement. Heinemann et al. and Chase highlight the importance of understanding the influence of networks on resettlement dynamics. In addition, the past experiences of war, displacement, and life in camps or other settings of insecurity may erode the capacity or readiness for social reciprocity and trust, as well as feelings of social cohesion human beings need to build social networks. Hence, social networks are not readily (re)formed upon resettlement. Rather, they grow incrementally over time, something emphasized by most authors in this volume.

Stadler, Lumley-Sapanski, Nelson, and Ramsay mention that while displacement happened due to national and global forces beyond refugees' control, emplacement is strongly influenced by their agency and their ability to recreate "original" and "secondary" relationships and to create new relationships, highlighting the concepts of integration and home. The primary focus of refugee resettlement agencies on economic independence and self-sufficiency as a condition for integration misses a more holistic notion of home and place. In some cultures, home does not mean independence but rather social dependence or an embeddedness in social networks. Lumley-Sapanski and Nelson illustrate how in some cultures personal debts to kin and close friends are far preferential to impersonal debts to banks (e.g., for the purchase of one's house), often prioritized by agencies as signs of economic independence and integration. Virtually all authors conclude that the emphasis of policies on employment as a measurement of integration foregoes the refugees' experiences of feeling integrated on the basis of well-being and inclusion into the host society.

Putnam's conceptual distinction between bonding and bridging social networks is a useful tool for gaining a better understanding of resettlement dynamics; community-based organizations as a type of more formalized social networks offering both bonding and bridging social support is another. The findings of anthropological analyses using these concepts across a variety of different cultural groups—even as they go through similar experiences—are, as could be expected, far from unanimous. Sienkiewicz et al. actually propose the conceptualisation of a new, an "in-between bonding and bridging" social network type, namely one of engagements and interactions between refugees of different backgrounds and cultures, which could in turn be interpreted as a refugee community organization. Hoellerer, on the other hand, argues that when the national government, aid agencies, and service providers set the parameters for refugee groups to legitimately organize themselves in order to defend their interests, rather than promoting integration, they risk perpetuating the refugees' marginality because of the missing link with society-at-large.

Numerous refugee resettlement studies have in the past already denounced the top-down bureaucratic policies and practices of agencies and government offices, and called for a more refugee-centric approach by adding an anthropological understanding of the specific cultural configuration of the refugees into the designing of support programs, as documented in a recent special issue on resettlement in the *Forced Migration* journal (February 2017). The authors in our volume rightly argue that creating specific resettlement policies for each and every refugee group is problematic, unpractical, and impossible. However, by using ethnographic approaches to shift the conversation from refugees as passive victims to active agents in the process of resettlement, they demonstrate how the various ways through which refugees reconfigure their social networks are in themselves a direct response to the structural limitations imposed by the resettlement policies. Further, their focus on the dynamic relationship between bridging and bonding capital of networks provided insights to not only critique current policy, but also to design effective interventions through a deeper understanding of the communities facing these problems.

Stadler, Rosales, and Heinemann et al. found that by strictly applying Putnam's concepts we risk focusing too much on surface-level relations, thus missing out on the deeper dynamics that shape the very possibility of social relationships as well as the subjective experiences of the actors that engage in them. Refugee resettlement policies, in order to be successful, must engage with and foster multiple sources of social support and social capital. Additionally, programs must respond to the dynamic and shifting relevance of social capital. Yotebieng et al., Rosales, Halsouet, and Stam illustrate that rather than a result of state policies aiming to facilitate assimilation and integration, bridging networks are often a consequence of the efforts of non-state agencies. Relationships based on bridging capital frequently develop in accidental and unintended ways as consequences of circumstances. Moreover, social networks are susceptible to the whims of personal preferences, and are often built on interactions through informal friendships and participation in formal events. In times of need, refugees tend to seek more informal resources than formal services.

We strongly suggest that workers in refugee resettlement consider the informal networks and networking both within the refugee community and outside of it in order to best facilitate integration into the host society. Sufficient attention needs to be given to the subjectivity of the refugees themselves in interpreting the lived experiences of integration. After all, communities are created through and operated within interactions and experiences. However, while not being a substitute for social networks in which the individual refugee can feel "at home" and integrated, refugee community organizations can help build social networks through offering practical arrangements, related for instance to language and transportation. In a similar sense, service providers can partner with community-based organizations instead of limiting themselves to delivering services. In order to have effective programs that can foster the establishment of new social relationships and networks, either bonding or bridging, it is essential to include (the subjectivity of) the refugees themselves in the designing stage. As the crux of refugee resettlement, assisting with and helping the development of resettled refugees' social networks will allow for their increased well-being and swifter all-round integration, to the benefit of both the refugees themselves as well as their host society.

NOTES

1. Up until the time of writing, August 2018, the European Union Resettlement Framework was still under debate.
2. Since 1980, the United States had always resettled more refugees than all other countries combined, thereby providing a new home to 3 out of the 4 million refugees resettled worldwide in this period (PEW Research Center 2018).
3. Per capita, Canada resettled the highest number of refugees (725 per 1 million residents) followed by Australia (618) and Norway (528). The United States resettled merely 102 refugees per 1 million US residents (Pew Research Center 2018).

REFERENCES

European Commission (EC). 2017a. *Fifteenth Report on Relocation and* Resettlement—Report from the Commission to the European Parliament, the European Council and the Council. Brussels, 6 September. Retrieved from eur-lex.europa.eu/legal-content.

———. 2017b. President Jean-Claude Juncker's State of the Union Address. Brussels, 13 September. Retrieved from Europa.eur/rapid/press-release_SPEECH-17-3165_en.htm.

European Migration Network (EMN). 2016. *Resettlement and Humanitarian Admission Programmes in Europe—What Works?* Retrieved from www.emn.lv/.../emn-informs-00_inform_resettlement_final_en.pdf.

PEW Research Center. 2018. *For the first time, U.S. resettles fewer refugees than the rest of the world.* Retrieved from http://www.pewresearch.org/fact-tank/2018/07/05/for-the-first-time-u-s-resettles-fewer-refugees-than-the-rest-of-the-world/.

Society for Applied Anthropology. 2015. *Conference Program – Continuity and Change.* Oklahoma City: Society for Applied Anthropology.

Suter, Brigitte and Karin Magnusson. 2015. *Resettled and Reconnected: Social Networks in the Integration Process of Resettled Refugees.* Malmö: Malmö Institute for Studies of Migration, Diversity and Welfare.

United Nations High Commission for Refugees (UNHCR). 2018. *Update of UNHCR's operations in Europe.* Retrieved from http://www.unhcr.org/5a9fd8b30.pdf.

———. 2014. *War's Human Cost: UNHCR Global Trends 2013.* Retrieved from file:///C:/Users/Carrefour/Downloads/5399a14f9.pdf.

Index

About the Contributors

Andrew Nelson, an applied cultural anthropologist at the University of North Texas (USA), works with Nepali-speaking migrant and refugee populations in the Americas. His research is positioned at the intersection of migration and urbanism with a focus on policy, mobility, labor, and emplacement. Since 2010, he has worked with Nepali-Bhutanese refugees as a language interpreter, advocate, ESL teacher, and researcher.

Alexander Rödlach, associate professor in medical anthropology and psychiatry at Creighton University (USA), is interested in issues at the intersection of health, religion, and volunteerism. He has worked with various refugee and migrant populations in Omaha since 2007, exploring the role of religion in shaping health outcomes.

Roos Willems, a cultural anthropologist at the University of Leuven (Belgium), worked for years with the International Organization for Migration and the United Nations High Commission for Refugees, and has research experience with self-settled Congolese, Burundi, and Rwandan refugees in Dar es Salaam (Tanzania).

Jhuma Acharya was born in Bhutan and lived in a refugee camp for twenty-one years. He has degrees from North Bengal University and Tribhuvan University (Nepal) and has taught at a high school and a college. After resettling in the United States, he became a case manager at Community Refugee and Immigration Services and established a community resource center in Columbus, Ohio (USA).

Surendra Bir Adhikari is a mental health administrator with the Ohio Department of Mental Health and Addiction Services (USA). He leads health equities research on diverse ethnicities and communities and has international health experience in Asia and Africa. He has a doctorate in medical sociology from the University of Akron (USA).

Bimala Bastola passed the Canadian High School exams only five years after arriving in Quebec (Canada) without any prior knowledge of French. She is now a supervisor at a Boston Pizza restaurant and is considering completing hotel management training.

Khada Bhandari originates from Bhutan but sought refuge in Nepal. In 2008, he and his family came to the United States and resettled in Dallas where he initially volunteered with resettlement agencies, such as Catholic Charities, International Rescue Committee, and World Relief to support incoming refugee families, and later became director of a refugee program.

Jay Breneman is a licensed social worker and former chairman of the Erie County Council in Pennsylvania (USA). He is a consultant for nonprofit and other organizations to improve their long-term viability and to promote favorable policy-making for civic groups. He lives with his wife in Erie with their three children.

Liana Chase is a doctoral candidate in anthropology at the at SOAS University of London (UK). Her research is situated at the intersection of anthropology and psychiatry, applying ethnographic methods to the study of suffering, resilience, and care in humanitarian settings. She has worked with survivors of conflict and natural disaster in Canada, the U.S. and Nepal.

Chaitri Desai is a first-year medical student at Creighton University's School of Medicine (USA). She holds a master's degree in biomedical sciences from Colorado State University (USA). She intends to combine her medical training with her anthropology and public health background to advocate for healthcare issues faced by vulnerable populations.

Juana Domingo Andrés has a degree in theology and taught for more than eighteen years at an elementary school in Guatemala. She worked as an assistant teacher and in other professions in Omaha, Nebraska (USA) where she has been an activist for the Maya and other immigrants and is co-founder of the Maya organization Pixan Ixim.

Margaret Evans holds a master's degree in social work and has more than six years of experience working with women, children, and families on maternal-child health, human rights, and gender-based violence. She provides outreach to underserved communities through a local nonprofit that serves victims and survivors of domestic violence in South Carolina (USA).

Béatrice Halsouet has a doctorate in religious studies. She recently coedited with Lilyane Rachédi "When Death Strikes the Immigrant" and is applying her research as an education consultant for primary school teachers receiving immigrant pupils in Laval (Canada).

Kiri Hata is a senior caseworker at the Development and Relief Agency Refugee Hub in Australia. She has worked with refugees and asylum seekers since 1991 and is a well-respected advocate for their rights and well-being in the Hunter and Central Coast regions of New South Wales and has been at the core of community development initiatives in those areas.

Laura Heinemann, associate professor in medical anthropology at Creighton University (USA), is interested in caregiving, home life, kinship, policy, and community in matters of health and health care. She currently serves as chair of the Department of Cultural and Social Studies at Creighton University. She also has a background in medical social work.

Claire Herzog has worked with refugees in various capacities for over fifteen years, including resettlement and early childhood services. She is especially interested in refugee behavioral health and completed her master's thesis in public administration on the capacity of local behavioral health providers to serve refugee populations.

Nicole Hoellerer earned a doctorate in anthropology at Brunel University in London (United Kingdom) where she conducted ethnographic research with Bhutanese refugees. Her academic expertise is in community development in resettlement. She works at Exeter University (United Kingdom), conducting research on asylum adjudication in the European Union.

Melanie Kim is a first-year dual-degree medical student at Des Moines University (USA) pursing a degree in osteopathy and public health. She intends to go to work in underserved communities. She has experience in nonprofit management, campus ministry, and currently volunteers on a health coalition in a transient neighborhood.

Jaclyn Kirsch has master's degrees in social work and public health from The Ohio State University (USA). She has worked with refugees for five years with a focus on the physical and mental health of newly arrived refugees. She currently works for a mental health agency in Columbus, Ohio (USA) serving refugees.

Jennifer Kue, an assistant professor in the College of Nursing at The Ohio State University (USA), is Hmong American and a former refugee from Laos. She has over fifteen years of experience working with refugees, immigrants and medically underserved minority populations to understand and address health disparities.

Audrey Lumley-Sapanski received a doctorate from Pennsylvania State University (USA). Her research evaluates the effectiveness of the US Resettlement and Admissions Program. She is associate director of the Refugee and Immigrant Community Services program at Heartland Alliance in Chicago (USA) and is currently at the Gran Sasso Science Institute (Italy) studying the integration of forced migrants.

Govin Magar, a native of Bhutan, became a refugee in Nepal, where he lived until he was twenty-two years old. In 2009, he resettled to the United States. He works for a resettlement agency as an Employment Specialist and received a bachelor's degree in mechanical engineering from the University of Nebraska-Lincoln (USA) in 2017. He currently manages a home care agency for the aged and disabled.

Margo Minnich, assistant professor in nursing at Creighton University (USA), has clinical nursing experience in family case management, communicable disease, and homeless health care. She works with several refugee and immigrant groups and other vulnerable populations, such as homeless and underserved populations.

Celeste Mitchell has over a decade of experience working at a community refugee resettlement site in Omaha, Nebraska, USA. For her masters' thesis in social gerontology, she explored the health beliefs of elderly Southern Sudanese refugees through a qualitative research study.

Sharon Morrison, an associate professor in the Department of Public Health Education at the University of North Carolina at Greensboro (USA), is interested in refugee protection, and refugee and immigrant integration and health outcomes. She is a board member of the Association of Immigration and Refugee Service Professionals (ARSP) and a fellow with the Center for New North Carolinians.

Laeth Nasir is a family physician and associate dean for community medicine at Creighton University (USA). He has a special interest in cross-cultural aspects of medical care and mental health care delivery in Middle Eastern countries. Over the years, he has served as a consultant to a number of organizations, including the World Bank and USAID.

Madhu Neupane, originally from Bhutan, is a program manager at Howard Center Developmental Services in Vermont (USA) that serves people with intellectual and developmental disabilities. Before coming to the United States he served as a teacher in Nepal and in refugee camps. Madhu has worked as a liaison for the Bhutanese Community and Burlington Schools.

Tracy Nichols, a professor of public health education at the University of North Carolina at Greensboro (USA), studies reproductive justice, marginalized motherhoods, and community-based health programming. She has expertise in program evaluation, qualitative methodology, and research poetics.

Natacha Nikokeza arrived to the United States as a refugee from Burundi. She has a master's degree in Law from Wake Forest University (USA) and interned with the UNHCR in Washington, DC. She worked at World Relief prior to her work with the Center for New North Carolinians (USA) where she coordinates programs for two community centers.

Maura Nsonwu, a professor of social work at North Carolina State University (USA), has practiced as a clinician, educator, and researcher in refugee resettlement, human trafficking, health care, child welfare, and social work education. She is president of the Association of Immigration and Refugee Service Professionals and a fellow with the Center for New North Carolinians.

Angela Plummer holds a law degree from The Ohio State University (USA) and is the executive director of Community Refugee and Immigration Services in Columbus (USA). She supported resettlement to Columbus of more than 7,500 refugees and the successful resolution of many family reunification and asylum cases.

Georgina Ramsay has a doctorate from the University of Newcastle (Australia) and currently works as a sociocultural and politico-legal anthropologist at the University of Delaware (USA). Her research focuses broadly on refugees, displacement, and sovereignty. She has conducted fieldwork in Australia and Uganda with refugees from the Democratic Republic of Congo, Burundi, and Rwanda.

Lance Rasbridge, a medical anthropologist, helped found in 1992 and continues to coordinate the Refugee Outreach Program for Parkland Hospital in Dallas (United States). He inaugurated the Dallas Fort Worth Metroplex Refugee Network, and served as past president of both Refugee Services of Texas and the Center for Survivors of Torture.

Martin Renzo Rosales, an assistant professor of anthropology at Creighton University (USA), is interested in themes related to economic and environmental anthropology as well as ethnicity and migration, engaging in research with urban, rural, and indigenous communities in Panama and Puerto Rico as well as with Mayan communities in Omaha (USA).

Holly Sienkiewicz holds a doctorate in public health, is the director of the Center for New North Carolinians at the University of North Carolina at Greensboro (USA), and serves as a board member with the Association of Immigration and Refugee Service Professionals. Her research focuses on integration benchmarks, family violence prevention, and health access with immigrants and refugees.

Joseph Stadler is a sociocultural anthropologist at the University at Buffalo (USA). His research interrogates the impacts of political economic shifts and neoliberal policy regimes on a vulnerable rust belt city and its most vulnerable new residents, Nepali-Bhutanese refugees.

Kathryn Stam is a professor of cultural anthropology at the SUNY Polytechnic Institute (USA). Her research in Utica focuses on the lives and stories of Bhutanese-Nepali, Karen, and Somali-Bantu refugees. She is the founder of the Refugees Starting Over project, an information hub by, for, and about resettled refugees.

Chris Sunderlin is the founder and executive director of the Midtown Utica Community Center, which serves the large, diverse refugee-population of Utica, New York (USA). He taught English as a Second Language to new refugee arrivals and immigrants for seven years, and received his master's degree in curriculum development and instructional design from SUNY Albany (USA).

David Thatcher is a community organizer, social worker, and multimedia specialist who has been working with refugee communities for over a decade. His work focuses on employment and self-sufficiency for newly arrived refugees, advocacy campaigns addressing displacement crises, and participatory storytelling projects.

John Tluang, originally from Chin State in Myanmar, resettled with his family in Kansas City (USA) in 2010. After relocating to Omaha, Nebraska (USA), John worked as an interpreter, employment specialist and Christian, pastor. He currently resides in Columbus, Ohio (USA) where he serves as an assistant pastor in a Chin Baptist Church.

Kelly Yotebieng is a PhD candidate with The Ohio State University's Department of Anthropology (USA). Her research focuses on hope, gender, and risk among urban refugees in the United States and Yaoundé, Cameroon. She has worked for over fourteen years in Central Africa on humanitarian and public health issues.

www.ingramcontent.com/pod-product-compliance
Ingram Content Group UK Ltd.
Pitfield, Milton Keynes, MK11 3LW, UK
UKHW041423091026
15587UKWH00023B/273

9 781498 588898